Valesa, I hop you enjoy devotions Janie Hornsby

Obeying the Gospel

Also by Gary Henry

Diligently Seeking God
Reaching Forward
Enthusiastic Ideas
More Enthusiastic Ideas

Obeying the Gospel

Daily Motivation to
Act on Our Faith

Gary Henry

WordPoints
Louisville, Kentucky
WordPoints.com

WordPoints Daybook Series - Volume 5
Obeying the Gospel
Daily Motivation to Act on Our Faith

ISBN13 978-1-936357-51-2 – Print Edition
ISBN13 978-1-936357-65-9 – EPUB Edition
ISBN13 978-1-936357-75-8 – PDF Edition

A bulk discount is available for 18 or more copies of any combination of books in the *WordPoints Daybook Series.* Email *garyhenry@wordpoints.com* to place an order and receive this bulk discount. The books ordered must not be for resale.

WordPoints
12123 Shelbyville Road, Suite 100-247
Louisville, KY 40243

(502) 682-2603

Web: *wordpoints.com*
Email: *garyhenry@wordpoints.com*

For

Dee Bowman

without whose friendship

this book would not exist

Contents

Preface

IT WAS DURING THE FIRST WEEK OF MAY IN 1999 that I began working on *Diligently Seeking God,* the earliest writing in what would later become the *WordPoints Daybook Series.* Many things have changed since then, yet one thing has never changed: I have loved writing these pages. This work has become my life's passion.

But now we come to a book that is different from the others. In *Obeying the Gospel,* we'll be looking at what is involved in becoming a Christian. If we're asking the question the Philippian jailer asked, "What must I do to be saved?" (Acts 16:30), surely we'll want that question answered in a truthful way. We'll want nothing more or less than the answer given in the Scriptures — and that is the answer *Obeying the Gospel* earnestly seeks to give.

It may seem strange that I would write on how and why to become a Christian in the form of a daily "devotional." Aren't devotionals for those who are Christians already? From a writing standpoint, it has certainly been a challenge to explain and emphasize obedience to the gospel within the format of 366 short, stand-alone pages. But I believe we need to see this topic in terms of our "devotional" lives.

We need to think of "devotional literature" not as emotional fluff (providing a sentimental boost for a minute or two each morning), but as writing that *challenges us to respond more obediently to the gospel in every situation* — even if we set out on the path of discipleship to Christ many years ago. As a writer, I want to help you see that *doing what is right always comes down to responding rightly to the gospel.* After you read this book, I hope you won't ever be able to get this question out of your mind: ***if the gospel is true, what would obedience to the gospel — the message of the apostles in the New Testament — look like in the circumstances of my life right now?***

In these days of instant digital communication all over the world, interacting with individuals who do not share our convictions is a more frequent experience than it used to be. In the interconnected environment of today, it is all the more necessary for us to be ready to do what Peter urged us to do: "in your hearts honor Christ the Lord as holy, always being prepared to make a defense to anyone who asks you for a reason for the hope that is in you; yet do it with gentleness and respect" (1 Peter 3:15). I have tried to write evangelistically, which is to say, in a way that is understandable to those who do not share any of the basic presuppositions of Christians (or know the lingo that Christians use when talking to one another).

Writing these pages has been a sometimes painful exercise in self-examination. I have grown spiritually as a result of this work, and while I hope others will profit from it, I'm sure no one needs to hear it any more than I do. I've come to have a deeper understanding of what it means to be a Christian. With every page, I became more excited to learn anew the wonders of the gospel plan of salvation. The more of the gospel we grasp, the more jaw-dropping is our amazement that God would put such a plan together for us.

It grieves me that some who dearly wanted to use this book did not live long enough to hold it in their hands. Laron Fleming, for example, my dear brother and friend in South Carolina, asked me after he was diagnosed with cancer, "Gary, how soon do you think you can get this book ready?" But the cancer took his life, and he is no longer with us. How I wish he could have employed this book in his evangelistic efforts, as he surely would have. Please forgive me, Laron, for not starting sooner and writing more urgently.

If you are a Christian. I hope you'll learn to obey the gospel more radically. Where have you failed? In what ways can you do better?

If you are not a Christian. My prayer is that you'll die with Christ in baptism and begin a life in which obedience to the gospel will be your guiding concern from now on, in every situation.

In any case, please know that I have written these pages because they say what I need to hear personally. The core truths of the gospel have been my companions for the last five years while I was writing, and now that the book is finished, I will do what I always do: *I will use it as my own daily devotional.* I have a very short memory, and I will not recognize many of these pages as having been written by me. So I look forward to reading this book, wrestling with my conscience, and thinking ever more deeply about what it means to obey the gospel. *I pray it will help me to respond rightly — every day — to the good news of salvation in Jesus Christ.*

GPH

Obeying the Gospel

Grant to me, O Lord,
to know what I ought to know,
to love what I ought to love,
to praise what delights you most,
to value what is precious in your sight,
to hate what is offensive to you.

Do not suffer me to judge according
to the sight of my eyes, nor to pass sentence according
to the hearing of the ears of ignorant men;
but to discern with true judgment
between things visible and spiritual,
and above all things to enquire
what is the good pleasure of your will.

— *Thomas à Kempis*

January 1

In the Beginning

In the beginning, God created the heavens and the earth.
Genesis 1:1

LONG AGO, GOD MADE THE WORLD, AND WHEN IT WAS NEWLY MADE, IT WAS PERFECT. In its original state, as yet unmarred by any rebellion on the part of its inhabitants, the world reflected the perfection and glory of its Creator, ideally and supremely.

God is the only uncreated being. As Meister Eckhart wrote, "Outside of God, there is nothing but nothing." Yet God was moved by His wisdom and love to bring into being other entities, created things that would be external to Himself.

The heavens and the earth in Genesis 1:1 were created as the habitat for a special class of personal beings — spiritual souls clothed in physical bodies. At the climax of His creative work, the triune God (having three personalities within Himself) said, "Let us make man in our image, after our likeness. And let them have dominion over the fish of the sea and over the birds of the heavens and over the livestock and over all the earth and over every creeping thing that creeps on the earth" (Genesis 1:26). So, according to the earliest record, "God created man in his own image, in the image of God he created him; male and female he created them" (Genesis 1:27).

"Man is heaven's masterpiece" (Francis Quarles). Each part of the earthly creation shows God's glory, but it is only human beings that bear His image. Endowed with intellect, emotion, and a free will, Adam and Eve, our most ancient ancestors, had a relationship with God that the lower creatures were not capable of. We can only imagine God's reasons. Did He deem the possibility of love — as a choice rather than a robotic response — worth the damage that would ensue if these creatures chose rebellion rather than love? Apparently so, especially if He could rescue some of them from the wreckage.

But Adam and Eve's creation in God's image meant they were subject to Him in unique ways. Brought into being by God, they had God as their King. He possessed the sovereign right to set the rules and bar them from any conduct He knew would harm them.

Every soul belongs to God and exists by his pleasure.
God being who and what he is, and we being who and what we are,
the only thinkable relationship between us is one of full lordship
on his part and complete submission on ours. We owe him
every honor that it is in our power to give him.

A. W. TOZER

January 2

SIN

And the LORD God commanded the man, saying, "You may surely eat of every tree of the garden, but of the tree of the knowledge of good and evil you shall not eat, for in the day that you eat of it you shall surely die."
Genesis 2:16,17

ADAM AND EVE WERE FREE, BUT THEY USED THEIR FREEDOM TO REJECT GOD RATHER THAN HONOR HIM AS THEIR MAKER. We must not underestimate the seriousness of their decision to do what God had said they must not do. Their choice amounted to open rebellion. They wanted a knowledge they had been forbidden to have, and they refused to submit to their Creator's authority in the matter.

Long ago, Augustine of Hippo said, "I enquired what iniquity was and found it to be no substance but the perversion of the will, turned aside from thee, O God." More recently, Charles Colson put it this way, "Sin is essentially rebellion against the rule of God." God, to whom we owe our existence, has the right to rule over us. He is absolutely sovereign. So disobedience should be seen for what it is: an act of defiance. When Adam and Eve grew discontent with God's restrictions, they refused to obey Him, as if to say, "We know what the laws of Your love are, but we will do as we please."

But as soon as they sinned, the promised penalty began to operate. They were alienated from God spiritually. Their face-to-face access to Him was revoked. Expelled from Eden, they were sent away to have their hearts broken in a difficult, unpredictable world now under the limitations of "futility" (Romans 8:20). They would live out their years in a world dreadfully unlike the one they were made for. In all of its terrible implications, the word *death* began to define human existence. The perfect world of Eden was gone.

And today, the law of sin and death still operates. Who among us can say we've never done what Adam and Eve did? Who can say he has never in his lifetime done anything he knew to be disobedient to God? If we're honest, we have to plead guilty to the charge of sin. We know ourselves to be rebellious subjects who have committed treason against the King — our Father and our Sovereign.

Perhaps we think some of God's laws are trivial. But God is not trivial, and willful disobedience is deadly. When we disobey the Creator of life, we die. It's that simple. And in our present condition, our conscience tells us this: *we're dead already, even while we live.*

No sin is small. No grain of sand is small in the mechanism of a watch.

JEREMY TAYLOR

January 3

SALVATION

I will put enmity between you and the woman,
and between your offspring and her offspring; he shall
bruise your head, and you shall bruise his heel.
Genesis 3:15

EVEN BEFORE SIN BROKE THE PERFECTION OF GOD'S CREATION, GOD HAD FORMULATED A RESCUE PLAN. A descendant of Adam and Eve would crush Satan, the one who had lied to them, enticing them to sin: "he shall bruise your head, and you shall bruise his heel." As it turned out, this One would live a perfect life and die a sacrificial death. Not deserving death, He would die anyway, "that through death he might destroy the one who has the power of death, that is, the devil, and deliver all those who through fear of death were subject to lifelong slavery" (Hebrews 2:14,15).

To hear that God has provided a way for us to be rescued is "good news" indeed. The New Testament uses the word *gospel* ("glad tidings") to refer to this plan. But it will not seem like particularly good news until we have understood the seriousness of the problem. Unless we see what it means to have rebelled against God, to be separated from Him, and to be under the penalty of death both now and forever, we will not be receptive to the message of salvation. The terribleness of the problem is what makes the solution so amazing. We must hear the fearful news of our doom before we can rejoice at the good news of our deliverance.

But once we face the eternal tragedy — and utter agony — of being lost, the fatherly love that moved God to provide for our deliverance will bring us tears of joy. He could have abandoned us to the consequences of our choice, but He was not willing to do so. "For God so loved the world, that he gave his only Son, that whoever believes in him should not perish but have eternal life" (John 3:16). We can't understand the kind of love that would prompt such a sacrifice — we can only respond to it thankfully.

But let us be clear: it is from *sin* that God proposes to save us. Sin is the root from which all the lesser problems in the world grow, and sin is what the gospel is about. In the gospel, salvation is not about the amelioration of social ills or earthly maladies. It is about (a) the forgiveness of our sins, and (b) learning to live again in reverence and gratitude before the Creator who loves us.

Salvation is bringing back to normal the Creator-creature relation.

A. W. TOZER

January 4

The Gospel of Jesus Christ

The beginning of the gospel of Jesus Christ, the Son of God.
Mark 1:1

WHEN THE TIME CAME AND GOD BROUGHT TO COMPLETION HIS PLAN TO PROVIDE SALVATION, THE PLAN WAS COMMUNICATED IN WORDS. In the Scriptures, this announcement of the deliverance from sin that God has made possible is called the "gospel."

It is an interesting fact that God chose to use the medium of human language as He did. Crucial to His rescue plan was its communication by means of words from one person to another. In 2 Corinthians 5:18,19, Paul refers to the work of the apostles as the "ministry of reconciliation," and he calls the gospel the "message of reconciliation." The NIrV aptly paraphrases this as "the message that people may be brought back" to God. And in Ephesians 1:13, Paul said the joys of salvation came to his readers only after they heard "the word of truth, the gospel of your salvation." The gospel, then, is not a magical or mysterious feeling — it is a *message.*

But here is the important (and indispensable) point: *the message is about Jesus Christ.* It is in Jesus that God is offering salvation. In 2 Corinthians 5, we hear Paul affirming that "in Christ God was reconciling the world to himself" (v.19). And concerning Christ, God "made him to be sin who knew no sin, so that in him we might become the righteousness of God" (v.21).

The message that God has opened up the way for us to be forgiven — and that Jesus is the Messiah (or "Christ") through whom this was accomplished — is "good news." Indeed, it is the best news the world has ever heard. In the familiar story of Jesus' birth in the Gospel of Luke, we hear the angel saying to the shepherds in the field, watching their flocks at night, "Fear not, for behold, I bring you good news of great joy that will be for all the people. For unto you is born this day in the city of David a Savior, who is Christ the Lord" (2:10,11). *These are wonderful words.*

"Though you do not now see him, you believe in him," Peter wrote, "and rejoice with joy that is inexpressible and filled with glory" (1 Peter 1:8). What could make our hearts sing with greater joy than knowing God has made it possible for us to come back to Him?

Euangelion (which we call *gospel*) is a Greek word, and signifies good, merry, glad, and joyful tidings, that makes a man's heart glad, and makes him sing, dance, and leap for joy.

WILLIAM TYNDALE

January 5

Obeying the Gospel

. . . in flaming fire, inflicting vengeance on those who do not know God and on those who do not obey the gospel of our Lord Jesus.
2 Thessalonians 1:8

The gospel of Jesus Christ is the "good news" of God's salvation. But at this point, we encounter a misconception that is firmly lodged in the minds of many people: the notion that the gospel is unconditional and requires no response on our part.

Now certainly, anything we might do would be no more than a response to what God has done. Having cut ourselves off from God by our sins, there is absolutely nothing we could do to work our way back to Him. Paul says that "while we were still helpless, at the right time Christ died for the ungodly" (Romans 5:6 NASB).

That, however, does not mean the gospel requires no response. It is a message, but it is a message that must be responded to. In the absence of the response required by God, the benefits of the message should not be expected. As I remember hearing preachers say when I was a child, "The gospel contains facts which must be believed and commands which must be obeyed." If we leave out either the facts or the commands, the gospel is no longer good news.

The expression "obey the gospel" should not be scoffed at or minimized. It is biblical language. More is involved than just our initial obedience (see tomorrow's reading), but if we're lost in sin, we need to hear first about the initial steps required. We are wanting to enter the realm of God's grace, *so in the New Testament, what does the gospel say we must do?* First, we must believe the truth that Jesus is the Christ, the Son of God (John 8:24; 11:27). Then, we must repent of our sins (Acts 3:19), confess our faith (Romans 10:9,10), and be baptized in order to receive God's forgiveness (Acts 22:16).

The gospel confronts us with a decision that is nothing less than life's biggest decision. If we refuse God's terms of pardon, we will have condemned ourselves by the stand we've taken. Jesus said, "The one who rejects me and does not receive my words has a judge; the word that I have spoken will judge him on the last day" (John 12:48). The gospel is a gracious invitation from God, and it is open to every person. But the invitation has to be accepted, and God has not left it to us to decide what the conditions of that acceptance will be.

No one is excluded from the gospel.
But many are excluded by the gospel.

Karl Barth

January 6

Continuing to Obey the Gospel

You were running well. Who hindered you from obeying the truth?
Galatians 5:7

PAUL'S QUESTION "WHO HINDERED YOU FROM OBEYING THE TRUTH?" WAS ADDRESSED TO A GROUP OF CHRISTIANS. He was concerned about some in Galatia who, having been baptized into Christ, were turning away from the truth. They were no longer obeying the gospel, and Paul was worried about their salvation.

Beginning with the initial response, culminating in baptism, that brings one into a forgiven relationship with God, the Christian embarks on a lifetime of obedience. It is not too much to say that "obeying the gospel" defines everything the Christian does. Every obedient thought, word, and deed is a grateful response to the good news of what God has done to save us.

But if it is possible to obey the gospel, it is also possible to *quit* obeying it. Faithfulness to God and gratitude for His grace are not automatic; we have to choose to live this way. And the Scriptures are clear: *if we quit living in obedience to the gospel, we will go back to being under condemnation for our sins.* The Letter to the Hebrews, for example, is a powerful warning against apostasy and a plea to remain true to Christ. It was written to some in the first century who were becoming unfaithful and were in danger of losing their hope of heaven, just as many in Israel left Egypt in the Exodus but failed to reach Canaan because of unfaithfulness (Hebrews 3:12-4:11).

So becoming a Christian involves making a *commitment*. To "confess" Christ is not merely a statement that we believe the truth of the gospel — it is a promise of obedience to His will for the rest of our lives. That is a serious commitment, obviously, and Jesus urged us to "count the cost" (Luke 14:25-33) before we make it.

Reading the New Testament even briefly, we can see there are two phases or stages in obeying the gospel: first, we accept God's forgiveness on His terms, and second, we live the rest of our lives under the lordship of Christ. To do the first but not the second is to deny Christ. Paul put it succinctly: "As you received Christ Jesus the Lord, so walk in him" (Colossians 2:6). So the question is not just whether we've accepted Christ at some point in the past — it's also whether the gospel is what we're obeying right now.

There are two things to do about the gospel — believe it and behave it.

SUSANNA WESLEY

January 7

The Hope of the Gospel

. . . if indeed you continue in the faith, stable and steadfast, not shifting from the hope of the gospel that you heard, which has been proclaimed in all creation under heaven.
Colossians 1:23

HOPE IS ONE OF THE MOST POWERFUL TRAITS WE CAN POSSESS. Without it, we languish, but with hope, almost no obstacle can keep us from our goal. And one reason the gospel of Christ is the greatest of all messages is that it offers the greatest of all hopes. In Christ there is the prospect of a perfect, eternal relationship with God when our lives right now have run their course.

Unfortunately, the hope of the gospel is often misrepresented in modern evangelism. Rather than the forgiveness of sins and the restoration of a right relationship with God, the point of the gospel is often said to be the diminishing of injustice and suffering in the world. Even worse, some say the gospel is about "health, wealth, and happiness" — as if God's primary intent in the sacrifice of His Son was to provide us a path to prosperity and earthly comfort.

Make no mistake, the Christian will help anyone who is suffering if he can. In the words of C. S. Lewis, "[The gospel] does not mean that we are to leave the present world as it is. If you read history, you will find that the Christians who did the most for the present world were those who thought most of the next."

But the gospel is not about our secondary problems; it's about our sin. Fixing that problem, the gospel offers the thing we need more than anything else: *eternal fellowship with the God who made us.*

In an age like ours, we need to grasp anew the grandeur of the gospel's hope. We must cherish it for the treasure it is, maintain it at all costs, and reach forward to it every day. Our beloved brother Paul had his priorities straight: "forgetting what lies behind and straining forward to what lies ahead, I press on toward the goal for the prize of the upward call of God in Christ Jesus" (Philippians 3:13,14). May heaven mean no less to us than it did to him.

God speaks to the crowd, but his call comes to individuals, and through their personal obedience he acts. He does not promise them success, or even final victory in this life. The goal of the adventure to which he commits them is in heaven. God does not promise that he will protect them from trials, from material cares, from sickness, from physical or moral suffering. He promises only that he will be with them in all these trials, and that he will sustain them if they remain faithful to him.

PAUL TOURNIER

January 8

HEARING THE TRUTH

Take care then how you hear.
Luke 8:18

IF THE GOSPEL HAS A PREREQUISITE, IT IS THAT WE MUST BE WILLING TO HEAR IT. The process that the gospel was meant to begin can go no further if there is anything that filters it out of our thinking. Whatever else it may be, the gospel is a *message,* and like any message, the gospel requires not just a hearing but *a fair hearing.*

First, we must be open to being persuaded. No amount of evidence will be enough if, deep down, we are simply unpersuadable. The adage is true: there are none so deaf as those who will not hear. So we must be "easy to be entreated" (James 3:17 ASV) or "open to reason" (ESV). The gospel won't have a chance if we don't give it a chance. So how open are we? Will prejudicial filters block the gospel out of our hearts? Are there any up-front limits on how far we would follow Jesus if the gospel were true?

Truth demands from us two qualities of character: *honesty* and *courage.* The question "What is true?" has to do with the facts. Getting the right answer to that question requires honesty. But the more important question is "What are we going to do with the truth?" Responding to truth takes courage, and here is where we stumble. When the truth calls for a difficult response, we hide from it, as Adam and Eve did following their sin (Genesis 3:8-10).

There are two different truths we must hear: *the sinful truth about ourselves* (the gospel's diagnosis of our malady) and *the saving truth about God* (the gospel's plan for our restoration). The second will mean little to those who have rejected the first, and the first is by far the hardest to accept. Confronting our sinfulness is painful, but the truth can't save us if we're unwilling to face the problem. Without the bad news, the good news will not be good.

Above all, we must guard against defining truth in terms of what we *want* the truth to be. Without recognizing it or admitting it to ourselves, we often reject ideas as "untrue" when there is no objective reason to do so. We simply don't *want* them to be true. But the truth is what it is — regardless of our preferences. And the more painful a truth may be to accept (at least in the short term), the more we must be adventurers — *going wherever the truth leads us.*

The truth is not always what we want to hear.

JEWISH PROVERB

January 9

Grieving Our Sins

For godly sorrow produces repentance leading to salvation, not to be regretted; but the sorrow of the world produces death.
2 Corinthians 7:10 NKJV

IN AN AGE WHEN "FEELING GOOD" OUTRANKS EVERY OTHER VALUE, IT IS HARD FOR MANY TO SEE THAT OUR FIRST RESPONSE TO THE GOSPEL MUST BE GRIEF. Yet if the gospel is about redemption from our *sins,* we are not ready for what the gospel offers until we see our sins for what they are and grieve them in a godly way.

Nowadays, the purpose of the gospel is often perverted. No longer do people understand it to be about the remission of sins and the restoration of a right relationship with God. It is no wonder, then, that godly sorrow and repentance are left out of modern preaching. Nevertheless, the gospel is about sin. *Godly sorrow grieves the treachery we have committed against God.* And it alone produces the repentance that leads to salvation (2 Corinthians 7:10).

In the life of Christ, it is interesting to note who the people were whom Jesus welcomed. It was not the poor, the underprivileged, or the oppressed. These social statuses meant little to Jesus unless people in these conditions came *penitently* — seeking His forgiveness with godly sorrow. If they came with this attitude, they were welcomed, but no more than people from any other status who came with the same penitence. Jesus was looking for those who saw their need for His forgiveness, regardless of their external circumstances. So if we ask which people would be "blessed," Jesus said it was "the poor in spirit . . . those who mourn . . . those who hunger and thirst for righteousness" (Matthew 5:3-6). To those whose hearts were not broken by sorrow for their own sins, Jesus had nothing to offer of any unique or lasting value.

But if the first thing the gospel produces is sorrow, doesn't that "negative" message turn people away? For some, it certainly does. It did in Jesus' day, and it does now. But let's not misunderstand. The gospel is the most positive "good news" the world has ever heard. But it produces the joy of forgiveness only when a person has first gone through the process of godly sorrow. It gives us a new beginning, nothing short of a "new birth." But the new life comes only after a conversion that is bathed in bitter tears.

Repentance is not a fatal day when tears are shed,
but a natal day when, as a result of tears, a new life begins.

ILION T. JONES

January 10

Counting the Cost

For which of you, desiring to build a tower, does not first sit down and count the cost, whether he has enough to complete it?
Luke 14:28

BEFORE EMBARKING ON A PROJECT, MOST PEOPLE THINK ABOUT WHETHER THEY ARE WILLING TO PAY THE PRICE. Halfway through the work is not a good time to start wrestling with whether the results are going to be worth the sacrifice. We should have already done that. So Jesus said those considering obedience to His gospel should "count the cost." It is disastrous not to do so.

When it comes to following Christ, however, we don't know what the cost is going to be, at least not specifically. We know that it may be very costly — in fact, it may cost us everything valuable in this life — but when we are baptized into Christ, we can't see very far down the road. All we know is that Jesus requires a nothing-held-back commitment: "If anyone would come after me, let him deny himself and take up his cross and follow me. For whoever would save his life will lose it, but whoever loses his life for my sake and the gospel's will save it" (Mark 8:34,35).

So to "count the cost" would be to ask ourselves whether we're willing to make that kind of commitment and then keep the promise even if it kills us. *Are there limits to our submission to His authority? Are there any conditions or fine print in our contract with Him? Is there anything we wouldn't do if following Him required us to do that?* These are deep, heart-probing questions, and the serious disciple is one who answered them decisively before he made his commitment. Solomon said about promises in general, "It is better that you should not vow than that you should vow and not pay" (Ecclesiastes 5:5). If all we can say is "maybe," we insult our God.

We should not be surprised that there is a cost to be counted. If rightful love for God is what the gospel calls for, that response will be costly. Love requires sacrifice, and the higher the love, the bigger the sacrifice. But what is the alternative? If we turn away from the gospel because of the costliness of the love it requires, there is nothing left but lesser loves — counterfeits that offer little more than disappointment, having cost us little more than what was convenient. *So will we rise to the highest love, pay its price, and receive its joy?* There is no more fundamental or far-reaching question in this world.

True love is always costly.

BILLY GRAHAM

January 11

TRUSTING OUR FATHER

. . . for my people have committed two evils: they have forsaken me, the fountain of living waters, and hewed out cisterns for themselves, broken cisterns that can hold no water.
Jeremiah 2:13

SIN IS THE RESULT OF FORSAKING THE TRUST WE WERE MEANT TO HAVE IN GOD. We see it first in the Garden of Eden, where as soon as Adam and Eve's confidence in God's goodness had been broken, they were willing to violate His will to get what they wanted (Genesis 3:1-6). Since then, the problem of sin has always been the same, and we're all guilty of it. Failing to trust that God's way is best, we've rebelled and committed treachery to get satisfactions we think are better than those God's way would allow.

If a broken trust in God is the root of sin, it makes sense that for the problem of sin to be fixed, trust is going to have to be put back in its rightful place. That is why faith is so important in God's plan for our restoration to His fellowship through Jesus Christ.

Faith begins with simple belief, an acceptance of the factual truth about God. But based on belief, faith also means trusting that God is good, His commands are always going to be better than our will, and in the end He is waiting for us in heaven *if we will adhere to His plan for our redemption.* When our immediate circumstances seem to cast doubt on these truths, it is only trust (based on the solid evidence of God's trustworthiness, especially in Jesus' resurrection) that will keep us faithful to our Father.

I love Adam Litmer's definition of trust: "unwavering belief that God's way is always the right way, without exception . . . and that our lives will always be best lived when lived for His glory." If we reject the "obedience of faith" (Romans 1:5), there is no salvation for us. We must dispense with the doubts about God and His law that started us down the path of disobedience in the first place.

Abraham is the great example of trust. "By faith Abraham obeyed when he was called to go out to a place that he was to receive as an inheritance. And he went out, not knowing where he was going" (Hebrews 11:8). Because he believed, Abraham obeyed. At God's bidding, he risked everything he had in this world *because he trusted God's promise.* Today, we can't be God's friends as he was without banking on God's promise as he did.

The pith, the essence of faith lies in this — a casting oneself on the promise.

CHARLES HADDON SPURGEON

January 12
Making the Commitment

Then Philip opened his mouth, and beginning with this Scripture he told him the good news about Jesus. And as they were going along the road they came to some water, and the eunuch said, "See, here is water! What prevents me from being baptized?" And he commanded the chariot to stop, and they both went down into the water, Philip and the eunuch, and he baptized him.
Acts 8:35-38

IF (1) GODLY SORROW IS MOVING US TO SEEK GOD'S FORGIVENESS, (2) WE BELIEVE JESUS CHRIST IS THE ONE SENT BY GOD TO SAVE US, AND (3) WE ARE WILLING TO BEGIN A LIFE OF REAL TRUST, WHAT SHOULD WE DO? A commitment to God must be made through Jesus Christ, and we have talked about counting the cost of that. But if we are ready, what must we actually do to make the commitment required by the gospel and receive all its joyful benefits?

Repentance. It would make no sense to seek the forgiveness of sins which we refuse to give up, so God requires that we lay down our rebellion and pledge allegiance to His rule. The gospel is a message of "repentance for the forgiveness of sins" (Luke 24:47), and that means committing ourselves to a changed life.

Confession of faith. Christ's acknowledgment of His true identity cost Him dearly, and He requires that we be equally open about our faith in Him. The apostle Paul wrote, "If you confess with your mouth that Jesus is Lord and believe in your heart that God raised him from the dead, you will be saved" (Romans 10:9).

Baptism. In Colossians 2:12, Paul wrote that we are "buried with him in baptism, in which you were also raised with him through faith in the powerful working of God, who raised him from the dead." If we are presently "in Christ," it was in baptism that we moved from condemnation to salvation — our forgiveness was not the result of the water itself or any meritorious quality of our obedience; it was our "faith in the powerful working of God."

As you can see, there is something special about the act of baptism. Whether we understand God's purpose in this or not, He has made baptism the doorway, or division, that separates the old from the new. In the gospel of Christ, it is in baptism that our sins are washed away (Acts 22:16). Urgently viewing Christ's command to be baptized, and trusting the Father to forgive us, we commit ourselves to Christ by dying with Him in baptism (Romans 6:3,4).

Baptism points back to the work of God,
and forward to the life of faith.

J. ALICE MOTYER

January 13

Dying with Christ

The saying is trustworthy, for:
If we have died with him,
we will also live with him.
2 Timothy 2:11

THE LITTLE WORD "IF" IS A POWERFUL WORD. If salvation depends on dying with Christ, it's important to know what this means.

Baptism. If it is in baptism that we die with Christ (Romans 6:3,4), we should not expect the benefits of Christ's death unless we are willing to die with Him in this way. But there is more.

Intent to die to sin. The objective fact of God's forgiveness of our sins at baptism is accompanied by a subjective fact in our hearts: we *intend* to die to sin. That is, we *commit* ourselves to walking "in newness of life" (Romans 6:4). Just as Christ died on the cross, the condemnation for our sins is removed when we die with Him in baptism. But it is not only the guilt of our sins in the past that must be done away with; the practice of sin in the present must also die. This part of dying with Christ must not be left out. We must *decide* that our old practices are dead and gone.

Putting sin to death daily. Having died with Christ in baptism and committed ourselves to living rightly, *we must carry out that commitment on a daily basis.* Our dying with Christ is a *fact* (it happened when we were baptized), but it is also a *command*. It was not to the unbaptized but those who had died with Christ that Paul wrote, "Put to death therefore what is earthly in you" (Colossians 3:5). We may have been very sincere in turning to Christ, but Satan will keep trying to destroy us — *so "put to death what is earthly in you" is a command we never get finished obeying in this life.* The older devotional writers used to talk about the "daily mortification of the flesh," and perhaps we need to get back to that kind of thinking. You may prefer more modern words than "mortification," but don't ever underestimate this aspect of dying with Christ.

So let's come back to that little word "if." According to Paul, we will live with Christ "if" we have died with Him. We would not have been baptized into Christ "if" we had not decided to die with Him. It was a choice. And our old self will not stay dead "if" we refuse to let go of what used to be important to us. We must deny ourselves and take up our cross. That is also a choice.

You will be dead so long as you refuse to die.

GEORGE MACDONALD

January 14

KEEPING THE FAITH

When he came and saw the grace of God, he was glad, and he exhorted them all to remain faithful to the Lord with steadfast purpose.
Acts 11:23

SADLY, SOME PEOPLE MAKE A COMMITMENT TO CHRIST, BUT THEY GET TO WHERE THE COMMITMENT DOES NOT MEAN ANYTHING TO THEM. They do not "remain faithful to the Lord," as Barnabas urged the new converts in Antioch to do. And the New Testament is clear about the consequence of unfaithfulness: *to go back on our commitment to Christ is to go back to being lost.* The writer of Hebrews said that "we have come to share in Christ, if indeed we hold our original confidence firm to the end" (Hebrews 3:14).

Jesus did not mince words about our commitment to His salvation. He said, "No one who puts his hand to the plow and looks back is fit for the kingdom of God" (Luke 9:62). So anytime we talk about obeying the gospel, let's also talk about *continuing* to obey it. "Let us run with endurance the race that is set before us" (Hebrews 12:1). Until the victory is fully ours, we must . . . *continue.*

Few of the virtues we might have are more important than faithfulness. To be reliable is one of the finest things in life. And, of course, to be a traitor is one of the most despicable. So we should aspire to trustworthiness and steadfastness in our commitment. We can count on God; He should also be able to count on us.

For persons broken by sin as we are, learning God's character — allowing Him to remake us — is a growth process that takes time. In Christ, we "are being transformed into the same image from one degree of glory to another" (2 Corinthians 3:18). Surely we must not give up before the process has reached its goal.

Ultimately, it is love and gratitude for grace that will keep us faithful. Forgiven, we *want* to grow. We *want* to continue. Our most fervent desire is to be all our Father wants us to be, forever.

Thine am I, I was born for thee,
What wouldst thou, Master, make of me?
Give me death or give me life
Give health or give infirmity
Give honor or give obloquy
Give peace profound or daily strife,
Weakness or strength add to my life;
Yes, Lord, my answer still shall be
What wilt thou, Master, have of me?

TERESA OF ÁVILA

January 15

SHARING THE FAITH

Tell everyone God's message. Be ready at all times to do whatever is needed.
2 Timothy 4:2 ERV

IN THE NEW TESTAMENT, ORDINARY CHRISTIANS WERE EVANGELISTIC. It wasn't just the evangelists — everybody "preached the Good News about Jesus wherever they went" (Acts 8:4 NLT). Even under persecution (*especially* under persecution, it seems) the followers of Jesus spread the word of forgiveness and eternal hope.

Today, it is tragically true that we who follow Jesus are not as evangelistic as they were. We are reluctant to talk about the gospel, and most of us rarely do it except when we are in the company of fellow believers. We have disengaged from the world in such a way that we have little evangelistic impact in our communities.

To be sure, not everyone is equally adept at talking with strangers, nor is every member of the Lord's church equally skilled at teaching. In the body of Christ, as in a human body, "the members do not all have the same function" (Romans 12:4).

But we can't receive the benefits of the gospel ourselves and not want to do *something* to share those benefits with other people. In some kind of personal way, we should want to reach those around us with the message that has brought us such great joy.

We can at least do what Jesus told the man in Mark 5:1-20. In that account, Jesus had healed a man of his demonic possession, and in profound reverence and gratitude, the man wanted to get in the boat and accompany Jesus back across the Sea of Galilee. But Jesus wanted him to do something that would be even better: "Go home to your friends and tell them how much the Lord has done for you, and how he has had mercy on you" (v.19).

If nothing else, we can explain what convinced us the gospel is true. "Always be prepared to give an answer to everyone who asks you to give the reason for the hope that you have. But do this with gentleness and respect" (1 Peter 3:15 NIV). If we had our own doubts, we can tell others what truths overcame those doubts.

For those forgiven of their sins, sharing the faith is not optional. There is no alternative. If we bottle up our faith and keep quiet about it, as if we were ashamed of Christ, our faith will die.

Our faith grows by expression. If we want to keep our faith, we must share it.

BILLY GRAHAM

January 16

With What Attitude Should We Come to Jesus?

Come to me, all who labor and are heavy laden,
and I will give you rest.
Matthew 11:28

THE GOSPEL ALWAYS HAS AN INVITATION ATTACHED TO IT. Jesus' invitation is, "Come to me." In His day, however, some came to Jesus seeking things other than what He offered, some came for wrong motives, and some were simply unwilling to accept Jesus' conditions and commandments. In our day, people still "come to Jesus" for a wide range of reasons. So let's ask this: in the New Testament, who were those who came to Jesus and were *received* by Him? If we expect Jesus' *welcome,* how should we come?

Seeking the forgiveness of our sins. Jesus could not have been clearer about the purpose of His mission. His blood would be "poured out for many for the forgiveness of sins" (Matthew 26:28). God is certainly the Giver of many gifts, but the forgiveness of sins (and consequently the hope of heaven) is the only blessing promised to *all* who are in Christ and *only* to those in Christ. If we come looking for "loaves and fishes," we will hear Jesus say, "Do not work for the food that perishes, but for the food that endures to eternal life, which the Son of Man will give to you" (John 6:27).

Committing ourselves to Jesus' lordship. If treason is the problem, fixing it surely requires that we lay down our rebellion and return to God as our rightful King. Doesn't that make sense? If we're not ready to quit saying *My will be done* and start saying *Thy will be done,* we're not ready for what Jesus offers. As a Christian, Paul went so far as to say, "I have been crucified with Christ. It is no longer I who live, but Christ who lives in me. And the life I now live in the flesh I live by faith in the Son of God, who loved me and gave himself for me" (Galatians 2:20). This is life's greatest commitment.

But as I've said, the gospel is always framed as an invitation. God does not force us to accept His forgiveness; He *invites* us to do so. Yes, a most serious commitment is required in order to receive His gift, and yes, if we refuse the gospel, we will not escape the justice of God's penalty for our sins. But let us never forget what we have lost and what God wants to give back to us. In Christ, our Father is offering to give us nothing less than Himself. Forever.

In commanding us to glorify him,
God is inviting us to enjoy him.

C. S. LEWIS

January 17

THE LIGHT OF THE WORLD

Again Jesus spoke to them, saying, "I am the light of the world. Whoever follows me will not walk in darkness, but will have the light of life."
John 8:12

SINCE THE BEGINNING OF HISTORY, LIGHT AND DARKNESS HAVE BEEN UNIVERSAL SYMBOLS. Light stands for truth/goodness; darkness stands for untruth/evil. When Jesus said He was the "light of the world," He was claiming to be the only truth through which the darkness of evil can be dispelled. If it was untruth that led us away from God, we can't come back to Him without coming back to the truth. So Jesus boldly said: "I am the way, and the truth, and the life. No one comes to the Father except through me" (John 14:6).

To receive God's forgiveness, we must believe the truth found in His Son, Jesus Christ. Certainly, we must embrace *the truth of who Jesus is.* But we must also believe *the truth that Jesus revealed about God, His Father.* And what is more, we must accept *the truth about ourselves and our need for reconciliation with God.* The joyful truth about God's salvation will have little impact if we haven't digested the sorrowful truth about our alienation from Him.

Both the sinful truth about ourselves and the saving truth about God require honesty and courage. We must be willing to *know* the truth (this requires honesty); then we must be willing to *obey* the truth (this requires courage). At all costs, the truth must be *accepted* — the truth must be *acted upon,* no matter how hard it is. Because of truth's demands, therefore, not many people are willing to be saved by the truth. "And this is the judgment: the light has come into the world, and people loved the darkness rather than the light because their works were evil" (John 3:19).

Many of us have been quick to point out the failures of other people's honesty and courage. But what about us? Even more to the point, what about me personally? Am I willing to hear *whatever* I need to hear, and am I willing to go *wherever* I need to go?

Confronted by the Great Physician (both His diagnosis and His treatment plan), a bold choice has to be made. We can have the comfort of staying in denial (and be lost) or we can accept the discomfort of the truth (and be saved). Initially, reality can be hard to deal with. But our only alternative is to stay in denial and die in sin.

Darkness is my point of view, my right to myself;
light is God's point of view.

OSWALD CHAMBERS

January 18

Alpha and Omega

I am the Alpha and the Omega, the first and the last, the beginning and the end.
Revelation 22:13

ALPHA IS THE FIRST LETTER IN THE GREEK ALPHABET, AND OMEGA IS THE LAST. From "alpha to omega" is, as we would say, everything "from a to z." When Jesus said, "I am the Alpha and the Omega," He was making a claim to be God Incarnate, nothing less than the Eternal God who came into the world in human form. But why should this be attractive to us? What is it about God's *eternity* that should be of particular interest?

We yearn. The most obvious fact in the world is that human beings are deeply dissatisfied. We groan and aspire, yearning for things our hearts do not have. And what we do have, we have to say grievous goodbyes to. It doesn't do any good to pretend. The only way not to weep is not to know what happens in the world.

But why do we yearn as we do? No other species yearns with the longings of the human heart. And no other species grieves the ravages of time. Could it be that we were meant for a stability no longer available in this world? Is the agony of imperfection and change a clue that this kind of world is not what we were created for?

In Jesus Christ, we can have what we yearn for. The truth is, we were created for a perfect, eternal joy with God, a joy not subject to change and decay. By our sin, the human race broke that perfection, but we still yearn for it. And in Christ, that is what is offered to us: restoration of the *eternal, unfading life* we were designed for.

"Blessed be the God and Father of our Lord Jesus Christ! According to his great mercy, he has caused us to be born again to a living hope through the resurrection of Jesus Christ from the dead" (1 Peter 1:3). This "living hope" is the very heartbeat of the gospel. Ultimately, it is all the Christian has that is unique. Every other blessing from God may be — and often is — enjoyed in this world by people who are not in Christ. But think twice before you disdain the value of this hope. Would you not give everything in this world to have what you know your heart needs most deeply? And if you gained everything you want right now but were banished from God in eternity, what would you have profited?

Change and decay in all around I see;
O Thou who changest not, abide with me!

HENRY F. LYTE

January 19

IN CHRIST: RECONCILIATION TO GOD

In Christ God was reconciling the world to himself, not counting their trespasses against them, and entrusting to us the message of reconciliation.
2 Corinthians 5:19

OF ALL THE EVENTS IN HUMAN HISTORY, THE COMING OF JESUS CHRIST WAS THE MOST IMPORTANT. And the gospel of Christ is the most important of all messages. But what is it about? If Jesus was truly the Son of God, what was the point of His being sent into the world? Paul the apostle, one of thirteen men appointed by Christ to preach the gospel authoritatively, wrote that *"in Christ God was reconciling the world to himself."* And what about the gospel itself? It is, as Paul said, the *"message of reconciliation."* These are weighty words. They need to be understood very clearly.

The seriousness of the problem. The fact is, we are alienated from the God who made us. Our sins have cut us off from Him, and there is no way we can work our way back into fellowship with Him by our own efforts. We are rebels, deservedly under the sentence of death. If nothing is done about our condition and we die in our rebellion, there will be nothing for us in eternity but to be banished from God's presence forever. In a word, we are *lost.*

The wonderfulness of the solution. Not willing to leave us in our lost condition, God provided a way for us to be reconciled to Him. In love (Romans 5:6-11), He opened the door for us to come back home. The human race has never received any better news. But the gospel has to be obeyed (even by Christians); its terms have to be accepted. So Paul could implore his readers, "We implore you on behalf of Christ, *be reconciled to God"* (2 Corinthians 5:20).

We should not underestimate either the seriousness of the problem or the wonderfulness of the solution. If all we can say is "That is nice" or "That is interesting," we are missing the point. It is only when we come to terms with our own sinfulness — and the horror of the word *lost* — that the gospel fills us with wonder.

But neither should we forget that *God is at the center of both the problem and the solution.* The gospel is not primarily about our broken social relationships. These are but symptoms of the real problem: our broken relationship with God. That is what the gospel wants to fix — and until it is fixed nothing else will help us much.

To reconcile man with man and not with God
is to reconcile no one at all.

THOMAS MERTON

January 20

GOD HAS MADE HIM BOTH LORD AND CHRIST

Let all the house of Israel therefore know for certain that God has made him both Lord and Christ, this Jesus whom you crucified.
Acts 2:36

WHAT IS THE MEANING OF THE TITLES ASSOCIATED WITH THE NAME OF JESUS IN THE NEW TESTAMENT? In particular, what are we to make of the fact that at least sixty times He is referred to as the "Lord Jesus Christ"? To see fully who He is in the gospel message, we need to understand all three of these designations.

Jesus. If you had lived in Nazareth where Jesus grew up, you might have known several Jewish men with this name. It was a common name, but it was highly regarded because in ancient Israel the Hebrew name *Yehoshua* joined the name of God with the word for *salvation* (rescue, deliverance). It meant *God is our Salvation.*

Christ. The Greek for *Christ* is equivalent to the Hebrew for *Messiah,* and both refer to the "anointed one" foretold by the Jewish prophets. To say that Jesus is "Christ" affirms nothing less than Jesus' identity as the coming King, the One who would vanquish every foe and rule over God's glorious kingdom forever.

Lord. This is a first-century designation of authority, but in Jesus' case, the authority goes far beyond any human rule. He is the "Lord of lords and King of kings" (Revelation 17:14). He has the authority to rule every person's life. But here is the point: if Jesus Christ *is* the Lord, we need to *submit* to His lordship. It is a mockery to say the words "Jesus is Lord" if it is not His will that actually governs us (Luke 6:46). Jesus is not our Savior (providing our forgiveness) if He is not also our King (receiving our obedience).

In the text above, Peter said that "God has made him both Lord and Christ, this Jesus whom you crucified." So Jesus Christ is the rightful Ruler of the universe whether we give Him permission to rule over us or not. But if we refuse His rule in this world, we will not dwell with Him in the next. When He sits in judgment, the King will banish from His realm every disloyal subject — "And then will I declare to them, 'I never knew you; depart from me'" (Matthew 7:23). Now is the time to be reconciled to Him and yield ourselves to His loving reign. But we should weigh our decision carefully. If He is truly going to be our Lord, there must be nothing about us that we won't let Him govern.

Jesus Christ will be Lord of all or he will not be Lord at all.

AUGUSTINE OF HIPPO

January 21

Repent and Be Baptized

Now when they heard this they were cut to the heart, and said
to Peter and the rest of the apostles, "Brothers, what shall we do?"
And Peter said to them, "Repent and be baptized every one of you
in the name of Jesus Christ for the forgiveness of your sins,
and you will receive the gift of the Holy Spirit."
Acts 2:37,38

WE GET THE BEST ANSWERS WHEN WE ASK THE RIGHT QUESTIONS. On the Day of Pentecost following Jesus' resurrection, a large crowd in Jerusalem heard Peter and the other apostles preach the gospel of Christ publicly for the first time. Many were "cut to the heart," and no one in the history of human inquiry has ever asked a better question than they did: *What shall we do?*

Repent and be baptized. The forgiveness of sins in Jesus Christ requires that we repent of the sins we seek to be forgiven of. In godly sorrow, we determine that we will put these things out of our hearts and lives. Then we must be baptized, which means to be immersed in water. We do this "in the name of Jesus Christ," as an act of faith (Colossians 2:12) required for our forgiveness.

For the forgiveness of your sins. Are we forgiven before or after we submit to baptism? Peter could not have been clearer when he instructed his hearers to repent and be baptized "for the forgiveness of your sins." This is consistent with the words of Ananias to Saul, "And now why do you wait? Rise and be baptized and wash away your sins, calling on his name" (Acts 22:16).

You will receive the gift of the Holy Spirit. Jesus had promised the giving of God's Spirit (John 7:37-39), and Peter says this is for those whose sins have been forgiven. But to what effect? Much might be said, but whatever may be the blessings of God's Spirit in the life of the Christian (and there are many), these all serve the ultimate purpose of our *salvation* — our final restoration to God's perfect glory.

The gospel which three thousand people obeyed in Acts 2 was the gospel of *Jesus Christ.* It was the message that God has made possible the forgiveness of our sins in Christ — resulting in a right relationship with Him, growth in godly character, and an eternal hope we could never have regained for ourselves if Jesus had not atoned for our sins. This is the gladdest of all glad tidings — and it is possible only because of the greatest sacrifice ever made.

We say that Jesus preached the gospel, but he did more.
He came that there might be a gospel to preach.

OSWALD CHAMBERS

January 22

JESUS: THE WAY, THE TRUTH, THE LIFE

Jesus said to him, "I am the way, and the truth, and the life.
No one comes to the Father except through me."
John 14:6

OF ALL THE REMARKABLE THINGS ABOUT JESUS CHRIST, NONE IS MORE POWERFUL THAN HIS VIEW OF WHAT OUR REAL PROBLEM IS, THE ONE PROBLEM THAT ALL OTHERS ARE MERELY SYMPTOMS OF. Both His mission and His message were aimed directly at the problem of sin. It was the salvation of our souls that He wanted to give us — *a home in eternity with the God who created us, the God we cut ourselves off from the first time we sinned by saying no to His will.*

First, think about our need for a "way." Having broken the relationship with God for which we were created, we have no means of being reconciled unless God Himself provides a way for us to be saved. That is exactly what God has done in His Son, and Jesus was unmistakably clear that the way back to God would only be through Him. "No one comes to the Father except through me."

Next, think about our need for "truth." If it was untruth about God that deceived us into breaking His law, then truth is going to have to be put back in its rightful place if the problem of sin is ever going to be fixed. Jesus came to reestablish the truth about God.

Finally, think about our need for "life." Untruth is the means the devil uses, but his objective is our death. And the first time we yielded to his temptation to commit sin, that is what happened: we died spiritually. So it was Jesus' desire to rescue us from this terrible death and give us back our birthright — *life in God.*

At one point, many of Jesus' disciples began to leave Him. "So Jesus said to the twelve, 'Do you want to go away as well?' Simon Peter answered him, 'Lord, to whom shall we go? You have the words of eternal life'" (John 6:67,68). The truth was becoming clear to Peter: we simply can't survive without what Jesus came to bring us. Apart from Him, there is no *way* back to God, no certainty of *truth* about God, and no *life* other than the desperate yearning of our earthly existence. Jesus Christ is not one of many ways to return to God. He is not even the best way. He is the *only* way.

Follow me: I am the way, the truth, and the life.
Without the way there is no going;
Without the truth there is no knowing;
Without the life there is no living.

THOMAS À KEMPIS

January 23

DISCIPLES, CHRISTIANS

So Barnabas went to Tarsus to look for Saul, and when he had found him, he brought him to Antioch. For a whole year they met with the church and taught a great many people. And in Antioch the disciples were first called Christians.
Acts 11:25,26

THE TERM "CHRISTIAN" IS QUITE FAMILIAR IN OUR CULTURE. It is the designation most often used for those who are followers of Jesus of Nazareth. Today, let's look at the use of this term in Acts 11:25,26, which is the first use of it in the New Testament. In particular, let's ponder the fact that before Jesus' followers were called "Christians" they were known simply as "disciples" of Christ.

Disciples. To be a "disciple" is to be a pupil, the student of a master teacher. But more than that, it means to be a follower of the teacher's way of life, one who emulates not just the teacher's ideas but the teacher himself. So Jesus' followers were not just admirers; they were disciples who modeled their character after His.

Christians. Our text says that in Antioch the disciples began to be called "Christians." What an honor this was (even if it was used derisively by the public). To wear the name of our Savior, the One who died for us, is a great privilege. So we strive "to walk in a manner worthy of the Lord, fully pleasing to him" (Colossians 1:10).

It is not a coincidence that the term "Christian" was first used in Antioch. In this city, for the first time, the congregation of disciples was made up of both Jews and Gentiles. God's plan was not complete until the Gentiles had been included, and when that was done, God's people were now ready to be called "Christians."

If we are Christians, it is important for us to understand what it means to be among those who have "obeyed the gospel." To be a "disciple" of Jesus Christ, and hence a "Christian," is to be among those who have been *forgiven.* It does not mean we're perfect right now — it means we're on our way to a perfection that will be ours in eternity. John the Apostle said it this way: "Beloved, we are God's children now, and what we will be has not yet appeared; but we know that when he appears we shall be like him, because we shall see him as he is. And everyone who thus hopes in him purifies himself as he is pure" (1 John 3:2,3).

The Christian is not one who has gone all the way with Christ. None of us has. The Christian is one who has found the right road.

CHARLES L. ALLEN

January 24

JUSTIFIED

Therefore, since we have been justified by faith, we have peace with God through our Lord Jesus Christ.
Romans 5:1

IN THIS VERSE, PAUL WRITES OF THE JUSTIFICATION AVAILABLE TO US IN JESUS CHRIST. Our situation before God is like that of a law-breaker in a courtroom. We have no hope of acquittal; because we are guilty (the evidence is clear that we've rebelled against God's law), we rightly stand under the law's penalty. In an "unjust" condition, what we need is to be "justified." And the gospel will not mean much to us until we see how desperate our plight is. If our lives end while we're still under the sentence of death for our treason, we will be banished and separated from the King forever.

Condemnation. The word *condemnation* is a strong word, but it is not too strong to describe our situation as people who have sinned against our Creator. We can't deny we've thought, spoken, and done things that we knew were against our Father's will, but we did them anyway, our conscience telling us all the while that we could not do these things and still be in a right relationship with God. We're all like the ones Paul spoke of whose sin was deliberate: they "know God's righteous decree that those who practice such things deserve to die" (Romans 1:32).

Justification. The good news of the gospel is that God was not willing to leave us in our lost state. He took our punishment upon Himself so we could be brought back into harmony with His justice — in other words, "justified" from our sins. Having given His Son's life for our transgressions, God is able to be both "just" and the "justifier" of those whose faith is in Jesus (Romans 3:23-26).

Peace with God. When we obey the gospel and are justified with God, the result is that "we have peace with God through our Lord Jesus Christ." This is not the subjective *feeling* of peace (although that is a by-product) but the objective status of *being* justified with God. We had put ourselves at enmity with God, but in Christ we have been "reconciled" to Him (Romans 5:10). This is what the gospel of Christ is about. And just as all of our worst problems stem from a wrong relationship with God, there is no real joy that does not flow from a right relationship with Him.

The doctrine of justification is the foundation that supports all of the other benefits we receive from Christ.

ERWIN W. LUTZER

January 25

EXULTING IN HOPE

Through him we have also obtained access by faith
into this grace in which we stand, and we
rejoice in hope of the glory of God.
Romans 5:2

HAVING POINTED IN THE PREVIOUS VERSE TO THE JUSTIFICATION FROM OUR PAST SINS, PAUL SPEAKS IN THIS VERSE OF THE PRESENT GRACE AND FUTURE HOPE OF THE GOSPEL. Because the alienation has been removed, the relationship we can now have with God is rich and good — it is a foretaste of the perfect, unblemished relationship we will be able to have with Him in eternity.

The grace in which we stand. It certainly took a marvelous measure of grace for God to wipe away the sins of our past, but salvation in Christ involves more than the removal of our guilty history. In the present moment, there is a grace "in which we stand." Grace, of course, has to do with blessing or favor, and the grace here is obviously God's. In Christ, we are surrounded by provisions and gifts from our Father that are beyond our power to imagine. In regard to our highest good, there is nothing we will ever truly need that God will withhold from us. "He who did not spare his own Son but gave him up for us all, how will he not also with him graciously give us all things?" (Romans 8:32).

By faith. Paul is very clear that our access to the grace in which we stand is an access gained "by faith." Although repentance (Acts 2:38), confession (Romans 10:9,10), and baptism (Acts 22:16) are required by God in our initial obedience to the gospel, the operative element in all of these is faith: trust in the saving work of God through His Son, Jesus Christ (Colossians 2:12).

Through Jesus Christ. It is Christ that Paul is referring to when he says it is "through him" we have been given access to God's grace. It was His sacrifice that made it possible. It is His lordship that we now submit to. And it is the hope of His return that energizes us. In this hope, Paul says, we *exult,* rejoicing more the closer we get to its realization. For those in Christ, the "hope of the glory of God" is simply the most dynamic force in the universe.

Make us thy mountaineers;
We would not linger on the lower slope.
Fill us afresh with hope, O God of hope,
That undefeated, we may climb the hill,
As seeing Him who is invisible.

AMY CARMICHAEL

January 26

THE OBEDIENCE OF FAITH

. . . to bring about the obedience of faith
for the sake of his name among all the nations.
Romans 1:5

TEXTS THAT INDICATE SOMEONE'S "PURPOSE" SHOULD BE STUDIED CAREFULLY. In Romans 1:5, Paul was speaking of the purpose of his preaching as an apostle of Christ: "to bring about the obedience of faith" among all nations. So what is the "obedience of faith," and why is it so important that Paul could say it was the goal or outcome that he hoped for in his preaching? The expression may be taken in two ways, both of which make a valid point.

Obedience to the faith. If the phrase is translated like this (as in the NKJV), the idea would be that the preaching of "the faith" is intended to produce obedience. This is clearly the thought in Acts 6:7 where "a great many of the priests became obedient to the faith" and is consistent with the language of texts like Romans 10:16.

The obedience of faith. The ESV and many other translations render the phrase in this manner. Looking at it this way, the passage points to the importance of faith as the source of the Christian's obedience. In other words, we rightly respond to the gospel only when our obedience is based on faith, or trust, in God.

Either way, there is a vital connection between faith and obedience. The two can never be separated. For one thing, the person who does not obey God is not telling the truth if he says he has faith. "True faith commits us to obedience" (A. W. Tozer). As James put it, "Faith by itself, if it does not have works, is dead" (James 2:17). But it is equally true that our obedience must be motivated by faith. Like Noah, Abraham, and many others, we must do what God says because we trust Him. So the old hymn "Trust and Obey" said it very well. Faith without obedience is useless, but so is obedience without faith. *Faith and obedience must work together.* What's in our hearts and what's in our actions must match up.

The "obedience of faith," then, makes obedience to the gospel of Christ a different kind of obedience. In the world, obedience is based on either feelings or legal obligation, but in the gospel it is based on *trust in God.* Confident that His way is the best, we obey. *No matter how things look to us, we trust His love to bring us home.*

The highest pinnacle of the spiritual life is not happy joy in unbroken sunshine, but absolute and undoubting trust in the love of God.

A. W. THOROLD

January 27

CRUCIFIED WITH CHRIST

I have been crucified with Christ. It is no longer I who live, but Christ who lives in me. And the life I now live in the flesh I live by faith in the Son of God, who loved me and gave himself for me.
Galatians 2:20

IN THE TEXT ABOVE, PAUL SPEAKS OF "THE LIFE I NOW LIVE." This, of course, stands in contrast to the way he lived previously, when "faith in the Son of God" was not his guiding principle. To say the least, obedience to the gospel of Christ creates a "before" and an "after" — a radical conversion or turning in a person's life.

God's ultimate intention for us. In Christ, God plans to do more than smooth out a few wrinkles from our lifestyles; He plans to renovate the depths of our hearts so radically that *our character will be just like that of Jesus Christ.* When our hearts have become miniature models of Christ's own heart, we will truly be His siblings, bearing as He does the unblemished image of our Father. God aims for us "to be conformed to the image of his Son, in order that he might be the firstborn among many brothers" (Romans 8:29).

Our commitment to think differently. Being "crucified with Christ" does not happen automatically. It is a *choice* we make, and it is one we make *continually.* Learning to "live by faith in the Son of God" is not easy. It requires the kind of commitment and discipline which says, "I am done with self-will and self-reliance. God being my helper, I will learn to move at His command because I *trust* Him." A human being cannot change at any deeper level than this.

What will motivate us to make the change? Nothing less than deep gratitude for God's forgiveness is powerful enough to produce the kind of change He plans for us. The difference between Paul's past and present was motivated by his love for the Son of God, "who loved me and gave himself for me." In another text, he said that "the love of Christ controls us . . . he died for all, that those who live might no longer live for themselves but for him who for their sake died and was raised" (2 Corinthians 5:14,15).

May we never underestimate the seriousness of what has to happen to us in Christ. *Crucifixion* is not too strong a word for it. It was doubt and distrust that drove us to sin. That must change. Forgiven, we must learn to "live by faith in the Son of God."

"Crucified" is the only really definitive adjective by which to describe the Christian life.

J. FURMAN MILLER

January 28

The Importance of Jesus' Miracles

Now Jesus did many other signs in the presence of the disciples, which are not written in this book; but these are written so that you may believe that Jesus is the Christ, the Son of God, and that by believing you may have life in his name.
John 20:30,31

CLAIMS AS RADICAL AS THOSE MADE BY JESUS OF NAZARETH REQUIRE STRONG SUPPORT. No one should be expected to believe them without sufficient evidence. So Peter began his argument that Jesus was the Messiah by saying to a crowd in Jerusalem not long after Jesus' crucifixion, "Men of Israel, hear these words: Jesus of Nazareth, a man attested to you by God with mighty works and wonders and signs that God did through him in your midst, as you yourselves know . . ." (Acts 2:22). The miraculous deeds the dwellers in Jerusalem knew Jesus had performed attested to the veracity of an astonishing fact: *Jesus was, in fact, who He claimed to be.*

The apostle John said he wrote about Jesus' miracles "so that you may believe." In other words, the miracles of Jesus (which had been seen by many eyewitnesses, including His enemies) authenticated the truth of what He claimed about Himself. That is why the miracles were called "signs." As observable events, they "signified" the truth of Jesus' identity as "the Christ, the Son of God."

And yes, it is important that the eyewitnesses were not just Jesus' friends. After Jesus raised Lazarus from the dead, "the chief priests and the Pharisees gathered the council and said, 'What are we to do? For this man performs many signs. If we let him go on like this, everyone will believe in him, and the Romans will come and take away both our place and our nation'" (John 11:47,48).

The simple truth is, there is no *historical* reason to reject the miracles of Jesus. Before even looking at the records, we may have already made a decision that miracles *cannot* take place, and if so, no amount of historical evidence will convince us. But if we let the evidence speak, we see that we can't discredit Jesus' miracles without resorting to explanations that would be even harder to believe than the miracles themselves. And that is where faith begins — *with a willingness to trust what the evidence tells us.* "Eternal life does not begin with death; it begins with faith" (Samuel M. Shoemaker).

Faith does not mean believing without evidence. It means believing in realities that go beyond sense and sight — for which a totally different sort of evidence is required.

JOHN BAILLIE

January 29

THERE IS NO FREEDOM EXCEPT IN THE TRUTH

. . . and you will know the truth, and the truth will set you free.
John 8:32

FREEDOM IS AN IDEA THAT RESONATES IN EVERY HUMAN HEART. We all long to be free. Many forces trap us and hold us back, but which one of our problems is the slavemaster that has harmed us the most? According to Jesus, it is sin. Whatever else may bind us, the practice of departing from what we know is our Creator's will is our worst problem. If we're old enough to know right from wrong, we've all been guilty of it over and over again. And sin is not a master we can simply decide to walk away from anytime we wish. On our own, we are helpless to repair the damage. Jesus said, "Everyone who practices sin is a slave to sin" (John 8:34).

But Jesus did more than just diagnose the problem. As the Son of God, He not only identified the central problem of the human race; He proposed to fix it Himself. He said that He would make us free. And He would not just make us free; He would give us a freedom that was abundant and everlasting. He said, "If the Son sets you free, you will be free indeed" (John 8:36).

But Jesus was very clear as to where the problem came from: it came from deception. Mankind never would have sinned if it had not believed the devil's lie (Genesis 3:1-6; Revelation 12:9); so the only path out of sin is the path that leads us back to truth. Truth — and particularly the truth about God — must be put back in its place. If not, the problem of sin will just get worse and worse.

So Jesus said, "You will know the truth, and the truth will set you free." But I must be frank: if we are to be set free from our sins, it is not just truth about the world (or even truth about God's "plan of salvation") that we must accept. It is the truth about ourselves. *The prospects for our future reality can never improve until we accept the bitter facts about our present reality.* "The difference between life as it is and life as it ought to be is a frightening and distressing bit of reality" (James C. Dobson). Coming to terms with the full, ugly truth about who we really are and what we've really done is hard, but there is no other way to salvation. Jesus deals in reality. He intends to do far more than soothe our feelings with a heartfelt "religion" that says, "You're fine just as you are."

Jesus Christ makes us real, not merely sincere.

OSWALD CHAMBERS

January 30

FAITH IN THE POWERFUL WORKING OF GOD

. . . having been buried with him in baptism, in which
you were also raised with him through faith in the powerful
working of God, who raised him from the dead.
Colossians 2:12

THERE IS A SENSE IN WHICH JESUS' DEATH AND RESURRECTION HAPPENED ONLY ONCE. But there is another sense in which these events occur every time someone is baptized into Christ.

Our baptism into Christ is not a mere ritual or insignificant act of obedience — it is the most decisive turning point in our lives. Concerning baptism, the "before" and "after" are so different that Paul can say we are "buried with him in baptism." It is as if we are put to death and buried along with Christ. In the waters of baptism, our old way of life dies and is sealed in a tomb, a vivid reenactment of the death and burial of Christ Himself.

But Christ did not remain in the grave and neither do we. Just as He was raised, we are "raised with him." In Romans 6:4, Paul wrote that we were "buried therefore with him by baptism into death, in order that, just as Christ was raised from the dead by the glory of the Father, we too might walk in newness of life." Our death, burial, and resurrection with Christ also look forward to the great day when we will be raised to live with God in eternity. "Now if we have died with Christ, we believe that we will also live with him" (Romans 6:8). Waiting for that day, we live very differently than we would if we were still dead in sin. "If then you have been raised with Christ, seek the things that are above, where Christ is, seated at the right hand of God. Set your minds on things that are above, not on things that are on earth" (Colossians 3:1,2).

Coming back to the text we began with, however, did you notice what Paul said about the active ingredient in baptism? The water itself does not wash away our sins, and by our obedience we certainly do not earn our salvation. *It is "through faith in the powerful working of God" that our new lives are created.* Baptism is an act of trust, a placing of our faith in the promise of God to save us.

But listen: doesn't all this talk of death tell you how serious sin is? Dealing with it requires our being killed and resurrected. It is only by dying with Christ that the death of sin can be defeated.

God salvages the individual by liquidating him and
then raising him again to newness of life.

A. W. TOZER

January 31

THE GOSPEL: THE POWER OF GOD FOR SALVATION

For I am not ashamed of the gospel, for it is the power of God for salvation to everyone who believes, to the Jew first and also to the Greek.
Romans 1:16

WHEN PAUL WROTE THIS TO THE CHRISTIANS IN ROME, HE HAD NEVER BEEN THERE. And his critics seem to have been saying that he didn't have enough courage to leave the hinterlands and come preach the gospel in Rome, the most powerful and sophisticated city in the world. But Paul was no less ready to preach there than anywhere else. "I am not ashamed of the gospel," he said.

Paul said the gospel is powerful, and that's an important point in itself. If it is "the power of God," we should expect that power to be great. But it is *salvation* that this power of God is for. Whatever secondary blessings may flow from Christ, His mission was to save us from our sins. We will not understand Jesus Christ until we see that sin is the problem He came to correct. Speaking of Himself as the Christ (or Messiah), He said to His apostles, "Thus it is written, that the Christ should suffer and on the third day rise from the dead, and that repentance for the forgiveness of sins should be proclaimed in his name to all nations, beginning from Jerusalem. You are witnesses of these things" (Luke 24:46-48).

But while the Jewish people were privileged to be the first recipients of the gospel, it would ultimately be a universal gospel, a message of forgiveness "to everyone who believes, to the Jew first and also to the Greek." If salvation had been limited to those under the Law of Moses, that would have restricted it to the Jews and Jewish proselytes. But all have sinned, both Jew and Gentile, and all need salvation. The gospel is God's power to save anyone and everyone, the condition being faith and not race or ethnicity.

Since it is about sin, the gospel is not the kind of message the world wants to hear. But we dare not change it to make it attractive to those who have no interest in the forgiveness of their sins. Paul said he was not ashamed of the gospel. Are we? Would we go into the halls of power and prestige today and declare the gospel clearly — not the modernized, culturally filtered message being presented as "Christianity," but the gospel of repentance and obedience as it was proclaimed by Jesus and His apostles?

Humble and self-forgetting we must be always,
but diffident and apologetic about the gospel, never.

JAMES S. STEWART

February 1

IT IS BY GOD'S GRACE THAT WE ARE SAVED

For by grace you have been saved through faith.
And this is not your own doing; it is the gift of God.
Ephesians 2:8

IN HIS MAGNIFICENT LETTER TO THE CHURCH IN EPHESUS, PAUL MAKES IT CLEAR THAT ALL THE SAVED HAVE BEEN SAVED BY GOD'S GRACE. The church in Ephesus was made up primarily of Gentiles, and he wanted them to be encouraged by the fact that God's grace had saved them, just as much as it had saved their Jewish brethren.

None of us who are in Christ deserved to be saved from our sins. It was an act of sheer grace. "But God, being rich in mercy, because of the great love with which he loved us, even when we were dead in our trespasses, made us alive together with Christ — by grace you have been saved — and raised us up with him and seated us with him in the heavenly places in Christ Jesus, so that in the coming ages he might show the immeasurable riches of his grace in kindness toward us in Christ Jesus" (Ephesians 2:4-7).

Then in v.8, we have our text: "For by grace you have been saved through faith. And this is not your own doing; it is the gift of God." In Acts 15:11, the apostle Peter, as a Jew, courageously admitted this: "We believe that we [the Jews] will be saved through the grace of the Lord Jesus, just as they [the Gentiles] will." He was right. It took as much grace to save the Jews as it did to save the Gentiles. If *any* of us are pardoned and given entrance into the kingdom, it will only be by the magnitude of the King's goodness.

As great as this truth is, many have misunderstood it. What had to happen for us to be included in God's kingdom was the forgiveness of our sins. The means whereby God was able to do that was the death of His Son — *and His grace consisted in the giving of that gift, thereby making salvation possible.* That does not mean there are no conditions we must obey or that God's "gift" will fulfill the conditions for us. To the contrary, if we believe God has offered us — by His grace — the gift of salvation, our question will be, "What must I do to be saved?" (Acts 16:30). And humility will move us to accept God's answer, grateful that there is any answer at all.

We need to better understand that God applies His grace to mankind in giving Jesus Christ as our Savior, and that He calls upon us as free moral agents to commit ourselves in submissive obedience unto Him in order to receive the promises He has conditionally placed before us.

ROBERT F. TURNER

February 2

THE WORDS OF ETERNAL LIFE

Simon Peter answered him, "Lord, to whom shall we go?
You have the words of eternal life."
John 6:68

IN JOHN 6, WHEN JESUS GAVE HIS DIFFICULT "BREAD OF LIFE" DISCOURSE, MANY OF HIS DISCIPLES DECIDED THEY WOULD NOT FOLLOW HIM ANYMORE. But when He asked His inner circle of disciples, the twelve apostles, if they also would turn away from Him, Peter said, "Lord, to whom shall we go? You have the words of eternal life." Peter understood something about Jesus that we most certainly need to understand in our own generation.

Jesus was a teacher, but He was much more than that. He claimed that what He taught came directly from the mind of God (John 8:38; 12:49,50). In fact, He claimed to be the Son of God, sent into the world to reveal truths about God that no one could know who was not God Himself (John 3:31-36; 6:41-48).

And what was the purpose of the words that Jesus spoke? It was not to satisfy anyone's intellectual curiosity, and it was not merely to transform this world into a better place. No, there was a much higher purpose. Comparing Himself to the manna given to Israel in the wilderness, which gave them physical life, Jesus said that He was the Bread of Life. To His disciples He said, "The words that I have spoken to you are spirit and life" (John 6:63).

Spiritually dead because of our sins and without hope, we need "life." Not just a better life in this world and not merely release from the fear of physical death — but the prospect of having *the kind of life God has.* What we lost in sin was not just physical or biological life, but the life we would have had as "sons of God." Jesus taught that, in Him, this "eternal" kind of life can be given back to us (Romans 8:29). And His teaching is the only path to that life.

So Jesus' utterances are more than mere words. *They are the truths and the instructions necessary if we are ever going to be reconciled to our Creator.* All the other words that have ever been spoken pale by comparison. To say the least, they are important. But are we *paying attention* to these, the most important words in the world?

Besides belonging to eternity, Christ belonged to his times;
on the outskirts of a dying civilization he spoke of dying in order
to live. Today, when our civilization is likewise dying, his words have
the same awe-inspiring relevance as they had then.

MALCOLM MUGGERIDGE

February 3

ARE WE WILLING TO LEARN FROM OUR LIMITS?

What is crooked cannot be made straight,
and what is lacking cannot be counted.
Ecclesiastes 1:15

GOD HAS MADE THE PRESENT WORLD AN UNPREDICTABLE PLACE. Lest we think figuring out which buttons to push will invariably get us what we want from the world's vending machine, God prevents us from having this much control. He makes sure we can't straighten out every crooked thing in our lives. Paul describes this by saying "the creation was subjected to futility" (Romans 8:20).

This means the future is frustratingly unknowable. We may push all the right buttons and life's candy bar still not be forthcoming. "I saw that under the sun the race is not to the swift, nor the battle to the strong . . . but time and chance happen to them all" (Ecclesiastes 9:11). Sometimes God allows our plans to materialize, but sometimes He does not. This unpredictability is meant to disabuse us of any notion that we're in control of what happens.

Human civilization. If we're honest, we have to admit that conditions in the world are getting worse and worse. For every problem we've solved, we've created several new ones, each more terrible than the last. But rather than confess our powerlessness, we suppose it is just a matter of time until science solves all the riddles. This is, as David Ehrenfeld called it, the "arrogance of humanism."

Individual lives. We may know non-religious folks who disregard God in making their plans, and we believe they will find out the hard way that human plans don't always pan out. They should be more humble, we think. But if the "human race" and "certain individuals" need to learn the limits of human endeavor, so do all the rest of us. Godly people certainly have some advantages in life, but they are not exempt from the restraints on human activity to which God has subjected the world. It's a bitter pill to swallow (and a blow to our religious pride), but not even the godliest can make things turn out the way they want them to all the time.

The truth is, none of us can figure this world out and control it — *none of us.* That is the message of the Book of Ecclesiastes. For that reason, Ecclesiastes is a powerful preparation for the gospel. Its purpose is to deny the predictability of our earthly activities, and if it defeats us in that way, a great victory will have been won.

There are some defeats more triumphant than victories.

MICHEL DE MONTAIGNE

February 4

When Comfort and Confidence Are Dangerous

For you say, I am rich, I have prospered, and I need nothing, not realizing that you are wretched, pitiable, poor, blind, and naked.
Revelation 3:17

AFFLUENT SOCIETIES ARE OFTEN THE LEAST OPEN TO THE GOSPEL OF CHRIST. People who can get whatever they want to satisfy their temporal desires pay little attention to their spiritual needs.

The problem is that material prosperity breeds a false confidence in ourselves. When our immediate desires are fulfilled, we are deluded into thinking that we are self-sufficient. We don't actually have what we need, of course, but wealth deceives us. Like candy which makes us think we don't need any food, physical comfort tends to push our spiritual needs into the background.

Even after becoming Christians, affluence can hinder us. The Christians in Laodicea, for example, were prosperous financially, but when the Lord looked at their hearts, He saw that they were "wretched, pitiable, poor, blind, and naked." Doing so well on the outside made it hard for them to recognize their wretchedness on the inside. There were no doubt other congregations in those days that were just as much in need of repentance, but the less wealthy congregations would have had an easier time *seeing* their need.

But what about us? What should we do? Honesty and courage are always the first steps toward spiritual progress, so the first thing is to come out of hiding and bring ourselves before God's throne. *Lord, help me to see my heart as You see it. Search me and try me. Expose every idol in my heart that has kept me from You. Take away from me every comfort in this world that has blinded me to my deeper needs. Open my eyes to see how much I need You and Your forgiveness.*

Whether we are rich or poor, comfortable or uncomfortable, we urgently need to understand the helplessness of our spiritual state. Our sins have put us in an absolutely *lost* condition before God, and we dare not let the comforts of our lives in this world distract us from our plight. What we need is more than a psychological boost to help us fill in the blanks and round out our worldly resumé — we need to be *saved.* The sooner we admit our woeful inability, the sooner we'll be ready to hear the gospel.

It is to the drowning man the Rescuer comes. To the brave swimmer who can fare well alone He comes not. And no rush of joy *can* be like that of a man towards his Rescuer.

A. J. RUSSELL

February 5

That We Should Not Perish

For God so loved the world, that he gave his only Son, that whoever believes in him should not perish but have eternal life. For God did not send his Son into the world to condemn the world, but in order that the world might be saved through him.
John 3:16,17

MANY PEOPLE WOULD SAY THIS TEXT IS THEIR FAVORITE. But favorite things have a way of becoming so familiar that they no longer challenge us as we need to be challenged. With a text like John 3:16,17, we need to be careful. It is a beautiful sentiment, certainly, but it was meant to do more than make us feel good.

If God had not given His Son for us, we would "perish." That is a strong word, but it is the only word strong enough to describe what happens when we separate ourselves from our Creator. Charles Colson was right when he said that "sin is essentially rebellion against the rule of God." It is a defiant declaration of independence against our Creator, and if sin is not remedied, its consequence is eternal banishment from the presence of God, attended by a corruption and anguish we can barely imagine right now. Of all the ways we might "perish," this would be the worst.

Amazingly, however, God was not willing to abandon us. Although He might have justly left us to our consequences, His love moved Him to provide pardon. He did not want us to perish. But ponder with me what had to happen if He was to forgive us without violating the laws of His own justice: *"he gave his only Son, that whoever believes in him should not perish but have eternal life."* If we do not perish (as we surely deserve to do), it will be because of the grace of a Father who was willing to make the ultimate sacrifice to save us. And that grace is found in His Son, Jesus Christ.

How, then, should we respond to the truth of John 3:16,17? As I said above, it needs to be more than just a beautiful sentiment. If we are to do more than just admire its beauty, our first response should be to *obey* the gospel. How could we not say *Yes!* to a Father who has paid such a high price to bring us back home?

But second, we should respond by loving the world as God loves it: *sacrificially.* If He loved us enough, in our unworthy state, to save us at such great cost to Himself, is there any price too high for us to pay to help those around us with their spiritual needs?

God loved the world. Go thou and do likewise.

ERWIN W. LUTZER

February 6

FAITHFUL LOVE

The LORD bless you and keep you; the LORD make his face to shine upon you and be gracious to you; the LORD lift up his countenance upon you and give you peace.
Numbers 6:24-26

WORDS OFTEN COME IN PAIRS. For example, consider the words *benevolent* and *malevolent.* The first means "good will" and the second, "ill will." To be benevolently inclined toward someone is to want to help them, but if a person is malevolently inclined, that means their basic disposition is to hurt and to harm.

It's important to understand that God's basic inclination toward us is benevolent rather than malevolent. Having given us a free will, He will not force us to obey Him, and if we refuse to do so, He will not, just for our personal benefit, suspend the laws of His creation, one of which is that the penalty of sin is death. But He loves us, and it will break His heart if we refuse His salvation.

If there is ever any alienation between us and God, there can never be but one reason: we have kept God away by insisting on continuing in our sin — *and by refusing to accept His forgiveness on His terms.* "Behold, the LORD's hand is not shortened, that it cannot save, or his ear dull, that it cannot hear; but your iniquities have made a separation between you and your God, and your sins have hidden his face from you so that he does not hear" (Isaiah 59:1,2).

But God's hope is that we will turn back to Him. As He said to Israel through Ezekiel, "I have no pleasure in the death of the wicked, but that the wicked turn from his way and live; turn back, turn back from your evil ways, for why will you die, O house of Israel?" (Ezekiel 33:11). And in Moses' day, he had said, "I have set before you life and death, blessing and curse. Therefore choose life, that you and your offspring may live" (Deuteronomy 30:19).

God's faithful love is like most things about Him: *it is sobering as well as encouraging.* It should encourage us to know that God is always at the door of our hearts, wanting us to open up and accept His gift of life. But it should sober us to know that if we refuse, He will remain outside — and if we die in our rebellion, we will be lost forever. So with life and death set before us, *let us choose life.*

Let a man go away or come back: God never leaves.
He is always at hand and if he cannot get into your life,
still he is never farther away than the door.

MEISTER ECKHART

February 7

What Sin Is

Everyone who sins breaks the law; in fact, sin is lawlessness.
1 John 3:4 NIV

IF THE GOSPEL OF CHRIST IS ABOUT SALVATION FROM OUR SINS, IT IS IMPORTANT FOR US TO SEE CLEARLY WHAT SIN REALLY IS. If we deny the thing we need to be saved from, we are a long way from accepting God as our Rescuer. Hard as it is, sin is a fact we must face.

To begin with, we need to understand that God has authority over us. As our Creator, He has the right to govern everything about us. He happens to be a benevolent King (and we should be thankful for that), but in any case, He is our King. If we still lived in a sinless relationship to God, our every thought, word, and deed — and even every motive — would be obedient to His will.

But, of course, we *have* departed from God's rule. Every last one of us has done this (at least those who are old enough to discern good and evil). Early in our lives, we began pursuing our own will, deliberately setting aside what we knew to be right. This is what sin is, and none of us can claim to be innocent.

Nowadays, we react negatively to words like *obedience* and *disobedience* (and that is one evidence of how much self-will is embedded in us), but the basic idea of obedience is essential to any realistic concept of God. In the final analysis, that is what sin comes down to: *disobedience to God.* It is a flouting of His law, His rule over our lives. Simply put, sin is "lawlessness" (1 John 3:4). As Benjamin Whichcote said, "Sin is defiance to the authority of God."

It is important to see that God's law is an *objective* standard for our behavior. The thing that is wrong when we sin is not merely that we do something that gives us subjective feelings of guilt, but that we transgress an actual standard of right and wrong, one that originates in the mind and character of God Himself.

Also, it is not just our actions that are sinful but our intentions (Hebrews 4:12,13). In fact, that is the main thing that is wrong with sin. "Sin is not wrong doing; it is wrong being, deliberate and emphatic independence of God" (Oswald Chambers). Only creatures made in God's image are capable of committing this crime.

Sin is an affair of the will. It is not a "vestige of our animal inheritance." That trivial notion comes from an unexamined, too-quickly swallowed doctrine of evolution. Why blame the brute creation? No self-respecting wolf would be guilty of our modern wars.

GEORGE ARTHUR BUTTRICK

February 8

Do We Deny the Lord's Diagnosis?

I counsel you to buy from me gold refined by fire, so that you may be rich, and white garments so that you may clothe yourself and the shame of your nakedness may not be seen, and salve to anoint your eyes, so that you may see. Those whom I love, I reprove and discipline, so be zealous and repent.
Revelation 3:18,19

IF THE GOSPEL IS ABOUT GOD SAVING US FROM OUR SINS, THE FIRST REQUIREMENT IS TO SEE OUR SINFULNESS IN ITS TRUE LIGHT. This is not an easy thing to do, especially in our age when the very concept of sin is often scoffed at. We may admit to having made a few mistakes, or even having some dysfunctional habits, but we do not see ourselves as sinful people who need the forgiveness of our Creator. We think of ourselves as good people who might profit from a little improvement. We just need to "come to Christ."

But Jesus' diagnosis of our problem cuts deeper. Not even the best of us has a heart anywhere close to the purity that would be needed to live with God in eternity. Deep down, we know we've been good when it suited us, but when it didn't suit us, we did as we pleased, often setting aside what we knew was God's will. We know, if we're honest, that self-will has been our master. The heart-penetrating light of truth shows us to be rebels against God.

Ironically, the more "respectable" our lives have been outwardly, the harder it is for us to see how rebellious we've been inwardly. That is why Jesus' message of repentance was rejected by the religious folks who should have been the first to welcome Him. As they saw things, they had no significant sins to repent of.

Even as Christians (maybe especially as Christians) we are hindered by an overly optimistic assessment of how well we're doing. To the Christians in Laodicea, who thought they were well-clothed, Jesus counseled them to buy from Him white garments so that "the shame of your nakedness may not be seen."

What should be our response when the Lord tries to burst the bubble of our self-righteousness? *We should accept the Lord's diagnosis.* Like David, we should admit that God is right and we are wrong: "so that you may be justified in your words and blameless in your judgment" (Psalm 51:4). If we're not willing to be honest about how sinful we've been, there is no hope for us to be forgiven.

God has nothing to say to the self-righteous.

DWIGHT LYMAN MOODY

February 9

What If We Could Solve Every Problem but One?

And he said, "I will do this: I will tear down my barns and build larger ones, and there I will store all my grain and my goods. And I will say to my soul, 'Soul, you have ample goods laid up for many years; relax, eat, drink, be merry.'" But God said to him, "Fool! This night your soul is required of you, and the things you have prepared, whose will they be?"
Luke 12:18-20

THE SUCCESSFUL, PROSPEROUS ESTATE OWNER PORTRAYED IN JESUS' STORY IS A FIGURE WE ARE FAMILIAR WITH. We may (if we're honest) see him when we look in the mirror, but even if we don't, we see him in our neighborhoods and communities. Especially in the wealthier nations of the world, the population is increasingly made up of people for whom God is largely irrelevant, but their lives have still been happy, healthy, and socially well-adjusted.

Religious people may suppose that secular people are not genuinely happy, but the truth is, we live in a world where it is possible to deny the existence of God and still get through life quite comfortably. Even more so today than ever before, with the advances that have been made economically and scientifically, a person can have a life that is long and enjoyable. Psychologically, there are techniques available to overcome dysfunction and unhappiness. And if a person adopts the secular moral principles of compassion and equality, he can relate healthily to those around him and lessen the amount of suffering in the world.

But what if the God whom we have denied really does exist? What if we have solved all our problems except the biggest one? The man in Jesus' story said, "Soul, you have ample goods laid up for many years; relax, eat, drink, be merry." His life had been built on the assumption that there was no problem to which a secular solution could not be found — but now the problem he had not paid attention to confronted him in all of its terrible, deadly reality.

Eventually, we will find out whether our decisions about God were wise or foolish. If the Scriptures are correct, a day is coming that will be the greatest of all judgment days (Acts 17:30,31). Until then, the worst mistake we can make is thinking that because the sun is still shining in our lives, sin must not be a problem for us.

Shallow natures tremble for a night after their sin, and when they find that the sun rises and men greet them as cordially as before, and that no hand lays hold of them from the past, they think little more of their sin — they do not understand that fatal calm that precedes the storm.

MARCUS DODS

February 10

Sowing and Reaping

Do not be deceived: God is not mocked, for whatever one sows, that will he also reap. For the one who sows to his own flesh will from the flesh reap corruption, but the one who sows to the Spirit will from the Spirit reap eternal life.
Galatians 6:7,8

One of the worst mistakes we can make is to disconnect our actions in the present from our destiny in the future. The doctrine of God's grace, for example, is sometimes misunderstood to mean that we will enjoy eternity with God in heaven no matter how we live our lives right now. But that is not true. If we persist in disobedience, we are going to be lost. "Do not be deceived," Paul says. "Whatever one sows, that will he also reap."

Our destination in eternity is going to be the end of a path we have followed in this world. As long as life lasts, we are free to change paths (and that is what the gospel implores us to do), but when death overtakes us, it will be too late. God's judgment will be His unalterable ratification of the choice that we have made. For those who have obeyed the gospel and walked in Christ, heaven will be the "result" or "end" (Greek *telos*) of their journey (1 Peter 1:9). There will be nothing arbitrary or unpredictable about it.

There is a certain kind of fool, however, who ponders what has just been said and thinks to himself, "I will live my life right now in whatever way I please, but at the very end I will turn to God and be saved." His foolishness consists of at least two dangerous assumptions. One is that his opportunity for salvation is not going to run out unexpectedly, before he has time to "repent." The other is that his deathbed repentance is going to be genuine. God will always accept genuine repentance, of course, but how sincere do you think a person's repentance will be who all his life *planned* to give God nothing but the last few leftovers of his life?

These thoughts are sobering, to be sure. But if we "sow to the Spirit," they should also be encouraging; we can be confident that we will "from the Spirit reap eternal life" (Galatians 6:8). Either way, the Law of the Farm is going to decide our destiny. While we can, let's start obeying the gospel. It will bring us back to our Father — *and He is eagerly waiting to welcome us home.*

He who lives in sin and looks for happiness hereafter is like him who sows cockle and thinks to fill his barn with wheat or barley.

John Bunyan

February 11

The Horrible Lie We Tell Ourselves

The pride of your heart has deceived you, you who live in the clefts of the rock, in your lofty dwelling, who say in your heart, "Who will bring me down to the ground?" Though you soar aloft like the eagle, though your nest is set among the stars, from there I will bring you down, declares the LORD.
Obadiah 3,4

THE PROBLEM OF PRIDE ADDRESSED IN THE LITTLE BOOK OF OBADIAH IS A UNIVERSAL PROBLEM. Specifically, it pertained to Edom, a nation that had grown proud because of the seeming invincibility of its power and geographical security. Through the prophet Obadiah, God promised He would bring devastating judgment on the sins of Edom, and they would learn that they were not, in fact, as secure as they supposed. But the problem that plagued Edom is a universal human problem. There is no nation — and no individual — who does not need to listen to Obadiah.

The term *hubris* is familiar to us from ancient Greek and Roman history. It referred to the pride that deludes a person into thinking he can do anything he pleases, a pride that results in tragic consequences. But *hubris* is not only the problem of tragic heroes in ancient history; it is the problem of every human being. If possible, it is more of a temptation today than it was back then.

If we believe our hands can achieve anything our minds can conceive, we are telling ourselves a horrible lie. As God said to Edom, "The pride of your heart has deceived you." And as He said to the prosperous landowner in the story of Luke 12:16-20: "You fool! Tonight you will die. Then who will get what you have stored up?" (CEV). The fact is, we are not as invincible as we like to think. We are not autonomous. And we are not the masters of our own destiny. If we think we are, we're being not only foolish but self-destructive. Sooner or later, God will humble us and remind us of the limitations we have refused to acknowledge.

Today, we live in an age of unparalleled scientific progress. But the paradox of progress is that the more we achieve by our own know-how, the more vulnerable we are. Our pride becomes our weakness. And the worst part of it is that it makes us think we're too powerful to need God, or the gospel of His salvation through Christ. We destroy ourselves by what we thought was our strength.

We are slaves to our gadgets, puppets of our power, and prisoners of our security.

BILLY GRAHAM

February 12

TRUSTING GOD'S CHOSEN MEANS

And the LORD said to Moses, "Make a fiery serpent and set it on a pole, and everyone who is bitten, when he sees it, shall live." So Moses made a bronze serpent and set it on a pole. And if a serpent bit anyone, he would look at the bronze serpent and live.
Numbers 21:8,9

THERE IS NO WAY TO KNOW WHY GOD CHOSE THIS WAY OF SAVING THOSE WHO HAD BEEN SNAKEBITTEN. As the people of Israel drew near to the Promised Land, they grew distrustful and spoke against God and Moses. "Then the LORD sent fiery serpents among the people, and they bit the people, so that many people of Israel died" (Numbers 21:6). But when they cried out in grief, Moses prayed for them, and God said to him, "Make a fiery serpent and set it on a pole, and everyone who is bitten, when he sees it, shall live" (v.8). So Moses did as he was instructed, and sure enough, "if a serpent bit anyone, he would look at the bronze serpent and live" (v.9). As we meditate on what's involved in obeying the gospel, several things about this incident merit our attention.

One is that, as we have said, we cannot know *why* God decided to save the people in this way. Presumably, He could have done it in other ways, some of which might have made more sense to us. But if we are looking for some self-explanatory link between looking at a bronze image on a pole and being cured of snakebite, we will look in vain. Any linkage that our "logical" minds might decipher would be nothing more than a guess.

But the second thing is, we don't *have* to understand God's rationale. It was His grace that chose to provide any cure at all — and if He required them to look upon the bronze serpent before His grace granted the cure, He certainly had the right to do so.

Today, it is common to hear individuals question why God would connect baptism (immersion in water) with the forgiveness of sins (Acts 2:38; 22:16). But we do not know the reason why God linked that action to that result — nor, for that matter, do we know why He decided to require faith (John 8:24), repentance (Acts 17:30,31), and the confession of our faith (Romans 10:9,10). But the fact remains, those are the requirements that He has decided on.

One last thing is obvious, however: *God's reasons are always good.* And He has never devised a plan that did not have amazing results.

What God does, he does well.

JEAN DE LA FONTAINE

February 13

BEGINNING WITH THIS SCRIPTURE

And the eunuch said to Philip, "About whom, I ask you,
does the prophet say this, about himself or about someone else?"
Then Philip opened his mouth, and beginning with this Scripture he
told him the good news about Jesus. And as they were going along
the road they came to some water, and the eunuch said, "See,
here is water! What prevents me from being baptized?"
Acts 8:34-36

IN ACTS 8, WE HAVE THE ACCOUNT OF A CHRISTIAN NAMED PHILIP TEACHING THE GOSPEL TO AN ETHIOPIAN OFFICIAL WHO WAS RETURNING FROM A TRIP TO JERUSALEM TO WORSHIP. When Philip approached, he was reading from Isaiah. Inviting Philip into the chariot, the man asked him about the passage he had been reading: "Like a sheep he was led to the slaughter . . ." (Isaiah 53:7,8). So "beginning with this Scripture," Philip "told him the good news." Jesus was the person the prophecy referred to, the Messiah through whom we must receive the forgiveness of our sins. Philip also explained how the gospel must be responded to, because when "they came to some water . . . the eunuch said, 'See, here is water! What prevents me from being baptized?'"

What happened here was typical of most of the evangelism in Acts: *Jesus was shown to be the Messiah by the messianic prophecies in the Scriptures.* In Acts 18:28, for example, Apollos showed "by the Scriptures that the Christ was Jesus." When taken as a whole, the Old Testament is seen to be a thoroughly messianic work. It is filled with passages that prefigured the coming of a Savior, not only for the Jews but for the whole world — and the detailed fulfillment of all of these in the life and work of Jesus of Nazareth cannot possibly be accounted for by chance or accident.

In Acts 8, there is a straight line that runs from this man's reading of Isaiah 53 to his baptism into Christ. Each step led quite reasonably to the next. First, he saw the fulfillment of Isaiah's words in Jesus. Then he concluded that Jesus, as the Messiah, was his Savior. Next, he listened to Philip's explanation about how the gospel must be obeyed. And finally, he asked to be baptized. Thankfully, the Ethiopian was an honest man: (1) willing to *see* the truth, and (2) wanting to *do* whatever the truth required of him.

The correspondence between the description of the Servant and the
events surrounding Jesus' life, death, and resurrection was so convincing
that the Ethiopian believed immediately and was baptized.

MICHAEL A. RYDELNIK

February 14

Appeal to God for a Good Conscience

Baptism, which corresponds to this, now saves you, not as a removal of dirt from the body but as an appeal to God for a good conscience, through the resurrection of Jesus Christ.
1 Peter 3:21

According to Peter, baptism saves us. Its effectiveness does not lie in the washing of dirt from the body. And even as an action that is considered spiritual or religious, being immersed in water would surely not produce the forgiveness of sins if somebody did that in a rote, mechanical way, with no genuine penitence or faith in Christ. Nevertheless, Peter says that baptism saves us — and we need to understand what he meant by saying that.

In v.20, Peter had mentioned Noah. It was in Noah's ark, built at God's command, that eight people were "saved through water" (NKJV). Then, in v.21, Peter said that baptism "corresponds to this." Building the ark was an act of faith (Hebrews 11:7), but the outward act was not optional. It was not as though Noah had already been saved and the ark was just a sign of his commitment to God.

In a striking way, baptism truly is parallel to Noah's situation. Like Noah's obedience, baptism is an act of faith (Colossians 2:12), but also like Noah, we will not be saved without doing what God said. If God says to be baptized for the remission of our sins (Acts 2:38), we need not expect the gift to be given until we obey Him.

But let us be clear: the critical factor in baptism is *what takes place in the heart*. When one is baptized, he is longing to be saved from his sins. Making "an appeal to God for a good conscience," he yearns for his conscience to be eased by the grace of God's forgiveness — and "calling on the name of the Lord" (Acts 22:16 NKJV), he does what God has commanded, crying out for salvation.

When the Ethiopian official in Acts 8 learned the gospel and was baptized while he was traveling on the road from Jerusalem to Gaza, the text says that he "went on his way rejoicing" (v.39). And the Philippian jailer, after being baptized in the "same hour of the night" was said to have "rejoiced" (Acts 16:33,34). Surely, if there is anything in the world that can turn our sorrows into a song, it is the relief that comes from our conscience being cleared, the burden of sin's grief having been lifted (Romans 8:1,2).

The gospel is like a fresh, mild, and cool air in the extreme heat of summer, a solace and comfort in the anguish of conscience.

Martin Luther

February 15

Despised and Rejected by Men

He was despised and rejected by men, a man of sorrows and acquainted with grief; and as one from whom men hide their faces he was despised, and we esteemed him not.
Isaiah 53:3

IF THE WORLD HAD BEEN ALLOWED TO DESIGN ITS OWN MESSIAH OR SAVIOR, IT WOULD HAVE COME UP WITH SOMETHING VERY DIFFERENT FROM WHAT GOD ACTUALLY PROVIDED. Jesus was, to say the least, a shock. He was offensive, if not ridiculous, to His enemies. At one point, even His family thought He was "out of his mind" (Mark 3:21). The multitudes, who at first thronged to hear Him, eventually concluded that His teachings were too bizarre to be taken seriously (John 6:60,66). Even His closest friends and disciples often had a hard time understanding how He fit the pattern of the way the Messiah was supposed to act (Mark 8:31,32).

Many centuries before Jesus was born, Isaiah had said the Messiah would be "despised and rejected by men . . . one from whom men hide their faces." In v.2, he said that "he had no form or majesty that we should look at him, and no beauty that we should desire him." This does not mean there is any inherent value in poverty, social backwardness, or physical unattractiveness. But it was no accident that when God entered the world as a human being, He did so in very lowly circumstances. We may not understand all the reasons why God did this, but this much seems clear: *God wanted those who would be attracted to the gospel to be people who were looking for something other than "niceness" as the world perceives niceness.* He wanted people who were looking for *forgiveness.*

The apostle Paul wrote, "We regard no one according to the flesh. Even though we once regarded Christ according to the flesh, we regard him thus no longer" (2 Corinthians 5:16). As long as Paul assessed Jesus by fleshly criteria, he saw nothing Messiah-like about Him. To see the truth about this "despised" man, he had to look below the surface, so to speak. But what about us today? If we were trying to find the Messiah, what characteristics would we be looking for? Would we recognize Him when we found Him?

Jesus was not crucified in a cathedral between two candles, but on a cross between two thieves; on the town garbage heap; at a crossroads so cosmopolitan that they had to write his title in Hebrew and Latin and Greek; at the kind of place where cynics talk smut, and thieves curse, and soldiers gamble.

GEORGE MACLEOD

February 16

With His Wounds We Are Healed

But he was pierced for our transgressions; he was crushed for our iniquities; upon him was the chastisement that brought us peace, and with his wounds we are healed.
Isaiah 53:5

As a Jewish rabbi, Paul stumbled over the crucifixion of Christ in the same way that many have. The Messiah was to be the King, God's "Anointed." How could He even be killed, let alone die by crucifixion? To be hanged on a tree was to be under God's curse (Deuteronomy 21:22,23). Surely that kind of death automatically eliminated a person from being the Messiah.

The point Paul did not realize until later, however, was that Christ was indeed under God's curse, but it was not for His own sins; it was for ours. He voluntarily submitted to an accursed death to free us from the curse. "Christ redeemed us from the curse of the law by becoming a curse for us — for it is written, 'Cursed is everyone who is hanged on a tree'" (Galatians 3:13).

Isaiah had prophesied about the substitutionary nature of the Messiah's death centuries before it happened: *"But he was pierced for our transgressions; he was crushed for our iniquities; upon him was the chastisement that brought us peace, and with his wounds we are healed."* God put Him to grief, making Him "an offering for guilt" (v.10). In v.11, He would "bear their iniquities." And in v.12, He "bore the sin of many, and makes intercession for the transgressors." All of these phrases in Isaiah 53 say what many other Scriptures affirm: *the Messiah's death was vicarious.* He suffered *for* us — substituting Himself on our behalf at the bar of God's justice and agreeing to take the penalty that we had incurred by our sins.

Had any of us witnessed what was done to Jesus and known that this abomination was being suffered for us, it is not likely that we could have borne the sorrow of that. Perhaps it was a mercy that the handful of Jesus' friends who were at the foot of the cross did not fully understand what they saw until later. Who could have seen that, understood it, and not been crushed by shame?

The cross of Christ, therefore, is the ultimate contradiction: *He was murdered that we might be resurrected.* Upon Him was laid the chastisement that brought us peace, and in His horror is our hope.

The cross is a picture of violence, yet the key to peace, a picture of suffering, yet the key to healing, a picture of death, yet the key to life.

David Watson

February 17

LIKE A LAMB

He was oppressed, and he was afflicted, yet he opened not his mouth; like a lamb that is led to the slaughter, and like a sheep that before its shearers is silent, so he opened not his mouth.
Isaiah 53:7

IT WAS A BASIC PRINCIPLE OF THE LAW OF MOSES THAT THE VICTIM OF A CRIME WAS NOT ALLOWED TO PUNISH THE WRONGDOER — OTHERS WERE TO TAKE CARE OF THAT. We have the same principle in our laws today. And this principle makes obvious sense, does it not? The victim would always tend to overdo the punishment, so that task is relegated to those who are likely to be more just.

When Jesus, the most innocent victim who has ever been put to death, was being accused before the authorities, He did not strike back at those who were doing such wrong to Him. He did not even retaliate verbally. He understood (as we should understand) that justice must always be left in the hands of God, who can be counted on to perfectly balance justice and mercy. So if vengeance is what is needed, it is God who should carry it out. Quoting Deuteronomy 32:35, Paul said, "Beloved, never avenge yourselves, but leave it to the wrath of God, for it is written, 'Vengeance is mine, I will repay, says the Lord'" (Romans 12:19).

Although we know this, none of us would have had the restraint that Jesus did. *"He was oppressed, and he was afflicted, yet he opened not his mouth; like a lamb that is led to the slaughter, and like a sheep that before its shearers is silent, so he opened not his mouth."* Perhaps we might have done it, but we would have done it with the warm glow of smug self-approval: "These are wicked people, but I am so morally superior that I can take their mistreatment silently. There aren't many people willing to be as meek and humble as I am." But there was no such fake humility with Jesus.

The portrayal of Jesus' silent suffering in Isaiah 53 is a part of that prophecy's depiction of what would happen to the Messiah as He underwent the punishment for our sins. Nothing else like that death has ever taken place in the history of the world. Who would have thought that we could be healed by wounds being inflicted on our Savior? The more we learn of our Savior, the more we are moved to fall before God's throne and say, "How great Thou art."

All heaven is interested in the cross of Christ, all hell terribly afraid of it, while men are the only beings who more or less ignore its meaning.

OSWALD CHAMBERS

February 18

THE KNOWABLE GOD

No one has ever seen God; the only God, who is at
the Father's side, he has made him known.
John 1:18

WHILE AN INFINITE GOD COULD NEVER BE KNOWN COMPLETELY BY HIS CREATURES, THAT DOES NOT MEAN THAT NOTHING CAN BE KNOWN ABOUT GOD AT ALL. Other than the facts of His existence and power, which can be inferred from the creation (Romans 1:20), we could not know much by our own unaided wisdom (Romans 11:33; 1 Corinthians 1:21). But the truth is, we have not been left to our own wisdom. God has revealed Himself to the world — and this has reached its culmination in Jesus Christ.

We should not hesitate to say that God is "knowable." He is not *completely* knowable, but He is *truthfully* knowable. What we can know of God is not exhaustive, but it is objectively true. And it is right for us to rejoice in the knowledge we *can* have of God.

In contemporary culture, it is acceptable to speak of God as a mystery, but the moment one affirms anything specific about God, that is not viewed as helpful. Religion is rejected in favor of spirituality, where God is the "cosmic mystery," and paradox and uncertainty are privileged over any affirmation of objective truth. (Apparently the only thing we can be certain of — and therefore dogmatic about — is that there is nothing we can be certain of.)

We cannot, however, simply wave aside the question of whether God has revealed Himself to the human race. That issue must be dealt with, and it actually involves two questions: (1) is supernatural revelation *possible,* and (2) if it is possible, has it actually *occurred?* We cannot judge the gospel of Christ with any fairness if we come to the New Testament with our minds already made up that God cannot have revealed Himself. So rather than simply disregard the issue, we need to wrestle with it honestly.

On the eve of His crucifixion, Jesus prayed, "This is eternal life, that they know you, the only true God, and Jesus Christ whom you have sent" (John 17:3). So here is the gospel's position: *God has, in Jesus Christ, made it possible for us to know Him.* Sin robbed us of the truth about God, but in His Son we can regain that knowledge — and knowing our Creator, we may truly live.

The characteristics of God Almighty are mirrored for us in Jesus Christ.
Therefore if we want to know what God is like, we must study Jesus Christ.

OSWALD CHAMBERS

February 19

All the Fullness of God

For in him the whole fullness of deity dwells bodily.
Colossians 2:9

THE CHURCH IN COLOSSAE WAS BEING THREATENED BY A DESTRUCTIVE TEACHING THAT CALLED INTO QUESTION THE SUFFICIENCY OF CHRIST FOR THE SALVATION OF MANKIND. Paul, however, emphasized that Christ is absolutely supreme, not needing to be supplemented in any way. In fact, He is the full embodiment of God Himself. It is in Christ that "the whole fullness of deity dwells bodily."

Listen to Paul as he wrote about Jesus Christ: "He is the image of the invisible God, the firstborn of all creation. For by him all things were created, in heaven and on earth, visible and invisible, whether thrones or dominions or rulers or authorities — all things were created through him and for him. And he is before all things, and in him all things hold together. And he is the head of the body, the church. He is the beginning, the firstborn from the dead, that in everything he might be preeminent" (1:15-18).

It is beyond the limits of our finite understanding, but Jesus was God in the flesh. Somehow, God took upon Himself the form of humanity, with the result that Jesus was both God and man (John 1:1-3,14,18). The ultimate proof of this, of course, was the resurrection. If that event took place, then Jesus was telling the truth in everything He said, including what He said about Himself.

And what did He say about Himself? He said, "I and the Father are one" (John 10:30). So it is a colossal, towering truth that Paul presents to us when he says that in Christ "the whole fullness of deity dwells bodily." *But nothing less than this will suffice for our salvation.* If God's Son died for us, then He is the One "in whom we have redemption, the forgiveness of sins" (Colossians 1:14).

Finally, here is a practical truth that should strengthen us: if it is in Christ that our sins can be forgiven, it is also in Him that our every need can be met as we live from day to day. He is not only our Creator and Savior; He is our Sustainer. We will never have a problem that is beyond His ability to help us overcome. Indeed, His power overflows the banks of our need — as does His love.

Just because the fullness of deity dwells in Christ, therefore believers, by abiding in him, receive the fullness of their spiritual life. In him every want is supplied . . . in Christ they have a source from which flows all needed grace and courage and wisdom and strength.

CHARLES R. ERDMAN

February 20

The Exact Imprint of God's Nature

Long ago, at many times and in many ways, God spoke to our fathers by the prophets, but in these last days he has spoken to us by his Son, whom he appointed the heir of all things, through whom also he created the world. He is the radiance of the glory of God and the exact imprint of his nature.
Hebrews 1:1-3

God's revelation of Himself to mankind has been progressive. As the writer of Hebrews points out, God disclosed bits and pieces of the truth to the prophets over a long period of time, and we have the record of many of these revelations in the Hebrew Scriptures. But it was in His Son, Jesus Christ, that God made the perfect and complete disclosure of Himself. Christ is "the radiance of the glory of God and the exact imprint of his nature."

It is truly an amazing phenomenon that we have in Jesus Christ: in Him the "invisible" God has been made "visible." That which could never have been known about God, it is now possible for us to know. Of course, Jesus did not by His bodily characteristics show us what God looks like. Rather, it was the *character* of God — and God's *will* for us — that Christ revealed. In other words, He "interpreted" God to mankind. As the NASB renders John 1:18, "No one has seen God at any time; the only begotten God who is in the bosom of the Father, He has explained Him."

It would have been a marvelous thing to interact with Jesus personally while He was on the earth. When Philip, one of His disciples, said to Him, "Lord, show us the Father, and it is enough for us" (John 14:8), Jesus said, "Have I been with you so long, and you still do not know me, Philip? Whoever has seen me has seen the Father. How can you say, 'Show us the Father'?" (v.9). But the record of Jesus' revelation of God is exactly what we have in the documents of the New Testament — and that is what we need to be seeking when we study: Jesus' revelation of God.

Since He was one with the Father (John 10:30; 12:44,45), He was not merely an approximate representation of God; He was the *exact* representation of Him. May we never diminish the importance of this great fact. The knowledge of God having been lost, misrepresented, and suppressed, it can now be regained! In His Son, we can come to know our beloved Creator and Redeemer.

As the print of the seal on the wax is the express image of the seal itself, so Christ is the express image — the perfect representation — of God.

Ambrose

February 21

A New Covenant

Behold, the days are coming, declares the LORD, when I will make a new covenant with the house of Israel and the house of Judah, not like the covenant that I made with their fathers on the day when I took them by the hand to bring them out of the land of Egypt, my covenant that they broke, though I was their husband, declares the LORD.
Jeremiah 31:31,32

THESE ARE WORDS THAT ARREST OUR ATTENTION. *Behold, the days are coming, declares the LORD.* This expression, "the days are coming," echoes many similar phrases throughout the prophetic writings, such as "in that day," "in those days," and "in the latter days." These refer to the arrival of a new age, one to be inaugurated when the Messiah (or "Christ") came. Familiar with the great texts like Jeremiah 31, the Jews in the time of the Roman Empire were stirred by fervent expectations — and when John the Baptist began preaching, matters grew even more intense (Luke 3:15).

But notice in Jeremiah 31 that God said He would make "a new covenant" (v.31). It would be new in two senses: (1) it would replace the agreement at Sinai, and (2) it would be "not like" (v.32) the previous covenant. By God's design, it would be different in kind, a covenant differing in its basic nature from the older one.

Tragically, God had to point out that the people of Israel had not kept their part of the old covenant: "they broke [it], though I was their husband" (v.32). Their breaking of the covenant was not the only reason for its replacement, for even had Israel kept it, the Mosaic law was an interim arrangement, one that played a preparatory role in God's plan to provide salvation for all (Galatians 3:24-26). But even so, Israel's unfaithfulness to the Mosaic covenant is sad — and the warning to us today should be clear (Romans 11:22).

When the time came for the new covenant to become a reality, it was offered first to the Jewish people. Only later were the Gentiles included, when the final dimension of God's eternal plan was ready to be put into place. But it was a distinct privilege for Israel — as the family of Abraham, the physical vessel God used to bring the Messiah into the world — to be the first in line to receive the new covenant, the gospel of Christ (Romans 1:16). But thanks be to God, the invitation is now for all of us. May we accept it obediently, gratefully, and faithfully — *trusting God as our Savior.*

Rock of Ages, cleft for me,
Let me hide myself in thee.

AUGUSTUS M. TOPLADY

February 22

WRITTEN ON THEIR HEARTS

For this is the covenant that I will make with the house of Israel after those days, declares the LORD: I will put my law within them, and I will write it on their hearts. And I will be their God, and they shall be my people.
Jeremiah 31:33

ALL OF THE PROPHETS EMPHASIZED HOPE. We tend to view them as doomsayers (especially Jeremiah), but the word of God's judgment upon sin was always accompanied by a message of great hope for those who would come back to Him. In our examination of the "new covenant" in Jeremiah 31, let's look today at what was said about the "hearts" of those within this covenant.

I will put my law within them. God has always wanted people to internalize His teaching and not let it go "in one ear and out the other" (as my mother used to say). In the new covenant, God's law would be "within them" — not just heard but truly appropriated.

I will write it on their hearts. To say that it would be within them, is to say God's law would be written "on their hearts." They would possess the *character* that God was looking for, rather than just going through the outward observances required by God.

I will be their God, and they shall be my people. There is a sense, obviously, in which physical Israel was God's special people (Romans 9:4,5), but Jeremiah foresaw a day when God would have an even greater people. To be one of God's people, then and now, entails both blessings and responsibilities. To respond rightly to God requires as much *reverence* as it does *gratitude.*

As we know, Adam and Eve went astray — and all the rest of us have done the same thing (Romans 5:12). So God is seeking people who will *return* to Him. When He made mankind, He was wanting beings who would reflect His glory and reciprocate His love. Sin broke that picture, but even before that tragedy, God had a plan to build a new people. In Jesus Christ, that plan is now complete, and all individuals are invited to take part in this work of "re-creation." Obeying the gospel, we can be forgiven and begin to have our hearts remade in God's image (2 Peter 1:3,4). We can be "a people for his own possession" (1 Peter 2:9) — those for whom God's *torah* (His teaching) is "written on their hearts."

[God's] stringent requirements of a faithful life on the part of mankind are aimed at making a "people" who would (a) seek after and find Him, (b) worship and recognize dependence upon Him, and (c) reciprocate His love — in a word, *glorify* God.

ROBERT F. TURNER

February 23

THEY SHALL ALL KNOW ME

And no longer shall each one teach his neighbor and each his brother, saying, "Know the LORD," for they shall all know me, from the least of them to the greatest, declares the LORD. For I will forgive their iniquity, and I will remember their sin no more.
Jeremiah 31:34

HERE WE HAVE ONE OF THE MOST OBVIOUS DIFFERENCES BETWEEN THE OLD AND THE NEW COVENANTS. The difference pertains to "knowing" God; so we need to think for a moment about what that means. Surely, it is impossible for a human being to know God completely, but even when the word *know* is used in reference to God, it denotes a very special interaction between personal beings. To *know* someone is to have more than just a formal acquaintance; it is to have entered deeply into an understanding of them: their way of thinking, their character, their will, their instructions, and much more. When God created us in His image, He desired to have beings who were capable of knowing Him — and He revealed Himself to them so they could know Him *in truth.*

In Israel, a person's birth put him into the covenant automatically and then, as he grew older, he came to know God. But the new covenant is different. Our physical birth does not put us into that covenant, but rather a spiritual birth does (John 3:3-5), and that birth can't take place until we're old enough to understand sin and obey the gospel "from the heart" (Romans 6:17). *No one is in the new covenant who has not come to know God.* "No longer shall each one teach his neighbor and each his brother, saying, 'Know the LORD,' for they shall all know me," God predicted through Jeremiah. So one way we might define those who are God's people in this new age is that *they are those who know God.* And don't misunderstand: they are those whom *God knows* to be those who know Him. "The Lord knows those who are his" (2 Timothy 2:19).

When God entered the world in the person of His Son, Jesus Christ, one of His purposes was to allow mankind to know Him more perfectly than had been possible before. In the words of John, "No one has ever seen God; the only God, who is at the Father's side, he has made him known" (John 1:18). And in Christ, the day will come when we "will see his face" (Revelation 22:4).

By faith we are led, not against reason but beyond reason, to the knowledge of God in himself.

GERALD YANN

February 24

OUT OF ZION SHALL GO FORTH THE LAW

And many peoples will come and say, "Come, let us go up to the mountain of the LORD, to the house of the God of Jacob; that He may teach us concerning His ways and that we may walk in His paths." For the law will go forth from Zion and the word of the LORD from Jerusalem.
Isaiah 2:3 NASB

IN THIS TEXT FROM ISAIAH, A DAY IS ENVISIONED WHEN GOD'S TEACHING WOULD GO FORTH FROM "ZION" AND BE EAGERLY RECEIVED BY "MANY PEOPLES." These honest souls would gladly listen to the law of "the God of Jacob," seeking Him diligently "that He may teach us concerning His ways and that we may walk in His paths."

Zion was more or less the same as Jerusalem, as we see in the parallel clauses at the end of this verse. And the prophet foresees a day when the "law" or "word of the LORD" will go forth from this ancient city. But has this prophecy been fulfilled? And if it has, what is the law, or word, that has gone out from Zion?

Anyone familiar with the Book of Acts in the New Testament can't help being struck by the detailed fulfillment of Isaiah 2 in the events of Acts 2. In Acts 2, the gospel of Christ was first preached in its complete fullness by Peter and the other apostles in Jerusalem on the first Day of Pentecost after Jesus' resurrection. From that beginning, the message spread out from Jerusalem to encompass the whole world, shaking the foundations of humanity. This unfolding of events was exactly as Jesus had said it would be. After His resurrection, but before His ascension back to heaven, He had told His apostles not to leave Jerusalem until the Holy Spirit had empowered them to begin preaching the gospel (Acts 1:4,5), assuring them, "But you will receive power when the Holy Spirit has come upon you, *and you will be my witnesses in Jerusalem and in all Judea and Samaria, and to the end of the earth*" (Acts 1:8).

But let's ask the most penetrating question of all. *On that day and in that place, what was it that began to "go forth"? In other words, what was it that began in Jerusalem on Pentecost?* It was not a civil government. It was not even a religious institution. *It was the preaching of the full and final truth about God's means of saving the world.* Since then, anyone who has heard that message — and obeyed it — has come into a forgiven relationship with God. This truth was first proclaimed in Jerusalem. But it did not end there!

There is nothing so powerful as truth — and often nothing so strange.

DANIEL WEBSTER

February 25

ADAM'S HELPLESS RACE

For while we were still helpless,
at the right time Christ died for the ungodly.
Romans 5:6 NASB

TO SAY THE VERY LEAST, WE DID NOT DESERVE WHAT CHRIST DID FOR US WHEN HE DIED FOR OUR SINS. But not only were we undeserving; we were *helpless.* His death provided a salvation we could never have achieved by any ability that we possessed. We were, as the Amplified Bible puts it, "powerless to help ourselves."

Unfortunately, there is a concept in many people's minds that I call the "balance-sheet plan of salvation." According to this view, we will be saved if our good deeds outnumber our bad ones. We may acknowledge that we used to be sinful people, but we believe that (if we have enough time left) we may be able to do enough good deeds that we'll end up with a positive credit balance.

But here is the problem: if we had only ever committed just one sin, a lifetime of perfection after that would not be enough to atone for that sin. The "wages of sin is death" (Romans 6:23). Sin — any sin — separates us from God (Genesis 2:16,17), and no amount of goodness after that can bridge the gap our sin has put between us and God. Sin is not a problem we can work our way out of.

We are all, of course, guilty of a good many more sins than one. We have *repeatedly* chosen our own will over God's, and "ungodly" is what we are. We are not good people who just need a little polishing up; we are proud, self-willed people who have alienated ourselves from God. And when we put ourselves in that predicament, what we needed was not merely a better moral example. We needed a sinless Savior who would die on our behalf.

The good news is that Jesus Christ is that Savior. He rescued us when there was no other way we could have escaped being banished from God. Lying in the dust, dead in our sins, we were lifted up to life — vibrant, glorious *life* — by the One who loved us even when we were lost. And Peter was not exaggerating when he said, "There is salvation in no one else, for there is no other name under heaven given among men by which we must be saved" (Acts 4:12).

He left his Father's throne above,
So free, so infinite his grace!
Emptied himself of all but love,
And bled for Adam's helpless race.

CHARLES WESLEY

February 26

Alive Together with Christ

But God, being rich in mercy, because of the great love with which he loved us, even when we were dead in our trespasses, made us alive together with Christ — by grace you have been saved — and raised us up with him and seated us with him in the heavenly places in Christ Jesus.
Ephesians 2:4-6

WE ALL KNOW ABOUT THE PHYSICAL ASPECT OF LIFE AND DEATH, BUT SPIRITUAL LIFE AND DEATH ARE NO LESS REAL. In today's text, for example, Paul speaks of Christians as being "alive together with Christ." What does this expression mean?

If we've obeyed the gospel, we are not any more alive physically than we were before, but we certainly possess a spiritual life we didn't used to have. When we were "dead in our trespasses," we were baptized for the remission of our sins and God "raised us up with him and seated us with him in the heavenly places in Christ Jesus." In another passage, Paul wrote to the church in Colossae that "having been buried with him in baptism . . . you were also raised with him through faith in the powerful working of God, who raised him from the dead" (Colossians 2:12).

It needs to be emphasized that the word "dead" is the right word to describe our condition as people who have disobeyed what we knew to be the will of our Creator. The "wages of sin is death," as Paul described it in Romans 6:23. As long as our sins stand between us and God, we are alienated from Him in the very worst way, and "dead" is exactly what we are. If there is another word that comes close, it is the word "lost" (Luke 19:10).

But the life that is possible in Christ has two dimensions: *one we can enjoy right now (the lesser) and another that is waiting for us in eternity (the greater).* Writing to his fellow Christians, Peter said God "has caused us to be born again to a living hope through the resurrection of Jesus Christ from the dead, to an inheritance that is imperishable, undefiled, and unfading, kept in heaven for you, who by God's power are being guarded through faith for a salvation ready to be revealed in the last time" (1 Peter 1:3-5). So before our opportunity runs out, may we obey the commands of the gospel and be brought back to life spiritually — so that when Christ returns we'll be resurrected to live with Him *eternally.*

The same power that brought Christ back from the dead is operative within those who are Christ's. The Resurrection is an ongoing thing.

LEON MORRIS

February 27

Perfection, Corruption, Restoration

For I consider that the sufferings of this present time are not worth comparing with the glory that is to be revealed to us. For the creation waits with eager longing for the revealing of the sons of God.
Romans 8:18,19

IF THE GOSPEL IS THE "GREATEST STORY EVER TOLD," IT'S IMPORTANT FOR US TO SEE THAT THE STORY HAS A PLOT OR STORY LINE. In essence, the gospel is about something being repaired that had been ruined. What makes it the greatest of all stories is that God is the Repairer, and we, His creatures, are those being repaired.

Perfection. When He had finished creating the world, God "saw everything that he had made, and behold, it was very good" (Genesis 1:31). It was a perfect creation, and human beings were the pinnacle of its perfection. They were *personal* beings, made in God's image and blessed with abilities far beyond any other creatures in this world (Genesis 1:26,27). We can only imagine the joy of Adam and Eve's perfection — unspoiled by any disobedience, rebellion, alienation, or estrangement. With everything perfectly connected, Creator and creation were a symphony of goodness.

Corruption. Tragically, the creation was broken when Adam and Eve yielded to the tempter (Genesis 3:1-24). Disregarding the will of God, their Creator, they went against what they knew He had commanded them — and when they did, they discovered the horrors of "death" and separation from God. What had been beautiful was now ugly. What had been joyful was now dreadful. What had been perfect was now corrupt. And like Paul many centuries later, Adam might have cried out, "Wretched man that I am! Who will deliver me from this body of death?" (Romans 7:24).

Restoration. The gospel of Jesus Christ is the story of God continuing to write the story of the human race. Although He might have let justice run its course, God was not willing to leave us in our hopeless condition. If we had ruined the perfection He had created us to enjoy, He would allow us to come back to Him — even if it meant taking upon Himself the punishment for our sin. For those willing to accept this restoration, the "glory that is to be revealed to us" (Romans 8:18) is a hope beyond all hopes. For those reconciled to God in Jesus Christ, the best is yet to come.

Jesus is risen! he shall the world restore!
Awake, ye dead! dull sinners, sleep no more!

JOHN WESLEY

February 28

The Resurrection of the Messiah

For you will not abandon my soul to Sheol,
or let your holy one see corruption.
Psalm 16:10

Speaking in the synagogue in Pisidian Antioch, Paul alluded to three Old Testament prophecies that pointed to the resurrection of Jesus Christ. To his fellow Jews, he said, "We bring you the good news that what God promised to the fathers, this he has fulfilled to us their children by raising Jesus, as also it is written in the second Psalm, *'You are my Son, today I have begotten you.'* And as for the fact that he raised him from the dead, no more to return to corruption, he has spoken in this way, *'I will give you the holy and sure blessings of David.'* Therefore he says also in another psalm, *'You will not let your Holy One see corruption'*" (Acts 13:32-35). The first of Paul's Old Testament references is Psalm 2:7, the second is Isaiah 55:3, and the third is Psalm 16:10.

In Psalm 16:10, David had portrayed the Messiah as saying to Yahweh, "Therefore my heart is glad, and my whole being rejoices; my flesh also dwells secure. For you will not abandon my soul to Sheol, or let your holy one see corruption." In context, the one speaking is talking about resurrection rather than a mere preservation from death — and that is exactly how Peter understood Psalm 16:10 in his sermon on Pentecost (Acts 2:25-31).

The One whom David foresaw in Psalm 16:10 is the only person in the world who, having been killed, did not "see corruption." His resurrection proved Him to be the Son of God (Romans 1:2-4). It proved everything about the gospel to be true — and therein lies our hope. Had Jesus been no more than what David was (a great ruler over the kingdom of Israel, a prophet, and a man after God's own heart), He would have died, as David did, and His body would have decayed, as David's did. But he was not David, and He did not remain dead. *He rose from the grave, just as David knew the Messiah would.* He now reigns at the right hand of God (Psalm 110:1) where He makes intercession for His faithful people (Romans 8:34). What this means is that our hope of salvation is no idle dream.

The king described in Psalm 16:10 . . . [is] one who is laid in the grave and does not experience decay. The description of this ideal king leads us to the same conclusion the apostle Peter came to in his first post-Pentecost sermon to the people of Israel: David cannot be speaking about himself!

Seth D. Postell

February 29

THIS JESUS IS THE CHRIST

Now when they had passed through Amphipolis and Apollonia, they came to Thessalonica, where there was a synagogue of the Jews. And Paul went in, as was his custom, and on three Sabbath days he reasoned with them from the Scriptures, explaining and proving that it was necessary for the Christ to suffer and to rise from the dead, and saying, "This Jesus, whom I proclaim to you, is the Christ."
Acts 17:1-3

TO A JEWISH AUDIENCE, THE CENTRAL CLAIM OF THE GOSPEL WAS THAT JESUS WAS THE MESSIAH PROMISED IN THE HEBREW SCRIPTURES. Jewish hearers already accepted God and the writings of the prophets as the word of God. But whether Jesus was the Messiah promised by the prophets was another matter. Jesus put it simply: "You believe in God; believe also in me" (John 14:1 NET).

We should note that with a Gentile audience, the argument had to start further back. They had to be persuaded that the God presented in the Hebrew Scriptures was the true God. It is interesting, however, that in both cases the apostles' argument rested on the resurrection. If their testimony to Jesus' resurrection was true, then Jesus was both Lord and Christ (Acts 2:32-36). To the Jews, this meant that Jesus was the Messiah, the Son of God. And to the Gentiles it meant there was a God for Jesus to be the Son of.

But let's go back to our text in Acts 17:1-3 and Paul's presentation of the gospel in the Jewish synagogue at Thessalonica. To convince them that Jesus was the Christ, he "reasoned with them from the Scriptures, explaining and proving that it was necessary for the Christ to suffer and to rise from the dead." Even to those who took the prophets seriously, it needed to be shown that the death and resurrection of the Messiah were predicted by the prophets (Psalm 16,22,110; Isaiah 53; etc.) and that Jesus had fulfilled not just some of the messianic prophecies but all of them.

Personally, I would love to have been there to see the excitement of those who were persuaded by Paul's exposition of the Scriptures. To have known these prophecies all one's life and then be able to exclaim, "Yes, this Jesus is, in fact, the Christ we've been looking for" — their jubilation must have been like fireworks!

According to those predictions [in the Hebrew Scriptures], the Messiah was appointed to suffer and then rise again from the dead. Both these experiences had been fulfilled in Jesus, and in nobody else; therefore, said Paul, this Jesus of whom I tell you is the promised Messiah.

F. F. BRUCE

March 1

The Gospel of God's Kingdom

Now after John was arrested, Jesus came into Galilee, proclaiming the gospel of God, and saying, "The time is fulfilled, and the kingdom of God is at hand; repent and believe in the gospel."
Mark 1:14,15

THE GREEK WORD TRANSLATED "GOSPEL" IN OUR ENGLISH BIBLES WAS FAMILIAR IN THE ROMAN EMPIRE. It meant the joyful proclamation of some great event, often one having to do with Caesar, the Emperor. But in the New Testament, it refers to the greatest of all proclamations: not one concerning Caesar, but glad tidings pertaining to God Himself, the very King of the universe. *God is establishing the kingdom predicted by the prophets, and He is offering the forgiveness of sins to everyone who will submit to His Son, Jesus Christ.*

The time is fulfilled. In Isaiah 9:6,7, Daniel 2:44, and many other places, the Hebrew prophets had foretold the coming of a kingdom ruled over by God, something unique in the entire history of the world since Adam and Eve sinned and were exiled from Eden. In his account, Mark tells us that the coming of this kingdom is what Jesus preached. The time foretold by the prophets had arrived.

The kingdom of God is at hand. What was about to happen, according to Jesus, was that God was going to establish His kingdom. A "kingdom," of course, is a realm where someone rules or exercises authority. But the kingdom Jesus spoke of would be nothing like any of the kingdoms of men. It would be nothing less than God's kingdom. Its citizens would live under His rule, reverently and lovingly acknowledging His right to be their Lord.

Repent and believe in the gospel. The news of the coming kingdom required a response. Even as it approached, before its actual establishment in Acts 2, the proper response was to "repent and believe in the gospel." If the problem was that God's rule over His world had been rejected, admission to the new kingdom would require that people cease their rebellion and come back to the King, believing the truth of everything the King said about (1) Himself, (2) the problem of sin, and (3) the salvation He was providing. So if the gospel says the true King has returned, the question we must ask is: *will we join His cause or continue to support the rebellion?*

Enemy-occupied territory — that is what this world is. Christianity is the story of how the rightful king has landed, you might say landed in disguise, and is calling us all to take part in a great campaign of sabotage.

C. S. LEWIS

March 2

ZACCHAEUS: A LOST SOUL NEEDING TO BE SAVED

For the Son of Man came to seek and to save the lost.
Luke 19:10

IN THE GOSPEL WE ARE CONFRONTED WITH THE FACT THAT GOD ENTERED THIS WORLD AND TOOK UPON HIMSELF HUMAN FORM IN THE PERSON OF JESUS OF NAZARETH. As the apostle John put it, "The Word became flesh and dwelt among us, and we have seen his glory, glory as of the only Son from the Father, full of grace and truth" (John 1:14). In accounts like the one in Luke 19:1-10, we have a chance to learn something about why this happened.

As Jesus was passing through Jericho, He entered the home of a certain man named Zacchaeus, who was "a chief tax collector and was rich" (v.1). Zacchaeus had shown extraordinary interest in Jesus, and he proved himself sincere in his desire to repent of the sins he had committed, especially as a tax collector. And Jesus pronounced a blessing upon him: "Today salvation has come to this house, since he also is a son of Abraham" (v.9).

As He often was, Jesus was criticized for entering the home of such a person as Zacchaeus. But Jesus was looking for people like Zacchaeus. *"The Son of Man came to seek and to save the lost."* The thing that distinguished Zacchaeus from so many others who crowded around Jesus was not that he was lost, for every person Jesus ever met fell into that category. The quality that made Zacchaeus special was *his recognition that he was lost.* He knew he needed what Jesus came to offer: the forgiveness of sins.

The miracle of the Incarnation was necessary if any of us were to be forgiven. To die for us and atone for our sins, God had to take upon Himself the form of a human being who could be killed. And those who would receive the benefit of that sacrifice would be people just like Zacchaeus, those willing to humble themselves in true penitence and seek the grace of a forgiving Father.

Just as Jesus was misunderstood in His day, He is often misunderstood today. He is usually looked upon as a teacher of ethics, a social worker, or a psychologist. But Jesus came to be none of these things. He came to be our *Savior.* To be like Zacchaeus, we need to dispense with our preconceived notions and personal preferences — and let Christ save us in the way He came to save us.

The more you know about Christ, the less
you will be satisfied with superficial views of him.

CHARLES HADDON SPURGEON

March 3

Why We Study the Scriptures

. . . from childhood you have been acquainted
with the sacred writings, which are able to make you
wise for salvation through faith in Christ Jesus.
2 Timothy 3:15

THERE ARE MANY REASONS WHY WE MIGHT STUDY THE SCRIPTURES, BUT FOR TODAY'S MEDITATION LET'S THINK ABOUT ONE PARTICULAR REASON. The Scriptures are able, Paul says, to make us "wise for salvation through faith in Christ Jesus." Whether we ourselves study them or someone else teaches us (as was the case when Timothy's mother and grandmother taught him the Scriptures in his childhood), it is through the Scriptures that the knowledge necessary for us to be saved is mediated to us. We do not rely on the subjective feeling that God may be speaking to us in our hearts, nor do we depend on the mystical transmission of esoteric knowledge. It is by the simple process of reading, understanding, and obeying the Scriptures that we learn what God wants us to know.

Notice especially that Paul says it is "through faith in Christ Jesus" that we can be saved and that the Scriptures are our means of coming to know about Him. If Jesus is who He claimed to be, the One who can save us from our sins, it is critically important that we know what He taught and what we must do to receive His salvation. He was, after all, a historical figure, and historical figures must be learned about through the documents that contain information about them. Rather than debating feelings, opinions, and prejudices, we would do well to immerse ourselves in the actual documents — and on that basis make our decision about Jesus.

The Bereans in Acts 17 had the right idea. They listened eagerly as Paul argued that Jesus was the Messiah, but as they listened they were "examining the Scriptures daily to see if these things were so" (Acts 17:11). The Scriptures were their final arbiter.

But here is the point I hope you'll get: *it is not only at the beginning but also throughout our lives as Christians that we must study the Scriptures.* We will never, in this life, outgrow our need to be more and more "wise for salvation." So we keep studying. The treasure house of wisdom in the Scriptures is inexhaustible. When it comes to salvation, our need is great — and the resources are rich.

Nobody ever outgrows Scripture;
the book widens and deepens with our years.

CHARLES HADDON SPURGEON

March 4

TRUSTWORTHINESS OF THE SCRIPTURES (1)

Paul, a servant of Christ Jesus, called to be an apostle, set apart for the gospel of God, which he promised beforehand through his prophets in the holy Scriptures . . .
Romans 1:1,2

PAUL UNDERSTOOD HIMSELF TO BE A MESSENGER. As an apostle, commissioned by Christ to proclaim the gospel, he saw his work as faithfully transmitting to others that which he had received. He made no attempt to be theologically inventive or original. Quite to the contrary, Paul, with the other New Testament writers, adhered to a strict standard of accuracy in regard to the received tradition (1 Corinthians 11:23; 15:3,4; Galatians 1:11,12). The whole value of their work lay in its absolute faithfulness to the truth of "what really happened." To deviate from factualness in regard to Jesus' life was tantamount to deserting the gospel itself.

As we see in Romans 1:1,2, Paul knew the gospel had been foretold in the prophetic writings of the Hebrew Scriptures. It was not a new theology, unheard of until the New Testament writers cobbled it together; rather, God had "promised [the gospel] beforehand through his prophets in the holy Scriptures." In fact, evangelism in the New Testament period consisted largely of showing the exact correspondence between what happened in Jesus' life and what had been prophesied about it ages before.

What sense would it make, then, for the evangelists of the Christian faith to hang their whole case on the fulfillment of the Old Testament in the events in Jesus' life, *if it could be shown that no such things ever really happened in the life of Jesus?* Evangelism would have been a farce if there was no correspondence between what had been "promised beforehand" and what later took place. And don't forget: the New Testament writings were completed in the first century — while those who were in a position to *know* what had occurred were still living. So we are left with what, to some, is an uncomfortable truth: the New Testament documents are a trustworthy account of the life and teachings of Jesus of Nazareth.

All of [the Gospel writers] are conscious of being reporters of real events played out by a real historical person. For all their effort to create a conviction about that person, and to testify to the divine power that operated through him, they are essentially reporters, not free to invent or falsify the data which the tradition of their churches presented as having happened in Galilee and Judea a generation earlier.

E. C. BLACKMAN

March 5

TRUSTWORTHINESS OF THE SCRIPTURES (2)

For I delivered to you as of first importance what I also received: that Christ died for our sins in accordance with the Scriptures, that he was buried, that he was raised on the third day in accordance with the Scriptures.
1 Corinthians 15:3,4

WHEN WE SPEAK OF THE NEW TESTAMENT RECORD OF JESUS' LIFE, DEATH, AND RESURRECTION, THERE ARE THREE LINKS IN THE CHAIN OF TRUSTWORTHINESS. First, there were the prophecies of the Messiah in the Old Testament. Second, Jesus fulfilled those prophecies with strict accuracy. And third, the New Testament writers reported the facts about Jesus' fulfillment of prophecy, again with strict accuracy. At each step of the way, the process depended on *faithfulness to the historical events behind the gospel.*

In between steps one and two, there was a gap of several centuries, and this adds to the credibility of Jesus' messiahship. When Jesus fulfilled the Hebrew prophecies, those predictions had been known publicly for at least two hundred years. The Septuagint (the Greek translation of the Old Testament) was begun around 250 BC. So even if none of the prophecies were any older than that (most were much older), the prophets could not possibly have known, that far in advance, what Jesus would do — yet virtually everything Jesus did matched up precisely with the prophecies.

But what about the gap between steps two and three? Here, we need a gap as small as possible, and that is exactly what we've got. If the New Testament writings had been made two or three centuries after Jesus lived, we might argue that their presentation of Jesus was legendary and not historical. But the gap between the events and the reporting of those events was not two or three centuries; it was only a few years. Paul's writings are the earliest, beginning as early as AD 50-51, but even the last of the New Testament writings were completed during the first century, while eyewitnesses to the recorded events were still living.

So as we said in yesterday's reading, the New Testament writings are trustworthy. We may reject the gospel as being a doctrine we're not interested in, but we may not, if we're historians, claim that Jesus never said or did the things that are attributed to Him.

The Christians may not have been interested in "history"; but they were certainly interested in the "historical." The preachers of the new faith may not have wanted to narrate *everything* about Jesus, but they certainly did not want to relate anything that was not real.

PIERRE BENOIT

March 6

SEEING THE SERIOUSNESS OF OUR OWN SINS

. . . but God shows his love for us in that while
we were still sinners, Christ died for us.
Romans 5:8

INSIDE ALL OF US IS A DEEP NEED TO SEE OURSELVES AS GOOD PEOPLE. We readily admit we've made mistakes, but we like to think that's all they were: just mistakes. If others knew the extenuating circumstances, they would see how hard we've had it and how understandable the errors have been. Even in our confessions of wrongdoing, we often come out of the experience with people thinking more highly of us for being so humble and courageous.

The gospel, however, asks us to see ourselves not as nice folks but as *sinners*. It was not the inadvertent slip-ups of good people that put Christ on the cross, but the rebellious acts of creatures unwilling to accept the will of their Creator. And lest I think that "sinners" is just a reference to the human race in general, I need to understand this: *if I were the only person God ever created, my sins alone would have been every bit serious enough to crucify Christ.*

But do we see ourselves that way? Probably not. If I'm giving a talk at the Lord's Table on Sunday, my eyes may fill with tears as I talk about how "sinful" and "unworthy" I am, but on Monday I may bristle with defensiveness if I find out that some of my peers actually do view me as a wicked person. I will probably feel that I've been judged unfairly and try to salvage as much of my reputation as I can. But if I cry, "God, be merciful to me, a sinner!" (Luke 18:13), I need to get comfortable wearing that suit of clothes honestly. If it's the truth and I really believe what I said about myself, why should I object if others see me the same way?

The gospel is indeed "good news." It's the message of a love so great that it moved God to give the life of His Son for our sins. Rightly do we celebrate the goodness of God's forgiveness. But those who appreciate it most are those who see the seriousness of their own sins most clearly (Luke 7:47). As long as we live in this world, godly sorrow and repentance will always be the springs from which our joy flows. We can't have the latter without the former. So when we say Christ died for us "while we were still sinners," let's be sure we understand exactly what we're saying.

None of us feels the true love of God till we realize how wicked we are.
But you can't teach people that — they have to learn by experience.

DOROTHY L. SAYERS

March 7

THE HIGHEST (AND HARDEST) KIND OF HONESTY

The heart is deceitful above all things,
and desperately sick;
who can understand it?
Jeremiah 17:9

ALL OF US WANT TO VIEW OURSELVES IN A POSITIVE LIGHT. As a result, we often tell ourselves what we'd like to hear rather than what we need to hear. The human heart is exceedingly "deceitful," as Jeremiah 17:9 says, and it takes an uncommon measure of honesty for us to see when we are lying to ourselves. Think about three areas where self-honesty is both important and very hard:

(1) What does God's word teach? Especially when a text calls for a change that would be difficult to make, we reason our way around it, convincing ourselves of the meaning we prefer the text to have. We tell ourselves we're "explaining" the passage when all we're really doing is draining the inconvenience out of obeying it.

(2) What kind of relationship do I have with God? Ideally, we should see our relationship with God exactly as it is, neither overestimating nor underestimating it. But rather than look at the facts honestly (2 Corinthians 13:5), we often allow our hearts to lie to us. We define reality in terms of whatever makes us feel good.

(3) What are my true motives, desires, and intentions? Here is the hardest area of all. If the question is *What is the real reason why I want to do this?* that can be a painful question to answer. It takes peeling off many successive layers of the "onion" in our hearts to get down to the real, true desires that are driving our decisions.

Edward White Benson remarked, "How desperately difficult it is to be honest with oneself. It is much easier to be honest with other people." And yet, this harder kind of honesty is also more important than the easier kind. If we're not willing to see (1) what God teaches us in the Scriptures, (2) the true status of our relationship with God, and (3) the true motives behind the decisions we make, then no amount of external honesty with other people is going to amount to much. It is God who is our Judge, and He knows "the thoughts and intentions of the heart" (Hebrews 4:12). We ought to embrace *all of what He knows to be true* — even about ourselves. Is it not the truth that will set us free?

Honesty consists of the unwillingness to lie to others; maturity, which is equally hard to attain, consists of the unwillingness to lie to oneself.

SYDNEY J. HARRIS

March 8

THE WORST WORDS WE CAN IMAGINE

And then will I declare to them, "I never knew you;
depart from me, you workers of lawlessness."
Matthew 7:23

HAVING BEEN MADE IN GOD'S IMAGE, OUR DEEPEST NEED IS FOR FELLOWSHIP WITH HIM. He created us as personal beings, and one of the characteristics of personal beings is their need for relationship with other persons, above all with their Creator. If it is hard for us to be alienated from other human beings, it is even harder to do without our Heavenly Father, although when we're alienated from Him we often misdiagnose the problem and try to fill the void in our hearts with other things besides God.

As Adam and Eve found out, sin cuts us off from the God whose fellowship we need so deeply. Outside of Eden, it may have taken them a while to realize just how much they had lost, but they lived a very long time after their separation from God and we can only imagine the emptiness and sorrow of their experience.

But God had a plan ready by which He would bring His Son into the world to die for mankind's sins and open up the door to forgiveness. Having been forgiven, those who accepted God's plan would have a partial fellowship with God restored to them in this world, but that blessing would only be a "down payment" on the perfectly restored fellowship they would have with God in eternity. This, in a nutshell, is the message of the gospel of Christ, and it centers on the *restored fellowship with God* we can have when He has brought the history of this sin-damaged world to its end.

Only by God's grace could such a thing be possible. Yet God has made receiving the benefits of His grace contingent on our accepting the terms or conditions which He has set. What if we say no to God's plan? What if we reject the good news of the gospel?

The answer is that the saddest thing in the whole creation will happen: *we will have rejected the very thing we were created for.* Fellowship with God — lost by our sin but offered back to us in the gospel — will be forever out of our reach when we hear Him say, "Depart from me." But for the time being, that horror is still an "if." We will hear those words "if" . . . *if we say no to our Savior.*

The pain of punishment will be without the fruit of penitence;
weeping will be useless, and prayer ineffectual. Too late they will believe
in eternal punishment who would not believe in eternal life.

CYPRIAN

March 9

THROUGH JESUS CHRIST, THE FORGIVENESS OF SINS

And he commanded us to preach to the people and to testify that [Jesus Christ] is the one appointed by God to be judge of the living and the dead. To him all the prophets bear witness that everyone who believes in him receives forgiveness of sins through his name.
Acts 10:42,43

THE GOSPEL MAY BE DEFINED AS THE PREACHING OF JESUS CHRIST. And it is in two different senses that it is "of" Jesus Christ. First it is the good news or glad tidings preached *by* Jesus, the gospel of the kingdom of God (Mark 1:14,15). But also, it is the message *about* Jesus. In the house of Cornelius, a Roman centurion and the first Gentile convert to Christ, Peter said that God "commanded us to preach to the people and to testify that he is the one appointed by God to be judge of the living and the dead."

It is a fact that the judgment of the world has been given into the hands of Jesus Christ, and we will give account of ourselves to Him. Speaking to a group of philosophers in Athens, Paul said that God "has fixed a day on which he will judge the world in righteousness by a man whom he has appointed; and of this he has given assurance to all by raising him from the dead" (Acts 17:31).

But if Jesus is our Judge He is also the Savior of those who accept Him. That is why the gospel is good news. As Peter said, "Everyone who believes in him receives forgiveness of sins through his name." And the consequence is that when God's wrath falls upon the world, those who are forgiven will be spared. Paul put it vividly when he described Jesus as the one "who delivers us from the wrath to come" (1 Thessalonians 1:10).

What makes Jesus so disliked, however, is the gospel's claim that forgiveness is *only* in Christ. To many, there is no more objectionable statement of Jesus than His saying, "I am the way, and the truth, and the life. No one comes to the Father except through me" (John 14:6). Yet that is what He said, and we must decide whether He was telling the truth. Great outcomes depend on our decision.

May we not quibble, but rather be grateful. For where else can we go but to Christ? As Peter said when Jesus asked him if he and the other disciples were going to turn away from Him, "Lord, to whom shall we go? You have the words of eternal life" (John 6:68).

By a Carpenter mankind was made, and only by that Carpenter can mankind be remade.

DESIDERIUS ERASMUS

March 10

The Sinner's Prayer

And with many other words he bore witness and continued to exhort them, saying, "Save yourselves from this crooked generation." So those who received his word were baptized, and there were added that day about three thousand souls.
Acts 2:40,41

In our day, when people ask "What must I do to be saved?" they are commonly told to pray the "Sinner's Prayer." According to its advocates, this prayer is how one "accepts" Christ, based on the premise that "faith only" is the requirement for the forgiveness of sins. There are many versions of the prayer, but they all run something like this: *"Dear God, I know I'm a sinner, and I ask for your forgiveness. I believe Jesus Christ is Your Son. I believe that He died for my sins and that you raised Him to life. I want to trust Him as my Savior and follow Him as Lord, from this day forward. Guide my life and help me to do your will. I pray this in the name of Jesus. Amen."*

A couple of remarks are in order. First, our conversion to Christ should certainly be accompanied by fervent prayer. If there is ever a time when prayer is appropriate, would it not be on the crucial occasion of our turning to Christ as our Savior?

But it is simply not true to the Scriptures to say that a prayer like the Sinner's Prayer is sufficient. We do not find in any of the conversions to Christ in the Scriptures anyone being instructed to pray such a prayer, as if that were all they needed to do to be saved.

But if we do not find in the Scriptures people being told to pray the Sinner's Prayer, what *do* we find? As in our beginning text in Acts 2:40,41, the gospel called for a response, and those who responded did not merely pray; they were baptized. Beginning on the first Pentecost after Jesus' resurrection in Jerusalem, when the gospel was first preached in its completeness, those who sought God's forgiveness submitted gladly to the gospel's command to be baptized into Christ. Their baptism was preceded by faith (John 8:24), repentance (Acts 2:38), and the confession of their faith (Romans 10:9,10). All of these were motivated by trust in God's power to save them (Colossians 2:12) and backed up by a very serious commitment (Luke 9:62). To tell the sinner to do anything less than these things is to share something less than the gospel with him.

In the New Testament, it was not by prayer that people became Christians but by receiving God's forgiveness as they died with Christ in baptism.

Dee Bowman

March 11

BORN AGAIN

Jesus answered him, "Truly, truly, I say to you, unless one is born again he cannot see the kingdom of God."
John 3:3

OBEYING THE GOSPEL INVOLVES THE DEEPEST CHANGE POSSIBLE IN A HUMAN BEING'S HEART. Dying to sin and living "in newness of life" (Romans 6:4) is more than adopting a different religious affiliation, accepting a different set of beliefs, or attending services at a different church. *It is becoming a different person.* Jesus said, "Unless one is born again he cannot see the kingdom of God."

In John 3:5, Jesus was more specific: "Unless one is born of water and the Spirit, he cannot enter the kingdom of God." What does this mean? It means, first, that the act of baptism (immersion in water) precedes our entrance into God's kingdom. But born of water, we are also born of the Spirit. At baptism, the Christian begins learning to lay aside his self-will and yield himself to the direction of God's Spirit. This guidance is available for us today in the Scriptures that were revealed by the Spirit (2 Timothy 3:16,17).

Paul wrote that God has saved us "by the washing of regeneration and renewal of the Holy Spirit" (Titus 3:5). Here we see once again the "water" and the "Spirit" of which Jesus spoke in John 3:5. Beginning with the remission of our sins at baptism, a strong renewal takes place. As we learn more of God's will, we begin to be led, directed, and governed by God's Spirit. And as we obey God's command to "walk in the Spirit," the "works of the flesh" begin to be replaced by the "fruit of the Spirit" (Galatians 5:16-26).

As you can see, being born again involves *something that happens to us* (the remission of our sins) and also *something we do* (live a new life). By His grace God has forgiven us, and He will help us obey Him, but to remain in the kingdom we must accept the rule of the King. As Paul said, "The Spirit has given us life; he must also control our lives" (Galatians 5:25 *Good News Bible*).

If the problem of sin is to be corrected, radical surgery must be done. The gospel does not deal in superficial solutions. According to Jesus, it is not our dysfunctional behavior that is the problem — *it is us.* It is in the deepest depths of our hearts that we need to change. We must, in fact, die and become new people altogether.

[Being born again] is a foundational fact. The characteristic of the new birth is that I yield myself so completely to God that Christ is formed in me.

OSWALD CHAMBERS

March 12

ABRAHAM, THE FATHER OF THE FAITHFUL

And [Abraham] believed the LORD,
and he counted it to him as righteousness.
Genesis 15:6

ABRAHAM WAS AN OLD MAN AND CHILDLESS WHEN GOD TOLD HIM HIS DESCENDANTS WOULD BE AS MANY AS THE STARS OF HEAVEN. Sarah, his wife, was well past the age of childbearing. Yet he knew enough of God's track record to believe that whatever God promised, that's what would happen. So he trusted God's promise, and the text says that God "counted it to him as righteousness."

The operative element in Abraham's faith was *an obedient confidence* — a trustful willingness to yield to God's word. "By faith Abraham obeyed when he was called to go out to a place that he was to receive as an inheritance. And he went out, not knowing where he was going" (Hebrews 11:8). And James wrote, "You see that faith was active along with his works, and faith was completed by his works; and the Scripture was fulfilled that says, 'Abraham believed God, and it was counted to him as righteousness' — and he was called a friend of God" (James 2:22,23).

Abraham is the person most often cited in the Scriptures as an example of faith's role in God's plan of salvation. "Know then that it is those of faith who are the sons of Abraham. And the Scripture, foreseeing that God would justify the Gentiles by faith, preached the gospel beforehand to Abraham, saying, 'In you shall all the nations be blessed.' So then, those who are of faith are blessed along with Abraham, the man of faith" (Galatians 3:7-9).

Abraham's faithfulness was the product of his decision to trust that God always tells the truth. Today, we very much need to get back to Abraham's kind of faith. Far from mere gullibility or blind faith, his faith was *a reasoned choice to believe the promises he knew God had made.* And unlike those who think that *feelings* of faith are sufficient, Abraham was *obedient* to God, even in situations that required great courage. Whether it was in the operation of his intellect, his emotions, or his will, Abraham's point of departure was always this: *what has God said?* And all these years later, he continues to be the spiritual forefather of those who take bold, sacrificial steps based on the dependability of what God has said.

Faith does not begin with what the human intellect
has discovered . . . [but] with what God has revealed.

WILLIAM BARCLAY

March 13

FAITH: THE MAINSPRING OF RIGHTEOUSNESS

. . . but the righteous shall live by his faith.
Habakkuk 2:4

IN THE WHOLE BIBLE THERE ARE FEW TEXTS MORE BASIC THAN THIS ONE. The principle embedded in this passage from Habakkuk is fundamental and far-reaching. And it illustrates an interesting fact about the Scriptures: the more basic the principle found in a passage, the more ways it may be applied in other passages.

In its original context in Habakkuk, "the righteous shall live by his faith" was a part of God's answer to the prophet's perplexity at God's use of a nation like Babylon to accomplish His purposes. Based on a human being's limited information, such may seem puzzling, but God has always proven Himself trustworthy, so those who are committed to justice will trust Him. Their trust in God will guide them through life's apparent contradictions.

In the New Testament, Paul quoted the familiar words of Habakkuk 2:4 in Romans 1:16,17 to emphasize one of the most basic truths of the gospel: it is faith (rather than race, social status, or any other criterion) that is the basis of righteousness before God. *No one is excluded; the gospel is open to any person who will make the choice to trust God obediently.* And no congregation needed to hear this more than the group in Rome, where the mixed Jewish and Gentile membership needed to keep in mind that they had all been accepted in Christ on the very same basis.

So here we have one of the key elements of the truth about our relationship to God. Beginning with Adam and Eve and coming all the way down to our own day, sin has always been a refusal to trust God enough to obey Him, and salvation has always required coming *back* to a trust that *will* obey Him. In the gospel, faith is required for our initial reconciliation to God and also our continuing lives in Christ. It is the mainspring of the watch (to use an antiquated illustration), the source of the energy that drives the mechanism. Yet real faith involves a good deal more than just accepting the facts of the gospel intellectually. That may be the starting point, since faith is based on what our minds recognize to be true. But as it grows to maturity, faith turns into *trust* — a trust that will risk everything in order to act on what God says about Himself and His will for us.

Faith is deliberate confidence in the character of God
whose ways you cannot understand at the time.

OSWALD CHAMBERS

March 14

Where the Righteousness of God Is Revealed

For in it the righteousness of God is revealed from faith for faith,
as it is written, "The righteous shall live by faith."
Romans 1:17

PAUL WANTED IT UNDERSTOOD THAT HE WAS NOT RELUCTANT TO COME TO ROME. Rome might have been the most powerful and prestigious city in the world of that day, but Paul was just as willing to preach the gospel of Christ there as he was anywhere else. "I am not ashamed of the gospel," he wrote to the church in Rome, "for it is the power of God for salvation" (Romans 1:16).

And then, still speaking of the gospel, Paul said, "For in it the righteousness of God is revealed from faith for faith, as it is written, 'The righteous shall live by faith'" (v.17). It is in the gospel that the righteousness of God is revealed. That sounds important, obviously, but what is "the righteousness of God" that Paul speaks of?

In the context of Paul's letter to the Romans, the phrase does not refer to God's personal righteousness but rather His way of making sinful man righteous — that is, God's chosen means of reconciling us to Himself, as opposed to any system of righteousness or plan of salvation by which we might try to save ourselves.

This contrast is clearly seen in Romans 10:3: "For, being ignorant of the righteousness of God, and seeking to establish their own, they did not submit to God's righteousness." Paul was speaking here of the Jews who had rejected the gospel. It grieved him, as a former rabbi, to point out that by preferring a Jewish system of moral credits to achieve their own salvation, his Jewish brethren had turned away from God's salvation: *the plan that He had provided for all mankind, one based on faith rather than Jewishness.*

God, as the Sovereign Ruler of the universe, has the right to set the criterion separating those who will be saved from those who will not, and it is in the gospel that He has revealed His choice. The righteousness that He is willing to provide is based upon faith in His Son, Jesus Christ. We might have preferred some other plan, but God's plan is what it is — and it is in the gospel that He makes it known. The "good news" is that, because of Christ's death, the door of forgiveness is open to the entire world. Only God could have opened this door. The wonder is that He did so.

Christ died that we might live — but live as he lives,
by dying as he died who died to himself.

GEORGE MACDONALD

March 15

The Sorrow That Seeks Salvation

Wretched man that I am! Who will deliver me from this body of death?
Romans 7:24

SORROWFUL. PENITENT. CONTRITE. These do not sound like positive words. But if we're looking at life from the perspective of the Scriptures, they are some of the most positive words in the dictionary — not because they are comfortable but because they are beneficial. Ponder with me their importance in our salvation.

There are a handful of texts in the Bible (I call them "fundamental" texts) that describe the heart of the person who is truly turned in God's direction. We might think, for example, of Micah 6:8 or Deuteronomy 6:4,5. Out of all the texts like these, none is more helpful to us than David's cry in Psalm 51:17: "The sacrifices of God are a broken spirit; a broken and contrite heart, O God, you will not despise." I believe this basic truth would have been the background of Jesus' statement of blessing in Matthew 5:3,4: "Blessed are the poor in spirit, for theirs is the kingdom of heaven. Blessed are those who mourn, for they shall be comforted."

Godly sorrow is not an end in itself; it is a part of the path that leads us back to God (2 Corinthians 7:8-11). Without sorrow for our sins, we will not seek salvation with any deep passion or fervent desire. And in the end, it is this sort of seeker who will be rewarded. It is not the one interested in intellectual information or theoretical philosophy, but the seeker of *salvation* who will find the object of his desire. And as often as not, it is our *tears* that show what is most important to us in regard to God (Luke 7:36-50).

If we're seeking salvation, we will naturally be eager to experience the joy God has promised to us. We long to be reconciled to Him. There is, however, no shortcut to salvation. The path to heaven passes through the territory of repentance, and as anyone knows who has been there, it is a painful place to be. But the horror of our sins has to become real to us. If that does not happen, the Promised Land will not seem much better than the wilderness. "Until sin be bitter — Christ will not be sweet" (Thomas Watson).

Ah! happy they whose hearts can break
And peace of pardon win!
How else may man make straight his plan
And cleanse his soul from sin?
How else but through a broken heart
May the Lord Christ enter in?

OSCAR WILDE

March 16

God's Promise to David

When your days are fulfilled and you lie down with your fathers, I will raise up your offspring after you, who shall come from your body, and I will establish his kingdom . . . And your house and your kingdom shall be made sure forever before me. Your throne shall be established forever.
2 Samuel 7:12-16

THIS TEXT IS ONE OF A HANDFUL OF OLD TESTAMENT TEXTS THAT ARE ABSOLUTELY CRITICAL FOR AN UNDERSTANDING OF THE NEW TESTAMENT. Much that is said in the New Testament about Jesus Christ would be incomprehensible without an understanding of what it was that God was promising to David in 2 Samuel 7:12-16.

Offspring. On the first Pentecost after Jesus' death, Simon Peter, a pious Jew, affirmed that he and others were eyewitnesses of the fact that Jesus had been resurrected. And Jesus' resurrection, he argued, fulfilled what the Scriptures had foretold about the much-anticipated Messiah. To make his point, he quoted Psalm 16:10, where David had said, "For you will not abandon my soul to Hades, or let your Holy One see corruption" (Acts 2:25-28).

Now follow very carefully what Peter said next: "Brothers, I may say to you with confidence about the patriarch David that he both died and was buried, and his tomb is with us to this day. Being therefore a prophet, *and knowing that God had sworn with an oath to him that he would set one of his descendants on his throne,* he foresaw and spoke about the resurrection of the Christ, that he was not abandoned to Hades, nor did his flesh see corruption. This Jesus God raised up, and of that we all are witnesses . . . *Let all the house of Israel therefore know for certain that God has made him both Lord and Christ, this Jesus whom you crucified"* (Acts 2:29-36).

Kingdom. God said to David, "Your throne shall be established forever." Just as "offspring" meant more than David's son Solomon, there would be more to David's "throne" than the government of Israel. *The kingdom of which God spoke to David would not be geographical but spiritual (John 18:36) — and this is the very kingdom over which Jesus Christ, the Messiah, now reigns.* So if we've obeyed the gospel, we may gladly say that God "has delivered us from the domain of darkness and transferred us to *the kingdom of his beloved Son,* in whom we have redemption, the forgiveness of sins" (Colossians 1:13,14).

The kingdom of God does not exist because of your effort or mine.
It exists because God reigns. Our part is to enter this kingdom
and bring our life under his sovereign will.

T. Z. KOO

March 17

An Indestructible Kingdom

And in the days of those kings the God of heaven will set up a kingdom that shall never be destroyed, nor shall the kingdom be left to another people. It shall break in pieces all these kingdoms and bring them to an end, and it shall stand forever.
Daniel 2:44

THIS TEXT IN THE BOOK OF DANIEL GIVES US THE MAIN POINT OF A DREAM THAT DANIEL INTERPRETED FOR NEBUCHADNEZZAR, THE KING OF BABYLON. It speaks of a kingdom that God would establish in the days of the Roman Empire, a kingdom that would be unlike any other kingdom that had ever been known to mankind.

A spiritual kingdom. If people thought the kingdom prophesied here was going to be just a more powerful type of earthly government, they were disappointed. When the King finally came, He did not set up a worldly regime: "My kingdom is not of this world. If my kingdom were of this world, my servants would have been fighting . . . But my kingdom is not from the world" (John 18:36).

A kingdom whose rule would not be transferred to succeeding rulers. Unlike earthly kingdoms in which rulers are always replaced by other rulers, there would be no line of succession in this kingdom — "nor shall its sovereignty be left to another people" (RSV).

An indestructible kingdom. The stability of this kingdom was such that it "shall stand forever." The ups and downs of history would not faze it, and no enemy could conquer it. With the Son of God as its King, this kingdom would be impossible to overthrow.

This kingdom, we now know, is the rule of God in Jesus Christ, inaugurated on the first Pentecost after Jesus' resurrection. In Christ, we submit to this rule and are saved (Colossians 1:13,14).

When we consider the majesty of God's plan to bring us back under the benevolence of His rule, we are struck with awe. And it is our privilege to honor Jesus Christ, "the ruler of kings on earth. To him who loves us and has freed us from our sins by his blood and made us a kingdom, priests to his God and Father, to him be glory and dominion forever and ever. Amen" (Revelation 1:5,6).

Only when God hath brought to light all the hidden things of darkness, whosoever were the actors therein, will it be seen that wise and good were all his ways, that he saw through the thick cloud, and governed all things by the wise counsels of his own will, that nothing was left to chance, or the caprice of men, but God disposed all strongly and sweetly, and wrought all into one connected chain of justice, mercy, and truth.

JOHN WESLEY

March 18

A New Creation in Christ

Therefore, if anyone is in Christ, he is a new creation.
The old has passed away; behold, the new has come.
2 Corinthians 5:17

NEW BEGINNINGS SHOULD BE WELCOMED INTO OUR LIVES. It is an exciting, strengthening experience to turn a corner and make a fresh start — and there is no more powerful new beginning than obeying the gospel of Jesus Christ. In Christ, our starting over is so deep and complete that we are said to be a "new creation."

Having died with Christ in baptism, we walk in "newness of life" (Romans 6:4). And what does that mean? Paul described it in Colossians 3:1-17. We have new *goals* (v.1), new *thoughts* (v.2), and new *habits* (vv.5-16). With Christ as our Lord, we live under a new *authority* (v.17). And most important, having been forgiven of the sins that separated us from God, we live with a new *hope* (vv.3,4).

At baptism, we commit ourselves to actually living like what we have become: *a new creation*. Growing to maturity in Christ takes time. We can be encouraged by the fact that God will be patient. He will provide the help that is necessary. But if we don't open our eyes and see what *needs* to change, we will be hindered.

Unfortunately, most of us fail to see how radical the surgery needs to be. We see ourselves as "good" people — we may stumble now and then, but basically, we think we've lived without any very serious errors. Yet nothing could be further from the truth (Matthew 3:7-9). We need more than a little polishing up; we need to be destroyed and completely rebuilt. There is only one word to describe what must be done: "re-creation." If we're going to be fit to live in God's presence, we're going to have to be "re-created."

But in Christ, what needs to happen *can* happen. What God offers us is absolutely unique. There is nothing else like it in the world. So Peter appealed to his hearers in Jerusalem, "Repent therefore, and turn back, that your sins may be blotted out, *that times of refreshing may come from the presence of the Lord,* and that he may send the Christ appointed for you, Jesus, whom heaven must receive until the time for restoring all the things about which God spoke by the mouth of his holy prophets long ago" (Act 3:19-21).

In the natural world it is impossible to be made
all over again, but in the spiritual world it is exactly
what Jesus Christ makes possible.

OSWALD CHAMBERS

March 19

GOVERNED BY GOD

So if the Son sets you free, you will be free indeed.
John 8:36

FREEDOM IS ONE OF THE PRIME BENEFITS OF THE GOSPEL. In a world characterized by rebellion against God, we find ourselves fettered and frustrated by sin. But we can be delivered from this slavery. "If the Son sets you free, you will be free indeed."

Yet freedom is often misunderstood. The very essence of sin is the attitude which says, "I do not wish to do anyone's will but my own. I wish to be free of any limitations, so that I can do as I please." And when we first hear about the gospel of Christ, we may see it as a ticket to this kind of freedom. No longer will we be bound by the petty rules of "legalism." We will be free!

But ponder these words by Charles Kingsley: "There are two freedoms: the false, where man is free to do what he likes; the true, where a man is free to do what he ought." True freedom is not the absence of any limits at all; it is being governed by the wisdom of God — within limits that help us to do what is right.

What Adam and Eve found was that throwing off the restrictions of God's law did not enable them to enjoy the "good life," as they had been led to believe. Contrary to the tempter's lie, they discovered that God had been telling the truth in the first place: *outside of His will, human life leads, in the end, to nothing but death.*

After the establishment of Christ's church in the first century, there began to be those who taught that what one does in the flesh is of no consequence to the spirit. Christians should pursue "freedom" and disregard the old-fashioned precepts of right and wrong. But these advocates of "liberty" were lying, just as the tempter had been lying back in the Garden of Eden. And Peter called them out when he said, "For, speaking loud boasts of folly, they entice by sensual passions of the flesh those who are barely escaping from those who live in error. They promise them freedom, but they themselves are slaves of corruption. For whatever overcomes a person, to that he is enslaved" (2 Peter 2:18,19).

Eric Hoffer said, "The best test of freedom is perhaps less in what we are free to do than in what we are free not to do." If that is true politically, it's also true spiritually. We'd do well to listen.

Christianity promises to make men free;
it never promises to make them independent.

WILLIAM RALPH INGE

March 20

DEFERRING TO GOD'S REVEALED WILL

There is a way that seems right to a man,
but its end is the way to death.
Proverbs 14:12

THE BASIC PRINCIPLE IN PROVERBS 14:12 IS APPLICABLE TO LIFE IN GENERAL, BUT IT HAS A VERY SPECIFIC IMPORTANCE IN REGARD TO OUR ETERNAL SALVATION. Our own opinions and feelings can be dangerously wrong, despite our self-confidence about what "seems right" to us. Sincerity about our salvation is no guarantee we're on the right track. So of all the questions in the world, this is the one where we need the most help in getting the right answers.

There is a way that seems right to a man. Our brains, given to us by God, are marvelous instruments for figuring things out. But if we were trying to figure out the way to be saved from our sins, there is no chance we would be able to do so. If God did not reveal His mind to us, we wouldn't know the first thing about any plan that He might have for our reconciliation (1 Corinthians 2:11). What we could do, of course, is exercise our rational powers to envision how we think God *would* or *could* (or even *should*) set up His plan, and then suppose that because such a plan "seems right" to us subjectively, it must be true objectively, even if it conflicts with what the Scriptures teach. And not content with that, we might even go further and suppose that our subjective feelings about our salvation were, in fact, God speaking to us in our hearts. No amount of objective evidence from any source would be enough to dislodge from our minds our idea of what "seems right" to us.

Its end is the way to death. The problem, as Solomon observed, is that what seems to a human being to be the right path is often "the way to death." History is replete with examples of people who acted with great inner feelings of reasonableness but their feelings turned out to be disastrously wrong. In fact, as George Moore observed, "The wrong way always seems the more reasonable."

But God has not left us to figure out the path that leads to Him. He has revealed that path in the Scriptures, objectively and for all time to come. As Paul reminded his friend Timothy, the Scriptures are able to make us "wise for salvation" (2 Timothy 3:15). Whatever may seem right to us, we would do well to listen humbly to what God has said and accept His plan gratefully.

Where God has put a period, do not change it to a question mark.

T. J. BACH

March 21

The Way of God More Accurately

[Apollos] began to speak boldly in the synagogue, but when Priscilla and Aquila heard him, they took him aside and explained to him the way of God more accurately.
Acts 18:26

THERE IS PERHAPS NO GREATER TEST OF OUR HONESTY AND HUMILITY THAN WHEN WE FACE THE KIND OF SITUATION THAT APOLLOS DID. Fervent and faithful, at least to the best of his previous understanding, he needed to be shown "the way of God more accurately." And to his credit, when Priscilla and Aquila showed him where his understanding had been lacking, he changed.

Today, we face a challenging set of circumstances. In some countries, like the United States, millions of people are devout members of religious groups that call themselves "Christian" in some sense. But in very many, if not most, cases, the doctrines and practices that are being followed are not true to the teaching of Jesus Christ and His apostles in the New Testament.

For those committed to a return to the "Way" reflected in the New Testament (Acts 9:2; 24:14), the challenge is to get people to take a second look at their convictions. There is no harder person to convert to Christ than the one who thinks he is already following Christ. The shell of popular "Christianity" is very hard to penetrate. And there are few who will do what Apollos did: humbly admit that his previous understanding was inadequate. People do not like to be shown that they've been on the wrong path.

There is nobody, including this writer, who does not need an "Apollos experience" now and then. Our salvation depends on our willingness to be instructed by others. But such "teachability" requires a humility that is hard. As Winston Churchill said, "I am always ready to learn, but I do not always like being taught."

So what are we to do when we sit across the table discussing the Scriptures with someone whose understanding is significantly different from ours? What did Apollos do when he was lovingly confronted by Priscilla and Aquila? In the end, it doesn't matter *who* is right; it only matters *what* is right. And the Scriptures must be our guide. Each of us must have the courage to adjust ourselves to the truth when we learn "the way of God more accurately."

We owe almost all our knowledge not to those who have agreed but to those who have differed.

CHARLES CALEB COLTON

March 22

OUR RELATIONSHIP TO GOD: FRIENDSHIP OR ENMITY?

For if while we were enemies we were reconciled
to God by the death of his Son, much more, now that
we are reconciled, shall we be saved by his life.
Romans 5:10

THE GOSPEL OF CHRIST CALLS ON US TO TAKE SIDES. To be more precise, it calls on us to *change* sides. Jesus was clear that if we have not cast our lot *with* Him, that amounts to a decision to stand *against* Him. "Whoever is not with me is against me, and whoever does not gather with me scatters" (Luke 11:23). If our present position (the status quo, if you will) is that we have said "No" to Christ. We are on the side of the enemy. But Christ invites us to change our minds and say "Yes." *He will makes us His friends and treat us just as if we had never left the rule of God in the first place.*

Having been enemies, we are urged to be "reconciled" to God. "For if while we were enemies we were reconciled to God by the death of his Son, much more, now that we are reconciled, shall we be saved by his life. More than that, we also rejoice in God through our Lord Jesus Christ, through whom we have now received reconciliation" (Romans 5:10,11). But this involves far more than simply a change in our legal status before God. To be reconciled means that we not only pass from a wrong relationship with God to one that is right — it means that our *character* is brought back into conformity to God's character. God having removed the barrier and made us His friends, we learn to think — and *act* — as His friends.

Writing to Christians who were not living as they should, James said, "You adulterous people! Do you not know that friendship with the world is enmity with God? Therefore whoever wishes to be a friend of the world makes himself an enemy of God" (James 4:4). Having changed sides, we need to make sure we don't live like people who are still friends with the enemy.

But what if we have not yet obeyed the gospel at all? We need to see the reality of the position we're in, without glossing it over or making it seem more innocent than it is. If the gospel is false, it should be rejected. But if it is true, indifference is not an option. If we die in our rebellion, it will not go well with us at judgment.

You may say you are far from hating God; but if you live in sin,
you are among God's enemies, you are under Satan's standard and
enlisted there. You may not like it, no wonder; you may wish
to be elsewhere. But there you are, an enemy of God.

GERARD MANLEY HOPKINS

March 23

WITHOUT OUR SAVIOR, OUR SINS WILL KILL US

I told you that you would die in your sins, for unless you believe that I am he you will die in your sins.
John 8:24

TO MODERN PEOPLE, PREOCCUPIED WITH WHAT WE NAIVELY CALL "REAL" LIFE, WORDS LIKE *SIN* AND *DEATH* SOUND HOPELESSLY OLD-FASHIONED. To us, "dying in our sins" is a ridiculous concept.

But Jesus really did say these things. We may have a personal distaste for it, but there is no historical reason to deny that these were the claims Jesus made. We must grapple with whether His claims were true. And frankly, there is no way around the radical nature of what Jesus taught. He said that salvation from our sins requires believing Him to be the Christ, the Son of God, and that if we do not believe in Him, we will die in our sins. In other words, Jesus taught that He was (and continues to be) the only path back to God. Without Him, there is no remedy for our sins.

It is hard for us to grasp the full import of Jesus' words: *"die in your sins."* For one thing, *sin* is not the serious word it used to be. It's not how we explain misconduct. We talk of dysfunctions, diseases, and undesirable habits, but not sin. But Jesus did talk about sin. He did not diminish the seriousness of our problem. In turning away from our Father's will, we have cut ourselves off from Him in the very worst way. And there is only one word that adequately describes the consequences of what we've done: *death.*

"Unless you believe that I am he you will die in your sins" is what He said. But let us be clear: if we die in our sins and are lost eternally, our lost condition will not be the penalty for not having come to Jesus. *It will be the penalty for our sins.* In sin, the status quo is that we are lost. "The wages of sin is death" (Romans 6:23). A friend of mine, Robert F. Turner, used to say that it's like a person bitten by a rattlesnake. If he dies before he gets to a doctor, he didn't die of "not getting to the doctor." He died of rattlesnake venom.

But if sin is the problem and Jesus is the solution, He is the *only* solution. He is the only "savior" who has the power to do what has to be done. Sin is no ordinary problem, and its cure will not be ordinary either. Only Jesus Christ, the very embodiment of God Himself, has the power to get rid of the condemned person we used to be and bring to life a new person, fit for eternity with God.

Only when the axe is put to the tree does the fruit of sin wither.

ERWIN W. LUTZER

March 24

The Path to Death Does Not Lead to Life

But what fruit were you getting at that time from the things of which you are now ashamed? For the end of those things is death. But now that you have been set free from sin and have become slaves of God, the fruit you get leads to sanctification and its end, eternal life.
Romans 6:21,22

IF WE COULD SEE OURSELVES AS GOD SEES US, WE WOULD PROBABLY BE SHOCKED AT HOW CONTRADICTORY OUR LIVES LOOK TO HIM. We say we desire life, but so much of what we do is inconsistent with that goal; it must be sad for our Creator to observe.

If we persist in sin, hell is the only place we can get to. *The path that leads away from God is never going to get us back home to Him.* But foolishly, that is what we seem to believe. We don't want to change *paths,* but somehow we suppose that the *destination* of the path might change. Yet the law of cause and effect applies to all of us. No special exceptions are going to be made. And one definition of insanity is, as we've been told, "doing the same thing over and over again and expecting different results."

Solomon observed, "There is a way that seems right to a man, but its end is the way to death" (Proverbs 14:12). That is the very point Paul made in the text above: "the *end* of those things is death." In other words, eternal banishment from God is not an arbitrary punishment — it is the *telos* (a Greek word meaning "goal" or "result") of our decision to refuse God's rule. God is not going to force us to love Him in eternity if it has been our decision not to love Him in this life. So it is a very serious thing to refuse (or even procrastinate) reconciliation to God. And we are not in a position to dictate to God what the terms of our surrender will be. If He has chosen that it is through Jesus Christ that He will save us, then refusing that plan can't be anything but disastrous.

As Robert Louis Stevenson famously said, "Sooner or later everyone sits down to a banquet of consequences." Ultimately, there are only two paths available. Jesus counseled us to be careful. "Enter by the narrow gate. For the gate is wide and the way is easy that leads to destruction, and those who enter by it are many. For the gate is narrow and the way is hard that leads to life, and those who find it are few" (Matthew 7:13,14). It's time to clear up our contradictions. *Let's choose the path that goes where we want to end up.*

The way to Babylon will never bring you to Jerusalem.

OLD SAYING

March 25

Our Faith Must Be Confessed

. . . if you confess with your mouth that Jesus is Lord and believe in your heart that God raised him from the dead, you will be saved. For with the heart one believes and is justified, and with the mouth one confesses and is saved.
Romans 10:9,10

CONFESSING OUR FAITH IS A PART OF WHAT JESUS CHRIST REQUIRES FOR OUR SALVATION IN HIM. He said, "Everyone who acknowledges me before men, I also will acknowledge before my Father who is in heaven, but whoever denies me before men, I also will deny before my Father who is in heaven" (Matthew 10:32,33).

To "confess" something is to acknowledge it. It means that we openly admit the thing to be true. So if we are believers in Jesus Christ and followers of His teaching, He expects us to confess our faith openly. We would not be His friends at all if we were no more than "fair-weather friends," abandoning Him when it might be unpopular, or even dangerous, to be one of His people.

It is entirely appropriate for us to be asked to confess that "Jesus is Lord" (Romans 10:9) before we are baptized. The confession of our faith is no less a prerequisite to the remission of our sins than is faith itself. But don't forget: the confession which Paul calls "the good confession" (1 Timothy 6:12) is not just a one-time act, checked off the list as nothing more than one of the "steps of salvation." Our confession prior to our baptism is the beginning of an *entire life* that will confess Christ from that point onward, in deed as well as word. And we dare not go back on the promise we made when we first began to confess Christ. "Since then we have a great high priest who has passed through the heavens, Jesus, the Son of God, *let us hold fast our confession*" (Hebrews 4:14).

Dag Hammarskjöld once said, "Never, for the sake of peace and quiet, deny your own experience or conviction." The idea is not to make trouble merely to be militant, nor does it mean being obnoxious to other people with an in-your-face kind of aggression. The confession of our faith is simply a matter of being genuine and authentic. I call it "courageous sincerity." We are not to hide the truth about who we really are. When questioned — or even threatened — we should be able to say what Martin Luther said, "Here I stand; I can do no other. God help me. Amen!"

Weak persons cannot be sincere.

FRANÇOIS DE LA ROCHEFOUCAULD

March 26

STUDYING "THE CHURCH" IN THE SCRIPTURES

And he put all things under his feet and gave him as head over all things to the church, which is his body, the fullness of him who fills all in all.
Ephesians 1:22,23

PAUL WROTE THAT GOD HAS MADE CHRIST "HEAD OVER ALL THINGS TO THE CHURCH." This is consistent with what Christ Himself said to the apostles prior to His ascension to heaven: "All authority in heaven and on earth has been given to me. Go therefore and make disciples of all nations, baptizing them in the name of the Father and of the Son and of the Holy Spirit, teaching them to observe all that I have commanded you" (Matthew 28:18-20).

In its widest, most universal sense, the word *church* encompasses all the saved everywhere. This is the sense in which it is used in Ephesians 1:22,23. But it can also refer to a group of the Lord's people in a particular place. So we read, for example, about "the church of the Thessalonians" (1 Thessalonians 1:1), "the churches of Galatia" (Galatians 1:2), and many others. In this local sense, the Lord's people don't just share a saved relationship to Christ; they are able to "assemble as a congregation" (1 Corinthians 11:18 AMP) and jointly participate in the Lord's work.

We need to recover the importance that first-century Christians saw in the Lord's church. In the local congregation, we need to see the essential nature of that arrangement as the Lord designed it. And beyond the local churches in which we take part, we need to value our connection to "the brotherhood" (1 Peter 2:17; 5:9) — a relationship bigger than the affairs of our own local assembly, and one, in fact, existing in heaven as well as on the earth (Ephesians 3:14,15). We hurt ourselves spiritually — and we hurt the Lord's work of evangelism — when we undervalue the church.

Above all, we need to emphasize the sovereignty of Christ over the church. It was God who made Christ "head over all things to the church." The church is "his body, the fullness of him who fills all in all." To be a part of that body, then, is a privilege. And it means we submit to Christ's headship lovingly, radically, and respectfully.

Christ is the head of His church. His word is authority; all things relative to the church are at His feet. Its characteristics must, therefore, be Christ-determined. Questions must be Christ-answered; and problems must be Christ-solved . . . If it is important enough to be an issue, it is important enough to let Christ settle — that is, there must be authority for our conclusion in the New Testament.

ROBERT F. TURNER

March 27

WHICH SYNAGOGUE? MESSIAH? CHURCH?

So the woman left her water jar and went away into town and said to the people, "Come, see a man who told me all that I ever did. Can this be the Christ?"
John 4:28,29

LIFE IS FULL OF DECISIONS, AND OUR RELIGIOUS LIVES ARE ESPECIALLY SO. If we are serious about wanting to have a right relationship with God, we will have to sort through the many options presented by the world around us and determine what His will for mankind really is. But first, let's go back two thousand years.

When the Samaritan woman in our text hurried back into town, having just talked with Jesus, she said to the people, "Can this be the Christ?" Her question illustrates two things: (1) people were in a state of expectation that the Messiah might soon appear, and (2) deciding whether a certain person actually *was* the Messiah was a matter that needed to be weighed carefully. If you were looking for the Messiah, Jesus wasn't the only one making that claim. You would have to consider the various claims and choose rightly.

If you were a Jew in the Roman age, there was also another choice to make: which synagogue to attend. By some estimates, there may have been several hundred synagogues in Jerusalem, and perhaps even more in big cities like Alexandria and Rome. No two synagogues were alike in demographics, doctrine, or practice. Would you go to a liberal Hellenistic synagogue or a conservative Hebraic one? Would it be simpler to just go wherever your friends went, those who shared your traditions, your likes and dislikes?

Today, if you begin to live as a Christian, you will have to decide what relationship you will have with other Christians. Just as in the first century when many synagogues claimed to follow Moses and many persons claimed to be the Messiah, there may be many churches near you claiming to follow Christ. The question of "church" is important. If you're serious about pleasing God, you'll want to worship where the Scriptures are followed most closely.

Complexity turns some people into cynics; they just give up. I hope you won't do that. Instead, I hope you'll pray and ponder the Scriptures diligently. If you truly want to do what is right, you'll get the information you need to make your choices. But be careful. Not all paths lead to God — *and making wise choices can be hard work.*

The choices of time are binding in eternity.

JACK MACARTHUR

March 28

WHAT KIND OF HEART IS THE LORD LOOKING FOR?

[Samuel] looked on Eliab and thought, "Surely the LORD's anointed is before him." But the LORD said to Samuel, "Do not look on his appearance or on the height of his stature, because I have rejected him. For the LORD sees not as man sees: man looks on the outward appearance, but the LORD looks on the heart."
1 Samuel 16:6,7

WE CAN BE GLAD THAT THE LORD IS MORE CONCERNED WITH OUR HEART THAN WITH OUR EXTERNAL APPEARANCE. He knows things about us that others can't see. That is a comforting thought (and to tell the truth, it is also sobering). When Samuel was sent to the house of Jesse to anoint Israel's new king, he naturally thought that Eliab, Jesse's oldest son, would be the Lord's choice. But no, God wanted David, the youngest son. God could see, below the surface, that David had the *character* that was needed.

Today, the Lord is not looking for the next king of Israel; He is looking for those who will be "a people for his own possession" (1 Peter 2:9) — those who will respond gratefully to the gospel and be eager to live in a reconciled, joyful relationship with Him. But if He is to have a people who are uniquely His possession, what will their character be like? What kind of *heart* is the Lord looking for?

Penitent hearts. "The LORD is near to the brokenhearted and saves the crushed in spirit" (Psalm 34:18). Are we humble individuals who know what the tears of godly sorrow taste like?

Committed to the Lord's ways. Of King Jehoshaphat, it was said that "his heart was courageous in the ways of the LORD (2 Chronicles 17:6). Then and now, God is looking for hearts like that.

Loyal to the Lord. God said of Solomon, "His heart was not loyal to the LORD his God" (1 Kings 11:4,6 NKJV). Of the traits that God desires, few, if any, are more important than loyalty and reliability.

When we obey the gospel, we begin to grow in these qualities. But there is a sense in which these are the traits that make a person responsive to the gospel in the first place. And lest we make excuses, let's admit this fact: *we ourselves choose whether we will have such hearts or not.* So let's choose wisely. With His help, let's learn to have the kind of heart the Lord is looking for.

O Lord, let me not henceforth desire health or life, except to spend them for thee, with thee, and in thee. Thou alone knowest what is good for me; do, therefore, what seemeth to thee best. Give to me, or take from me; conform my will to thine.

BLAISE PASCAL

March 29

No Turning Back, No Turning Back

But we are not of those who shrink back and are destroyed,
but of those who have faith and preserve their souls.
Hebrews 10:39

IF WE DECIDE TO FOLLOW CHRIST, WE WILL MOVE IN A FORWARD DIRECTION AS LONG AS WE FOLLOW HIM. But having decided to follow Him, we must never change our minds and revert to going backward, the way we used to live. As the writer of Hebrews put it, we must not be among those who "shrink back and are destroyed."

Whether we ever turn back or not, one thing is certain: we will be *tempted* to do so. It is nothing but naive to think the Christian will never be discouraged or have second thoughts. Our enemy, the devil, will do all he can to get us back. And make no mistake, if we do return to his bondage, we will once again be in a lost condition, just as Peter wrote, "For if, after they have escaped the defilements of the world through the knowledge of our Lord and Savior Jesus Christ, they are again entangled in them and overcome, the last state has become worse for them than the first" (2 Peter 2:20).

Surrounded by difficulties and distractions every day, there is little chance we'll hold out if we haven't made a *commitment* to hold out. Becoming a Christian is more than a mood or a whim — it comes from (1) a sober assessment of the evidence, and (2) a commitment to take a stand that is lifelong and binding. Looking at it more personally, obeying the gospel involves *a commitment of love for Christ Himself.* Since we love Him, we will never betray Him. He can count on the faithfulness and obedience of our love.

Such a great commitment is more than a one-time act. As our lives unfold, we will find it needful to get a fresh grip on our commitment from time to time, meditating and reminding ourselves of the evidence that our decision rests upon and vowing anew that we will never be a traitor to our Lord. Every Lord's Day, we will make new promises of faithfulness to Him when the church gathers and we remember His death in the Lord's Supper.

So the Christian life is a long sequence of stronger and stronger commitments. But it all begins very simply. Whether we say it out loud or not, at baptism our hearts are entering into this pledge: *From this day forward, I will follow Jesus faithfully, so help me God.*

I have decided to follow Jesus.
No turning back, no turning back.

OLD GOSPEL SONG

March 30

Is Jesus the Only Way?

She will bear a son, and you shall call his name Jesus,
for he will save his people from their sins.
Matthew 1:21

WHEN JESUS WAS BORN, THE CHILD WAS NOT MERELY ANOTHER HUMAN BEING. He was God in the flesh, come into the world to "save his people from their sins." This is an astonishing claim.

Several years later, after Jesus had ascended back to the Father following His death and resurrection, His apostles were directed by the governing authorities in Jerusalem not to preach anymore in His name. Respectfully, they refused to comply with this order. "This Jesus," they said, "is the stone that was rejected by you, the builders, which has become the cornerstone. And there is salvation in no one else, for there is no other name under heaven given among men by which we must be saved" (Acts 4:11,12).

The idea of Jesus being the only way makes a good deal more sense when we consider the nature of the problem that has to be fixed. If all we needed was a little moral instruction or the example of a noble life, there might be many teachers and many paths to the goal. But if the problem is actually *sin,* then we have a very different situation: this problem will have only one solution.

God. If we have, in fact, alienated ourselves from our Creator by rebellion against His rule, only He has the right to set the terms of our return to Him. Facts are stubborn things, and reality is what it is. We need not expect that the path to reconciliation with God will involve anything less than the real truth about God — and that truth will inevitably exclude everything except itself.

Sin. A part of our problem is our insistence on writing our own rules. But if sin is the objective violation of the will of a God who truly does exist, the rectification of that problem will require letting God define exactly where we have gone wrong.

Salvation. If the gospel is about sin, that means "salvation" must be seen from a different perspective. Various proposals by the "world's greatest teachers" will not be enough. What we need is a grace that only our God can supply, and it is God who has said, "This is my Son, my Chosen One; listen to him!" (Luke 9:35).

Anyone can devise a plan by which good people may go
to heaven. Only God can devise a plan whereby sinners,
who are his enemies, can go to heaven.

LEWIS SPERRY CHAFER

March 31

COME, ONE AND ALL

The Spirit and the Bride say, "Come." And let the one who hears say, "Come." And let the one who is thirsty come; let the one who desires take the water of life without price.
Revelation 22:17

HAVING SEPARATED OURSELVES FROM GOD, WE NEED TO COME BACK TO HIM. By His grace, in the death of His Son to atone for our sins, He has made it possible for us to come back. By accepting the gospel, we can be baptized into Christ's death and receive the forgiveness of our sins (Romans 6:3-5). And as Paul said, "if we have been united with him in a death like his, we shall certainly be united with him in a resurrection like his" (v.5). But the question is: will we do this? Will we make the decision to receive what God is offering? *He invites us, but what will we do?*

All that stands between us and God's mercy is our stubborn will, our persistent refusal to accept His invitation. The Book of Revelation, the last book in the Scriptures, ends by emphasizing the desire of God for everyone to come and partake of the salvation He has provided. The fifth-from-the-last verse in the very last chapter of that hopeful book says, *"The Spirit and the Bride say, 'Come.' And let the one who hears say, 'Come.' And let the one who is thirsty come; let the one who desires take the water of life without price."*

We accept this invitation, initially, when we repent of our sins, confess our faith, and are baptized into Christ. As a child, I heard Charlotte G. Homer's hymn sung often as an "invitation song," inviting people, at the end of a sermon, to come and obey the gospel. *"Hear the invitation, come, whosoever will; praise God for full salvation, for whosoever will."* Powerful words, these. We are the losers if we have heard them so often they have lost their appeal.

In its most far-reaching application, Revelation 22:17 is an invitation to drink of the "water of life" *in eternity.* There is no conflict of meaning here — we drink of this water now, as a foretaste, but it will also be ours to enjoy in eternity, in an even greater sense. But we need to bear this in mind: *only in the here and now can we accept God's invitation.* When this life is over, it will be too late for us to decide that, yes, we would like to enjoy the water of life.

Hear the invitation,
Come, whosoever will;
Praise God for full salvation,
For whosoever will.

CHARLOTTE G. HOMER

April 1

An Everlasting Dominion

I saw in the night visions, and behold, with the clouds of heaven there came one like a son of man, and he came to the Ancient of Days and was presented before him. And to him was given dominion and glory and a kingdom, that all peoples, nations, and languages should serve him; his dominion is an everlasting dominion, which shall not pass away, and his kingdom one that shall not be destroyed.
Daniel 7:13,14

THE KINGDOM THAT GOD WAS GOING TO ESTABLISH THROUGH THE MESSIAH WAS REVEALED TO DANIEL IN VARIOUS WAYS. He was enabled by God to interpret a dream of Nebuchadnezzar's in which four earthly kingdoms were envisioned, but in the days of the fourth kingdom (which was the Roman Empire), "the God of heaven will set up a kingdom that shall never be destroyed, nor shall the kingdom be left to another people" (Daniel 2:44).

Later, we hear very similar language in 7:13,14. During the reign of Belshazzar, Daniel saw a vision in which "one like a son of man" came with the clouds of heaven and was given by God, the Ancient of Days, "dominion and glory and a kingdom, that all peoples, nations, and languages should serve him."

This prophecy was fulfilled when Jesus ascended back to heaven after His resurrection and was seated at the right hand of God (Acts 2:32-36). It is the coronation of the Messiah, God's Anointed One, predicted in Psalm 2:7-9, where we hear the Messiah say of God, His Father: "The LORD said to me, 'You are my Son; today I have begotten you. Ask of me, and I will make the nations your heritage, and the ends of the earth your possession.'"

The kingdom of the Messiah is now a reality. It was established in the days of the Roman Empire, and as Daniel had said in 2:44, it shall not "be left to another people." That is, there will never come a time when it falls apart and its place is taken by some other kingdom. This kingdom is permanent. It is indestructible. In fact, not even the end of this world will bring it to a close; it will continue in eternity. When we become members of this kingdom, our "citizenship is in heaven" (Philippians 3:20,21) — and we need not fear the rise and fall of any of the kingdoms of this world.

The kingdoms of earth pass away one by one,
But the kingdom of heaven remains;
It is built on a rock, and the Lord is its king,
And forever and ever He reigns.

HENRY R. TRICKETT

April 2

A DIFFERENT KIND OF KINGDOM

Jesus answered, "My kingdom is not of this world. If my kingdom were of this world, my servants would have been fighting, that I might not be delivered over to the Jews. But my kingdom is not from the world."
John 18:36

IT TOOK A LONG TIME FOR JESUS' DISCIPLES TO UNDERSTAND THE KIND OF KINGDOM HE CAME TO ESTABLISH. They assumed that the Messiah, when He came, would lead His people in throwing off the shackles of any earthly empire (like Rome) that might be ruling over them and reestablish the Davidic dynasty of kings in Jerusalem. We see this misunderstanding in the disciples' question in Acts 1:6, even after Jesus' resurrection. But we shouldn't be too quick to criticize them. If we had been in their shoes, we wouldn't have understood things any better than they did.

Today, many people still strongly desire for Jesus, as the Messiah, to be the king of some sort of earthly government or nation-state. That, however, was not His aim. "My kingdom is not of this world," He said. We would do well to consider how His rule is different from the kingdoms that *are* of this world.

It does not have a capital city. David had a physical throne situated in a particular city, but Christ's government does not have a "home office" anywhere on the globe. He does indeed rule, but He does so from His seat at the right hand of God (Colossians 3:1).

It does not have a territory defined by geographical boundaries. In political science, we can hardly think of a "kingdom" without thinking of the physical "territory" it controls. But the kingdom of Christ is not defined by the boundaries of any earthly territory — nor are its citizens defined as those born inside a certain territory.

It does not grow by means of military conquest. Earthly kingdoms have armies that fight, either to defend their territory or to expand it, and Jesus was being honest when He said, "If my kingdom were of this world, my servants would have been fighting." But it is not *territory* that Jesus wishes to rule over — it is the *hearts* of men and women, no matter where their earthly citizenship is. His kingdom exists wherever there are people who have truly given their hearts to Him, so that their "citizenship is in heaven" (Philippians 3:20).

Jesus made clear that the Kingdom of God is organic and not organizational. It grows like a seed and it works like leaven: secretly, invisibly, surprisingly, and irresistibly.

OS GUINNESS

April 3

Kingdom and Church

But when they believed Philip as he preached good news about the kingdom of God and the name of Jesus Christ, they were baptized, both men and women.
Acts 8:12

STUDIED TOGETHER, THE WORDS *KINGDOM* AND *CHURCH* HAVE A GREAT DEAL TO TEACH US. The first emphasizes authority, and so the expression "kingdom of God" has to do with God's rule or authority as King (1 Timothy 1:17). The second conveys the idea of being an assembly of persons "called out" from the world to belong to Him (Matthew 16:18). Perhaps we might say that *kingdom* focuses more on God and His sovereignty, while *church* looks more specifically at the people — those who have answered the call to come back to God, be forgiven, and live under His rule.

As far as the citizens of the kingdom are concerned, one cannot be a member of the Lord's church and not be a citizen in His kingdom. The reverse is also true. To be in the kingdom is to be in the Lord's church (with some responsibilities to other "called out" ones). This is an important point because of the popularity of the "spiritual but not religious" concept. Many who speak favorably of the "kingdom of God" would quickly say they have no desire for anything that could be called "church." However, in the New Testament, those who were members of God's kingdom were the same people as the members of Christ's church, and vice versa. They weren't two different groups; they were the same group.

In regard to kingdom and church, there is another confusion we need to avoid. The Scriptures do not teach that we are in the "church age" now but the "kingdom age" will begin when Christ comes back and establishes a government on the earth. The kingdom age is right now, and so is the church age. In fact, the very thing that *defines* the church is that God has "transferred us to the kingdom of his beloved Son" (Colossians 1:13). That's what a Christian is: a loyal subject in God's kingdom, joyfully accepting all that Jesus taught about how God's rule should govern our lives. Jesus Christ did not fail. He began His kingdom, as He said He would. We can accept the gospel — *and the kingdom* — right now.

As saints and faithful brethren in Christ at Colosse were delivered from the power of darkness and "translated into the kingdom of the Son of His love" (Colossians 1:12-14), so the true people of God today are citizens in Christ's kingdom and a manifestation that His power is yet very much alive.

ROBERT F. TURNER

April 4

The Unseen God Is Not Unreal

At that time I will search Jerusalem with lamps, and I will punish the men who are complacent, those who say in their hearts, "The LORD will not do good, nor will he do ill."
Zephaniah 1:12

THROUGH ZEPHANIAH, AS THROUGH THE OTHER HEBREW PROPHETS, GOD PROMISED SURE JUDGMENT UPON THOSE WHO LIVED WITH NO REGARD FOR RIGHT AND WRONG. Then, as now, there were many who had declared independence from God, for all practical purposes. Perhaps still believing in His existence, they saw no need to take Him into daily account. He could be disregarded. "The LORD," they said, "will not do good, nor will he do ill."

Might not this "practical atheism," as I call it, have been partly the result of God's unseen nature? The people of Jerusalem could not see Him with their eyes, so eventually their minds drifted into a lazy disobedience. "If He expects us to obey Him, why doesn't He show Himself openly?" is what they might have been saying.

There is no denying that the things our physical senses can experience — right now, in the present moment — seem much more real to us than intangible realities. Even things that can be experienced physically don't seem as real if they are in the past or the future. What is "here and now" has such a powerful pull on our minds, it sometimes blots out everything else. We know full well that the "here and now" is not all there is, but it has such a strong gravitational force that its orbit is very hard to break out of.

Yet God expects us to use the powerful minds He gave us. We are able to deal responsibly with unseen realities, and if we do not, there will come a day of reckoning. The foolish man who "says in his heart, 'There is no God'" (Psalm 14:1) is not necessarily the philosophical atheist. He may be the man who simply disregards God in his daily affairs. "Out of sight, out of mind," as we say.

Yet we do not diminish God by disregarding Him. He created us, and it is He "to whom we must give account" (Hebrews 4:13). He continues to be a benevolent Father whose promises have never failed to be fulfilled when the time was right. So let us not suppose that a mere "nevermind" on our part will make Him disappear.

Were every man on earth to become an atheist, it could not affect God in any way. He is what he is in himself without regard to any other. To believe in him adds nothing to his perfections; to doubt him takes nothing away.

A. W. TOZER

April 5

It Was Foretold That the Messiah Would Suffer

My God, my God, why have you forsaken me? Why are you so far from saving me, from the words of my groaning?
Psalm 22:1

PSALM 22 IS A PROPHECY OF THE MESSIAH'S SUFFERING. The familiar words of v.1 were spoken by Jesus while He was in the throes of death, as recorded in Matthew 27:46 and Mark 15:34. Among those expecting a personal Messiah, many would have been horrified at the very thought of the Messiah being killed — but that is exactly what David, as a prophet (2 Samuel 23:1,2), had predicted. Psalm 22 ends on a note of triumph (vv.21b-31), indicating that the Messiah's death would not be the end of the story, but it is v.1 that Matthew and Mark single out. Their quotation of Jesus' cry of agony on the cross showed God allowing Him to suffer, exactly as David had said in Psalm 22 that the Messiah would suffer.

When Jesus began to tell His disciples what was going to happen to Him, they did not comprehend it (Luke 9:43-45; 18:31-34). After it happened, however, Jesus explained that His suffering had to take place. *"These are my words that I spoke to you while I was still with you, that everything written about me in the Law of Moses and the Prophets and the Psalms must be fulfilled . . . that the Christ should suffer and on the third day rise from the dead, and that repentance for the forgiveness of sins should be proclaimed in his name to all nations, beginning from Jerusalem" (Luke 24:44-47).* The Messiah's death was not an unexpected interruption of God's plan. It was the most important part of the plan, foretold in the Scriptures long before.

We will look at some of the details of Psalm 22 in tomorrow's reading, but for now, I ask you simply to get a Bible and read the Psalm. It is the gruesome, heartbreaking picture of an innocent person being tortured to death. Death by crucifixion was intended to be torture, and Jesus was certainly not the only man to be put to death in this way by the Roman government, but as you read Psalm 22, just contemplate what it means that the Son of God was subjected to a death like this — and that even the particulars of it were foreseen ten centuries before it took place.

Psalm 22 makes it clear that Messiah was first to come and die for the sins of the world. It is a picture of the crucifixion, years before crucifixion was a method of capital punishment. The parallels between this Psalm, written nearly 1,000 years before Jesus, and the Gospel account are uncanny.

MITCH GLASER

April 6

THE MESSIAH'S HUMILIATION

I can count all my bones — they stare and gloat over me; they divide my garments among them, and for my clothing they cast lots.
Psalm 22:17,18

ALL FOUR OF THE GOSPELS IN THE NEW TESTAMENT ALLUDE TO THIS PART OF PSALM 22. In Matthew 27:35; Mark 15:24; Luke 23:34; and John 19:24, there are references to the dividing of Jesus' garments by the soldiers at His crucifixion. John specifically mentions that this was a fulfillment of prophecy. Yet this is only one of several details in Psalm 22 that describe Jesus' death. Let's look at some of the others, and as we do, ask yourself how these could all have been fulfilled so vividly and specifically in the death of Jesus if He were not, in fact, the person being pictured in this Psalm.

(1) There is, as we saw yesterday, Jesus' cry of agony from the cross, "My God, My God, why have you forsaken me?" (v.1), which is quoted in Matthew 27:46 and Mark 15:34. (2) The mocking that was hurled at Jesus, recorded in Matthew 27:39-43, is powerfully depicted in vv.6-8 of Psalm 22. (3) The devastation of the body of one being crucified is pictured realistically in v.14. (4) The thirst described in v.15 is emphasized in John 19:28. (5) In v.16, there is the saying, "They have pierced my hands and feet." This wording, while controversial, is supported by the LXX, Syriac, and Vulgate translations and is attested by the earliest manuscript of Psalm 22 discovered among the Dead Sea Scrolls. (6) Finally, there is in v.18, as we saw above, the gambling for the garments of the one being executed. This point is included in all four of the gospels.

In addition to these points, there is the general impression in Psalm 22 — an absolutely profound impression — that one is reading an actual description of what happened when Jesus died. If it was only a vague resemblance, one might argue that the similarity was just a coincidence. But an account with this many specifics, and corresponding to Jesus' death so closely, can be explained in only one way: David was enabled by God's Spirit to predict what he could not have known about in any other way.

So we come back to the point we began with yesterday. How can it be that the Messiah, of all people, would die such a death? It is simply that His death was required for our atonement. He reigns in glory today, but the cross had to come before the crown.

It is suffering and then glory.

ROBERT CRAWFORD MCQUILKIN

April 7

I Am the Resurrection and the Life

Jesus said to her, "I am the resurrection and the life.
Whoever believes in me, though he die, yet shall he live, and
everyone who lives and believes in me shall never die. Do you believe
this?" She said to him, "Yes, Lord; I believe that you are the Christ,
the Son of God, who is coming into the world."
John 11:25-27

LAZARUS HAD DIED SEVERAL DAYS BEFORE, AND MARTHA, ONE OF THE SISTERS OF LAZARUS, RAN TO MEET JESUS WHEN SHE HEARD THAT HE HAD ARRIVED IN THE VILLAGE. "Your brother will rise again" (v.23), Jesus said, and she expressed confidence that he would indeed rise again in the resurrection at the last day.

But Jesus had something more in mind than what Martha was thinking of. He intended to raise Lazarus from the grave, then and there. But He wanted Martha to understand something. Any resurrection from the dead, now or at the end of time, would always be by His power. "I am the resurrection and the life," He said. "Whoever believes in me, though he die, yet shall he live, and everyone who lives and believes in me shall never die." Jesus' own resurrection would prove Him to be the Son of God (Romans 1:4) — and as God, the Giver of life, Jesus held the power of life and death. In John 5:21, He had made this momentous claim, at once sobering and hope-giving: "As the Father raises the dead and gives them life, so also the Son gives life to whom he will."

Martha not only saw the force of what Jesus said; she believed that He was telling the truth. "I believe," she said, "that you are the Christ, the Son of God, who is coming into the world." She saw that the Messiah prophesied in the Old Testament was not to be an earthly ruler over a restored kingdom of Israel; He would be nothing less than God Himself, breaking the power of sin and death — founding a kingdom where the redeemed people of God could enjoy *a life that was eternal in every sense of the word.* This life, then, is our great hope, as Jesus promised: "This is the will of my Father, that everyone who looks on the Son and believes in him should have eternal life, and I will raise him up on the last day" (John 6:40).

The resurrection of Jesus is our hope today. It is our assurance
that we have a living Savior to help us live as we should now, and that
when, in the end, we set forth on that last great journey, we shall
not travel an uncharted course, but rather we shall go on
a planned voyage — life to death to eternal living.

RAYMOND MACKENDREE

April 8

Jesus, the Author and Finisher of Our Faith

. . . looking unto Jesus, the author and finisher of our faith, who for the joy that was set before Him endured the cross, despising the shame, and has sat down at the right hand of the throne of God.
Hebrews 12:2 NKJV

IF WE ARE FAMILIAR WITH THE GOSPEL OF JESUS CHRIST, WE MUST NOT GET TO THE POINT WHERE WE TAKE IT FOR GRANTED. We must never fail to appreciate the magnitude of what God has achieved in His Son, Jesus, who is the "author and finisher of our faith."

The author and finisher of our faith. Faced with persecution, the original readers of Hebrews needed to fix their eyes on Jesus and His faithfulness in hard circumstances. He is the supreme example of faith: both the *archegos* ("leader, pioneer") and the *teleiotes* ("completer, perfecter") of faith's endurance. As far as "the faith" is concerned, He is both the Originator and the Consummator of it.

Has sat down at the right hand of the throne of God. Following His resurrection and ascension, Jesus took His place at the right hand of God, in fulfillment of the prophecies of the Messiah (Psalm 110:1; Acts 2:32-35). He rules today over the kingdom of God as the King of kings. "And he is the head of the body, the church . . . that in everything he might be preeminent" (Colossians 1:18).

All of these great things are leading up to a climax that will occur at some point in the future. Concerning our resurrection at the return of Christ and the ultimate victory that will then have been won over Satan and his forces, Paul wrote, "Then comes the end, when [Christ] delivers the kingdom to God the Father after destroying every rule and every authority and power. For he must reign until he has put all his enemies under his feet. The last enemy to be destroyed is death" (1 Corinthians 15:24-26).

So when we say, as we often do, that Jesus is our "Savior," we are saying a great deal. If we don't see the magnificence of that, it is because we don't see the horror of what we had to be saved from or we don't appreciate the wisdom, love, and power that it took to rescue us. After we cut ourselves off from God, we could never have gotten back to Him. To be delivered from death, it took more than a Great Teacher or even a Courageous Martyr. It took a Savior.

God has set a Savior against sin, a heaven against hell, light against darkness, good against evil, and the breadth and length and depth and height of grace that is in himself for my good, against all the power and strength and subtlety of every enemy.

JOHN BUNYAN

April 9

THE BLESSINGS OF THE BROKEN HEART

But this is the one to whom I will look: he who is humble and contrite in spirit and trembles at my word.
Isaiah 66:2

WHO IS THE PERSON WHO RECEIVES GOD'S SPECIAL CARE? To those who worship self-confidence, the answer is surprising: *he who is humble and contrite in spirit and trembles at God's word.*

A text very similar to Isaiah 66:2 is Psalm 34:18, where David said, "The LORD is near to the brokenhearted and saves the crushed in spirit." When we hear this perspective expressed, we can't help but think of the "Beatitudes" of Jesus in the New Testament: "Blessed are the poor in spirit, for theirs is the kingdom of heaven. Blessed are those who mourn, for they shall be comforted" (Matthew 5:3,4). While these words sound almost absurd to modern ears, the truth is still the truth. When it comes to the most important parts of life, the broken heart is not a problem; it's a blessing. As long as sin is a reality in our lives, we will need to see it for what it is and, in godly sorrow, seek God's forgiveness.

What we see in both the Old Testament and the New is that the door to God's blessing is opened not by satisfaction with our lifestyles or a sense of our own fullness, *but by a sense of how empty we are.* If we humble ourselves before God, what we see is that in the presence of His holiness we are not wealthy; we are bankrupt. Especially in the so-called "developed" nations of the world, we need hearts that are more broken. To the self-satisfied, James put it clearly: "Be wretched and mourn and weep. Let your laughter be turned to mourning and your joy to gloom. Humble yourselves before the Lord, and he will exalt you" (James 4:9,10).

It is true — and what a wonderful truth it is — that joy comes from God's forgiveness (1 Peter 1:3-6). But who are the forgiven? It is those who come to God with their hearts broken (2 Corinthians 7:9,10). And we see no better illustration of this than the description of Saul of Tarsus grieving because of his new awareness of the need for God's forgiveness. He had fasted for three days before the Lord knew he was ready to be told what he must do to have his sins washed away (Acts 9:8-19; 22:11-16). In this world, even in Christ, it will always be the penitent who are able to find true joy.

The only things that are improved by breaking are the hearts of sinners.

ANONYMOUS

April 10

A New Prophet Like Moses

The LORD your God will raise up for you a prophet like me from among you, from your brothers — it is to him you shall listen.
Deuteronomy 18:15

TOWARD THE END OF MOSES' LIFE, HE TOLD ISRAEL THAT IN THE FUTURE GOD WOULD RAISE UP ANOTHER PROPHET LIKE HIM. At Sinai, Moses had received God's word and brought it back down the mountain to the people. So, Moses said, the time would come when another spokesman would act as God's representative, revealing things about God that the people could not have known if God had not spoken to the prophet, and the prophet, to the people.

We see here the meaning of "prophet": a spokesman or mouthpiece (Exodus 7:1,2). We often think of prophecy as a prediction of the future (and sometimes it is), but the basic idea is that of one who represents God and speaks in His name. The prophet is one through whom God reveals His word to the people.

We should not miss the importance of this point. The will of God cannot be discovered by human efforts such as divination, mystical experience, subjective emotions, or philosophical effort. Anything true we may know about God will have been *revealed* to us by Him — *using an authoritative spokesman.* The prophet could say, "Thus sayeth the Lord . . ." and not simply, "I feel that . . ."

By the Roman era, the Jews were expecting the coming of the new prophet who would be like Moses. When John the Baptist began preaching, some thought he might be this prophet: "When the Jews sent priests and Levites from Jerusalem to ask him, 'Who are you?' He confessed, and did not deny, but confessed, 'I am not the Christ.' And they asked him, 'What then? Are you Elijah?' He said, 'I am not.' 'Are you the Prophet?' And he answered, 'No'" (John 1:19-21). It was John's mission to prepare for the One who *was* the coming Prophet, Jesus the Messiah.

"It is to him you shall listen" is what Moses had said in Deuteronomy 18:15. And when Jesus was transfigured and seen by His disciples talking to Moses and Elijah, God spoke from heaven and said, "This is my beloved Son; *listen to him*" (Mark 9:7).

Moses predicts that the Lord will raise up another prophet like to himself . . . This promise received its complete fulfillment when God finally spoke through His own Son. Such was the definite assertion of Peter concerning Christ: "Moses said, 'The Lord God will raise up for you a prophet like me from your brothers'" (Acts 3:22).

CHARLES R. ERDMAN

April 11

God's Promise to Abraham

Go from your country and your kindred and your father's house to the land that I will show you. And I will make of you a great nation, and I will bless you and make your name great, so that you will be a blessing. I will bless those who bless you, and him who dishonors you I will curse, and in you all the families of the earth shall be blessed.
Genesis 12:1-3

This text records God's famous call for Abraham to leave his home in Ur. It also summarizes the remarkable promises that God made to Abraham concerning the future of his family.

First, God was going to lead Abraham to a *land* that would be given (over four hundred years later) to the family of Jacob, one of Abraham's grandsons. Next, God said He would make Abraham's descendants so numerous that they would constitute a great *nation.* And finally, God said the whole world would be blessed "in you," i.e., "in your *seed*" (Genesis 22:18 NKJV). Since "seed" here is singular rather than plural, this is a reference to Christ, the Savior who descended from Abraham, as Paul points out in Galatians 3:16.

Of these three, only the *Seed* promise was universal and ultimate in its scope. The *land* that God gave to Abraham's descendants has fulfilled its purpose in the history of salvation, and so has the physical *nation* of Israel. The Messiah having come and God's plan being complete, the preliminaries have been laid aside (Galatians 3:24-26). Consequently, the people of God are those from every tribe and tongue who have been justified by faith, the same kind of trust that Abraham was known for. Of course, not even Abraham could have been justified by his faith without the sacrifice of Christ, so Christ's sacrifice works backward in time just as it works forward (Hebrews 9:15; 11:1-40). *Every person who inhabits heaven will have gotten there on the same basis as Abraham: the obedience of faith, based on the sacrifice of Christ.* Abraham, then, is the prime example of how salvation works; he is the forefather of all who trust in God's promises enough to actually *walk* by faith. And when the whole host of Abraham's spiritual family gets together in heaven, what a reunion that's going to be!

The physical aspects of God's promise to Abraham were but a means to the far more important and eternal end of salvation from sins for all mankind. "There is neither Jew nor Greek . . . you are all one in Christ Jesus. And if you are Christ's, then you are Abraham's seed, and heirs according to the promise" (Galatians 3:26-29).

Robert F. Turner

April 12

Kingdom of Priests, Holy Nation

Now therefore, if you will indeed obey my voice and keep my covenant, you shall be my treasured possession among all peoples, for all the earth is mine; and you shall be to me a kingdom of priests and a holy nation.
Exodus 19:5,6

IN THIS AGE OF THE WORLD, "KINGDOM" AND "PRIEST" ARE NOT EVERYDAY CONCEPTS, LET ALONE "HOLY NATION." But what did God mean by these terms in speaking to Israel at Sinai, and what relevance do they have to us in thinking about the gospel of Christ?

My treasured possession. This is what physical Israel was then, and it is what spiritual Israel is today. Those who have been reconciled to God are uniquely His people, His "special property" (BBE).

A kingdom of priests. In the Law of Moses, the priests were to represent Israel to God, but they were also to represent God to Israel. By extension, then, Israel was to be "a kingdom of priests;" that is, they were to represent God to the rest of the world. Today, it is Christians, coming from both the Jewish and Gentile races, who represent God before the watching eyes (and listening ears) of the world. So, for example, the Book of Revelation begins with this doxology: "To him who loves us and has freed us from our sins by his blood *and made us a kingdom, priests to his God and Father,* to him be glory and dominion forever and ever. Amen" (1:5,6).

A holy nation. God wanted Israel to be what His people in Jesus Christ would later be: a group of people who were "holy." In other words, they would be devoted exclusively to Him, set apart for His use and reserved for the accomplishment of His purposes.

Writing to Christians, Peter used all of these ideas: "You are *a chosen race, a royal priesthood, a holy nation, a people for his own possession,* that you may proclaim the excellencies of him who called you out of darkness into his marvelous light" (1 Peter 2:9).

Much more could be said about being a kingdom of priests and a holy nation, but I want to end with the most important way in which those who are God's people represent Him to the world: we are to be those who speak God's *truth* to the world. And the ultimate goal is always the same: people who, based on God's truth, come to share His likeness and enjoy His presence in eternity.

We are called to be God's transmitters, to be completely separated from all thoughts which are contrary to his thinking, so that we may transmit his thoughts to others.

HANNAH HURNARD

April 13

A Child Is Born, A Son Is Given

For to us a child is born, to us a son is given; and the government shall be upon his shoulder, and his name shall be called Wonderful Counselor, Mighty God, Everlasting Father, Prince of Peace.
Isaiah 9:6

IN THIS MEMORABLE TEXT, ISAIAH PORTRAYED THE MESSIAH'S DOMINION IN MAJESTIC, SWEEPING LANGUAGE. He would rule as God's sovereign King ("the government shall be upon his shoulder"), and He would be entitled to the most exalted praise. "Wonderful Counselor, Mighty God, Everlasting Father, Prince of Peace" are epithets that could apply only to a divine ruler, receiving both the *love* and *reverence* that are reserved for God.

The words "to us a child is born, to us a son is given" should remind us of the "Immanuel" prophecy in 7:14: "Therefore the Lord himself will give you a sign. Behold, the virgin shall conceive and bear a son, and shall call his name Immanuel." Indeed, our text for today in 9:6 should be seen within the context of the entire section of chapters 1-12, a section filled with messianic hope. The messianic King who was to come would be no ordinary king. He would be even greater than David: a descendant of David physically, but one who would be miraculously born and nothing less than the Son of God — Immanuel ("God with us").

The King in Isaiah 9 would rule "from this time forth and forevermore" (v.7). This is exactly what Gabriel the angel told Mary about the Son that she would bear: "You will conceive in your womb and bear a son, and you shall call his name Jesus. He will be great and will be called the Son of the Most High. And the Lord God will give to him the throne of his father David, and he will reign over the house of Jacob forever, and of his kingdom there will be no end" (Luke 1:31-33). And when the Child was born and taken by His parents to Jerusalem for the required sacrifices, an aged man named Simeon took Him in his arms and said, "Lord, now you are letting your servant depart in peace, according to your word; for my eyes have seen your salvation that you have prepared in the presence of all peoples, a light for revelation to the Gentiles, and for glory to your people Israel" (Luke 2:29-32).

The point of Isaiah 9:1-7 was to alert the house of David that the virgin-born King for whom they were to look would only come after a long period of darkness. Nevertheless, He would indeed come, possessing a divine nature, to establish a righteous and eternal kingdom.

MICHAEL A. RYDELNIK

April 14

The King's Unpromising Birth

But you, O Bethlehem Ephrathah, who are too little to be among the clans of Judah, from you shall come forth for me one who is to be ruler in Israel, whose coming forth is from of old, from ancient days.
Micah 5:2

THIS TEXT IS ONE OF MANY FROM THE HEBREW PROPHETS QUOTED OR ALLUDED TO IN THE WRITINGS OF THE NEW TESTAMENT. It foretells that the Messiah ("Anointed One") would be born in the village of Bethlehem — just one of the numerous details about the Messiah that were fulfilled in Jesus Christ (Matthew 2:1-6).

If you had lived in the first century and were looking for the coming of the Messiah, you probably would have been looking for a kingly figure more majestic than Jesus. Bethlehem was an unpromising place to begin, but Nazareth, the village where Jesus grew up, was even more lowly. He was a peasant. How could He be the king who would lead Israel in its freedom-fight against Rome?

But what was the "territory" Jesus promised to reclaim and rule over? It was the human heart. His was a mission to defeat Satan, the great usurper. And He did exactly that. In Jesus Christ, God "has delivered us from the domain of darkness and transferred us to the kingdom of his beloved Son" (Colossians 1:13).

There is a marvelous irony in Jesus' humble birth in a place like Bethlehem. If the God of the Old and New Testaments is indeed real, and if in fact He did enter the world and take upon Himself human form, who would have expected that it would be in such lowly circumstances? Yet when we think about it for a moment, it seems altogether appropriate. If it is our pride that is the root of our sin, there can be no deliverance for us if we won't humble ourselves once again before our King. But are we not beautifully moved to do so when we see the humility of the King Himself? Although He is unimaginably powerful and glorious, He was willing to accomplish our rescue by sharing our weakness. He conquered the consequences of our pride not by arrogant command but by the ultimate act of submission.

Breath, mouth, ears, eyes
he is curtailed who overflowed all skies, all years.
Older than eternity, now he is new.
Now native to earth as I am,
nailed to my poor planet,
caught that I might be free.

LUCI SHAW

April 15

THE KEYS OF THE KINGDOM

I will give you the keys of the kingdom of heaven, and whatever you bind on earth shall be bound in heaven, and whatever you loose on earth shall be loosed in heaven.
Matthew 16:19

WHAT ARE WE TO MAKE OF CHRIST'S "KEYS OF THE KINGDOM" STATEMENT? If Roman Catholics have read too much into this text, Protestants have often read too little. Jesus' saying is of fundamental importance, and it should impact our thinking significantly.

To Peter, and by extension the rest of the apostles, Christ said that the "keys of the kingdom of heaven" would be given to them. Obviously, they would not have the authority to legislate the law of the kingdom, for God alone can do that, but to the apostles would be given *the role of communicating that law authoritatively.* The terms of entrance into the kingdom revealed by the apostles, and also the rules for living in the kingdom, would be those which God had decided on. When the apostles taught (or wrote), you could no more disregard what they said than you could disregard Christ Himself. (Ponder the implications of 3 John 9). The keys of the kingdom had, by God's design, been placed in their hands, so the normative nature of their work must be taken seriously. *We are the church of the Lord today only to the extent that we conform to what the apostles directed the church to be in the first century.*

The apostles, therefore, played a pivotal role in the New Testament period. No one since then has possessed Christ's authority as they did, and their teaching will always be the benchmark against which everything must be measured. So are we free to "develop" the apostolic teaching to make it more relevant to our times? Paul, the thirteenth and last of the apostles, left no doubt: "Even if we or an angel from heaven should preach to you a gospel contrary to the one we preached to you, let him be accursed" (Galatians 1:8). And what did John say to brethren being disturbed by the advocates of a more enlightened gospel? "Let what you heard from the beginning abide in you" (1 John 2:24).

Christian theology is anchored not only to certain historical events, culminating in the saving career of Jesus, but to the authoritative apostolic witness to, and interpretation of, these events. The Christian can never weigh anchor and launch out into the deep of speculative thought. Nor can he forsake the primitive teaching of the apostles for subsequent human traditions.

JOHN R. W. STOTT

April 16

THE LORDSHIP OF DAVID'S LORD

The LORD says to my Lord: "Sit at my right hand,
until I make your enemies your footstool."
Psalm 110:1

IN PSALM 110, DAVID SPOKE OF THE RULE OF A PERSON HE REFERRED TO AS "MY LORD." Who was this person? Whoever it was, Yahweh is pictured as saying to him, "Sit at my right hand, until I make your enemies your footstool." Some have said David was speaking of himself, but there is no other place in the Scriptures where a king spoke of himself as "my Lord." And David would not refer to any of the later kings on the throne in Jerusalem as "my Lord."

(1) Jesus argued in Matthew 22:41-46 that David was speaking of the Messiah. The Pharisees had agreed that the Messiah would be "the son of David" (v.42), but Jesus countered, "How is it then that David, in the Spirit, calls him Lord, saying, 'The Lord said to my Lord, "Sit at my right hand, until I put your enemies under your feet"'? If then David calls him Lord, how is he his son?" (vv.43-45).

(2) Peter, in his sermon on Pentecost, quoted from Psalm 110 and applied it to Jesus: "For David did not ascend into the heavens, but he himself says, 'The Lord said to my Lord, "Sit at my right hand, until I make your enemies your footstool."' Let all the house of Israel therefore know for certain that God has made him both Lord and Christ, this Jesus whom you crucified" (Acts 2:34-36). (On this point, read 1 Corinthians 15:24-28 with Daniel 7:13,14 in mind.)

(3) That Psalm 110 is messianic is also seen in v.4 where Yahweh says to the one at His right hand, "You are a priest forever after the order of Melchizedek." Unlike the Levites, the Messiah would be a priest-king, like Melchizedek in Genesis 14:18-24. Hebrews 7:1-28 argues that this "priest forever after the order of Melchizedek" is Jesus.

Psalm 110, then, is one of the most powerful prophecies of the Messiah — and every part of it meshes seamlessly with the person and work of Jesus Christ. It is no wonder that the New Testament writers saw in the language of this great Psalm clear and forceful references to the identity of Jesus as the Messiah, the One who is now seated at the right hand of God (Hebrews 1:3,13; 10:12,13).

There are in fact strong reasons to conclude that the original author of the psalm intended to speak of a divine lord. David, Israel's most exalted king, was looking forward to the coming of a future ruler even more exalted than himself.

MICHAEL A. RYDELNIK

April 17

FAITH AND REASON

But many of those who had heard the word believed,
and the number of the men came to about five thousand.
Acts 4:4

BETWEEN "HEARING" THE GOSPEL AND "BELIEVING" IT, A PROCESS OF REASONING HAS TO TAKE PLACE. Contrary to the popular notion that faith and reason are incompatible, reason is necessary in the creation of a genuine faith in God. Without the solid foundation of reasonable thinking, faith is nothing but a feeling that is subject to the winds of ever-changing circumstances. Tried by persecution, a merely emotional faith would not stand the test.

Evaluating the evidence. Anyone who has sat in the jury box in a criminal trial knows that in order to reach a decision as to the defendant's guilt or innocence, your reason has to evaluate the evidence provided by witnesses. The same is true with the New Testament. No faith in the deity of Jesus is possible without making a rational ("reasoned") decision as to the quality of the evidence.

Reaching right conclusions from the evidence. Going back to our courtroom analogy, it is one thing to get the facts straight as to what happened, but it is another to see clearly what is *implied* by those facts. Both of these — *What are the facts?* and *What do the facts mean?* — require reasoning. In the New Testament, the witnesses claim that they found Jesus' tomb empty, and we have to decide whether the record is believable. If the tomb was empty, we have to decide whether its emptiness means that Jesus was resurrected. Finally (and most importantly), we have to decide whether, if Jesus was resurrected, that means "God has made him both Lord and Christ" (Acts 2:36). Reason is required at each step.

Deciding to trust God. Ultimately, our faith must be in *the character of God* — and that, like everything about the gospel, requires that we reason carefully from the facts to the meaning of the facts. What the gospel aims to produce is not simply a person who participates in a certain religion and keeps the right commandments. It is a person who, believing the facts of the gospel, is willing to stake his whole life on God — *the very God whom the gospel is about.*

Faith and sight are set in opposition to each other in Scripture, but not faith and reason . . . True faith is essentially reasonable because it trusts in the character and the promises of God. A believing Christian is one whose mind reflects and rests on these certitudes.

JOHN R. W. STOTT

April 18

FAITH AND TRUST

And the LORD said to Moses, "How long will this people despise me? And how long will they not believe in me, in spite of all the signs that I have done among them?"
Numbers 14:11

ONE MEASURE OF THE MATURITY OF OUR FAITH IS HOW MUCH WE TRUST GOD. If we believe in the existence of God, that is a good thing. But as believers, do we trust Him enough to do things His way when that path looks very dangerous and difficult?

In Numbers 14, when the spies came back from their reconnaissance of the land of Canaan, all but two of them reported that it would not be possible for Israel to occupy the land. Discouraged, the nation wanted to reject Moses' leadership and return to Egypt. That is when God pointed to the real problem: *the people's lack of trust in Him.* "How long will they not believe in me, in spite of all the signs that I have done among them?" They had not gotten the point of the miracles God had done to prove His dependability.

God's character. If all we mean is that Israel accepted God's existence, they were "believers." But they showed, when the going got tough, that they were not believers in the sense of *trusting* God. In fact, God said, "How long will this people despise me?" Having thrown away everything God had demonstrated to them about His trustworthiness, they had little confidence in God's character.

God's promises. We call Canaan the "Promised Land" for a reason: God had promised it to Israel and powerfully confirmed His promise. They had seen God's power in the plagues in Egypt, heard His thunderous voice from Sinai, and received His provision of manna in the wilderness. Nevertheless, they had no confidence that God would actually keep the promises He had made.

God's commandments. Worst of all, Israel showed a lack of trust by refusing to obey what God had commanded. Here, perhaps, is the main area where we all find out whether our faith has matured into trust: *will we or won't we do what God has said?* We can deplore the lack of trust that caused Israel to back away from God's command, but do we do any better? When it comes to obeying the gospel of Christ, do we trust the God we believe in enough to do what He has told us, confident that His wisdom is always best?

Trustfulness is based on confidence in God, whose ways I do not understand. If I did, there would be no need for trust.

OSWALD CHAMBERS

April 19

Baptism Is Immersion

We were buried therefore with him by baptism into death,
in order that, just as Christ was raised from the dead by the glory
of the Father, we too might walk in newness of life.
Romans 6:4

WHEN A PERSON IS BAPTIZED, WHAT IS THE PHYSICAL ACTION THAT TAKES PLACE? Biblically, there is no evidence that baptism was ever anything other than complete immersion in water. Of John, the prophet sent by God to prepare the way for Christ, it was said that he "was baptizing at Aenon near Salim, because water was plentiful there" (John 3:23). We are told that "when Jesus was baptized, immediately he went up from the water, and behold, the heavens were opened to him" (Matthew 3:16). In Acts, in the account of the Ethiopian official's baptism by Philip, the text says that "as they were going along the road they came to some water, and the eunuch said, 'See, here is water! What prevents me from being baptized?' And he commanded the chariot to stop, and they both went down into the water, Philip and the eunuch, and he baptized him. And when they came up out of the water, the Spirit of the Lord carried Philip away, and the eunuch saw him no more, and went on his way rejoicing" (Acts 8:36-39).

In the New Testament, baptism is a vivid picture of the death, burial, and resurrection of Christ — a physical act which shows that in obeying the gospel a person is dying with Christ. Paul reminded the Colossians that they had been "buried with him in baptism, in which you were also raised with him through faith in the powerful working of God, who raised him from the dead" (2:12). And to the Romans, he used this analogy in an even more extensive way (Romans 6:3-5). So if we let the Scriptures decide the issue, we'll have to conclude that baptism is immersion.

In practical terms, this burial and resurrection in baptism marks the beginning of a new life, so much so that it can be said that *a new person has come into existence,* one whose allegiance is now to Christ and not the world. And more than all the other blessings combined, what this new person has now that he didn't have before is hope — the hope of life eternal (Titus 1:2; 3:7).

Buried with Christ, my blessed Redeemer,
Dead to the old life of folly and sin;
Satan may call, the world may entreat me,
There is no voice that answers within.

T. O. CHISHOLM

April 20

The Return of Elijah

Behold, I will send you Elijah the prophet
before the great and awesome day of the LORD comes.
Malachi 4:5

MALACHI IS THE LAST BOOK IN THE OLD TESTAMENT. After this oracle was delivered, God did not speak prophetically to His people again until John the Baptist appeared preaching in the wilderness of Judea over four hundred years later. When John began to preach, his message was simple: "Repent, for the kingdom of heaven is at hand!" (Matthew 3:1,2). The Messiah was soon to appear, and to be ready for Him and the kingdom that He would inaugurate, the people needed to turn away from their sins.

In the days when John the Baptist appeared preaching in the Wilderness of Judea, the Jews were familiar with this text in Malachi, and they were expecting the return of Elijah. Yet it was not Elijah himself that Malachi had spoken of; it was John the Baptist. By preaching the message of repentance with the same power as Elijah, John prepared the people's hearts for the Messiah.

Jesus, on more than one occasion, identified John as the Elijah who was to come. For example, in Matthew 11:13,14, He said, "For all the Prophets and the Law prophesied until John, and if you are willing to accept it, he is Elijah who is to come." There is in the Old Testament no prediction that is any more clearly and specifically explained than the one in Malachi 4:5 about the return of Elijah.

But we miss the point if we fail to see the importance of what Elijah, John, and Jesus preached. If there was to be a kingdom populated by those whose sins had been forgiven, the first thing that obviously had to take place was for the people to be brought to a realization of their *need* for forgiveness — and then for them to be willing to *repent* of those sins as they sought God's forgiveness. The only preaching that could have prepared them for the Messiah was the message that John (and before him, Elijah) preached.

But who are the people who will repent of their sins? It is those who are *humble* enough to do so. If it is pride that produces sin in the first place, then getting rid of pride — returning our hearts to a posture of humility before God — must be the first thing that happens in the process of our salvation. And frankly, there is nothing harder for modern people to hear than this.

Humility is a necessary prerequisite for grace.

BERNARD OF CLAIRVAUX

April 21

A Tragic Disregard for God's Requirements

Now Nadab and Abihu, the sons of Aaron, each took his censer and put fire in it and laid incense on it and offered unauthorized fire before the LORD, which he had not commanded them.
Leviticus 10:1

BEGINNING WITH ADAM AND EVE'S BOLD EXPERIMENT WITH INDEPENDENCE FROM GOD, EVERY MEMBER OF THE HUMAN RACE HAS STRUGGLED WITH THE SAME PROBLEM. Somehow, we just can't believe that God really means business when He reveals His will for the way things are to be done. We can't resist the thought that His requirements are arbitrary, unreasonable, and legalistic — and that no harm will come if we choose to do things differently.

The story of Nadab and Abihu in Leviticus 10 is one of the most striking examples of how displeased God is with the human desire to do as we please, regardless of His instructions. Sons of Aaron, the high priest, Nadab and Abihu put fire in their incense burners that was "unauthorized." The text does not say specifically in what way their fire was in violation of the Lord's command, but they surely would have known. They deliberately did that "which he had not commanded them." And because the Lord could not allow such disrespect to stand on such a great occasion, "fire came out from before the LORD and consumed them, and they died before the LORD" (v.2). In a manner that was no doubt shocking to everyone, especially Aaron, their father, God demonstrated to His people that His instructions are to be taken utterly seriously.

Like it or not, there is a link between the *character of God* and the *commands of God.* When God has given any instruction to regulate our behavior, we cannot disrespect His *word* without disrespecting *Him.* There is no such thing as "reverent disobedience."

In our thoughts on obeying the gospel, we've pointed to the importance of the question, "What must I do to be saved?" (Acts 16:30). *That is the one question we must be the most willing to let God answer.* Whatever our preferences may be as to what God *should* require, the only thing that matters is what He *does* require — and the only way we can know this is by the Scriptures. We may not understand God's rationale for setting things up as He has, but we must respect His right to do so. It is to be hoped that we'll honor Him more reverently than Nadab and Abihu did.

Understanding can wait, but obedience cannot.

GEOFFREY GROGAN

April 22

God Will Not Be Trifled With

Then Moses said to Aaron, "This is what the LORD has said: 'Among those who are near me I will be sanctified, and before all the people I will be glorified.'" And Aaron held his peace.
Leviticus 10:3

WHEN NADAB AND ABIHU DISRESPECTED GOD BY FLOUTING HIS INSTRUCTIONS FOR THE TABERNACLE WORSHIP, THEY PAID FOR IT WITH THEIR LIVES. Having offered "unauthorized fire before the LORD, which He had not commanded them . . . fire came out from before the LORD and consumed them" (Leviticus 10:1,2). And in the aftermath, God clearly stated the point He wanted the people to take from the event: *"Among those who are near me I will be sanctified, and before all the people I will be glorified"* (v.3). What does this statement mean, especially the first part where God says, "I will be sanctified"? Two interpretations are possible, and both of them involve truths that are clearly taught in the Scriptures:

(1) The NIV words it this way: "Among those who approach me I will show myself holy." If this is how the Hebrew is to be taken, it means that those who come near God (the priests) will be vessels through whom He will exhibit His holiness. The NLT has, "I will display My holiness through those who come near Me."

(2) But there is another possibility, as shown in the NKJV rendering: "By those who come near Me I must be regarded as holy." This means, as the CEV tersely puts it, "I demand respect from my priests." To come near God is a serious thing. Disrespect and disobedience will not be tolerated in those allowed to approach Him.

As we've said, both of these lines of thought are true. Either way, the main point is that God is holy. He must be *treated* as holy — with deep respect for His commandments — and He will also *display* His holiness in His dealings with those who come near — even if that means punishing those who play fast and loose with His instructions and "worship" Him presumptuously.

When it comes to God's plan for our salvation, only He has the right to decide the terms of our forgiveness. In the matter of obeying the gospel, as in all else, it is He who writes the rules and not we. So we need to dispense with the popular notion that we can "love" God with a "positive" (and wholly subjective) theology that pays little attention to the requirements of His holiness.

Saying yes to God means saying no to things that offend his holiness.

A. MORGAN DERHAM

April 23

WITH ALL YOUR HEART AND SOUL

But from there you will seek the LORD your God and you will find him, if you search after him with all your heart and with all your soul.
Deuteronomy 4:29

THE BASIC IDEA CONTAINED IN THIS TEXT IS FOUND THROUGHOUT THE SCRIPTURES. I have not counted them, but if you took all the occurrences of "with all your heart and soul" (and all the variations thereof) and put them together, it would be an impressive list. Clearly, what God wants is for us to seek Him *wholeheartedly.*

In our text, however, Moses was not just speaking of a generic seeking of the Lord; he was talking about Israel *returning* to God after having forsaken Him. His point was that God would be willing to forgive them and bless them if they returned *with all their hearts.* No apathetic or lackadaisical return would be accepted.

Wholeheartedness may be thought of in various ways. If we said somebody did something "with all his heart," that would mean his effort was diligent, passionate, focused, and committed. All of these, and more, are involved when God said that Israel must return "with all your heart and with all your soul."

If a person has not yet obeyed the gospel (Acts 2:37-41), the idea of wholeheartedness should be given careful consideration. To seek God's forgiveness of our sins is a serious matter, as is committing ourselves to lifelong faithfulness after we've been forgiven. Jesus urged us to "count the cost" of discipleship (Luke 14:25-33). If we're not willing to throw the doors open and give God access to *every* room in our hearts (even the "secret" ones), it is doubtful that our intentions are as serious as they should be.

There is a sense in which becoming a Christian is a "return" to God. We were born into this world innocent of any sin and in a relationship with God that was beautifully right. It was only when we first went against what we knew to be God's will that our fellowship with Him was broken and we found ourselves, somewhat like Israel, banished to a foreign land, spiritually speaking. The gospel of Christ offers restoration to those who return — but only to those who come back with a commitment befitting the majesty and love of God. Our loyalty must be absolutely unconditional. Surely, our Heavenly Father — our Merciful King — deserves this.

To my God, a heart of flame; to my fellowmen,
a heart of love; to myself, a heart of steel.

AUGUSTINE OF HIPPO

April 24

SETTING APART CHRIST AS LORD IN OUR HEARTS

But in your hearts set apart Christ as Lord. Always be prepared to give an answer to everyone who asks you to give the reason for the hope that you have. But do this with gentleness and respect.
1 Peter 3:15 NIV

ONE WAY TO DEFINE THE CHRISTIAN'S UNIQUENESS IS TO SAY THAT HE HAS MADE CHRIST THE "LORD" OF HIS HEART. When he turned away from his sins, confessed his faith, and was baptized into Christ, the Christian began to follow a new leadership. Whatever may have directed his life before, he now looks to Christ as the deciding factor in every aspect of his character and conduct.

This is what Peter had in mind when he said we should "set apart Christ as Lord" in our hearts. While not as familiar now as it was in the first century, the concept of "lordship" is critically important. The word *lord* means "master" or "one who has authority," but in the case of Jesus Christ the term is all-encompassing. For the Christian, Christ has *all* authority. There is nothing about the Christian's life that the will of Christ does not govern — from the innermost thoughts of his heart to the outermost aspects of his behavior. *No step is taken unless he is confident that Christ approves.*

Paul put it this way: "Whatever you do, in word or deed, do everything in the name of the Lord Jesus, giving thanks to God the Father through him" (Colossians 3:17). And this principle does not just apply to the "religious" aspect of life or "church" activities. It applies to everything the Christian does, publicly and privately.

Peter said Christ is to be set apart as Lord "in your hearts." The Christian fights a losing battle against sin if he has not first given his *heart* to Jesus Christ. It is only when Christ has been given control of our *thinking* that progress begins to be made.

This decision to "set apart Christ as Lord" is the main ingredient in conversion to Christ. The changes that occur on the "outside" of our lives are the result of a change on the "inside": our thoughts are now under the rule of Jesus Christ. But living *consistently* under Christ's lordship requires growth. We have to learn to yield our hearts *completely* to His direction. At our baptism, we're just getting started in learning how to let Christ be our Lord.

If you desire Christ for a perpetual guest, give him all the keys of your heart; let not one cabinet be locked up from him; give him the range of every room and the key of every chamber.

CHARLES HADDON SPURGEON

April 25

Do We Really Mean Our Nice-Sounding Words?

Oh that they had such a heart as this always, to fear me and to keep all my commandments.
Deuteronomy 5:29

God's statement in this verse came after Israel had said they would obey the Law that God would give to Moses on Mount Sinai. "Go near and hear all that the Lord our God will say," they had said, "and speak to us all that the Lord our God will speak to you, and we will hear and do it" (v.27). That was a fine statement, which God acknowledged (v.28), but God knew that Israel would end up *not* keeping the Law, so He said, "Oh that they had such a heart as this always, to fear me and to keep all my commandments" (v.29). Although some of the people may have been sincere in what they said at Sinai, the fact is, it was easier to *say* those nice-sounding words than it was to *keep* them.

This is not an argument against saying the words that express our highest ideals and best intentions. There is value in verbalizing these things, even when we know our performance is going to be imperfect. Often our words serve the purpose of saying what we *want* to be true. Yet we still need to be careful. Surrounded by other religious people, it's easy to say nice things. But talk is cheap, as they say. *We need to mean every promise we make to God.*

Finally, I wish to suggest another aspect of this topic. All of us have had the experience of saying things nonchalantly that turned out to be far more "real" than we imagined at the time. A similar thing happens sometimes when we speak of God. For example, we might casually and superficially talk about God being "a consuming fire." Those are true words, as we find in Hebrews 12:29, but if the time ever comes when we actually *experience* the wrath of God that we spoke about so glibly, we will tremble to realize that, whether we really meant it or not, we spoke far more truth than we knew. All of which is to say: words are powerful things. And if the words we speak are about God and they happen to be true, their truth may come crashing down on us eventually — even if we didn't really mean them when we said them.

There comes a moment when people who have been dabbling in religion ("man's search for God") suddenly draw back. Supposing we really found Him? We never meant it to come to that! Worse still, supposing He had found us?

C. S. Lewis

April 26

WE HAVE TO BE TAUGHT WHAT WE NEED

And you shall remember the whole way that the LORD your God has led you these forty years in the wilderness, that he might humble you, testing you to know what was in your heart, whether you would keep his commandments or not. And he humbled you and let you hunger and fed you with manna, which you did not know, nor did your fathers know, that he might make you know that man does not live by bread alone, but man lives by every word that comes from the mouth of the LORD.

Deuteronomy 8:2,3

IN THE WILDERNESS, GOD KEPT ISRAEL FROM STARVING TO DEATH, BUT NOT WITHOUT LETTING THEM FEEL THE EXPERIENCE OF HUNGER. The purpose of this was to teach Israel their need for Him, especially their need for His truth. Moses said that God "humbled you and let you hunger and fed you with manna . . . that he might make you know that man does not live by bread alone, but man lives by every word that comes from the mouth of the LORD."

It is a fact that we need our Creator. He created us to need not only Him *but a right relationship with Him.* Yet we forget this, living our lives as if no notice need be taken of the God who made us. On Thanksgiving Day we may say grace before we eat, but more often we live as if what we need is going to come from marrying well and making smart career moves — matters that "we control."

So if it was said to Israel that "he humbled you and let you hunger," the same might be said of us. Food might not be the thing we have to do without, but there will be some deprivation, some unmet needs. God will see that this happens. He will grant us the gift of "need" — to teach us that we are *not* self-sufficient.

The fact is, we have to be taught what our greatest needs are. We think we know what these are, but our priorities can become dangerously disordered. We have to be taught (sometimes the hard way) that it is by God's word that we live, not by bread alone.

All of this relates to the gospel in a powerful way. There is no greater barrier to a person's reception of the gospel than the sense of not needing what the gospel offers. If we don't need God at all, we certainly don't need His forgiveness, least of all by yielding ourselves to some plan that He might have for our "salvation." But there is coming a day of reckoning. If our doom ends up being that of those who have disregarded God, it won't be because He did not try to break through our hard shell of self-sufficiency.

God's restrictions were given to show us more keenly our need of him.

ERWIN W. LUTZER

April 27

A Bag with Holes

You have sown much, and harvested little. You eat,
but you never have enough; you drink, but you never have your fill.
You clothe yourselves, but no one is warm. And he who earns
wages does so to put them into a bag with holes.
Haggai 1:6

DESPITE OUR DILIGENCE IN THIS WORLD, SOMETIMES IT SEEMS THE RESULTS OF OUR WORK ARE NOT COMPLETELY SATISFACTORY. In our more honest moments, we recognize the existence of yearnings and aspirations that show no signs of going away. This is true collectively in societies, and also personally in individuals.

In Haggai 1:6, God used the analogy of a man putting his wages into "a bag with holes." This man may believe in the power of positive thinking, but if his bag has holes in it, pouring more coins into it is going to be futile. *And it is God who determines whether any particular bag will have holes in it or not.* It is simply not within our power to reach every goal we set (James 4:13-16). At any time, God can withhold the profit we intended from our goals (putting holes in our bags), so that, despite our energy and optimism, we are left with the feeling that we didn't really get what we were after.

Now think carefully. *What is true of specific activities in life is also true of life in general.* When mankind rebelled against Him, God subjected the world to "futility" (Romans 8:20,21). That is, God set limitations that would prevent the human race from controlling everything it wanted to control, and having everything it wanted to have. These limitations should be a constant reminder of man's need for God. The fact that, in this world, our "bag" will always have "holes" in it does not mean that God is cruel. *Rather, He lets us experience this earthly unsatisfaction in order to draw us back to Him.*

In Deuteronomy 8:3, Moses reminded Israel about the hunger God had allowed them to suffer in the wilderness: "And he humbled you and let you hunger and fed you with manna, which you did not know, nor did your fathers know, that he might make you know that man does not live by bread alone, but man lives by every word that comes from the mouth of the LORD."

The sooner we grasp this point, the sooner we'll be ready for the gospel. It will be a huge step forward when we come to see the human race — and ourselves — as being empty rather than full.

We are all beggars, each in his own way.

MARK TWAIN

April 28

Repentance from the Heart

Let us lift up our hearts and hands to God in heaven.
Lamentations 3:41

IN HIS COLLECTION OF SORROWFUL SONGS FOLLOWING THE DESOLATION OF JERUSALEM BY THE BABYLONIANS, JEREMIAH CAPTURES THE PENITENT SPIRIT THAT ISRAEL SHOULD HAVE HAD AT THIS TERRIBLE TIME. "Let us lift up our hearts and hands to God in heaven," he says. Although God had brought judgment upon Israel (just as He had said He would if they did not cease their idolatry), their future could still be bright with hope if they would repent.

Repentance is a sincere turning of the heart back to God. In our outward actions, repentance involves ceasing to do what is wrong and starting to do what is right, but these outward results of repentance proceed from *a heart that is sorry for the sins that have been committed against God* (cf. 2 Corinthians 7:9-11). Theoretically, a person might change his ways for a number of reasons that have nothing to do with God. Repentance, however, is the reformation of one's thoughts, words, and deeds *because of godly sorrow.* It has to do with God and it requires a certain kind of heart (Acts 26:19,20).

This doesn't mean that the outward aspects of repentance are optional or unimportant. There are some individuals who, when they hear that something depends on what is in the heart, conclude that as long as their heart is right it doesn't matter what they do in their outward life. But if that is ever true, it certainly is not true with regard to repentance. John the Baptist rebuked the Pharisees, all of whom would have said their hearts were deeply devoted to God: "Prove by the way you live that you have repented of your sins and turned to God" (Matthew 3:8 NLT).

Any honest person who has been a Christian very long will confess that repentance must be engaged in *continually.* Yes, it is one of the initial requirements for becoming a Christian, but to become a Christian is to enter a process of godly growth that will require repentance anytime we see that we've failed to trust and obey God. In fact, one of the evidences of spiritual maturity in Christ is that we live with a penitent "frame of mind," instantly going to God in prayer the moment we see that we've not responded rightly to His love. It's a new and better way of thinking.

Repentance is an attitude rather than a single act.

RICHARD OWEN ROBERTS

April 29

YOU WILL BE MY PEOPLE, I WILL BE YOUR GOD

I will take you to be my people, and I will be your God, and you shall know that I am the LORD your God, who has brought you out from under the burdens of the Egyptians.
Exodus 6:7

AFTER ISRAEL WAS DELIVERED FROM CAPTIVITY, WHAT THEN? That is a question God answered even before He liberated them: "I will take you to be my people, and I will be your God." Having rescued them from four centuries of servitude, God would enter into a "covenant," a special two-way agreement, with them. He would be their God in a unique sense, but as His people, they would have some responsibilities along with their blessings. "You yourselves have seen what I did to the Egyptians, and how I bore you on eagles' wings and brought you to myself. Now therefore, *if you will indeed obey my voice and keep my covenant,* you shall be my treasured possession among all peoples, for all the earth is mine" (Exodus 19:4,5). Israel would have to keep their part of the agreement.

In Leviticus 26:12, God said to Israel, "I will walk among you and will be your God, and you shall be my people." Surrounded by the moral and religious corruption of Canaan, they would need to keep themselves free of those influences, so that they could truly be God's people, in practice as well as in name.

Paul quotes Leviticus 26:12 in the New Testament and applies it to Christians living in environments like Corinth: "For we are the temple of the living God; as God said, 'I will make my dwelling among them and walk among them, and I will be their God, and they shall be my people'" (2 Corinthians 6:16). If it was true of Israel, it is also true of Christians — if God is to "walk among" us, we must do more than rely on the privilege of a special status; we must maintain *a purity in our actual lives* that identifies us as belonging to God. God said then the same thing He says now, "You shall be holy, for I am holy" (Leviticus 11:45; 1 Peter 1:16).

For here is the truth of the matter: we haven't really been liberated or "saved" if, for all practical purposes, we continue to live in "Egypt." God requires that we leave our chains behind, not only as a group, but also inwardly, privately, and individually.

O Thou, to whose all-searching sight
The darkness shineth as the light!
Search, prove my heart; it pants for Thee.
Oh, burst these bonds, and set it free!

GERHARD TERSTEEGEN

April 30

THE GOSPEL: WORDS AND POWER

. . . our gospel came to you not only in word, but also in power and in the Holy Spirit and with full conviction.
1 Thessalonians 1:5

PAUL'S ENEMIES IN THESSALONICA WERE PROBABLY SAYING THAT HE WAS A FAKE. The gospel of Christ was false, they would have said, and what is more, Paul knew it to be false. He was deceiving people deliberately, for reasons that were purely selfish. So Paul was anxious about those who had obeyed the gospel in Thessalonica. Knowing of their persecution and that they were hearing hateful charges against him, Paul was concerned — not about his reputation but about their steadfastness. The last thing he wanted was for their faith to be overthrown by doubts about him.

To these brethren, Paul wrote, "We give thanks to God always for all of you, constantly mentioning you in our prayers . . . For we know, brothers loved by God, that he has chosen you, because our gospel came to you not only in word, but also in power and in the Holy Spirit and with full conviction. You know what kind of men we proved to be among you for your sake" (1 Thessalonians 1:2-5).

Paul wanted several things to be clearly understood. (1) Although the gospel is communicated by words, it was far more than the reasonableness of the words that had moved the Thessalonians to believe. (2) In addition to the words, there had been "power." This is a reference to the miraculous powers by which the apostles guaranteed the truth of their message (Luke 24:44-49; Acts 1:4,5; Hebrews 2:3,4). (3) The Thessalonians also needed to remember that the gospel had come to them "in the Holy Spirit". This may be a second way of referring to the miracles, but it probably also points to the *source* of the gospel. The message had come from the Holy Spirit and not from Paul's intellect (1 Corinthians 2:11-13). (4) Finally, the gospel had been presented "with full conviction." Paul believed the gospel deeply. He and his coworkers might be many things, but they were not charlatans or liars. "You know," he said, "what kind of men we proved to be among you."

This text merits our careful attention. Even though the apostles are no longer preaching personally, the foundation has been laid and the record stands firm. The gospel, as preached and confirmed by the apostles, is just as powerful for us as for the Thessalonians!

The world has many religions; it has but one gospel.

GEORGE OWEN

May 1

EZRA'S GODLY SORROW

O my God, I am ashamed and blush to lift my face to you,
my God, for our iniquities have risen higher than our heads,
and our guilt has mounted up to the heavens.
Ezra 9:6

EZRA DID NOT DOUBT GOD'S READINESS TO FORGIVE, BUT NEITHER DID HE DOUBT THE REQUIREMENT OF REPENTANCE. His grief was an indication of his deep reverence for God, coupled with a recognition that sin is never a trifling matter. It must be dealt with boldly, bravely, and with a commitment to return to God's will.

In 2 Corinthians 7:10, Paul contrasted "godly sorrow" with the "sorrow of the world" or mere self-pity: "For godly sorrow produces repentance leading to salvation, not to be regretted; but the sorrow of the world produces death" (NKJV). While selfish sorrow will certainly produce misery, it does not produce repentance. Only godly sorrow does that. When we recognize the seriousness of our transgressions against God and how much He loves us, we are strongly moved to lay aside our sin and come back to obeying Him.

A lack of godly sorrow is one reason the "repentance" of many people disappears so quickly. Never having pondered how seriously their sins affected their Heavenly Father and His work in this world, they are not powerfully motivated to repent. If they make any commitment to repentance at all, it is little more than "I guess I'll give it a try." But godly sorrow is a more potent force. It produces, as Paul says, "repentance leading to salvation."

In an age when feeling good is the highest priority, the process of godly sorrow is often short-circuited. Many of us know the value that God places upon "a broken and contrite heart" (Psalm 51:17), but we rush past that stage pretty quickly. Eager to be happy again, we do not grieve our sins in a way that would put us on the path to a true and deep reformation of our character.

If repentance is an essential part of God's plan of salvation (and it certainly is), then the godly sorrow that leads to repentance is critically important. It requires humility, certainly. But if we are willing to bow before God in the honest recognition of our sins' seriousness, we may be sure that He is ready to help us and heal us.

It does not need to be a formal prayer: the most stumbling and broken cry — a sigh, a whisper, anything that tells the heart's loneliness and need and penitence — can find its way to God.

PHILLIPS BROOKS

May 2

WHAT GOD HAS GRACIOUSLY REVEALED TO US

The secret things belong to the LORD our God, but the things that are revealed belong to us and to our children forever, that we may do all the words of this law.
Deuteronomy 29:29

THERE ARE SOME THINGS WHICH GOD HAS NOT REVEALED TO THE HUMAN RACE. In fact, it seems likely that only a small portion of what God knows has been revealed to us. We can think of many reasons why God has not spoken of some things. Some would be beyond our ability to understand even if He should tell us. Others are none of our business, which is to say, we have no need to know them. Other things are more than we could bear — it is in mercy that He has not spoken to us of these. But whatever the case may be, "the secret things belong to the LORD our God."

Yet the main point of Moses' statement in Deuteronomy 29:29 is about the things that *have* been revealed. These, he said, "belong to us and to our children forever, that we may do all the words of this law." God would surely be pleased if we paid more attention to the "do-able" and "obey-able" aspect of His revelation. He has not revealed Himself merely to inform us or to satisfy our curiosity. It is, instead, for the purpose of our obedience. If the problem of sin boils down to our refusal to obey God, that problem can't be corrected until we're brought back to a wholesome sense of *the goodness of God's law.* Even in the revelation of His character, God is wanting not just to correct our *intellectual* misunderstandings of His nature or improve our *emotional* responses to Him. He is wanting to bring us back to the blessings of a creaturely *will* that is conformed obediently to its Creator (as reflected in Psalm 19:7-14).

Blaise Pascal made a good point when he said, "Instead of complaining that God has hidden himself, you should give him thanks for having revealed so much of himself." Given our rebellion against Him, the wonder is that God has spoken to us at all! And if we are thinking rightly, we will drink in every bit of truth about Himself that God has shared with us, eagerly wanting not only to know it but to act on it, hoping always to respond to God with a more perfect blend of reverence and gratitude.

Faith instructs us in the depths of God. Faith stands above any human system, no matter how valid; it is concerned with the revealed data, with that glory which cannot be named by any human name, yet has desired to make itself known to us in words which all may understand.

JACQUES MARITAIN

May 3

God's Glory in the Church and in Christ Jesus

Now to him who is able to do far more abundantly than all
that we ask or think, according to the power at work within us,
to him be glory in the church and in Christ Jesus throughout
all generations, forever and ever. Amen.
Ephesians 3:20,21

PAUL'S WORDS HERE CONSTITUTE A "DOXOLOGY." From the Greek *doxa* ("glory, honor"), a doxology is an expression of praise to God. To God be glory, Paul says, throughout all generations.

In Christ Jesus. Everything about Christ results in God's glory. On the evening before He died, Jesus prayed, "Father, the hour has come; glorify your Son that the Son may glorify you" (John 17:1). So we may certainly pray that God will be glorified in Christ.

In the church. Because it deals with human beings, this part of the passage is hard for some to understand, and yet it is no less true. The work of Christ in accomplishing the Father's purposes resulted in *a people saved from their sins.* God is glorified by the very existence of these people. Even prior to their perfection in heaven, those saved "in Christ" are those in whose redemption God is greatly glorified.

Our prayer should be that God will receive glory "in the church and in Christ Jesus." Yes, we do need to resist sectarian, institutional, and "party" concepts of the church, but we must not be so preoccupied with false doctrine that we fail to emphasize important truths that should be preached positively. I fear that some can't even hear the mention of a passage like Ephesians 3:21 without hastening to remind hearers of what it does *not* mean. But surely, what the passage teaches is extremely important, and we shouldn't be hesitant to proclaim it. *May God be glorified in Christ Jesus. And may He be glorified in the church, as Paul teaches us.*

God chose that Christ's glory would be closely related to the glory of His people, people who have been saved from their sins by His own blood. These people — broken, fallible, but forgiven people, growing in holiness as they learn from their mistakes — are the people who "embody" Christ and glorify God the Father. If you have obeyed the gospel of Christ, you are a part of Christ's body, His church. In your new relationship with God, you are not alone. You are part of a people, each of whom it glorified God to rescue.

In Your church, Lord, be glorified, be glorified.
In Your church, Lord, be glorified today.

BOB KILPATRICK

May 4

CHRIST AND THE CHURCH

For the husband is the head of the wife even as Christ is the head of the church, his body, and is himself its Savior. Now as the church submits to Christ, so also wives should submit in everything to their husbands.
Ephesians 5:23,24

THESE VERSES OCCUR IN A PASSAGE THAT SEEMS TO BE ABOUT THE HUSBAND-WIFE RELATIONSHIP. There is certainly an analogy between this relationship and that of Christ to His church, but Paul is clear that the Christ-church relationship is the primary idea, and the other is the one serving as an illustration. "This mystery is profound, and I am saying that it refers to Christ and the church" (v.32). So while we could profit from studying God's will for the marriage relationship, let's think today about Christ's relationship to the church, which is His bride (Revelation 19:7; 21:2,9; 22:17).

First, Paul emphasizes that Christ is the "head" of His church. In fact, He is its only head. He has no "vicar" on earth. His will for the church was recorded in the New Testament writings, and if His headship is to be respected, those writings cannot be disregarded.

Next, notice that the church is the "body" of Christ. Many practical lessons can be drawn from this, but one is that if the body ever becomes disconnected from the head, it dies. In John 15:5, He used a different analogy (vine and branches), but the point is still the same: "apart from me you can do nothing."

Finally, meditate on Christ being the "Savior" of the church. In its universal sense, that is what the church is: *those who have been saved by Christ.* But the danger is that the church will forget that it has been saved, or even that it *needed* to be saved. Surely, we ought to sing more often the great hymn "Hallelujah! What a Savior!"

All of this should impress us with *Christ's preeminence in all things relating to His people.* He is "first" in every sense of the word. He said, "All authority in heaven and on earth has been given to me" (Matthew 28:18). But it is in *grace* and *benevolence* that Christ's authority is exercised, at least toward those who have laid down their rebellion and received His amnesty. To those individuals — His church — His rule results in their highest good. If we are "in Christ," there is no rightful need that He does not gladly supply.

Christ is full and sufficient for all his people. He is . . . a Foundation to support, a Root to quicken, a Head to guide, a Treasure to enrich, a Sun to enlighten, and a Fountain to cleanse.

JOHN SPENCER

May 5

CHRIST GAVE HIMSELF UP FOR THE CHURCH

Husbands, love your wives, as Christ loved
the church and gave himself up for her.
Ephesians 5:25

HERE, WITHIN THE SPACE OF JUST A FEW WORDS, WE HAVE ONE OF THE PROFOUNDEST STATEMENTS OF THEOLOGY EVER MADE. *Christ loved the church and gave himself up for her.* Here is the heart of the truth about Jesus Christ and also our main motivation for obeying His gospel. And since the statement is part of Paul's discussion of husbands and wives, we should add: if husbands are to love their wives with anything close to the love Christ had for the church when He went to the cross, they've got their work cut out for them.

Christ loved the church. When Jesus said to His disciples, "I will build my church" (Matthew 16:18), He spoke of a future event. Even when He died, the church He said He would build did not yet exist. So how can it be said that He gave Himself up because He "loved the church"? We can say that He loved the church *prospectively,* knowing it would soon come into existence, but it was not the church in the aggregate that He died for. He died for individuals who needed to be saved. So when Christ died, those whom He loved were the individuals who would obey the gospel and receive the forgiveness His death would make possible. We all need to see ourselves in this picture. Even if I am one who has not yet obeyed the gospel, I need to envision myself coming to be a part of the church that Christ loved so much. How could I not want to do so?

And gave himself up for her. None of us could have been saved without Christ's sacrifice. It was His death that atoned for the guilt of our transgressions and opened up the door of God's grace to us. Surely no one in the history of this world has ever made a greater sacrifice for others than Jesus made when He put Himself in our place and was executed. And for whom did He do this? *His church.*

When all is said and done, it is sacrifice that shows the extent of love. Christ did more than speak words of love; *He gave Himself up for us.* So let us celebrate Christ's sacrifice. And let's not be reluctant to celebrate the church which, by His love, became His bride.

For Christ, our dear Redeemer,
For Christ, the crucified;
For the church His blood hath purchased,
The church, His holy bride.

E. E. HEWITT

May 6

MEMBERS OF HIS BODY, NOURISHED AND CHERISHED

For no one ever hated his own flesh, but nourishes and cherishes it, just as Christ does the church, because we are members of his body.
Ephesians 5:29,30

HUSBANDS ARE EXHORTED TO NOURISH AND CHERISH THEIR WIVES "JUST AS CHRIST DOES THE CHURCH." As the head of the body, Christ is deeply concerned about the body's healthy functioning. It is more than a minor interest of His. He died to make the church possible, but having done that, there is nothing He wouldn't do to provide for the ongoing needs of the church. His nurturing of those who are His special people is without measure.

Paul made this point in Romans 8:32 also. Speaking of God the Father, he wrote, "He who did not spare his own Son but gave him up for us all, how will he not also with him graciously give us all things?" As the CEV words it, "If God did this, won't he freely give us everything else?" The cross proves everything we need to know about our Lord's benevolent intentions toward the saved.

As those who have obeyed the gospel and been saved from our sins, we are, as Paul says, "members of his body." This is one of many ways that Christians are described in the New Testament. In other passages we are spoken of as a kingdom, a household, a vineyard, and so forth. Even "church" is a metaphor, comparing the Lord's people to an assembly or gathering. But to speak of the Lord's saved ones as His "body" is a very special way of speaking. Every time we Christians partake of the Lord's Supper on the first day of the week, we are reminded that His body was broken for us *in order that we might become His body.* And again, if He would make such a difficult sacrifice, should we doubt that He desires to nourish and cherish the body that He has brought into being?

Christians have been saved in order to serve. Whatever blessings we've received, we are to view those as resources to be used rather than treasures to be hoarded. Similarly, we can say that the "nourishing" and "cherishing" of the church by Christ are not meant to be enjoyed selfishly but evangelistically. How could a cared-for people not care for others? How could they fail to serve — and sacrifice for — the spiritual needs of those around them?

The church was not designed to be a reservoir, ever-receiving and retaining for itself God's spiritual blessings, but rather a conduit, conveying them on and out to others everywhere.

ROBERT HALL GLOVER

May 7

The Hand That Made Us Is Divine

For what can be known about God is plain to them, because God has shown it to them. For his invisible attributes, namely, his eternal power and divine nature, have been clearly perceived, ever since the creation of the world, in the things that have been made.
Romans 1:19,20

HAVE YOU EVER HEARD THE EXPRESSION "PREPONDERANCE OF THE EVIDENCE"? It's a cumbersome string of words, I'll grant you, but it contains a useful idea. The preponderance of the evidence means "the greater weight of evidence." Disputed questions are (or should be) settled this way. When all the evidence has been heard and all the arguments made, on which side does the evidence weigh more heavily? In which direction do the scales tip?

The existence of God is a disputed question, to say the least. And it seems that disbelief is the "trending" position right now. Yet the evidence has not changed; it is what it has always been. And no matter what the social, cultural, and political pressures may be, our task also remains unchanged. We must decide whether the evidence is heavier on the side of belief or disbelief.

Now, it is one thing to sit safely in Starbucks and debate the existence of God. But what if your life depended on it? Suppose you were going to be asked whether God exists, an envelope would be opened revealing the truth of the matter ("May I have the envelope, please?"), and if your answer is wrong, you would be taken outside and shot to death. What would you do? You would ignore opinions and prejudices, and simply choose the position that had the greater weight of evidence. With your life on the line, you would ignore your prejudices. Only one thing would matter: *the actual evidence.*

Paul argued that God's "eternal power and divine nature" are clearly seen "in the things that have been made." Many have agreed, including Joseph Addison, who was no fool when he wrote, "The Hand that made us is Divine." It is *reason* (based on thoughtful observation and not childish simplicity) that urges this conclusion.

What though, in solemn Silence, all
Move round the dark terrestrial Ball?
What tho' nor real Voice nor Sound
Amid their radiant Orbs be found?
In Reason's Ear they all rejoice,
And utter forth a glorious Voice,
For ever singing, as they shine,
The Hand that made us is Divine.

JOSEPH ADDISON

May 8

THE SPACIOUS FIRMAMENT ON HIGH

The heavens declare the glory of God, and the sky above proclaims his handiwork. Day to day pours out speech, and night to night reveals knowledge. There is no speech, nor are there words, whose voice is not heard. Their voice goes out through all the earth, and their words to the end of the world.
Psalm 19:1-4

THE HEAVENS DECLARE THE GLORY OF GOD. So said David, a man who would have pondered the sky on many occasions, especially in the days of his youth as a shepherd. Every part of the world is full of wonder, obviously, but there is something special about the sky. We need to admire it more — and think more deeply about why it is that the sky moves our hearts as it does.

The heavens do not just declare the existence of God (although that is a point of immense importance in itself); it is His "glory" that is proclaimed. The word *glory* literally means "brightness" or "splendor," but I want to propose an idea. When we are speaking of God, might we not think of glory as *the joining of beauty and power?* I think so, and I suspect that the blending of these two is why God's creation has such an impact on us.

There are those who are not much moved by beauty. For them, power is of more interest. And then, there are those for whom beauty has more appeal than power. But whoever you are, I predict that in the presence of something equally beautiful and powerful, your heart would melt. If you don't shut it down, your heart will tell you the truth: the heavens declare the glory of God. *God is real.*

I used to doubt it, but I doubt it no more. Even though, for me, the "days of trouble" have come (Ecclesiastes 12:1 NIV), my heart has been ravished with Beauty and Power. The Beauty is too powerful, and the Power too beautiful, to resist. The truth is not only true; it is a glorious, magnificent reality. And when I shall have been mended and made whole by the God who became Man, I will thrill to the joy of being a part of His rescued people, forever.

The Spacious Firmament on high,
With all the blue Ethereal Sky,
And spangled Heav'ns, a Shining Frame,
Their great Original proclaim:
Th' unwearied Sun, from day to day,
Does his Creator's Pow'r display,
And publishes to every Land
The Work of an Almighty Hand.

JOSEPH ADDISON

May 9

LISTEN TO HIM

And a cloud overshadowed them, and a voice came out of the cloud, "This is my beloved Son; listen to him."
Mark 9:7

WHEN GOD SPEAKS, WE OUGHT TO LISTEN. Other people may say things we have little interest in, but surely, when the Creator of the universe is addressing us, as He does in our day through the Scriptures, the least we can do is sit up and take notice.

It was an extraordinary claim when Jesus said that His teaching was authoritative because He was God in the flesh (Matthew 11:27; 28:18; John 5:18-27; 8:28; etc.). This was not merely the claim of a prophet, a human being whom God was using as an ad hoc spokesman; this was an assertion of equality with God and ultimate authority, a status far greater than Moses or Elijah ever had. "And after six days Jesus took with him Peter and James and John, and led them up a high mountain by themselves. And he was transfigured before them, and his clothes became radiant, intensely white, as no one on earth could bleach them. And there appeared to them Elijah with Moses, and they were talking with Jesus . . . And a cloud overshadowed them, and a voice came out of the cloud, *'This is my beloved Son; listen to him'*" (Mark 9:2-4,7).

It is sobering to realize that our destiny depends on how we listen to God's Son. Jesus pointed to the problem of those who have heard but not obeyed when He said, "If anyone hears my words and does not keep them, I do not judge him; for I did not come to judge the world but to save the world. The one who rejects me and does not receive my words has a judge; the word that I have spoken will judge him on the last day" (John 12:47,48). In the end, it will be a painful recollection if we have to remember that we walked away from the words that could have saved us.

These days, it would be a rare person anywhere in the world who has not "heard" the gospel. Printed Bibles are everywhere, and digital copies of the Scriptures are even more universal. So for most of us, the main question is what we've done with what we've heard, however much or little that may be. Or perhaps we could put it another way: the question is not whether we've heard; it's whether we've *listened.* We've heard enough truth to save the whole world. But are we paying attention? Is the truth sinking in?

Hearin' is one thing and listenin' is another.

WILLIAM FREND DE MORGAN

May 10

The Scriptures

. . . just as our beloved brother Paul also wrote to you according to the wisdom given him, as he does in all his letters when he speaks in them of these matters. There are some things in them that are hard to understand, which the ignorant and unstable twist to their own destruction, as they do the other Scriptures.
2 Peter 3:15,16

In this text, Peter, who was one of the apostles of Christ, alludes to the letters written by Paul, another one of the apostles. As a Jew, Peter makes an astonishing claim. He classifies the letters of Paul as a part of the "Scriptures," a Jewish expression referring to the documents accepted as having originated in the mind of God. Peter would have known the Pentateuch, the Hebrew prophets, and certain other books to have been inspired by God; but he also recognized Paul's writings as a part of this canon, the authoritative collection of books that, taken together, constitute God's written word to the human race.

Just the other day, I happened to be reading in Deuteronomy where Moses was anticipating the day when Israel would have a king. The king would need to be, above all else, a godly man, faithful in his adherence to God's teaching. But being a godly man would depend on his attention to the writings that *contained* that teaching. These writings could not be neglected. "He shall write for himself in a book a copy of this law . . . it shall be with him, and he shall read in it all the days of his life, that he may learn to fear the Lord his God by keeping all the words of this law and these statutes, and doing them . . . so that he may continue long in his kingdom, he and his children, in Israel" (Deuteronomy 17:18-20).

We have to stretch our minds to accept that there could be books written in human language that ultimately came from God's own spirit (2 Peter 1:21), but that is exactly the claim made for "the Scriptures." Yes, human writers were involved. They were the agents through whom God brought these books into the world, but somehow, the writings are from God Himself. If we "twist" them, as Peter says, we do so to our "own destruction." The Scriptures are given to us by God's grace. They can make us "wise for salvation" (2 Timothy 3:15) — but since they are a communication from our Creator, we dare not bandy them about carelessly.

The Bible is a supernatural book.

A. W. Tozer

May 11

RESPONDING RIGHTLY TO GRACE

But by the grace of God I am what I am, and his grace toward me
was not in vain. On the contrary, I worked harder than any of them,
though it was not I, but the grace of God that is with me.
1 Corinthians 15:10

OBEDIENCE TO THE GOSPEL IS A RESPONSE. We do not initiate the process; God does. Whatever we do, we do in response to what His love has done to make our salvation possible. And surely, God wants our response to be *wholehearted.* That is, each of the components of our hearts should respond rightly to the gospel.

Intellect. Sin resulted from Satan lying to Adam and Eve about the character of God (Genesis 3:1-6), and ever since then, untruth has been at the root of mankind's broken relationship with God. The gospel wants to put truth back in its proper place, and if our intention is to respond to God rightly, we're going to have to study and learn and yield our intellects back to His truth.

Emotion. This part of the gospel is emphasized nowadays, almost exclusively, but even in our emotional response to God we are sometimes dangerously imbalanced. God created us with a very wide range of emotions, all of which are healthy. As we see in the Psalms, we are to respond to God with all of our emotions — not just the warm and fuzzy ones, which most people like the best.

Will. In its most basic sense, sin is the rebellion of our will against God (1 John 3:4). The gospel proposes not only to forgive our past disobedience but to transform us back into persons who submit to the will of their Creator. So there can be no rightful response to God's grace without obedience. As Jesus said, "Why do you call me 'Lord, Lord,' and not do what I tell you?" (Luke 6:46).

There are, in fact, many ways our response to God might be less than wholehearted, but most of these come down to one thing: *a response that is merely passive rather than active.* In other words, we do not really *respond* to the gospel; we are content just to bask in the glow of thinking about how gracious God is. But that was not the response of the apostle Paul, and we need to ponder his words frequently: "By the grace of God I am what I am, *and his grace toward me was not in vain.* On the contrary, I worked harder than any of them, though it was not I, but the grace of God that is with me."

Those things, good Lord, that we pray for,
give us also the grace to labor for.

ANONYMOUS

May 12

Soul Health

Beloved, I pray that all may go well with you and that you may be in good health, as it goes well with your soul.
3 John 2

IN JOHN'S PRAYER FOR GAIUS, HIS BROTHER IN CHRIST, THERE IS AN INTERESTING ORDER OF PRIORITIES. Whereas most people would think first about a friend's physical state and then also hope they were doing well spiritually, John prays that "you may be in good health, as it goes well with your soul." In other words, John knew that Gaius was doing well spiritually, and that was the main priority. If he was also healthy physically, that would be a nice extra.

There is such a thing as "soul health," and it is a much more important issue than most people acknowledge. In these days of emphasis on holistic health and wellness, many people do pay attention to "spirit" and "mind," but in the New Testament, the health of the soul goes a good bit deeper than peace of mind, tranquillity, emotional balance, and a sense of oneness with the universe. If the gospel of Christ is true, we are not in good spiritual health if we are not in a right relationship with the God who is our Creator — and that requires the objective, actual forgiveness of our sins through obedience to the message of salvation in Christ.

The evidence of a right relationship with God is not in our feelings but in the text of the Scriptures. If there is consistency between our commitment to Christ and what the New Testament teaches must be true for us to have eternal life, then our soul is in good health. The hope — and therefore the joy — we have is based on the objective promise of God in the Scriptures, and not on the feelings of peace generated by meditation or mindfulness.

This is not to say that the neurological and psychological kinds of tranquillity that come from meditation are of no use at all. They can be extremely helpful in many ways — and this writer is a devoted practitioner of mindfulness. But tranquillity should not be confused with rightness of relationship to God. And if, not having been saved from our sins by the gospel of Christ, we do not enjoy justification with God, all the tranquillity and wellness we might have achieved by worldly means will come to a screeching halt when we die. Bodily health, including emotional serenity, is well enough. But of far greater import is how well our souls are faring.

Body: not a home but an inn — and that only briefly.

SENECA

May 13

Don't We Remember What We Saw?

O foolish Galatians! Who has bewitched you? It was before your eyes that Jesus Christ was publicly portrayed as crucified.
Galatians 3:1

THERE IS NOTHING THE HUMAN MIND IS NOT CAPABLE OF FORGETTING, EVEN THE THINGS WE NEED TO REMEMBER THE MOST. Sometimes surprisingly quickly, we get to the point where even the most vivid experiences no longer have any impact. So when the Galatian Christians began to waver in their faith, Paul was amazed. "It was before your eyes," he said, "that Jesus Christ was publicly portrayed as crucified." Paul himself had preached the cross to them, and they had understood what Jesus' death meant. How could they now be drifting away from what they knew?

The problem the Galatians had is one most of us are familiar with: we forget things we need to remember. The truths that should keep us faithful to God slip away from our conscious awareness.

Yet the problem goes deeper than mere forgetfulness. All of us "know" that Jesus died for our sins — but in too many cases, the *significance* of what we know hasn't really sunk in. The devil is perfectly content for us to "remember" Christ's death as long as it never dawns on us what the implications of that event really are.

Even worse, however, we don't see the *personal* significance of the cross. We may, on some level, grasp that Jesus' crucifixion was a monumental event in human history, but rarely does that truth come home to us individually. *Do I see that Jesus bled and died for MY sins? Do I understand the personal consequences of really believing that?*

Clearly, we need to take two steps. First, what we know of the cross must be constantly *deepened*. If we don't understand what happened at the cross more deeply today than we did last year, our love for God is probably not growing and we may be headed in the same direction as the Galatians. But second, what we know must constantly be *refreshed*. The Lord's Supper each first day of the week is a public memorial that Christians share, but we need to ponder the cross in our private devotions as well. *Every day of the week is not too often to remember what Jesus suffered and feel anew the full, shattering impact of His death.* We must make up our minds that having seen Jesus crucified for our own sins, we will not forget what we saw.

O my Savior, make me see
How dearly thou has paid for me.

RICHARD CRENSHAW

May 14

Knowing God, Eternal Life

And this is eternal life, that they know you, the only true God, and Jesus Christ whom you have sent.
John 17:3

IT IS FASCINATING TO CONTEMPLATE WHAT IT MUST HAVE BEEN LIKE FOR ADAM AND EVE TO KNOW GOD. Prior to their tragic decision to rebel against His will, they would have had a perfect relationship with their Creator: knowing Him, revering Him, and loving Him. But once that relationship was broken, the knowledge of God would have become an increasingly distant memory.

In John's record of Jesus' prayer on the night of His betrayal, we hear the Son of God praying: "Father, the hour has come; glorify your Son that the Son may glorify you, since you have given him authority over all flesh, to give eternal life to all whom you have given him" (John 17:1,2). And then we have this remarkable statement: "And this is eternal life, that they know you, the only true God, and Jesus Christ whom you have sent" (v.3).

To "know God" means more than knowing *about* God. The devil has a good bit of information about God, but that doesn't mean he "knows God." And it means more than having feelings of closeness to God, for many people feel that way, even quite passionately, while still being outside of Christ and lost in their sins.

One thing is for sure: there is no knowing God apart from the knowledge of Him made possible by Jesus Christ. In Jesus alone is the truth about God made accessible to mankind (John 14:6). But God cannot be known apart from the Scriptures, even if we seek Him through Jesus Christ. The Scriptures contain the only objective information we have about Jesus' revelation of the Father.

Obeying the gospel, then, we begin to partake more and more of God's true nature, anticipating the time when we will meet Him face to face (Revelation 22:4). In Christ, we have what might be considered a foretaste of eternal life — or a down payment on it (Ephesians 1:14) — but the fullness of that life is something that will be ours only in eternity (Titus 1:2; 1 Peter 1:3,4). When it is finally ours, however, it won't be eternal just in *duration* — it will be a *quality* of life no one has ever known before except Jesus, the Son of God, who will graciously share with us the life He has always had.

[Christianity] is a revelation of the true way of living, the way to know God, the way to live life of eternal quality.

J. B. PHILLIPS

May 15

A Ransom for All

For there is one God, and there is one mediator between God and men, the man Christ Jesus, who gave himself as a ransom for all, which is the testimony given at the proper time.
1 Timothy 2:5,6

BETWEEN GOD AND MANKIND THERE IS A GREAT SEPARATION. We are cut off from our Creator by our sins. And this alienation is a problem we can't solve by our own wisdom or human effort.

Mediator. Paul states that Jesus Christ is able to serve as a "mediator" between God and us. This does not mean that Jesus serves as an arbiter to work out a compromise between God's position and ours. It means that He is a "go-between" enabling God to have a relationship with us that would be impossible otherwise.

Ransom. Jesus makes possible our reconciliation with God because he "gave himself as a ransom for all." In other words, He paid the price for us to be released from our condemnation, dying in our place and thereby "atoning" for our sins. So God is now able to forgive us without violating the integrity of His own law. As Paul wrote to the Romans, God is able at once to be both "just and the justifier of the one who has faith in Jesus" (Romans 3:26).

On one occasion, John the Baptist saw Jesus and said, "Behold, the Lamb of God, who takes away the sin of the world!" (John 1:29). Freely and voluntarily, He "gave himself" as our ransom. In 1 Peter 2:24, Peter put it this way: "He himself bore our sins in his body on the tree, that we might die to sin and live to righteousness. By his wounds you have been healed."

But notice in our beginning text what Paul said about Jesus. Just as there is one God, there is only one mediator between God and men. Without Him, our sins will kill us. And this is exactly what Jesus said: "I told you that you would die in your sins, for unless you believe that I am he you will die in your sins" (John 8:24).

In this life, we can improve ourselves a little bit, but we can't save ourselves from sin. We may be able to elevate ourselves, but we can't grasp eternal life. And even when we come to Christ, we can't have the life He offers except by dying with Him in baptism and accepting the kind of life He has for us in the here and now.

The death of Jesus is the only entrance into the life he lived. We cannot get into his life by admiring him, or by saying what a beautiful life his was, so pure and holy. To dwell only on his life would drive us to despair. We enter into his life by means of his death.

OSWALD CHAMBERS

May 16

If Our Concept of God Is Wrong

Therefore God gave them up in the lusts of their hearts to impurity, to the dishonoring of their bodies among themselves, because they exchanged the truth about God for a lie and worshiped and served the creature rather than the Creator, who is blessed forever! Amen.
Romans 1:24,25

IF WE THOUGHT THAT "THEOLOGY" WAS AN INTELLECTUAL PURSUIT WITH NO PRACTICAL CONSEQUENCE, WE WOULD BE WRONG. Our theology is our view of God (His existence, His nature, His purposes, His will), and of all the ideas in our heads, our ideas about God are the most powerfully practical. What we think of our Creator is the main determinant of our character and our conduct.

We don't use the word *idolatry* much anymore, but it is still a concept that needs to be considered. To worship an idol is to worship a god that does not exist. If a person bowed down before a physical object (perhaps one that he himself had made) and called that God, he would be engaging in idolatry. But if we conceive of God in ways that are false, even if it's only in our minds, we are worshiping not God but an idol, created by our imagination. And that kind of idolatry is still very much a problem in the world.

In the text above, Paul spoke of certain ones who "exchanged the truth about God for a lie." Tragically, our ignorance of God is often this very kind of *willful* ignorance, as the apostle indicated a few verses later when he said that "since they did not see fit to acknowledge God, God gave them up to a debased mind to do what ought not to be done" (v.28). In the final analysis, the person may not have been wrong who said that sin consists of having a wrong idea about God and deliberately acting as if that idea were true.

So out of all the subjects we think about, let us be the most careful when we are thinking about God. False notions about God will derail even the best of our thinking on other subjects, including morality and our treatment of other human beings. And most important of all, if we view God wrongly, we are going to have wrong beliefs about the reality of sin and the question of our fellowship with God. The gospel will mean little to us if our beliefs about God are such that we see no need for what Christ made possible at the cross. *We need to be careful about our "theology."*

The wrong concept of God leads to the wrong concept of sin, self, and salvation.

RICHARD OWEN ROBERTS

May 17

THE BODY OF CHRIST

And [Christ] is the head of the body, the church. He is the beginning, the firstborn from the dead, that in everything he might be preeminent.
Colossians 1:18

STRICTLY SPEAKING, THERE IS NO ONE OVER WHOM CHRIST IS NOT HEAD. But there is a special sense in which He is the head of His body, the church. After having refused His rule, these individuals have returned to their rightful King, sought His forgiveness, and sworn allegiance to Him from now on. Christ is truly their head — not just legally or theoretically, but in the way they live.

We could spend a lifetime unfolding different aspects of the truth that the people of Christ are His "body." It is a fascinating metaphor, to say the least. All of us have bodies, governed (at least in our best moments) by our heads, so when the Scriptures say we are related to Christ in ways that resemble the link between our own head and body, that is an analogy that resonates with us.

For one thing, the fact that Christ is the head of His body should never become so commonplace that we forget how important that truth is. His rule over the church does not require our permission, nor are His instructions for the church subject to our preferences. We serve Christ, and we do not serve Him in an "advisory" capacity. To repeat: He is the head of the church.

He is the head of the church *because He was made the head of it by God.* Paul affirmed this when he wrote, "[God] put all things under [Christ's] feet and gave him as head over all things to the church, which is his body, the fullness of him who fills all in all" (Ephesians 1:22,23). And Jesus said, "All authority in heaven and on earth has been *given* to me" (Matthew 28:18). When this world comes to an end, the kingdom will be turned back to God (1 Corinthians 15:24), but for now, God has put all things under the feet of Christ, the Son who rules from the right hand of His Father (Mark 16:19; Hebrews 1:3) until the last enemy has been defeated.

Every Sunday when Christians observe the Lord's Supper, they remember that *their inclusion in the spiritual body of Christ is possible only because His physical body was sacrificed for them.* By submitting to the agonizing limitations of a "body," He gained a "body" of saved people whose own bodies are no longer prisons.

From his imprisonment my freedoms grow, find wings.
Part of his body, I transcend this flesh.

LUCI SHAW

May 18

OBTAINED WITH CHRIST'S BLOOD

Pay careful attention to yourselves and to all the flock, in which the Holy Spirit has made you overseers, to care for the church of God, which he obtained with his own blood.
Acts 20:28

WHAT COULD MAKE US VALUE THE LORD'S CHURCH ANY MORE HIGHLY THAN TO KNOW THAT IT WAS OBTAINED AT THE COST OF HIS BLOOD? No higher purchase price is imaginable. And if we think we can appreciate the Lord without valuing the church for which He died, we are deluded. John wrote, "Everyone who believes that Jesus is the Christ has been born of God, *and everyone who loves the Father loves whoever has been born of him*" (1 John 5:1).

Going back to Acts 20:28, Paul's statement about the church was made to the elders of the church at Ephesus as he said farewell and exhorted them to care for the saints under their oversight. Paul was speaking of the congregation in Ephesus when he said that the elders should "care for the church," for in the New Testament elders never had oversight over any Christians except those in the local congregation. But what a charge! If those for whom the elders were to care were people who belonged to the Lord — *having been paid for with His blood* — well might Paul say, "Pay careful attention." No duty ever deserved an attention more careful.

But if the reference in Acts 20:28 is to the local church, it is no less true that the universal church (the saved in *all* places) is comprised of blood-bought individuals. In the great throne scene in Revelation, the Lamb, who is Christ, is triumphantly praised: "for you were slain, and by your blood you ransomed people for God from every tribe and language and people and nation" (5:9). That is one reason the Lord loves His church so much. They are the people whom He has saved by His blood, His ransomed ones.

Each of these thoughts points us emphatically to Jesus Christ — His love, His authority, His majesty. If He bought the church with His blood, it is not our church to do with as we wish; it is *His* church. *The Lord's church.* May we never quit calling it what it is. The church of God. The church which He bought with His blood. The church that belongs to Christ. *The Lord's church.*

The church's one foundation is Jesus Christ her Lord;
She is His new creation by water and the word;
From heav'n He came and sought her to be His holy bride;
With His own blood He bought her, and for her life He died.

E. E. HEWITT

May 19

We Can't Exclude God and Still Have Him

For who knows a person's thoughts except the spirit of that person, which is in him? So also no one comprehends the thoughts of God except the Spirit of God. Now we have received not the spirit of the world, but the Spirit who is from God, that we might understand the things freely given us by God. And we impart this in words not taught by human wisdom but taught by the Spirit, interpreting spiritual truths to those who are spiritual.
1 Corinthians 2:11-13

RATIONALISM ARGUES THAT WE SHOULD REJECT (OR AT LEAST DE-EMPHASIZE) ALL SOURCES OF KNOWLEDGE EXCEPT HUMAN REASON. If knowing a thing requires the operation of something in addition to human reason, that thing should not be classified as "knowledge." In particular, "faith" is distinguished from "knowledge." If God exists at all, we cannot "know" that He exists or what His nature is; we can only "believe" . . . and hope for the best.

It is a fact that we could not know much about God if we had nothing but our reason to work with. Paul makes the point that God's existence and His power can be inferred from the world around us: "For his invisible attributes, namely, his eternal power and divine nature, have been clearly perceived, ever since the creation of the world, in the things that have been made" (Romans 1:20). But if reason had no outside help, God's existence and power would be about as far as we could go. We would have no way of knowing what God's nature is or what His will for us might be.

But God has revealed Himself so that we can know a good deal more about Him. (Go back and ponder 1 Corinthians 2:11-13.) His revealing of Himself culminates in Jesus Christ. "And the Word became flesh and dwelt among us, and we have seen his glory . . . No one has ever seen God; the only God, who is at the Father's side, he has made him known" (John 1:14,18).

Do you see the dilemma of rationalism? It wants to disallow any knowledge that might come from revelation, yet there are many rationalists who still want to believe in some kind of God. But we can't have it both ways. If we rule out the possibility of God revealing Himself, then we should get used to the idea of having no God at all. The only God that unaided human reason can believe in is a God who is little more than a question mark. There is no room within rationalism for a God who can save us.

The failure of rationalism is that it tries to find a place for God in its picture of the world.

WILLIAM RALPH INGE

May 20

THE SIN OF SELF-SUFFICIENCY

Yet he sent prophets among them to bring them back to the LORD. These testified against them, but they would not pay attention.
2 Chronicles 24:19

THE GOSPEL IS POWERFUL, BUT IT CAN'T OVERCOME THE WILL OF A PERSON WHO DOESN'T SEE THAT HE NEEDS TO BE SAVED. And for this reason, the gospel will not be of much interest to people today. Living in an age when the concept of "sin" is no longer taken seriously, we should not expect the gospel to be widely received. It is only the penitent who will come to Jesus Christ.

Actually, that last statement is not true. It is a fact that many today do "come to Christ" without any consciousness of the sins they need to have forgiven. They come seeking relief from a wide range of temporal troubles: poverty, social oppression, physical ailments, psychological disorders, and emotional distress, to name just a few. Yet when people "become interested in Christianity" for these reasons, they are seeking something other than what Jesus went to the cross to provide. Jesus is not unconcerned about the lesser problems that we have, but He was very clear what His mission was: "to seek and to save the lost" (Luke 19:10).

Jesus, then, is our *Savior.* But is that what we want Him to be? We might prefer Him to be our surgeon, psychologist, or social worker, but the fact remains, He came to be our Savior. And the sooner we acknowledge that we are lost, the sooner His message will make sense to us. Not only are we lost, but we cannot save ourselves. In a helpless spiritual condition, we are doomed to die in eternity if we do not let Him redeem us from our rebellion.

But our self-sufficiency is not easy to give up. These days, science and technology seem to be a better hope. If there is a problem the scientific method can't solve, that is a problem we need not worry about. And as long as we believe that, we will view the gospel of Christ as little more than a relic of pre-modern superstition.

Indeed, until we humble ourselves before the painful recognition of our sin, we will find Jesus Christ to be insulting and offensive. We will not only be uninterested; we will be angry. How dare this ignorant peasant from ancient Galilee tell us, "Unless you believe that I am he you will die in your sins" (John 8:24)?

There's nothing more irritating than a Savior
when you aren't ready to be saved.

D. SUTTEN

May 21

The Messiah's Rule

Ask of me, and I will make the nations your heritage,
and the ends of the earth your possession.
You shall break them with a rod of iron
and dash them in pieces like a potter's vessel.
Psalm 2:8,9

POWER CORRUPTS. And if this is true of individuals, it is even more true of groups. Consider governments, for example. Can it be denied that governments tend toward corruption, that they always move in the direction of greater self-will? "The kings of the earth set themselves, and the rulers take counsel together, against the LORD and against his Anointed, saying, 'Let us burst their bonds apart and cast away their cords from us'" (Psalm 2:2,3).

But God cannot successfully be ignored. From His perspective, the presumption of human rulers that they can do as they please is so out of touch with reality that it is laughable. "He who sits in the heavens laughs; the Lord holds them in derision. Then he will speak to them in his wrath, and terrify them in his fury, saying, 'As for me, I have set my King on Zion, my holy hill'" (vv.4-6).

In God's Son, the Messiah ("Anointed" or "Commissioned One"), a kingdom has been set up that is above all the kingdoms of men. To Him, the nations have been granted as a gift: "I will make the nations your heritage, and the ends of the earth your possession" (v.8). And God leaves no doubt as to what the Messiah will do in dealing with the nations: "You shall break them with a rod of iron and dash them in pieces like a potter's vessel" (v.9).

Jesus, the "Christ" or Messiah, said after His resurrection, "All authority in heaven and on earth has been given to me" (Matthew 28:18). But has He broken the kingdoms of men, dashing them in pieces? If so, the kingdoms seem not to have gotten the memo. They pay no attention to the Messiah whatsoever.

But the rule of the Messiah does not come about by physical revolution (or democratic voting). He breaks the nations not by dismantling them (for now, at least) but by reestablishing *the truthful ideas and words* they have denied. "From his *mouth* comes a sharp sword with which to strike down the nations" (Revelation 19:15). When the nations have come and gone, this truth will still be true.

God did not abolish the fact of evil; he transformed it.
He did not stop the Crucifixion; he rose from the dead.

DOROTHY L. SAYERS

May 22

King of Kings, Lord of Lords

Then I saw heaven opened, and behold, a white horse! The one sitting on it is called Faithful and True, and in righteousness he judges and makes war . . . From his mouth comes a sharp sword with which to strike down the nations, and he will rule them with a rod of iron. He will tread the winepress of the fury of the wrath of God the Almighty. On his robe and on his thigh he has a name written, King of kings and Lord of lords.
Revelation 19:11-16

WHOSE AUTHORITY IS THE HIGHEST? In the affairs of this world, that question never has any permanent answer. One person may be the most powerful figure in the world at a particular moment, but that individual is always subject to being surpassed by a more powerful person in the future. Only in Jesus Christ do we encounter a King who is above all kings — both now and forever.

Read the description of Jesus Christ in Revelation 19:11-16 and let its vivid imagery sink in. If the claim of absolute sovereignty embedded in these words is false, the New Testament should be rejected decisively. But what if this claim is true? Here is a figure whose power and authority are not only supreme but unconquerable, a leader who can be followed without the slightest fear that He will ever be defeated. Here is One in whom our *faith* can rest.

It is crucial, however, for us to understand the sort of King Jesus is. He did not liberate His fellow Jews from the Roman government in the first century, and He does not promise to break the shackles of any particular tyranny today. To be sure, all of the kingdoms of men — every last one of them — will be destroyed eventually, but the gospel of Christ is primarily about deliverance from our own sins. "You will know the truth," He said, "and the truth will set you free" (John 8:32). It is from the bondage of *untruth* that Jesus wants to liberate us, and if we don't let Him set us free from the untruth in our own hearts, it won't matter whether our political situation in this world is one of freedom or slavery.

Against the destructive lies with which the devil has done his work, Jesus came into the world to overcome falsehood and repair its damage. For the time being, it often looks as if the enemy is still winning, and frankly, the appearance of that can be discouraging. But the war has already been won. The outcome of history is now a foregone conclusion. And to keep resisting this King (as the kingdoms of men always do) is to fight a losing battle.

God will have the last word, and it will be good.

Robert Harold Schuller

May 23

THE CHURCHES IN ASIA

He who has an ear, let him hear what the Spirit says to the churches.
Revelation 2:7

WHAT MUST IT HAVE BEEN LIKE TO GET A LETTER LIKE THOSE RECEIVED BY THE CHURCHES OF ASIA? Toward the end of the first century, Christ sent a letter to each of the seven churches in Asia. (Contained in the second and third chapters of Revelation, which went to all of the churches, each of the letters were read, it seems, by all seven of the churches.) Each message depicted the condition of that congregation as the Lord saw it, providing a personal diagnosis of their health from the Great Physician Himself. Some of these groups were in better shape than others, but every letter ended the same way: *"He who has an ear, let him hear what the Spirit says to the churches."* It would do little good for a church to get a diagnosis from the Lord if it paid no attention and made no changes.

Churches (by which we mean congregations or local assemblies of Christians) can depart from the Lord just as individual Christians can (Galatians 1:1-7). So there is a need, both congregationally and individually, for us to make frequent mid-course corrections and realign ourselves with the intentions of Christ.

Today, the Lord is not going to send a personalized letter to a congregation, but in a sense, that is what the entire New Testament is. When we read what was happening in that era, when the affairs of the churches were being guided by the authority of Christ's apostles, we are wasting our time if we don't apply what we read to our own congregations today. Christ would say the same thing to us that He said to those churches: *"He who has an ear, let him hear what the Spirit says to the churches."*

A diagnosis can be painful news to hear, of course, whether it is from a medical doctor or from Jesus Christ. But if we are truly committed to being saved, we will want the truth and nothing but the truth — in order to act on it and change our practices.

The ability to "hear" is an endowment with some serious responsibilities attached to it. Given our tendency to drift away from Christ, our only hope is in our *willingness to be warned*. Christ loves us too much not to call us back to the right way, but His call will not help us if we don't see that it applies to us very personally.

Before the service speak to God. During the service let God speak to you. After the service speak with your neighbor.

OLD SAYING

May 24

WE PREFER

[Jeroboam] went up to the altar that he had made in Bethel on the fifteenth day in the eighth month, in the month that he had devised from his own heart. And he instituted a feast for the people of Israel and went up to the altar to make offerings.
1 Kings 12:33

WHEN JEROBOAM DECIDED TO SET UP AN ALTERNATIVE TO THE WORSHIP IN JERUSALEM, A WORSHIP THAT HAD BEEN DIVINELY AUTHORIZED, HE MADE A NUMBER OF CHANGES. As a substitute for the Feast of Booths in the seventh month, he organized a feast in the eighth month, "the month that he had devised from his own heart." Having dispensed with any loyalty to what God had prescribed, he saw no reason not to do whatever he pleased.

Unfortunately, this has always been the tendency of human beings. Refusing to admit that God has laid down any real norms or requirements that we must adhere to, we feel we are free to simply choose what we "prefer," like customers at a delicatessen.

The existence of God. Are there those who disbelieve because it would suit them better if there were no God and others who believe just because they want to? Probably. But either way, it really doesn't matter what we prefer. The truth is what it is.

The nature of God. If there is a God, most of us would like Him (or Her, or It) to be a certain kind of God. But what is congenial to us really doesn't matter. The only question is: what are the facts?

The meaning of the Scriptures. Do we twist the Scriptures to make them mean what we prefer them to mean? If so, we are no more honest than those who prefer to reject them entirely.

The contents of our own conscience. When we listen to our conscience, do we hear only what we prefer? Can we tell when what sounds like "ought to" is nothing more than the voice of "want to"?

It takes a person of uncommon honesty to say simply, "What is the truth? That's what I want, period." But that is the very essence of faith and humility, the willingness to trust God and lean upon His wisdom when what He wants is not what we prefer.

O Lord, help each one of us to learn how to bow more humbly before You and seek Your will more simply and truly. Help us to have the courage to go wherever the truth takes us. At whatever cost, may we follow the path that leads us to see Your shining face throughout eternity.

Man prefers to believe what he prefers to be true.

FRANCIS BACON

May 25

CHRIST JESUS, OUR HOPE

Paul, an apostle of Christ Jesus by command
of God our Savior and of Christ Jesus our hope . . .
1 Timothy 1:1

IN OUR WORLD TODAY, HOPE OFTEN SEEMS IN SHORT SUPPLY. Despite the prodigious efforts of humanism and secularism to convince us that things are getting better, we all know that there is great cause for concern. For every specific problem that our science and philosophy seem to improve, there are always unintended consequences that, in the greater scheme of things, make things worse. We can only be optimistic if we ignore many of the obvious facts.

The gospel of Christ is nothing if not a message of hope. But the hope it offers is different from what most people are looking for. Ironically, it tells us that things are going to get better by telling us that things are *not* going to get better (at least in this world). By fixing the *cause* of the problem — our sin — the gospel offers a hope that is unaffected by the worsening condition of the world.

God our Savior. Any honest look at our plight tells us that we were lost. "But when the goodness and loving kindness of God our Savior appeared, *he saved us,* not because of works done by us in righteousness, but according to his own mercy" (Titus 3:4,5).

Christ Jesus our hope. Look closely at how God has saved us. Paul says that it was "by the washing of regeneration and renewal of the Holy Spirit, whom he poured out on us richly *through Jesus Christ our Savior,* so that being justified by his grace we might become heirs according to *the hope of eternal life*" (Titus 3:5-7). These are powerful phrases. They reflect the truth that is on every page of the New Testament: it is in Jesus Christ that God is providing protection from the condemnation that we have brought upon ourselves.

If Christ is our hope, however, we ought to actually *invest* our hope in Him, in our deeds as well as our words — and we ought not to hedge our bets by putting some of our hope in worldly sources of confidence (just to be on the safe side). It is, in fact, only when we give up on the hope that we can fix any of our own problems that Jesus Christ is able to save us. But oh, what a Savior! He is waiting to bless us more abundantly than we can imagine.

All we want in Christ, we shall find in Christ. If we want little, we shall find little. If we want much, we shall find much; but if, in utter helplessness, we cast our all on Christ, he will be to us the whole treasury of God.

HENRY BENJAMIN WHIPPLE

May 26

IS THE GOSPEL UNLIKELY? IS THE GOSPEL TRUE?

Philip found Nathanael and said to him, "We have found him of whom Moses in the Law and also the prophets wrote, Jesus of Nazareth, the son of Joseph." Nathanael said to him, "Can anything good come out of Nazareth?" Philip said to him, "Come and see."
John 1:45,46

WHETHER SOMETHING SEEMS "LIKELY" IS USUALLY DETERMINED BY OUR CULTURE AND OUR CONDITIONING. If you had asked somebody two thousand years ago whether it was likely that people would ever travel to Mars, they would have said no. Today, however, that feat does not seem as unlikely as it did back then.

But we should not be so arrogant as to think that we have broken free from the limitations of culture and conditioning. We may be freer to see the likelihood of *some* things than ancient people were, but in all honesty, we are less free than they were to see the likelihood of other things —including the truth of the gospel.

The inherent likelihood of the resurrection of Christ (and therefore of the truth of the gospel) has not changed since the first century. If it seems more improbable today, it is only because we come to the question with a set of prejudices that ancient people were not bound by. Before even considering the historical evidence, we have already made up our minds that there is no God who could have caused the event, so we dismiss it out of hand.

But if you have ever sat on a jury in a courtroom and had to evaluate evidence, you know how wrong you can be when you start thinking, "It just doesn't seem possible that this could have happened." If the evidence is sufficient, you have to revise your opinion of what is possible and go with the evidence. The operative question is not "Is this likely?" but "Is this true?"

And so it is with the gospel. However unlikely, implausible, or even impossible it may seem, the gospel story must be judged on the basis of the evidence, even if we don't want it to be true. As C. S. Lewis once said, "I do have moods in which the whole thing looks very improbable; but when I was an atheist, I had moods in which Christianity looked terribly probable." Fortunately, C. S. Lewis did not let his moods determine his beliefs one way or the other.

So if our sense of likelihood tells us that "nothing good can come out of Nazareth," the gospel simply says, "Come and see."

The gospel is wildly improbable — except that it happened.

MICHAEL HORTON

May 27

The Honest Acknowledgment of Our Sins

For I know my transgressions, and my sin is ever before me.
Psalm 51:3

THE KNOWLEDGE OF OUR SINS IS PAINFUL, BUT IT IS POWERFUL. If we're willing to look honestly at our sins against God, the door can be opened to confession, repentance, and salvation.

The problem at the root of sin is always pride. It is pride that moves us to sin in the first place (we refuse to submit humbly to a will higher than our own), but having sinned, it is also pride that prevents us from acknowledging what we've done. Rather than confess our sins and seek God's forgiveness, we suppress the truth with all manner of evasions, defenses, and rationalizations.

But if the gospel is about redemption from our sins, we must acknowledge our need for redemption. The first prerequisite to the gospel, therefore, is humility — the willingness to bow before the painful truth about ourselves. We must lay down not only our rebellion but the excuses we have been offering for our rebellion.

We usually think of the confession of sin in two directions: confession to God and confession to others. But I suggest that there is a confession that must precede both of these, and it may be the hardest confession of all. *We must admit the truth to ourselves.* Only when we ourselves face the facts will we be ready to acknowledge those facts to God and to those we've sinned against.

But let's go a little deeper. The honest acknowledgement of sin requires more than a generic "I have sinned." We must be willing to confess our actual sins and call them by their right names. In our human relationships, we wouldn't feel an apology was sufficient if someone said no more than, "I haven't treated you as I should." An honest apology requires stating specifically the error that was committed. But again, the real difficulty lies in making that acknowledgement to ourselves. We won't seek the forgiveness of God (or the forgiveness of others) if we haven't fully digested the truth about our guilt and laid aside our excuses.

Personally, I know of no part of the plan of salvation that is any harder than this. It is gut-wrenching. But look at the doors that are opened. Humbled, we are ready to come to the foot of Jesus' cross and say, "What must I do to be saved?" (Acts 16:30).

The knowledge of sin is the beginning of salvation.

EPICURUS

May 28

A Broken and Contrite Heart

The sacrifices of God are a broken spirit;
a broken and contrite heart, O God, you will not despise.
Psalm 51:17

WHETHER WE HAVE A "BROKEN AND CONTRITE HEART" IS ONE OF THE MAIN FACTORS IN OUR READINESS TO ACCEPT THE GOSPEL. If, as the Scriptures teach, the gospel is about the forgiveness of our sins, we won't listen to it if we don't believe that sin is a problem for us. It is "godly sorrow" that puts us in touch with our need for the grace that is available in Christ, and while grief for our sins is not pleasant, it is the one experience that opens us to the gospel.

But godly sorrow is an experience that not everybody has had. Consequently, the gospel will seem like just another "religion" in the world — one more system of social ethics and personal well-being. And seen as such, the gospel may not compare very favorably with the humanistic psychology and social ethics we've been using up to now. The lives we've put together in this world may not be perfect in every respect, but they are very good, at least for many of us. Absent the grief that comes from seeing our sins realistically, the gospel will seem silly and superfluous. Jesus Christ is an answer to questions we are not even asking.

But a broken and contrite heart changes all of that. "And behold, a woman of the city, who was a sinner . . . began to wet [Jesus'] feet with her tears and wiped them with the hair of her head and kissed his feet and anointed them with the ointment . . . And he said to her, 'Your sins are forgiven'" (Luke 7:37,38,48).

So is there no joy in the gospel of Christ? Yes, there is a greater joy than can be found anywhere else. But here is the catch: this greater joy is available only when we've accepted the loss of our lesser joys, especially those of self-sufficiency and pride. As long as we're content to believe that we're doing all right — and that any remaining problems are within the power of science and psychology to solve — we will cut ourselves off from the highest of all joys: reconciliation with the God who created us. Ironically, then, it is only a broken and contrite heart that is in a position to receive the joy that human beings were created to experience.

Christianity is certainly not despair; it is, on the contrary, good news — for the despairing; but for the frivolous it is certainly not good news, for it wants first of all to make them serious.

SØREN KIERKEGAARD

May 29

FROM DEATH TO LIFE

Do not present your members to sin as instruments for unrighteousness, but present yourselves to God as those who have been brought from death to life, and your members to God as instruments for righteousness.
Romans 6:13

IN JESUS CHRIST, BOTH LIFE AND DEATH TAKE ON A NEW MEANING. Having obeyed the gospel, the death we used to fear has no more power over us, and we find ourselves growing toward a kind of life that used to mean very little to us.

Death. For many people, physical death is the worst thing imaginable, the one thing to be avoided at all costs. There is, however, something worse: *being dead spiritually even though we're still alive physically.* If we are alienated from God, whatever "life" we have right now is only a hollow shell, a sad reminder of the true life we were created for. It's only a matter of time until our lives run out, and without a right relationship to God, nothing we do in this world is anything more than rearranging chairs on the deck of the Titanic. To change the metaphor, our vehicle may still be going down the road, but we're running on empty. Cut off from God, we are dead even while we live (1 Timothy 5:6).

This "living death" is, as I say, far worse than death itself. Indeed, physical death is a matter of small concern compared to the question of whether we are dead or alive in regard to God.

Life. In Christ, we are delivered from bondage to the fear of death (Hebrews 2:14,15). It no longer has power over us, and for that we're grateful. But more important, we're grateful to have passed from death to life *in the highest sense.* It doesn't matter whether our sojourn on this planet is long or short — *we are truly alive.*

There is even a sense in which the longer we live (and the closer we get to physical death), the more alive we become each day. Paul, a man whose entire life as a Christian was lived under the threat of being put to death, was growing toward a greater life the whole time. He said, "Though our outer self is wasting away, our inner self is being renewed day by day" (2 Corinthians 4:16).

So the Christian truly has "been brought from death to life" (Romans 6:13). And there is a wonderful irony in this. It was, after all, by dying that Jesus "abolished death and brought life and immortality to light through the gospel" (2 Timothy 1:10).

Salvation is moving from living death to deathless life.

JACK ODELL

May 30

WHO ARE THE "PEOPLE OF GOD"?

For if Joshua had given them rest, God would not have spoken of another day later on. So then, there remains a Sabbath rest for the people of God.
Hebrews 4:8,9

THE "PEOPLE OF GOD" IS A PHRASE FAMILIAR TO US IN THE SCRIPTURES, BUT WHO ARE THE INDIVIDUALS TO WHOM THE EXPRESSION APPLIES? In the widest sense, these words apply to every person whom God ever created. But in the Scriptures, the phrase often refers to a subset of the human race: a group with a special relationship due to having been redeemed or rescued by God.

At the time when the Law of Moses was in effect, the tribes of Israel were God's people in a unique sense. They were the physical family through whom God was going to bring the Messiah, or Christ, into the world. That mission having been accomplished, however, and the special role of Israel having been laid aside (Hebrews 8:1-13), who are the ones today who are the "people of God"? *It is those who obey the gospel of Christ.* The nation of Israel, in fact, pointed forward to this greater Israel, a spiritual people belonging to God (1 Peter 2:9,10). If you want to know whether you are among these "people of God," ask yourself these questions:

(1) Have I been reconciled to God on His terms? God's people are His *forgiven* ones, having died to sin in baptism (Romans 6:3-5).

(2) Do I offer to God what He is seeking from His creatures? God has always looked for those who would love Him with all their hearts and live accordingly (Deuteronomy 10:12,13; Micah 6:8).

(3) Do I live on the basis of faith in God? I am not one of God's people if my life doesn't show that I *trust* Him — taking risks to do things His way. "The righteous shall live by faith" (Romans 1:17).

It is only the people of God who can look forward to the eternal *rest* that He has promised. For Israel, Canaan was the land in which they hoped to rest, but as Hebrews 4:8,9 points out, God spoke even then of a greater rest awaiting His people. "For if Joshua had given them rest, God would not have spoken of another day later on. So then, there remains a Sabbath rest *for the people of God.*" May God hasten the day when all His foes have been vanquished and He reigns over all His faithful people forever.

Come, Thou almighty King, help us Thy name to sing, help us to praise!
Father all-glorious, o'er all victorious,
Come and reign over us, Ancient of Days.

CHARLES WESLEY

May 31

When the Old Self Is Crucified

We know that our old self was crucified with him
in order that the body of sin might be brought to nothing,
so that we would no longer be enslaved to sin.
Romans 6:6

CHRIST DIED BY CRUCIFIXION, AND WHAT HAPPENS WHEN WE ARE CONVERTED IS COMPARABLE TO HIS MANNER OF DEATH. We are, so to speak, crucified with him. And the thing that is put to death is our "old self," as Paul describes it. The "body of sin" is killed, resulting in the situation that we are no longer "enslaved to sin."

Baptism should be seen as a unique link in this chain of events. Because it takes place by an act of immersion, it aptly represents a burial. In baptism, our "old self" dies and is buried, and our "new self" comes to life (Colossians 2:12). "We were buried therefore with him by baptism into death," Paul wrote, "in order that, just as Christ was raised from the dead by the glory of the Father, we too might walk in newness of life" (Romans 6:4).

Think about the physical circumstances when a person was crucified. Fastened to a cross, the person being executed could not move, not even to twist around and look behind him. Similarly, when we are crucified with Christ, we look ahead to our lives in Him — our crucifixion does not allow us to look at anything else.

Obviously, Roman crucifixion was fatal. On the cross, a person could not decide to reverse his course of life. To be crucified is to be set on a path that goes in only one direction. Just so, our death with Christ is the most decisive turning point of our lives.

But finally, and most importantly, death by Roman crucifixion robbed a person of anything that could be called his own. He was stripped of his clothes, nailed to a cross, and deprived of whatever plans he may have had for his life before that moment. In an even deeper sense, our being crucified with Christ means that we die to our previous lives, including the self-will with which we used to talk about "our" lives. With Paul, we can say, "I have been crucified with Christ. It is no longer I who live, but Christ who lives in me. And the life I now live in the flesh I live by faith in the Son of God, who loved me and gave himself for me" (Galatians 2:20).

There are three marks of one who is crucified. One, he is facing in only one direction. Two, he can never turn back. And three, he no longer has any plans of his own.

A. W. TOZER

June 1

THE TEMPTING LURE OF "SELF-REALIZATION"

So when the woman saw that the tree was good for food, and that it was a delight to the eyes, and that the tree was to be desired to make one wise, she took of its fruit and ate, and she also gave some to her husband who was with her, and he ate.
Genesis 3:6

CREATED TO GROW AND DEVELOP WITHIN THE BOUNDARIES OF GOD'S WILL, THE HUMAN RACE HAS NOT BEEN CONTENT. Deceived, we have proceeded on the assumption that the really good life lies outside those boundaries. When Eve, and then Adam, disobeyed God, they did so because they had lost confidence in God's goodness. Satan had suggested that God's restrictions were unfair, and that, in fact, it was selfish of God to keep them from the knowledge they desired. They were seduced by Satan's lie when he said, in effect, "Seize what is yours. Take what you have a right to enjoy. Break the rules, and be your true self."

Well, we are not fully developed, that much is true. But if we believe there is some true "self" we were meant to be, and "realizing" that dream requires disobeying God, then we have bought into the very same lie that destroyed Adam and Eve. God created us with great potential (we hardly have the imaginations to comprehend it), but fully becoming all that is possible for us requires staying *inside* the Creator's will. Despite what the devil may say, down the road of disobedience there is nothing but *death.*

The fact is, we are not our own. Created by God, we belong to Him. We exist for His purposes. Any declaration of independence from Him is an act of rebellion, all the more serious because it is an abuse of the freedom we were given. God wanted us to use this freedom to obey Him — not as robots but as loving children — but we have chosen to pursue our own path, in defiance of His will. How sad it must be to our Father that not only do we not see our sin; we glory in it. We think we're building heaven on earth. We're the masters of our destiny. We're "fulfilling our human potential."

If we don't turn around, we are going to spend eternity in a place where, without any more interference from God, we will be completely "free to be ourselves." And it will be our little "self" (now fully "realized" and "actualized") that will make hell, hell.

The sin that shocks God is the thing which is highly esteemed among men — self-realization, pride, my right to myself.

OSWALD CHAMBERS

June 2

Salvation Is Not Earned, but It May Be Forfeited

Therefore we must pay much closer attention to what we have heard, lest we drift away from it.
Hebrews 2:1

NONE OF THE INHABITANTS OF HEAVEN WILL DESERVE TO BE THERE. Having sinned, we deserve to be punished, and if mere justice were allowed to run its course, we would all be lost. But the wonder of the gospel is that in Jesus Christ we may hope to receive what we do not deserve to receive: forgiveness. By His grace God has made it possible for us to be restored to His fellowship — and to enjoy eternity with Him in a perfect relationship.

But sometimes we leave the wrong impression. When we are emphasizing our undeservedness and the graciousness of God's forgiveness, we lead people to believe that salvation has nothing to do with our conduct. But, in fact, it has very much to do with our conduct, and I want to mention one way in which that is true.

When we obey the initial terms of the gospel and come into a forgiven relationship with God, God begins at that point to renovate our character and make our hearts those which will be in perfect tune with His heart in eternity. We are required to participate in this process of character rehabilitation. It calls for choice and decision on our part, not to mention diligence and sacrifice.

If we don't enter into this process of spiritual growth (or if having entered into it in the past, we've quit growing in the present), we begin to decline. On nearly every page of the New Testament, we see warnings about this (Acts 20:31; 2 Peter 3:14,17; etc.). There is no question that those to whom these warnings were written were actually Christians. They were "in Christ" and saved by His grace. But in many cases, they were in danger of forfeiting their salvation by complacency, neglect, and apostasy.

To the church in Ephesus, for example, the Lord communicated this warning: "You have abandoned the love you had at first. Remember therefore from where you have fallen; repent, and do the works you did at first. If not, I will come to you and remove your lampstand from its place, unless you repent" (Revelation 2:4,5). The fact is, we are never in greater danger than when we — presuming upon God's grace — think we don't need to be warned.

The safest road to hell is the gradual one — the gentle slope, soft underfoot, without sudden turnings, without milestones, without signposts.

C. S. Lewis

June 3

The Incarnate Word

In the beginning was the Word, and the Word was with God, and the Word was God. He was in the beginning with God . . . And the Word became flesh and dwelt among us, and we have seen his glory, glory as of the only Son from the Father, full of grace and truth.
John 1:1,2,14

THE INCARNATION (GOD TAKING UPON HIMSELF HUMAN FLESH) IS THE HEART OF THE GOSPEL. It is, as C. S. Lewis put it, the "Grand Miracle" that makes all the other miracles, including the Resurrection, meaningful. It is very important to understand this.

Out of all our problems, there is only one that required God to become flesh: the problem of sin. To fix that problem God had to die in our place, and to do that He had to become a man capable of being killed. In the words of John Donne, "God clothed himself in vile man's flesh so he might be weak enough to suffer."

Toward the end of the first century, there began to be those who denied the Incarnation. Influenced by the attitudes of Gnosticism, some began to suggest that Jesus was not really God in the flesh. They denied that "the Word became flesh and dwelt among us," offering what purported to be a more advanced gospel. Sadly, this revision of the gospel is still extremely popular.

If the Incarnation is not true, however, then the gospel of Christ is just another religious philosophy. Take away the Incarnation, and what you have left is something that is antithetical to ("against") Christ and His gospel. John saw this error for the perversion that it is: "Many deceivers have gone out into the world, those who do not confess the coming of Jesus Christ in the flesh. Such a one is the deceiver and the antichrist" (2 John 1:7).

It would be nice if our worst problem was nothing worse than poverty, disease, injustice, or emotional distress. God could have alleviated those kinds of hardship without the Incarnation. But there was a deeper sickness that required a more drastic solution, and we can be thankful He was willing to do what had to be done.

The gospel is about the forgiveness of sin — and our need for forgiveness is why God had to become a man and die. May we not water the message down. The Incarnation is astonishing and hard to believe, but it is not optional. If it was not God who died on the cross, the gospel may be an interesting story, but it cannot save us.

If we waver on the Incarnation we cease to be Christian.

ZACH KINCAID

June 4

Sin Strikes Deeper Than We Admit

For the word of God is living and active, sharper than any two-edged sword, piercing to the division of soul and of spirit, of joints and of marrow, and discerning the thoughts and intentions of the heart. And no creature is hidden from his sight, but all are naked and exposed to the eyes of him to whom we must give account.
Hebrews 4:12,13

MOTIVES MAKE A DIFFERENCE, DO THEY NOT? When we fail to use good judgment, we hope people will see that "we meant well." But there is another side to this. Actions that are good, at least in their outward appearance, may be contaminated by impure motives. If everybody could see what God sees in our hearts, they would have to reevaluate even the best of our deeds.

So the question I must always ask is not only *What did I do?* but *Why did I do it?* The outward deed is certainly important (2 Corinthians 5:10), but the inward motive is even more so (Acts 8:20,21). God, of course, is the only one who knows our motives completely. We are "naked and exposed to the eyes of him to whom we must give account." He knows not only our words and deeds, but He knows "the thoughts and intentions of the heart."

All of this means that when we're considering the problem of sin, we need to see how deep it really goes. (And please understand, I'm talking about our *own* sinfulness, not that of other people.) Sin strikes deeper than we admit. If all that had gone wrong was that our behavior had become dysfunctional, that problem would be relatively easy to fix. But the problem is that our hearts have become rebellious. Selfishness taints nearly everything we do, sometimes so subtly that we don't even see it ourselves.

And if the problem is this deep, *we should expect the remedy to be radical.* Bringing our innermost hearts back to a position of utter unselfishness, God will have to do some serious work. The battle to "take every thought captive to obey Christ" (2 Corinthians 10:5) will take more than a few days. And the process will not be painless.

It may be that our most pressing need is for greater self-honesty — and deeper repentance. The human heart is "deceitful above all things" (Jeremiah 17:9). So when we find ourselves doing something for multiple reasons, do we have the honesty to ask, "Deep, deep down, what was the *real* reason why I did that?"

Man sees your actions, but God your motives.

THOMAS À KEMPIS

June 5

Jesus' Final Instructions to His Apostles

And Jesus came and said to them, "All authority in heaven and on earth has been given to me. Go therefore and make disciples of all nations, baptizing them in the name of the Father and of the Son and of the Holy Spirit, teaching them to observe all that I have commanded you. And behold, I am with you always, to the end of the age."
Matthew 28:18-20

JESUS' FINAL INSTRUCTIONS TO HIS APOSTLES SHOULD BE OF MORE THAN PASSING INTEREST. If we wanted to know how Jesus viewed His own mission, we would need to look at the entire body of His teaching, of course, but His last words would be pertinent in a special way. What were the marching orders He gave to those whom He had selected to carry forward His work in the world?

Disciple is not a word we use much today, but it is a crucial word. The basic meaning is "pupil" or "learner," but the extended meaning involves something deeper. A disciple is not merely under the *instruction* of a teacher; he or she is a *follower* of that person, one who emulates the life and character of the teacher. And that is what Jesus sought: not just students but *disciples.* His command to "make disciples" was a charge to proclaim the gospel to all who would listen and then to baptize those who sought the forgiveness of their sins. But while baptism was essential (there could be no discipleship without having "died with Christ"), baptism was just the beginning. Now forgiven and restored to God's fellowship — and with the hope of heaven in their hearts — those baptized were to be taught "to observe all that I have commanded you."

So the mission assigned to the apostles was *disciple-making,* and that could only be done through *evangelism,* the proclamation of the gospel itself. Whatever the apostles might have thought was more relevant, Jesus' command never changed: *make disciples.*

We need to keep coming back to the central concern of Jesus. Yes, He helped people physically and emotionally, but His greater concern was always with their spiritual needs. "For what will it profit a man if he gains the whole world and forfeits his soul?" (Matthew 16:26). If we follow Jesus, our concern must be for the eternal welfare of people's souls. So let's not lose our focus. By God's grace, let's do what Jesus told His apostles: *teach people how they can be with God when their broken lives in this world are done.*

The church has many tasks but only one mission.

ARTHUR PRESTON

June 6

Delivered from the Power of Death

Since therefore the children share in flesh and blood, he himself likewise partook of the same things, that through death he might destroy the one who has the power of death, that is, the devil, and deliver all those who through fear of death were subject to lifelong slavery.
Hebrews 2:14,15

WHEN JESUS ARRIVED AT BETHANY AFTER HIS FRIEND LAZARUS HAD DIED, HE FOUND MARY AND MARTHA GRIEVING THE LOSS OF THEIR BROTHER. To Martha, Jesus said, "Your brother will rise again" (John 11:23), and she replied, "I know that he will rise again in the resurrection on the last day" (v.24). Then Jesus said these words to her: "I am the resurrection and the life. Whoever believes in me, though he die, yet shall he live, and everyone who lives and believes in me shall never die. Do you believe this?" (vv.25,26).

It is a fundamental fact of the gospel that by dying Jesus enabled those who accept His salvation to have a whole new perspective on death. To be able to die, He had to take upon Himself human flesh (John 1:14), but as the Hebrew writer points out in 2:14,15, by sharing in our "flesh and blood" and then dying for us, He took away from Satan the power of death and delivered "all those who through fear of death were subject to lifelong slavery."

We shall all have to die physically, of course, unless we happen to be alive when Christ returns. That is because when Adam and Eve were expelled from Eden, they and their progeny were barred from the Tree of Life — the physical immortality that would have come from eating of that tree was forfeited (Genesis 3:22-24).

But in Christ, the *fear* of death has been broken. The assurance of our own resurrection makes all the difference. In short, it is *hope* — the anticipation of what is *beyond* death — that "gives us the victory through our Lord Jesus Christ" (1 Corinthians 15:57).

But actually, what Jesus did was better than just giving us a new perspective on death: on the other side of death, He opened the door *to a life much better than what we call "life" right now.* I expect heaven will be even better than what Adam and Eve had in the Garden of Eden. Although it seems ironic that Christ gave us this life by dying, that is the good news. He died that we "might become heirs according to *the hope of eternal life*" (Titus 3:7).

Jesus audaciously abolished death, transforming it from a door that slammed to, into one that opened to whoever knocked.

MALCOLM MUGGERIDGE

June 7

FROM GOD, FOR OUR PROFIT

All Scripture is breathed out by God and profitable for teaching, for reproof, for correction, and for training in righteousness, that the man of God may be complete, equipped for every good work.
2 Timothy 3:16,17

MANY OF US, LIKE TIMOTHY, HAVE BEEN ACQUAINTED WITH THE SCRIPTURES SINCE WE WERE CHILDREN. But we, also like Timothy, need to be reminded of the extraordinary nature of these books that comprise the sacred writings. In 2 Timothy 3:16,17, Paul points to several fundamental facts about these documents:

Scripture. The Jews, and later the Christians, recognized a very special body of writings which they knew as "Scripture." The word literally means "writings," but when referring to this unique collection, it meant writings that came from God. Of all the writings in the world, these are the most treasured and the most authoritative.

Breathed out by God. The uniqueness, and hence the authority, of the Scriptures derives from their having been "breathed out by God," as Paul says. We do not know precisely the process through which this took place (indeed, the writer of Hebrews indicates, in 1:1,2, that it was not always in the same way), but the end result is clear: the books that can be called "Scripture" originated in the mind of God. In the words of Peter, "men spoke from God as they were carried along by the Holy Spirit" (2 Peter 1:21).

Profitable. The Scriptures are not merely for our study; they are for our profit. God has revealed Himself for the purpose of our betterment. When mankind departed from God, one of the most tragic results of this alienation was the loss of the knowledge of God. But God has reached across the gap and progressively reintroduced us to the truth about Himself. So the record in the Scriptures of this revelation is profitable to us: *"for teaching, for reproof, for correction, and for training in righteousness."*

We are right to say that the Scriptures are unfathomable. That is not to say they are mysterious or impossible to understand, but simply that they are inexhaustible. No matter how many years we study, there is always more to learn — and more to profit from. Indeed, the inexhaustible nature of the Bible is one of the clues that it was not produced by merely human wisdom.

God's Book is packed full of overwhelming riches; they are unsearchable — the more we have the more there is to have.

OSWALD CHAMBERS

June 8

What We Need to Be Saved From

For out of the heart come evil thoughts, murder, adultery, sexual immorality, theft, false witness, slander.
Matthew 15:19

THE CANCER THE GOSPEL WAS MEANT TO CURE IS MUCH MORE SERIOUS THAN MANY PEOPLE ARE WILLING TO ADMIT. If we want any help at all, it is usually just with our outward behavior or our external circumstances. But the gospel proposes to help us with our *character* — which in the Scriptures is often called our "heart." It is our character that produces our conduct, and so the gospel works on the cause of the problem and not just its symptoms.

Sin is any transgression of the will of God, but sin may occur at different levels, some more basic than others. We may sin by doing things "on the surface" that are not right, but these sins are the symptoms of a deeper problem: *our hearts are in rebellion against God.* Looking back at Matthew 15:19, Jesus said that it is "out of the heart" that evil thoughts and sinful deeds arise. That is where the real problem lies, and that is what we most need help with.

One of the most fascinating of the prophecies in the Hebrew Scriptures is Ezekiel 36:26,27, where God said, "I will give you a new heart, and a new spirit I will put within you. And I will remove the heart of stone from your flesh and give you a heart of flesh. And I will put my Spirit within you, and cause you to walk in my statutes and be careful to obey my rules." Jews in the first century who were looking for the coming of the kingdom of the Messiah could not have done better than to be longing for the new *hearts* the Messiah would make it possible for them to have.

One of the most important things in life is to take responsibility for our faults. In the gospel of Christ, we are asked to take responsibility at the deepest level possible. If we are to be saved from our sins, we must humbly acknowledge not just that we have done sinful deeds, but that we are sinful people. Whatever sins we have done outwardly, it is from our hearts that such deeds have come. We need to be saved not just from the penalty for our sins, but from the sinfulness of being the kind of people who would do such things. Recognizing this is the first step toward repentance.

Christ's definition of sin penetrates far deeper than a list of sins on a membership card. It goes to our inner desire, motivations, and secret thoughts.

ERWIN W. LUTZER

June 9

SAVED FROM, SAVED FOR

. . . by which he has granted to us his precious and very great promises, so that through them you may become partakers of the divine nature, having escaped from the corruption that is in the world because of sinful desire.
2 Peter 1:4

THE QUESTION "NOW WHAT?" IS ONE OF LIFE'S MOST IMPORTANT QUESTIONS. Unfortunately, many of us who have sought salvation *from* our sins do not understand what salvation is *for.* Like ancient Israel, we've been rescued from "Egypt," but we don't have a good grasp of the goal God had in mind when He set us free.

The past. If the Christian has "forgotten that he was cleansed from his former sins" (2 Peter 1:9), that is not good. Now that we follow Christ, the dominant note in our lives should be *gratitude:* "thanks be to God, that you who were once slaves of sin have become obedient from the heart to the standard of teaching to which you were committed" (Romans 6:17). But we dare not define ourselves solely in terms of the things we don't do anymore.

The future. Nature abhors a vacuum, as they say, and the gospel was meant to do more than subtract the evil from our lives (Luke 11:24-26). The question is, why did God want certain things removed from our lives and what does He want to put in their place? We are not what we used to be, but what comes next?

Having forgiven us, God wants us to "become partakers of the divine nature" (2 Peter 1:4). His plan is to repair the damage of sin (Peter described it as "corruption") and transform us into people who think and act as creatures made in His image. *In fact, He plans to makes us into people who have the same character as His Son, Jesus Christ.* "For those whom he foreknew he also predestined to be conformed to the image of his Son, in order that he might be the firstborn among many brothers" (Romans 8:29).

So a glorious destiny awaits us in Jesus Christ, and even now, we "are being transformed into the same image from one degree of glory to another" (2 Corinthians 3:18). And it's not just our *character* but also our *conduct* that is being renovated. "For we are his workmanship, created in Christ Jesus for good works" (Ephesians 2:10). *So let's be frank: are we participating in God's plan . . . or not?*

We have been holding the letter of truth while at the same time we have been moving away from it in spirit because we have been preoccupied with what we are saved from rather than what we have been saved to.

A. W. TOZER

June 10

The Importance of the Apostles

But you will receive power when the Holy Spirit has come upon you,
and you will be my witnesses in Jerusalem and in all Judea
and Samaria, and to the end of the earth.
Acts 1:8

IN GOD'S PLAN TO SAVE US FROM OUR SINS, THE APOSTLES HAD AN IMPORTANCE THAT NEEDS TO BE UNDERSTOOD. The entire message of the gospel depended on the resurrection of Christ (1 Corinthians 15:13-17), and the apostles served, first and foremost, as eyewitnesses of that event. Each of them had seen Jesus after He had been raised (Acts 1:21,22). And while the apostles were not the only eyewitnesses (1 Corinthians 15:3-8), their testimony was invested with nothing less than the authority of Christ Himself (Matthew 28:18-20; Acts 1:8). In addition, the apostles could perform miracles that guaranteed the truthfulness of their account (Hebrews 2:3,4). So the apostles were not just Christians; they were the definitive, authoritative emissaries of Christ. They could regulate the practice of the church in its foundational period. And what we have today in the New Testament is the written record of their definitive teachings. These documents provide the permanent, unchangeable "constitution" of the Lord's church.

In the first century, of course, many people claimed to be apostles who were not. So to separate the false apostles from those actually appointed by Christ, the true apostles were able to miraculously confirm their authority. Paul wrote to the Corinthians (some of whom were questioning his apostleship), "The signs of a true apostle were performed among you with utmost patience, with signs and wonders and mighty works" (2 Corinthians 12:12).

Jesus said that after His resurrection the Holy Spirit would finish revealing to the apostles the things He had only just begun to teach them (John 14:25,26; 16:12-15). So to get all of Jesus' teaching, we have to study not only what He personally taught, but also what was revealed to His apostles. Taken together, this body of teaching is definitive. It is authoritative and foundational. So we must not say, as many do, that we should ignore the apostles and only study the "teachings of Jesus." *We can't have Jesus without the apostles.* They were His designated, not-to-be-ignored spokesmen.

Jesus chose the twelve apostles for a unique, unrepeatable
role in the history of redemption.

JOHN PIPER

June 11

Normative Nature of the Apostles' Teaching

Now I would remind you, brothers, of the gospel I preached to you, which you received, in which you stand, and by which you are being saved, if you hold fast to the word I preached to you — unless you believed in vain.
1 Corinthians 15:1,2

WHEN WE ARE ADRIFT, WE NEED AN ANCHOR. But when it comes to the gospel of Christ, it is extremely important what anchor we choose to employ. Changing the metaphor, we might say that our standard of measurement is important. If we need to know whether a particular belief or practice is valid, we won't get a helpful answer if we measure by the wrong yardstick.

For Christians, the Scriptures are the definitive standard by which beliefs and practices are judged. Starting with Genesis and culminating in the writings of the apostles of Christ, these documents are normative. That is, they define what is and what is not an authentic part of the "Way" (Matthew 7:13,14; John 14:6; Acts 24:14). The Bible is, in effect, the "constitution" of Christianity.

In the late first century, several decades after the beginning of the gospel, many began to abandon the teaching of the apostles and promote progressive views of discipleship. Against this departure, the apostle John wrote a heartfelt plea to his brethren urging them to ground themselves in what they had been taught by the apostles (1 John 1:1-4; 2:24; 4:1,6). If they left this teaching, they would have departed from Christ (1 John 2:18,19; 2 John 9-11).

The crisis in John's day was the beginning of a trend that continues today. At present, it is fashionable to say that there is no norm — Christianity is whatever we wish it to be. If there is any standard, it is our own subjective feelings. As for the Bible, it is viewed as a "living" book whose meaning changes over time.

Yet this goes against the way the apostles themselves viewed the gospel. There was, for example, no hope that the problems in Corinth would be solved if the Corinthians didn't remember what Paul had taught them as an apostle. "Now I would remind you, brothers, of the gospel I preached to you, which you received, in which you stand, and by which you are being saved, if you hold fast to the word I preached." And what if they did not hold fast? Paul left no doubt that they would have "believed in vain."

A Christian cannot live by philosophy. Only the light of Christian revelation gives the end as well as the means of life.

JOHN JAY CHAPMAN

June 12

THE APOSTLES: DOUBTERS WHO BECAME EVANGELISTS

. . . who was descended from David according to the flesh and was declared to be the Son of God in power according to the Spirit of holiness by his resurrection from the dead, Jesus Christ our Lord.
Romans 1:3,4

PHYSICALLY, JESUS WAS A DESCENDANT OF DAVID. But that does not tell the whole story about Him. He was also, as Paul said, "declared to be the Son of God . . . by his resurrection from the dead." Even if a person had not been convinced by the other miracles Jesus performed (John 20:30,31), His resurrection could not be explained in any other way. If that took place, He was indeed the Son of God — and His gospel is to be believed and acted upon.

Jesus' own disciples, especially the twelve apostles, are an interesting case. They had seen all of the miracles, and they had heard all of Jesus' preaching. On some level, they had become believers (Matthew 16:13-16). But when Jesus was crucified, their hopes were dashed: He was dead, so how could He be the Messiah? But when they saw Him with their own eyes after His resurrection, they understood what the resurrection meant.

Thomas (who has often been called "Doubting Thomas") was perhaps the hardest to convince. Not present when the Lord first appeared to the apostles after His resurrection, Thomas declared that he would need to see Jesus for himself. But later, when Jesus appeared and Thomas was present, Thomas drew exactly the right conclusion: "My Lord and my God!" (John 20:28).

If the resurrection took place, there is simply no other conclusion we can reach. And we can't argue that the stories of Jesus' post-resurrection appearances were made up and later added to the records of His life. There simply wasn't enough time for this myth-making process to occur. The New Testament documents began to be written within 20-30 years after the resurrection. Those who wrote them knew beyond a doubt whether the resurrection had taken place — and rather than deny an event which they knew had actually come to pass, they were willing to die for their testimony. Having been doubters, they became evangelists. And it was the resurrection that turned them around.

The fact that Jesus did arise from the dead was the only thing that brought absolute conviction to the hearts of even his disciples that he was the Son of God. His resurrection from the dead left in their minds no trace of doubt.

ROBERTSON L. WHITESIDE

June 13

DOES JESUS' RESURRECTION REALLY MATTER?

And if Christ has not been raised, then our preaching is in vain and your faith is in vain. We are even found to be misrepresenting God, because we testified about God that he raised Christ, whom he did not raise if it is true that the dead are not raised.
1 Corinthians 15:14,15

THERE IS A VERSION OF "CHRISTIANITY" IN WHICH ALL OF THE MIRACLES ARE ELIMINATED FROM THE SCRIPTURES. Many people today take it for granted, based on their philosophy and worldview, that such a thing as a miracle is simply impossible, so the scriptural accounts of Jesus' miracles are assumed to be fictitious.

In particular, the resurrection of Jesus is held to be a legend — an idea created by later Christians and injected into the accounts of Jesus' life and death. Many ministers who occupy pulpits on Sunday morning may preach on the resurrection, but if you ask them privately, they will tell you that it didn't really take place.

But what do we have left if we leave the resurrection out of the gospel of Christ? Not much. We may have a positive-mental-attitude system of emotional uplift and benevolent motivation, but we do not have the Christian message of salvation, for originally that gospel promised the forgiveness of sins and eternal life. Paul spoke with remarkable candor when he wrote to the church in Corinth that if Christ was not raised from the dead, *"our preaching is in vain and your faith is in vain. We [the apostles] are even found to be misrepresenting God, because we testified about God that he raised Christ."* Some seem to think that it is only in modern times that people began doubting the resurrection, but as Paul indicates, many people doubted it from the start. And he is very clear as to the choice we must make: either we accept that the resurrection occurred and obey the gospel that is based upon it — or we deny the resurrection and dispense with the gospel as nothing more than a myth whose believers are *"most to be pitied"* (v.19).

Like it or not, sin is real and we are lost. But no alternative to Christ is available for our forgiveness. *"If Christ has not been raised . . . you are still in your sins"* (v.17). To be sure, wishful thinking must not make our decision. If the gospel is false, we must face the facts. But let's not water down what's at stake here: *hope vs. no hope.*

The resurrection of Jesus is at the heart of apostolic preaching and upon it rests the truth of the gospel.

PAUL EARNHART

June 14

Assurance That Jesus Will Be Our Judge

. . . because he has fixed a day on which he will judge the world in righteousness by a man whom he has appointed; and of this he has given assurance to all by raising him from the dead.
Acts 17:31

CONCERNING GOD, THE IDEAS OF "ACCOUNTABILITY" AND "JUDGMENT" ARE NOT CONGENIAL TO THE MODERN MIND. Those who believe there is a God do not usually think in terms of being judged by Him, such that their eternal destiny will be dependent on that judgment. Yet God's judgment is one of the things affirmed about Him in the Scriptures. Consider the text in Acts 17:16-34.

In this passage, there is the account of Paul's presentation of the gospel of Christ in Athens. Invited to speak to a group of philosophical inquirers, Paul talked first about the nature of God as a personal Creator, and then he spoke of God's judgment.

A time has been appointed, Paul said in v.31, when the world will be judged by God. And this will be done "in righteousness," which is to say, God's verdict will be exactly the right verdict in every case, rendered in perfect justice. What is more, Paul said that God has entrusted this judgment into the hands of "a man whom he has appointed." This is Jesus Christ, and "of this [God] has given assurance to all by raising him from the dead."

The resurrection established the truth of many things, not the least of which is Jesus' deity, His identity as the Son of God. But Paul shows that Christ's resurrection also verified His role as the One before whom we must stand in judgment. If someone wanted proof that judgment is coming and that Jesus will be the Judge, no greater proof would be possible than His resurrection.

This, then, is one of the Messiah's roles. In addition to being our High Priest and King, *He is our Judge.* "For as the Father has life in himself, so he has granted the Son also to have life in himself. And he has given him authority to execute judgment, because he is the Son of Man" (John 5:26,27). For those who have accepted the gospel faithfully, the judgment holds no fear, only love. But one way or the other, judgment is coming. Of that we may be sure.

Paul does not refer directly to the human figure — the "one like a son of man" — of Daniel 7:13; but this is "the man" whom he has in mind, the one in whom God's eternal purpose finds its fulfillment, the one to whom the Father has given "authority to execute judgment, because he is the Son of Man" (John 5:27).

F. F. BRUCE

June 15

An Insurmountable Objection

Now when they heard of the resurrection of the dead, some mocked. But others said, "We will hear you again about this."
Acts 17:32

THERE IS NO PROPOSITION SO COMPELLING THAT EVERYONE ACCEPTS IT. No matter what is affirmed, some objection or other is always possible. So with any idea, the question is not whether anyone can come up with objections but whether those objections are valid. Taking an opinion poll won't help us much either. Regardless of which way the opinions of the majority may be running, the only question worth asking is always: *is this idea true?*

When Paul was asked to speak to a group of philosophers in Athens about Jesus Christ, he first talked about the nature of God. But as his argument progressed, he came to Jesus' resurrection. At this point, "some mocked." However, some said, "We will hear you again about this." They all heard the same words — but the response of the audience was a split decision. In the end, the gospel was not received as obediently in Athens as it was elsewhere, and perhaps this is not surprising. But Paul's preaching was acted on affirmatively by some who heard it: "some men joined him and believed, among whom also were Dionysius the Areopagite and a woman named Damaris and others with them" (v.34).

Today, we could make a long list of objections that people offer to the resurrection of Christ. Some of these are based on misunderstandings which can be cleared up, while others come from a lack of acquaintance with the evidence. But there is one objection that can't be overcome by supplying additional evidence: the belief that the resurrection *cannot* have taken place. If a person approaches the question maintaining that such a thing is inherently impossible, he will not believe it no matter how much evidence there is.

So when it comes to miracles, and especially the resurrection, our presuppositions are crucial. In these days of discovery, haven't we learned to use the word *impossible* very sparingly (if at all)? It is a strange world, is it not? Let us, then, be open-minded enough to admit the possibility that the resurrection *could* have happened — and then have the courage to assess the historical evidence fairly.

If anything extraordinary seems to have happened, we can always say that we have been the victims of an illusion. If we hold a philosophy which excludes the supernatural, this is what we always shall say.

C. S. LEWIS

June 16

DIFFERENT SOILS, DIFFERENT HEARERS

Other seeds fell on rocky ground, where they did not have much soil, and immediately they sprang up, since they had no depth of soil, but when the sun rose they were scorched. And since they had no root, they withered away. Other seeds fell among thorns, and the thorns grew up and choked them.
Matthew 13:5-7

IN THE PARABLE OF THE SOWER, JESUS MADE THE POINT THAT THOSE WHO HEAR THE GOSPEL DON'T ALL HAVE THE SAME KIND OF HEART. He used the analogy of four different kinds of soil to teach the lesson — just as the seed sown by a farmer doesn't always fall on productive soil, the gospel doesn't always fall into receptive hearts.

(1) Along the path (vv.4,19). Some seed is picked up by the birds and never germinates at all. This is the person whose lack of interest in understanding the truth gives it no chance to affect him.

(2) Rocky ground (vv.5,6,20,21). Some seed falls into soil that is shallow, resulting in short-rooted plants that die when the sun gets hot. This is the person who is not a commitment keeper, so when it comes to the gospel, he can't be counted on to remain steadfast. Hardship causes him to change his mind about the Lord.

(3) Among the thorns (vv.7,22). Some seed sprouts but the plants are choked by thorns. "The cares of the world and the deceitfulness of riches choke the word, and it proves unfruitful" (v.22).

(4) Good soil (vv.8,23). Other seed, however, falls into fertile ground. It germinates, grows, and produces a crop. In Luke's account, Jesus said this soil is like those who "hearing the word, hold it fast in an honest and good heart, and bear fruit with patience" (Luke 8:15). This kind of hearer is obviously the one Jesus was always seeking, and He often found such hearers in unlikely places.

But how often do we, when we think of the Parable of the Sower, raise the question of *our own receptivity* to God's word? It may be that for all our talk about the need for honesty and courage, we ourselves do not bow before the truth as receptively as we should. To tell the truth, it is a rare human being who is willing to follow the truth wherever it goes (and sadly, we preachers are often the least willing). Today, as we contemplate obeying the gospel, let's challenge ourselves. God does not decide what kind of heart we have; we decide. So let's make the decision a good one.

A sound head, an honest heart, and an humble spirit are the three best guides through time and to eternity.

SIR WALTER SCOTT

June 17

LETTING THE SCRIPTURES DECIDE

And Paul went in, as was his custom, and on three Sabbath days he reasoned with them from the Scriptures.
Acts 17:2

IN THE TEXT ABOVE, NOTICE THE STANDARD OF AUTHORITY TO WHICH PAUL APPEALED. With the task of convincing a Jewish audience that Jesus' claims were true, he "reasoned with them from the Scriptures." If Jesus was the promised Messiah, everything about Him would match up with the portrait of the Messiah in the prophecies of the Hebrew Scriptures. And if the case for Jesus could *not* be made from the Scriptures, it would be reasonable for Paul's Jewish hearers, and everyone else, to reject the gospel.

The Scriptures are our only worthy standard. Having originated in the mind of God (John 5:39; 2 Timothy 3:16,17; 2 Peter 1:20,21), the Scriptures are able to make us "wise for salvation" (2 Timothy 3:15). To say that they are dependable is a considerable understatement. Jesus went so far as to say, "Scripture cannot be broken" (John 10:35). So these writings are no ordinary documents. To disregard the authority with which God speaks to us in the Scriptures is to do a very foolish thing. In all the great issues of life, it is the standard of the Scriptures to which we should appeal.

When we are considering controversial matters, it is hard to keep our feelings from influencing our decisions. When I served on the jury for a very sensitive child molestation trial many years ago, I well remember the judge's instructions to the jury: "Your decision should be based solely on the evidence, not on your feelings, preferences, or personal opinions." She was right. And when it comes to questions about our relationship to God, it is even more important to have an objective standard by which to measure.

At this point in history, however, few people believe there is any objective standard by which we can navigate. Most people assume that personal feelings and experience are the "voice of God" within them. But God has not left us to the chaos of such subjective uncertainty, and His servant David was on the right track long ago. "The law of the LORD is perfect, reviving the soul; the testimony of the LORD is sure, making wise the simple" (Psalm 19:7).

We must guard against grounding our spiritual commitment on the quicksands of fluctuating experiences. Experience . . . must be constantly tested and verified by the objective truths of the Word of God.

ERWIN W. LUTZER

June 18

A Powerful Clue to God's Nature

. . . as even some of your own poets have said, "For we are indeed his offspring." Being then God's offspring, we ought not to think that the divine being is like gold or silver or stone, an image formed by the art and imagination of man.
Acts 17:28,29

THE WORLD WE LIVE IN IS FULL OF WONDERS. It is, as Tolkien said, "full of strange creatures beyond count." But surely, the strangest of these by far is the human race. Human beings are so different from any of the other creatures, the more we learn about our human qualities, the more we see just how wide the gap is. (If you want to read a book that will make you think, get a copy of Mortimer J. Adler's *The Difference of Man and the Difference It Makes.*)

In Acts 17:28,29, Paul pointed out that the personal nature we know we possess is a clue to the nature of God. The Greek poets had acknowledged that we are the "offspring" of God. If that's true, Paul argued, how can we think God is any less personal than we are? He was right. If we have personal minds, those minds can't be explained by impersonal forces. Even if our physical brains could have evolved, what scientists call the "mind" is a phenomenon the brain simply cannot produce by itself.

Today, neuroscience believes it is making progress in explaining human consciousness in completely naturalistic, biological terms. We are told it's only a matter of time before we can see how the physical brain produces the "mind." But honestly, the campaign promises of that bold project will be hard to fulfill.

Human "personhood" is very familiar to us (it may be hard to define, but we know it when we see it), and it can't be explained from *below* itself — its origin can only be from *above* itself. The nonpersonal could never have produced the personal, no matter how many trillions of years it had to work with. And our physical brains can never be, all by themselves, the generative source of our rational thought and free will. In our heart of hearts, we know this. We know that what we are can only be explained by the creative act of a Personal Being who had the power to make us in His image.

I can't understand man, Agnos, without invoking the transcendent, the supernatural, the immaterial . . . Augustine once confessed, "The manner in which the spirit is united to the body cannot be understood by man, but it is the essence of man." Even with theism man remains a puzzle, but to me the puzzle is augmented geometrically if theism is false.

ARLIE J. HOOVER

June 19

That Where I Am You May Be Also

Let not your hearts be troubled. Believe in God; believe also in me. In my Father's house are many rooms. If it were not so, would I have told you that I go to prepare a place for you? And if I go and prepare a place for you, I will come again and will take you to myself, that where I am you may be also.
John 14:1-3

IT IS EXTREMELY ENCOURAGING FOR US TO READ OF THE DEPTH OF JESUS' CONCERN FOR HIS DISCIPLES. As He came down to the bitter end of His life, even on the night before He knew He would be crucified the next day, His concern was for them — to comfort them, reassure them, and establish hope in their hearts. In the Gospel of John, we hear Him saying, "You have sorrow now, but I will see you again, and your hearts will rejoice, and no one will take your joy from you" (John 16:22). And, "I have said these things to you, that in me you may have peace. In the world you will have tribulation. But take heart; I have overcome the world" (16:33).

So in our text in John 14:1, we find the familiar words, "Let not your hearts be troubled." But what idea did He want them to be encouraged by? *He wanted them to keep in mind that, although He would be leaving, He would come back and take them to His eternal abode.* "If I go and prepare a place for you, I will come again and will take you to myself, that where I am you may be also" (v.3).

This is the hope that lies at the heart of the gospel of Christ. Having responded obediently to the gospel and been reconciled to God, we can anticipate the time when our Lord will return for us. And when He does, He will take us to be with Him forevermore.

Whatever imagery may be used to portray eternity with God, this should be the aspect of it that moves us most deeply: *we will be with God.* Having lived all our lives in this broken world, frustrated by our inability to have direct, face-to-face access to our Father, imagine what it will be like to actually be with Him!

To be with God where He is, of course, will require the removal of the imperfections that remain within us at present: the sinful attitudes, ungodly habits, and broken relationships. We will need to be, as one of my favorite songs says, "mended and whole." But therein will lie the joy of heaven. Our relationship with God, our Heavenly Father, will have been perfected — and sin will no longer interfere with the exchange of love between us and Him!

Where imperfection ceaseth, heaven begins.

PHILIP JAMES BAILEY

June 20

LESSONS FROM NAAMAN

So Naaman came with his horses and chariots and stood at the door of Elisha's house. And Elisha sent a messenger to him, saying, "Go and wash in the Jordan seven times, and your flesh shall be restored, and you shall be clean" . . . So he went down and dipped himself seven times in the Jordan, according to the word of the man of God, and his flesh was restored like the flesh of a little child, and he was clean.
2 Kings 5:9,10,14

NAAMAN WANTED TO BE CLEANSED FROM HIS LEPROSY, BUT HE DIDN'T LIKE WHAT HE WAS TOLD TO DO. When Elisha told him to dip himself in the Jordan River seven times, not only would such a menial act have been a blow to his pride, but he would not have seen any logical connection between the command and the benefit he hoped to receive. So he balked. But when his servants persuaded him to humble himself and obey Elisha, "his flesh was restored like the flesh of a little chid, and he was clean."

If we're honest, we probably see something of ourselves in Naaman. If God were to require of us something grand and glorious, our obedience would be prompt. And if we think we see *why* God would require something (the instruction "makes sense" to us), we are willing to go along with Him. But when God commands things that seem lowly, arbitrary, or irrational, we dismiss those items as "works" only a legalist would view as "required."

The fact is, it takes humility as well as trust to do things God's way. If we only obey when it suits us and when the act commends itself to our sense of logic, we are not really obeying God — we are doing as we please. And such self-will is what got us into trouble in the first place. If God is ever going to be allowed back on the throne of our hearts, *obedience* is the thing we must learn.

Naaman's obedience certainly did not *earn* him the cleansing of his leprosy. It had no "merit" that would cure him. But there is no denying this: if he had not been humble enough to accept the conditions that were stipulated, his leprosy would have remained.

An old adage says, "Understanding can wait; obedience cannot." Abraham wouldn't have understood why he should offer up Isaac, Noah wouldn't have understood what a flood was, and Israel wouldn't have understood going in circles around Jericho. *But it was in their obedience that God would have started making sense to them.*

Obedience is the key that unlocks the door
to every profound spiritual experience.

DOROTHY KERIN

June 21

The Fallacy of Original Sin

The soul who sins shall die. The son shall not suffer for the iniquity of the father, nor the father suffer for the iniquity of the son. The righteousness of the righteous shall be upon himself, and the wickedness of the wicked shall be upon himself.
Ezekiel 18:20

IN THIS OFTEN-QUOTED TEXT, A PRINCIPLE OF GREAT IMPORTANCE IS ENUNCIATED: THE PRINCIPLE OF INDIVIDUAL ACCOUNTABILITY. Our eternal destiny will be determined not by the deeds of others but by our own. As for righteousness, we won't go to heaven just because we're in a group of good people, and as for sin, we won't be sentenced to death because of someone else's ungodliness.

Physically, we die as a consequence of Adam's removal from access to the tree of life (Genesis 3:22-24). The false doctrine of Calvinistic "original sin," however, goes much further than this. *It teaches that we are all born guilty of the sin that Adam committed.* Standing under the condemnation of God for what Adam did, we are in a lost spiritual condition because of our eldest forefather.

If original sin were true, there is no reasonable way the principle found in Ezekiel 18:20 could be said to be valid. In the world we presently live in, it's an obvious fact that we can be impacted by other people's sins. Every day, people are hurt by the deeds of others, either directly or indirectly. But to say that even as infants we are guilty of Adam's sin and are *in a lost spiritual condition* because of what Adam did is to make a cruel joke out of Ezekiel's statement, "The wickedness of the wicked shall be upon himself." The wickedness of Adam would not only be "upon" us; it would be upon us in a much more devastating way than is ever the case when we suffer in this life as a consequence of someone else's sin.

To make matters worse, the doctrine of original sin is part of a package of other beliefs, as we will see in the next two readings. These doctrines, if true, would mean we are cosmic game pieces, moved around by a God who decides who will be saved and who will not. But thankfully, the gospel of Christ tells a different story.

Behind these errors is the long history of a misconception of the grace of God that denies man has free will, and accepts the doctrine of total hereditary depravity. The idea is that man is so depraved and wholly separated from God that without miraculous aid he can do nothing to bring about his redemption. The idea finally ends in the doctrine of preservation: once God has saved a person, He could never allow him to be lost.

ROBERT F. TURNER

June 22

SCRIPTURAL TEACHING ABOUT GOD'S "ELECTION"

Who shall bring any charge against God's elect? It is God who justifies.
Romans 8:33

TO "ELECT" IS TO "CHOOSE." So if we were talking about our salvation by God and we said that it's a matter of His "election" or "choosing," what would we mean? John Calvin (and various others before him) argued that before God created the world He chose which individuals would be saved. Yet it goes far beyond the truth concerning God's election in Romans 8:33 to teach that God *unconditionally* elected some *individuals* to *salvation*. Each of these terms makes a difference. Let's take them in reverse order:

Salvation. The Scriptures teach that, before the boys were born, God chose Jacob and not his twin brother, Esau, to father the family through whom the Messiah would come into the world (Romans 9:10-12). So yes, God did choose some persons to play specific roles in His plan to bring about salvation. But that is very different than choosing those persons to be eternally saved or lost.

Individuals. Paul spoke of the Colossians as "God's chosen ones, holy and beloved" (3:12). Salvation is surely a matter of God's choice, and His divine prerogative is where the emphasis should always be kept. It was God who chose whom He would save, but what He chose was a *class* of people defined by a *criterion:* the "obedience of faith" (Romans 1:5). This group is open to all who will obey. No one is barred by an eternal, unchangeable edict of God.

Unconditional. In the New Testament, people decided whether they would obey the gospel or not (Acts 2:40,41). Yet without any conditions that can be accepted or rejected, the gospel "call" is not really an invitation. Indeed, the whole enterprise of evangelism is meaningless if God has ordained who will be saved and salvation is not contingent on anyone's decision as to the gospel's requirements.

If the Bible teaches anything about God, it teaches that He acts with justice — He "shows no partiality" (Acts 10:34). But if Calvinism is true, T. W. Brents was correct when he said that God cannot possibly be considered a fair and righteous judge.

But if the doctrine . . . is true — that before the foundation of the world was laid, according to an immutable and eternal purpose of His own, without any foresight of faith, good works, or any thing else in man, God unconditionally elected some men and angels to eternal life, and at the same time foreordained the residue to dishonor and eternal wrath — then we know not how to avoid the conclusion that He is a respecter of persons.

T. W. BRENTS

June 23

God's Grace Is Not "Irresistible"

Working together with him, then, we appeal to you not to receive the grace of God in vain.
2 Corinthians 6:1

IN THE SCRIPTURES, ONE OF THE MOST TOUCHING CHARACTERISTICS OF GOD IS THE FERVENCY WITH WHICH HE APPEALS TO HUMAN BEINGS. In many dire circumstances, God is shown pleading with people to let Him save them. But there was always a choice to be made by those needing God's help: *would they receive God's grace or not?* The basic situation of mankind is summed up well in Paul's heartfelt exhortation to his brethren in Corinth in which he said, *"We appeal to you not to receive the grace of God in vain."*

Sadly, there are those (many of whom I admire for their sincerity) who teach that God's grace cannot be rejected. Believing that we are born with the "original sin" of Adam's transgression and are so depraved in our nature that we couldn't even respond to an offer of salvation if we tried, these teachers insist that God must decide who will be saved — *and those whom He decides to save, He infuses with the "enabling power" of the Holy Spirit.* This grace is "irresistible" by the recipients, or so says the doctrine. God having decided who will be saved, the chosen ones do not have the power to reject the saving influence which God sends upon them. But surely, many *have* refused God's efforts to win their hearts. When, for example, Jesus lamented Jerusalem's rejection of Him (Matthew 23:37), it is woefully inadequate to say that, since they refused, it must not have really been salvation that He was offering them.

As with all the concepts that are central to Calvinism, the doctrine of irresistible grace rests on a mistaken notion of God's sovereignty. The Calvinist argues that if anyone can say no to God, that means God is not sovereign. In other words, if we can, by the exercise of our will, keep God from saving us, that means God is not all-powerful. But actually, that argument is the one which limits God. It says that God could not have decided to make creatures endowed with a free will. But that is exactly what God did when He created us. And the result is that those who accept Him, whether many or few, do so freely and lovingly — rather than under the compulsion of their "irresistible" programming.

It is a denial of the sovereignty of God to say that He could not create persons capable of freely rejecting him.

CURTIS BYERS

June 24

THE LORD'S SUPPER, THE LORD'S PEOPLE

On the first day of the week, when we were gathered together to break bread, Paul talked with them, intending to depart on the next day, and he prolonged his speech until midnight.
Acts 20:7

IN THIS VERSE, WE FIND THE CHRISTIANS IN THE CHURCH AT TROAS DOING SOMETHING THAT WAS MORE IMPORTANT IN THOSE DAYS THAN MANY PEOPLE THINK IT IS TODAY. They gathered together on the first day of the week to "break bread," which in this context is a reference to what we know appropriately as the "Lord's Supper."

The Lord's Supper is a partaking of unleavened bread and fruit of the vine in memory of Jesus' death for our sins. The bread represents Christ's body which was crucified and the fruit of the vine, the blood which He shed. It was instituted by Christ on the night before His execution (Matthew 26:26-29), and we find more teaching about it in texts like 1 Corinthians 10:16,17 and 11:17-34.

In the assembly. The Lord's Supper is not a private observance. Every word spoken about it in the New Testament presumes that it is to be done when the Lord's people have come together.

Every Lord's Day. Just as it is linked to the assembly, it is also linked to the first day of the week — the Lord's Day — that being the day of the Lord's resurrection (Luke 24:1-3) and the day, a few weeks later, when the gospel was first preached in its completeness (Acts 2:1-4). And it was *every* Lord's Day, as we infer from Acts 20:7 (cf. 1 Corinthians 16:1,2; Revelation 1:10). Historically, it was sometime later before the Supper became separated from the Lord's Day.

But this essay is not meant as a general discussion of the Lord's Supper; it is written to emphasize the connection between *the Lord's Supper* and *the Lord's people.* Against the argument that one may be a Christian and not have anything to do with a local congregation, this is a point that needs to be pondered. If we reject "organized" religion and adopt the "spiritual but not religious" approach, where does that leave the Lord's Supper? It is not Christianity that we are practicing today if we don't take seriously an observance that, in the New Testament, was so extremely important to Christians on the first day of every week.

O Father, bless this solemn day,
When we assemble, sing and pray,
To honor Christ, Thine only Son,
Who tasted death for everyone.

CRAIG A. ROBERTS

June 25

God's Steadfast Love

"For the mountains may depart and the hills be removed, but my steadfast love shall not depart from you, and my covenant of peace shall not be removed," says the Lord, who has compassion on you.
Isaiah 54:10

One of the great anchors of our confidence in God is the steadfastness of His love. Unlike our human love, which is tragically fickle and fluctuating, God's love will still be there though "the mountains may depart and the hills be removed."

The Hebrew noun *hesed* is translated as "steadfast love" by some modern translations. Like many of the most meaningful words in any language, *hesed* is almost impossible to translate. There is no rendering for it that is entirely satisfactory, so translators have struggled to do it justice. Basically, *hesed* meant "mercy," and in many contexts it comes close to the idea of "grace." And yet it also has the connotation of "kindness." To make matters even more complicated, when used in reference to God, *hesed* often connotes the covenantal aspect of God's love, hence "steadfast love." God's love is enduring. It is, as Lois Tverberg says, "long acting love."

It would often take a sentence in English to say what Hebrew could say in one word, *hesed* — but for today's meditation, let's stick with "steadfast love." Because God has entered into a "covenant" or "contract" with us, we can count on Him to be loving, kind, merciful, and gracious to us *because He promised He would.*

The steadfastness of God's love does not mean He will never discipline us. Indeed it is His love that will move Him to discipline us when that is what we need (Hebrews 12:5-11). Nor does God's love mean He will not banish us from His presence in eternity if we persist in our earthly resistance to Him and refuse His offer of salvation. But until we have completely exhausted our opportunity to come back to Him and died in our rejection of His forgiveness, He will not give up on us. *He will keep His covenant.*

I don't know about you, but I'm mighty glad that God's love is steadfast. Were it not for His lovingkindness, this weak son of His would have been disinherited long, long ago. And, in Christ, I yearn for the sweet day when I shall be able to thank Him more properly.

The love of God is consistent and cannot be altered or deterred.
His love stands firmly fixed as the motive for all He asks
and for all He provides. His love never changes.

Dee Bowman

June 26

LEARNING ABOUT THE FATHER FROM THE SON

No longer do I call you servants, for the servant does not know what his master is doing; but I have called you friends, for all that I have heard from my Father I have made known to you.
John 15:15

IF YOU HAD DOUBTS ABOUT THE EXISTENCE OF GOD, WHAT IF SOMEONE TOLD YOU HE HAD COME FROM THE PRESENCE OF GOD AND COULD PERSONALLY VOUCH FOR GOD'S EXISTENCE? And suppose that person gave compelling evidence that he was telling the truth? Well, that is exactly what we have in the case of Jesus.

If (1) Jesus of Nazareth lived in the world as a real person, we need to pay attention to the historical data that can be known about Him. And if (2) a historical case can be made for the fact that His resurrection actually occurred, then He was not just a man but the Son of God. This crucial fact means that (3) of all the people who have ever lived, Jesus is the one who had the most direct information about God: *everything Jesus said about God should inform our thinking on this, the most important issue in our lives.*

Jesus is described as "the faithful witness" (Revelation 1:5), which means He told the truth in everything He reported to mankind about God. He claimed He came from God, had direct knowledge of Him, and bore accurate testimony about Him. To one audience, He said, "I speak of what I have seen with my Father" (John 8:38). And He said to His disciples, "All that I have heard from my Father I have made known to you" (John 15:15).

These are bold claims, but the resurrection proved them to be true. If Jesus said God is real, His testimony should supersede the doubts of us who have never been where God is. If Jesus, by His teaching and example, contradicts our opinions about the nature of God, He was in a better position to know what God is like than we are. If Jesus gave commandments for our obedience, these must be seen as having the authority of God. And finally, if Jesus taught that God's plan for our salvation was based on His death, we can stake our lives on that. It simply can't be emphasized too much: *Jesus is the ultimate proof of God — and of God's true nature.*

Jesus' claim to speak the things which he had "seen" in the Father's presence (John 8:38) echoes his language in John 6:46: "he who comes from God, he has seen the Father" . . . But no one can speak of heavenly realities except one who has come down from heaven and imparts to his hearers on earth what he has seen and heard in that transcendent realm.

F. F. BRUCE

June 27

Jesus' Mission: He Came to Save Sinners

The saying is trustworthy and deserving of full acceptance, that Christ Jesus came into the world to save sinners, of whom I am the foremost.
1 Timothy 1:15

Even before Jesus died, people disagreed as to what His purpose was. And those disagreements continue today. Whatever He may have done or not done, what was it that He *intended* to do? What was His mission (and His apostles' mission) in this world? What is the main point of the gospel of Christ? In other words, if the gospel is the solution, what is the problem it solves?

Writing to his young coworker Timothy, Paul left no doubt about the object of Jesus' work: "Christ Jesus came into the world to save sinners" (1 Timothy 1:15). This echoes Jesus' own words, "For the Son of Man came to seek and to save the lost" (Luke 19:10).

Many secondary benefits flow from the forgiveness of our sins, but we must never forget the message Christ commanded to be preached in His name. Paul never forgot it, because many years later he recalled that Christ had sent him to the Gentiles "to open their eyes, so that they may turn from darkness to light and from the power of Satan to God, that they may receive forgiveness of sins and a place among those who are sanctified by faith in me" (Acts 26:18). Christ ordered Paul to preach a specific message — and that message was about the forgiveness of sins.

But going back to 1 Timothy 1:15, did you notice what Paul said about himself? Christ came into the world to save sinners, *"of whom I am the foremost."* If we see the gospel as providing what others need most, the forgiveness of their sins, each of us should see our own need for the gospel very personally. And when forgiven, we must not suppose it took any less of God's grace to forgive us than might have been required for a really "sinful" person.

So let's not misunderstand what Jesus came to do, and in our preaching, let's not misrepresent what the gospel offers. Tempted to get lost in details and side issues, let's come back to the center. The cancer the gospel proposes to cure is this: *our sins against God.*

We shall never understand anything of our Lord's preaching and ministry unless we continually keep in mind what exactly and exclusively his errand was in this world. Sin was his errand in this world, and it was his only errand. He would never have been in this world, either preaching or doing anything else, but for sin. He could have done everything else for us without coming down into this world at all; everything else but take away our sin.

Alexander White

June 28

Learning About Love from God

Jesus said to him, "Have I been with you so long, and you still do not know me, Philip? Whoever has seen me has seen the Father. How can you say, 'Show us the Father'?"
John 14:9

NOTHING IS MORE IMPORTANT THAN OUR CONCEPT OF GOD. What we think of our Creator — both His character and His will — is the principal force that shapes our lives. Since ideas have consequences, the bigger the subject, the more our ideas need to be true. There being no bigger subject than God, we should be extremely careful. In the end, the way we have lived will have been the outworking of our real (not our pretended) beliefs about God.

When Jesus said that "the truth will set you free" (John 8:32), He had more in mind than just the truth about God's plan of salvation. I believe He meant, first and foremost, the truth about God Himself. The path that He has designed for our redemption must be accepted (untruths about God's plan are deadly), but out of all the errors that must be corrected, none are more crucial than wrong ideas about God. The problem of sin arose when we started acting on the basis of falsehoods about Him, and if the problem is to be fixed, those falsehoods must be rooted out of our thinking.

So let me ask you a practical question: what do you think about the "love of God"? And more importantly, where did you get those ideas? Most of us have some concept of what love is and how it behaves, but unfortunately those notions have often been picked up from pop psychology, pop theology, and even pop culture. Rather than letting our definition of love be formed by God, we imagine love as the world has taught us to see it, and we then transfer that shallow, sentimental view to God. Even when we flatter ourselves that we've gone beyond the worldly view to an understanding of "unconditional" love, we are still limited by the world's concept of what love would actually do in specific situations. Clearly, our minds are still fettered by a good bit of untruth.

Nothing about Jesus was more revolutionary than His exemplification of love. If we take *all* of what He did (and not just our favorite parts), even our most "advanced" ideas about love will be disrupted. It will be a disturbing, and truly liberating, experience.

The Christian does not understand God in terms of love; he understands love in terms of God as seen in Christ.

JOSEPH FLETCHER

June 29

AWAY FROM THE PRESENCE OF THE LORD

They will suffer the punishment of eternal destruction, away from the presence of the Lord and from the glory of his might, when he comes on that day to be glorified in his saints, and to be marveled at among all who have believed, because our testimony to you was believed.
2 Thessalonians 1:9,10

THE STARK TRUTH IS THAT OUR CHOICES WITH REGARD TO GOD WILL HAVE ETERNAL CONSEQUENCES. Having been created in the image of an eternal God, we also are eternal. Whether we accept Him or reject Him, we will live eternally. And as Paul taught in the text above, those who reject God will have an eternity "away from the presence of the Lord and from the glory of his might."

The doctrine of eternal punishment is not acceptable to the modern mind. The current trend, even among conservative Christians, is toward "universalism," the belief that all human beings are going to be saved (or at least that the unsaved will simply be annihilated rather than punished eternally). Francis Chan worded it well: "Does everyone go to heaven? Based on what I hear at funerals, the answer is an overwhelming 'Yes!' How many funerals have you attended where this was even in question?" Yet, as Chan has forcefully argued, the Bible simply cannot be taken seriously if the reality of eternal punishment is not accepted.

Unfortunately, many people do *not* take the Bible seriously. Universalism is fueled not by biblical exegesis but by emotional preferences. Hell is simply incongruent with the way people want to feel about God. As Arthur Climenhaga has said, "The issue of the new universalism is no longer 'God hath spoken' but 'Man hath reasoned.'" So this debate presents a challenge. Will we let Jesus be our Teacher in texts like Matthew 10:28 or will we not?

The knowledge that those who are lost right now will, if they fail to receive salvation in the gospel of Christ, be lost in eternity is the reason our evangelism should be so urgent. So let me ask you: is the reason why we Christians are not any more urgent in our evangelism the fact that we don't really believe the lost will be lost? Why is there so little passion to rescue the lost? Concerning hell, non-Christians need to accept what the Scriptures teach — *and the evidence suggests that many Christians need to believe it too.*

The true universalism of the Bible is the call to universal evangelism in obedience to Christ's universal commission. It is the conviction not that all men will be saved in the end, but that all men must hear the gospel.

JOHN STOTT

June 30

The Resurrection of Condemnation

Do not marvel at this; for the hour is coming in which all who are in the graves will hear His voice and come forth — those who have done good, to the resurrection of life, and those who have done evil, to the resurrection of condemnation.
John 5:28,29 NKJV

RESURRECTION! The very word stirs the soul — it is the very essence of the gospel. It was Jesus who said, "I am the resurrection and the life. Whoever believes in me, though he die, yet shall he live" (John 11:25). So Paul wrote these unforgettable lines, speaking for all who have obeyed the gospel and live in hope: "Behold! I tell you a mystery. We shall not all sleep, but we shall all be changed, in a moment, in the twinkling of an eye, at the last trumpet. For the trumpet will sound, and the dead will be raised imperishable, and we shall be changed" (1 Corinthians 15:51,52).

But resurrection is a double-edged sword. Go back and read our text in John 5:28,29. There, Jesus said that "the hour is coming in which all who are in the graves will hear His voice and come forth — those who have done good, to the resurrection of life, and those who have done evil, to the *resurrection of condemnation."* For some, the resurrection will be one of "life," but to others it will be one of "condemnation." Human beings have eternal souls — souls that will spend eternity, if not *with* God, then *away* from Him.

In Revelation 21:8, the eternal destiny of those who have refused God's salvation is called "the second death." Jesus said that to suffer that death is far worse than to die physically: "I tell you, my friends, do not fear those who kill the body, and after that have nothing more that they can do. But I will warn you whom to fear: fear him who, after he has killed, has authority to cast into hell. Yes, I tell you, fear him!" (Luke 12:4,5). And when He taught on hell, He used graphic language. At the judgment, the ungodly will hear the words, "Depart from me, you cursed, into the eternal fire prepared for the devil and his angels" (Matthew 25:41). These, Jesus said, "will go away into eternal punishment" (v.46).

Our human freedom entails *accountability to our Creator.* And if, in the end, we have rejected Him, it will be useless to deny the choices we made. While there is time, let's make the *right* choice.

Hell is paved with great granite blocks hewn from the hearts of those who said, "I can do no other."

HEYWOOD BROUN

July 1

Whole Heart, Willing Mind

And you, Solomon my son, know the God of your father and serve him with a whole heart and with a willing mind.
1 Chronicles 28:9

SOLOMON WOULD BE A NEW KING WITH SOME SERIOUS RESPONSIBILITIES. His father David having subdued all the surrounding enemies of Israel, Solomon (whose name meant "peace") would have to lead his people in the rightful, godly enjoyment of the peace that David had made possible. But not only that, he was also charged with building the temple of the Lord in Jerusalem which David had planned and made provision for. So in his charge to Solomon, David encouraged his son with the most important advice he could have given him: "know the God of your father and serve him with a whole heart and with a willing mind."

Know the God of your father and serve him. Human beings can't "know" God in the same sense that we know one another, but God's character can be known through His revelation of Himself. On the basis of this knowledge, it is possible to enter into a deep personal relationship with God, and no one illustrates that any more than David. Yet God must also be "served;" that is, He must be obeyed. That is the essence of what made David a man after God's own heart. Unlike his predecessor Saul, David could be counted on to carry out the Lord's instructions. Even in his repentance, David's disposition was to bow humbly before God's law.

With a whole heart and with a willing mind. A "whole heart" is one that is given to God completely, with no places in the heart reserved for other "gods." Likewise, a "willing mind" is one that serves God gratefully rather than grudgingly. When these two are combined — a whole heart and a willing mind — a person's character is well on its way to the devotion that God desires.

But all of these traits result from *personal choice.* David would not have charged Solomon to know God and serve Him with a whole heart and a willing mind *if Solomon could not have chosen to have that kind of character.* Excuses are futile. It is our hearts that God is seeking, and it is only we who can give our hearts to Him.

And what kind of habitation pleases God? What must our natures be like before he can feel at home within us? He asks nothing but a pure heart and a single mind. He asks no rich paneling, no rugs from the Orient, no art treasures from afar. He desires but sincerity, transparency, humility, and love. He will see to the rest.

A. W. TOZER

July 2

PRESENT KINGDOM, FUTURE KINGDOM

The Lord will rescue me from every evil deed and bring me safely into his heavenly kingdom. To him be the glory forever and ever. Amen.
2 Timothy 4:18

IS THE KINGDOM OF GOD SOMETHING THAT EXISTS IN THIS WORLD OR IS IT SOMETHING THAT WILL EXIST IN ETERNITY? The answer, if we let the Scriptures be our authority, is that it is both.

Present. The Scriptures clearly teach that the kingdom is a present reality. Jesus said it was "at hand" (Mark 1:15), and in Mark 9:1, He said, "There are some standing here who will not taste death until they see the kingdom of God after it has come with power." The kingdom began on the first Pentecost after Jesus' resurrection (Acts 1:1-2:47), and it has existed ever since. Anyone can be in the kingdom who accepts the requirements of God's forgiveness and lives under the loving rule of God. Paul wrote that God "has delivered us from the domain of darkness and transferred us to the kingdom of his beloved Son" (Colossians 1:13).

Future. The Scriptures also teach that the kingdom is a future reality, one the saints greatly anticipate but have not yet entered into (2 Timothy 4:18). Peter urged his fellow Christians to "be all the more diligent to confirm your calling and election, for if you practice these qualities you will never fall. For in this way there will be richly provided for you an entrance into the eternal kingdom of our Lord and Savior Jesus Christ" (2 Peter 1:10,11).

In 1 Corinthians 15, Paul wrote at length about our resurrection when Christ returns. The events surrounding Christ's return will conclude the history of this world and bring it to its climax. For those who have obeyed the gospel and remained faithful to the commitment they made, that will be the time when they pass from the kingdom of God in this present world to His kingdom in eternity. "Then comes the end, when he delivers the kingdom to God the Father after destroying every rule and every authority and power. For he must reign until he has put all his enemies under his feet. The last enemy to be destroyed is death" (vv.24-26).

To say that we are in the kingdom implies that we have submitted our lives unto the rule of God in His Son. But God's rule was never intended to be confined in space and time, for it is an eternal kingdom. We simply submit to God's rule now so that we may live under the rule and care of God forever. We enter the kingdom now . . . in order that we may "be heirs of the kingdom which he promised to those who love him" (James 2:5).

TOMMY POARCH

July 3

Some Strong Statements About the Kingdom

Then, hearing this, a number of his disciples said,
This is a hard saying; who is able to take in such teaching?
John 6:60 Bible in Basic English

JESUS' TEACHINGS WERE NOT ALWAYS EASY. Some of His sayings were, for various reasons, hard to understand, but other things He taught were simply hard to *accept*. As the disciples said in the text above, "Who is able to take in such teaching?" Let's look at some of Jesus' bold statements concerning the kingdom of God:

"Unless your righteousness exceeds that of the scribes and Pharisees, you will never enter the kingdom of heaven" (Matthew 5:20). The disciples may have been shocked to hear this. How could anyone's righteousness exceed that of the Pharisees, of all people?

"Not everyone who says to me, 'Lord, Lord,' will enter the kingdom of heaven, but the one who does the will of my Father who is in heaven" (Matthew 7:21). The kingdom could not be entered without accepting the lordship of Christ, but more would be involved in accepting it than a merely *verbal* acknowledgment of His authority.

"It is easier for a camel to go through the eye of a needle than for a rich person to enter the kingdom of God" (Matthew 19:24). Material wealth does not, by itself, disqualify us from the kingdom, but it tends to pull us away from God and most people allow that to happen.

"The kingdom of God will be taken away from you and given to a people producing its fruits" (Matthew 21:43). Blessings not used are eventually taken away (Isaiah 5:1-7), and so it is with God's kingdom. If we don't say yes to its invitation, there are others who will.

"No one who puts his hand to the plow and looks back is fit for the kingdom of God" (Luke 9:62). It is a strong dose of medicine to hear the Lord say that some are not "fit" for the kingdom, but that is the truth. And we are the ones who decide whether we're fit or not.

If we find ourselves challenged by what Jesus taught concerning the kingdom, it's because we *need* to be challenged. Whether we will allow God to rule in our hearts or not is the central concern of the gospel. And it's not a comfortable subject because, truth to tell, there is still in our hearts a good bit of *resistance* to God's rule.

The importance of this subject may be inferred from the fact that the New Testament contains more than 100 references to the kingdom. Jesus spent the three and one-half years of His ministry "preaching the gospel of the kingdom" (Matthew 4:23). Everything He said and did during this period of His life was related to the kingdom.

SEWELL HALL

July 4

TO HIM BE GLORY AND DOMINION

. . . from Jesus Christ the faithful witness, the firstborn of the dead, and the ruler of kings on earth. To him who loves us and has freed us from our sins by his blood and made us a kingdom, priests to his God and Father, to him be glory and dominion forever and ever. Amen.
Revelation 1:5,6

HERE, IN JUST TWO VERSES, IS A WORLD OF TRUTH ABOUT JESUS CHRIST. In his greeting to the seven churches of Asia at the beginning of Revelation, the apostle John ascribed glorious praise and honor to "him who loves us and has freed us from our sins by his blood." We could spend a rich lifetime pondering these two verses, learning to more deeply appreciate the King of kings and Lord of lords who has given us salvation and eternal hope.

The faithful witness. One of the claims of Jesus was that, having come from the Father, He brought us information about heavenly things that we could not know about otherwise. Speaking of Jesus, John the Baptist said, "He who comes from heaven is above all. He bears witness to what he has seen and heard, yet no one receives his testimony" (John 3:31,32). And Jesus Himself said, "I speak of what I have seen with my Father" (John 8:38). So when Jesus is said to be "the faithful witness," the point is that His testimony is *true* — whatever Jesus said about God can be believed and trusted.

The firstborn of the dead. When He was raised from the dead, Jesus became the "firstfruits" (or "guarantee") of our own resurrection (1 Corinthians 15:20,23). He has broken the power of death, the worst weapon of Satan (John 11:25,26; Hebrews 2:14,15).

The ruler of kings on earth. Jesus has been given "all authority in heaven and on earth" (Matthew 28:18). Earthly rulers are all answerable to Him; none is independent of His power. The kingdoms of men rise and fall only with His permission, and at any instant He can depose any ruler whose power stands against His eternal purposes (Psalm 2:1-12; Daniel 2:44; 7:13,14; Revelation 11:15).

Here, then, is One whom we may love and worship. *"To him be glory and dominion forever and ever."* Eternal with God the Father, He is the Alpha and the Omega. The world was created through Him, and He is moving history toward its final destination. For us, salvation means this: being found "in Christ" when He returns.

Christ himself is living at the heart of the world; and his total mystery — that of creation, incarnation, redemption, and resurrection — embodies and animates all of life and all of history.

MICHAEL QUOIST

July 5

What the Heirs Will Inherit: Eternal Life

. . . so that being justified by his grace we might become heirs according to the hope of eternal life.
Titus 3:7

PAUL'S MEMORABLE STATEMENT OF HOPE IN THIS VERSE IS SET IN THE CONTEXT OF A LARGER STATEMENT ABOUT GOD'S SALVATION. After speaking in v.3 of our sinfulness, he said that "when the goodness and loving kindness of God our Savior appeared, he saved us" (vv.4,5). To be in Christ is not to occupy some position which we have achieved by our own goodness. It is to have been rescued by a God whose tender love reached out and *saved* us.

In v.7, then, Paul wrote that those who are in Christ have been "justified." This language is from the courtroom, and it describes the fact that in forgiving us, God moved us from being "guilty" before His law to being "innocent." We stood before Him as lawbreakers, but He now treats us as those who have kept His law.

As Paul emphasizes, it was "by his grace" that God justified us. He "saved us, not because of works done by us in righteousness, but according to his own mercy" (v.5). How humbling this is! And yet, the way in which it humbles us is not humiliating. It energizes us, filling us with a wholesome desire to spend the rest of our days expressing our gratitude to God for His kindness.

The result of God's justification is that we are "heirs." Far beyond the greatness of any legacy we could receive from an earthly father, our inheritance from God is valuable in the highest sense of that word. When the time comes, we will hear Christ say, "Come, you who are blessed by my Father, *inherit the kingdom* prepared for you from the foundation of the world" (Matthew 25:34).

As heirs, we envision our inheritance daily: *we live fervently and serve faithfully in "the hope of eternal life."* The life we enjoy in Christ right now is a foretaste of the banquet that is coming, and we should be extremely thankful for it. But our inheritance is still ahead, so we must not lose our focus. *"Therefore gird up the loins of your mind, be sober, and rest your hope fully upon the grace that is to be brought to you at the revelation of Jesus Christ" (1 Peter 1:13 NKJV).*

In the cross is health, in the cross is life, in the cross is protection from enemies, in the cross is heavenly sweetness, in the cross strength of mind, in the cross joy of the Spirit, in the cross the height of virtue, in the cross perfection of holiness. There is no health of the soul, no hope of eternal life, save in the cross.

THOMAS À KEMPIS

July 6

SAINTS

To the saints and faithful brothers in Christ at Colossae:
Grace to you and peace from God our Father.
Colossians 1:2

THE WORD *SAINTS* IS A DESIGNATION FOR THE PEOPLE OF GOD. As we see in the text above, Paul addressed his letter to Colossae to "the saints and faithful brothers in Christ" in that place. (We see this same usage in Romans 1:7; 1 Corinthians 1:2; 2 Corinthians 1:1; and other letters.) All of the biblical terms used for God's people are helpful to study, since they give us important information about what God expects of those who are committed to Him. Today, let's focus on "saints" (and also "faithful brothers").

Meaning. To be a "saint" is to be "separate." A saint has accepted God's call to be redeemed from sin — seeking salvation, he has obeyed the gospel. But since not everyone has done that, those who have done so are "set apart." They are in a unique category, and they have a distinct identity. The apostle Peter put it this way: "you are . . . a people for [God's] own possession" (1 Peter 2:9).

Privilege. Considering the price that had to be paid for our sins, it is the highest of privileges to be among the saints. There is no room for a condescending attitude, for no one who is in Christ deserves to be there. All are there by God's grace. But surely, we can't appreciate grace and fail to see the honor which it bestows.

Responsibility. There are certain things — love for God and moral purity, for example — that are expected of those set apart for Him. God is patient, but ultimately, He will disown those of His saints who reject His lordship over their lives (Matthew 7:21-23).

But finally, notice that Paul also describes the saints in Colossae as "faithful brothers." In Christ, our common attachment to God as our Father creates a bond between us as siblings. We love those who, like us, have been baptized into Christ's death and are being prepared for an eternity with Him (2 Corinthians 4:16-18). In this family, each of the siblings is a saint. Set apart unto God, each has accepted both the privilege and the responsibility of living in this world as a person reserved exclusively for God.

[The word "brothers"] is a beautiful description of that surprising new fellowship which the church constituted. It was composed of masters and slaves, of rich and poor, of Greeks and barbarians, of Gentiles and Jews; yet all these members recognized themselves as forming an actual brotherhood, a household of faith.

CHARLES R. ERDMAN

July 7

THE LION OF JUDAH

Judah is a lion's whelp; from the prey, my son, you have gone up.
He bows down, he lies down as a lion; and as a lion, who shall rouse him?
The scepter shall not depart from Judah, nor a lawgiver from between his
feet, until Shiloh comes; and to Him shall be the obedience of the people.
Genesis 49:9,10 NKJV

WHEN JACOB BLESSED HIS SONS BEFORE HE DIED, HE UTTERED A VERY SPECIAL PROPHECY CONCERNING THE DESCENDANTS OF JUDAH. "Gather together," he said to his sons, "that I may tell you what shall befall you in the last days" (Genesis 49:1 NKJV). The expression "the last days" is a familiar prophetic expression, so Jacob was being moved by God's Spirit as he made these pronouncements to his sons. This is seen most clearly in his words concerning Judah: the time would come when a person from Judah would arise and "to Him shall be the obedience of the people."

Judah was the tribe from which David came, and it was to David that God made this promise: "When your days are fulfilled and you rest with your fathers, I will set up your seed after you, who will come from your body, and I will establish his kingdom . . . your house and your kingdom shall be established forever before you. Your throne shall be established forever" (2 Samuel 7:12-16 NKJV).

Genesis 49:9,10 looked ahead to the kingship of David — and more importantly, it looked beyond that to an even greater King. Jacob foretold that Judah would be the royal tribe, the tribe which held the "scepter" (the rod in the hand of a king symbolizing his sovereignty). But there would come another king whose sovereignty would extend far beyond that of any Davidic king. "To Him shall be the obedience of the people," said Isaiah.

Jacob said that Judah would be a "lion." It is no coincidence that Jesus is described in Revelation 5:5 as "the Lion of the tribe of Judah, the Root of David." *He is the King prophesied by Jacob when he blessed his sons.* His is an eternal kingdom that overarches every other kingdom that has ever existed. Since this kingdom is not "of this world" (John 18:36), it has no earthly throne or apparatus — *yet all the kingdoms of this world rise and fall at the will of this King.*

. . . we are more than justified in concluding that [Genesis 49:10] is a messianic text that adds to the Messiah's credentials the fact that he will govern, not only the nation of Israel, but all the nations of the world. The reason he can claim such a high prerogative is because it is his right to do so, for all rule and authority are derived from him.

WALTER C. KAISER, JR.

July 8

The Excitement of Finding the Messiah

One of the two who heard John speak and followed Jesus was Andrew, Simon Peter's brother. He first found his own brother Simon and said to him, "We have found the Messiah" (which means Christ).
John 1:40,41

TO BE A JEW IN FIRST-CENTURY JUDEA WAS TO BE IN A CULTURE OF GREAT CHANGE. Politically, socially, and religiously, the pot was boiling with trends and movements. If you cared about what was right, you would have had a number of decisions to make.

As various individuals turned up claiming to be the Messiah of Jewish prophecy, their conflicting claims needed to be examined. Were any of these people telling the truth? You could have been cynical (as many people are today in the face of religious confusion) or, realizing what was at stake, you could have dug in, studied the Scriptures carefully, and looked for the right answers.

But think for a moment about the *hope* involved in these world-changing events. Read Isaiah 52:13-53:12, for example, and ask yourself how you would feel if you lived back then and found out that this person had been born and was now proclaiming the gospel of God's kingdom. Could there have been a more exciting prospect than the idea that the Messiah might actually have come into the world? If you, like Andrew, could truthfully say, "We have found the Messiah," would you not be full of hope? Andrew did not yet understand much of what was involved in Jesus' messiahship, but he had seen enough to know that Jesus was the One the prophets had predicted. And he was eager to share the news.

Andrew's example is one we should meditate on. Perceiving that Jesus was the Messiah, he first found his brother and shared the good news with him. As one of the twelve who would become the Lord's apostles, Andrew would later preach the gospel to many people, but he began with his brother. Those closest to us may not listen as receptively as Peter listened to Andrew, but they should be the first ones with whom we share the exciting truth.

Andrew is characteristically the man who was always introducing others to Jesus. There are only three times in the gospel story when Andrew is brought into the centre of the stage. There is this incident here, in which he brings Peter to Jesus. There is the incident in John 6:8,9 when he brings to Jesus the boy with the five loaves and two small fishes. And there is the incident in John 12:22 when he brings the enquiring Greeks into the presence of Jesus. It was Andrew's great joy to bring others to Jesus.

WILLIAM BARCLAY

July 9

BOTH JUST AND THE JUSTIFIER

It was to show his righteousness at the present time, so that he might be just and the justifier of the one who has faith in Jesus.
Romans 3:26

THERE WAS PROBABLY MORE THAN ONE PURPOSE IN GOD'S GIVING THE LAW OF MOSES TO THE PEOPLE OF ISRAEL. But one thing was *not* in His purpose: to give them a tool whereby they could, as sinful people, work their way back into a perfect relationship with Him. No person who is guilty of sin, regardless of when he lived or what expression of God's law he lived under, has ever been able to keep enough of God's commandments to regain the perfection of holiness necessary for eternal life. By law-keeping, we can't pile up enough credits to counterbalance our debits. It simply can't be done.

But the penalty of sin is death (Genesis 2:16,17; Romans 5:12), and God cannot set aside that law arbitrarily. If He desires to save us from our sins, how can He do that? Is there any way He can maintain His own justice and at the same time justify us from our lawlessness? The answer, of course, is the cross of Christ. By taking upon Himself the death that was our due, He satisfied the law's demand, but He also made it possible to forgive us and treat us as if we had not sinned. In this way, God became both "just" and "the justifier of the one who has faith in Jesus."

It was a masterful plan, but it was very costly. It required the ultimate sacrifice on God's part, and our wildest dreams are not enough to imagine that kind of love. Yet the plan also has a requirement on our end: *we must be willing to accept it on God's terms.* We must give up the idea that we can ever be righteous enough to save ourselves — we have to accept that we will be saved "not because of works done by us in righteousness" (Titus 3:5) but by a "righteousness from God that depends on faith" (Philippians 3:9).

Obviously, such a plan leaves no room for us to boast. No human being, from Adam and Eve until the end of time, will ever have succeeded in being good enough to tip the scales of justice in their favor. It was on the cross of Christ that God tipped those scales — and it is "in Christ" that we enjoy the benefits of that.

In the self-offering of Christ, God's own righteousness is vindicated and the believing sinner is justified. For Christ occupies a unique position as God's representative with man and man's representative with God. As the representative Man He absorbs the judgment incurred by human sin; as the representative of God He conveys God's pardoning grace to men.

F. F. BRUCE

July 10

You Shall Not Add or Take Away

You shall not add to the word that I command you,
nor take from it, that you may keep the commandments
of the LORD your God that I command you.
Deuteronomy 4:2

THE FACT THAT GOD HAS SPOKEN TO MANKIND IS A MARVELOUS REALITY. But not satisfied with the contents of God's revelation, the human race has always had a tendency to "improve" His instructions, trimming away the objectionable parts and adding in other things more suitable. But Moses reminded Israel of the seriousness of this error. Speaking to the nation prior to their entrance into Canaan, he said, "You shall not add to the word that I command you, nor take from it." As someone has said, "Where God puts a period, we are not to put a question mark."

On the side of "adding to," the problem is that we tend to make rules where God has not. Concerning the gospel, for example, if I decided that to receive the forgiveness of sins a person had to be born in Brazil, I would have added to what God has revealed. But an example of "taking away" would be saying that the act of baptism is not necessary, perhaps arguing that it's "a good idea" to be baptized but it's not required for one's forgiveness.

Obviously, we need to be careful to take God's word as it is — making it *neither more nor less* restrictive than it is. Our study of the Scriptures must be diligent, and our attitude that of young Samuel: "Speak, LORD, for your servant hears" (1 Samuel 3:9,10).

If we accept that God has, in fact, revealed His will, the question is not whether we'd like to *modify* it but whether we're going to *do* it. And this confrontation with the word of God is a test of our character. There can be no salvation for us if we won't humble ourselves before God, and it is in our attitude toward the commandments of God that we get some of our first feedback as to how far along the road of humility we are. If we would be so presumptuous as to add to God's word or take away from it, then we've got some adjustments to make before any further steps can be taken in accepting the gospel. No doubt this need for adjustment is one reason that relatively "few" (Matthew 7:13,14) will follow Christ.

Once you and I are face to face with the Word of God . . . we can only accept or reject it. Jesus becomes the two-edged sword that cuts right down the middle, dividing us into believers and nonbelievers.

JOHN POWELL

July 11

When I See the Blood

For I will pass through the land of Egypt that night, and I will strike all the firstborn in the land of Egypt, both man and beast; and on all the gods of Egypt I will execute judgments: I am the LORD. The blood shall be a sign for you, on the houses where you are. And when I see the blood, I will pass over you, and no plague will befall you to destroy you, when I strike the land of Egypt.
Exodus 12:12,13

READY TO LEAVE EGYPT AS SOON AS THE WORD CAME, ISRAEL HAD BEEN TOLD TO STAY IN THEIR HOMES AND WAIT. Each family had eaten their Passover lamb, according to God's command, and the blood of the lambs had been put on the doorposts of their dwellings. As God went through the land in judgment that night, the people of Israel waited, trusting the protection of God's promise: "When I see the blood, I will pass over you, and no plague will befall you to destroy you, when I strike the land of Egypt."

Blood represents life, and the sacrifice of the lambs that night was a vivid reminder that death is the consequence of sin (Genesis 2:16,17). If the one who sins is not to die, the blood (i.e., the life) of another must be offered, one without sin and not under the penalty of death. Now, if the Hebrews were spared God's judgment on that night, it wasn't because they were free of idolatry (Joshua 24:14). It was in *grace* and *mercy* that God exempted them — "passing over" those in the homes where a lamb had been slain. This is a powerful object lesson. What can we learn from it about the gospel of Christ?

In the New Testament, there was an occasion when John the Baptist saw Jesus and said, "Behold, the Lamb of God, who takes away the sin of the world!" (John 1:29). Unlike the lambs in Egypt, which by themselves could never take away sin, Jesus was the perfect sacrifice, providing our full atonement. And if it was God's right to say that He would spare only those who put the blood on their doorposts, He can also set the conditions upon which His Son's blood will provide atonement. In neither case do those spared deserve to be spared. But in His mercy, God "passes over" those who will reverently accept the conditions of His grace. Before time began, it was always His plan to make this gift possible.

Before lambs bled in Egypt, One was given.
Before the worm tore Eden, pain was faced.
Somewhere, before earth's cornerstone was placed,
a hammer crashed in heaven — nails were driven.

KEITH PATMAN

July 12
You Shall Be Holy

For I am the LORD who brought you up out of the land of Egypt
to be your God. You shall therefore be holy, for I am holy.
Leviticus 11:45

BEGINNING WITH ABRAHAM, GOD BUILT A FAMILY THROUGH WHICH HE WOULD BRING INTO THE WORLD HIS SON, THE MESSIAH ("ANOINTED ONE"). When Abraham's family became numerous enough to be a nation, He delivered them from slavery in Egypt and established them in the land He had promised to Abraham. But prior to their entry into this land, God gave them this striking command: *"You shall therefore be holy, for I am holy."*

The root idea of *holiness* is *separateness.* Synonyms that come to mind are distinctness, uniqueness, unlikeness, difference, and the like. Unfortunately, we often limit our discussions about holiness to moral purity, but moral purity is only one of the ways that those who belong to God are to be separate. God's holiness does not consist solely in His moral difference; it includes every way in which His character is different from that of His adversaries. And if He commands us to be holy, we must learn to have a character that is distinct in the same ways that His character is distinct.

Israel's separateness from the world of its day anticipated the holiness of God's redeemed people in Christ, made up of Jews and Gentiles. Writing to Christians in the Roman Empire living under the threat of persecution, Peter quoted from Leviticus 11:45: "As he who called you is holy, you also be holy in all your conduct, since it is written, 'You shall be holy, for I am holy'" (1 Peter 1:15,16).

Sometimes holiness requires physical separation (and we are extremely foolish if we don't understand this). But with or without physical separation, holiness requires that our principles, our values, and our decision-making — i.e., our *character* — be different. And how could it not be? If we've repented of our rebellion against God, will that not make us unlike those still in rebellion? James asked it this way: "Do you not know that friendship with the world is enmity with God?" (James 4:4). For you and me today, this is an issue that requires some serious thinking and courageous choices.

It is time for us Christians to face up to our responsibility
for holiness . . . It might be well if we stopped using the terms *victory*
and *defeat* to describe our progress in holiness. Rather we should
use the terms *obedience* and *disobedience.*

JERRY BRIDGES

July 13

A Dangerously False Sense of Security

In the pride of his face the wicked does not seek him;
all his thoughts are, "There is no God." His ways prosper at all times;
your judgments are on high, out of his sight; as for all his foes, he puffs
at them. He says in his heart, "I shall not be moved; throughout
all generations I shall not meet adversity."
Psalm 10:4-6

THERE ARE MANY WAYS TO DISREGARD GOD. In addition to the obvious atheism of denying that God exists, there are many other varieties of atheism. In fact, millions of "religious" people are guilty of the kind of attitude reflected in Psalm 10 (and Psalm 14). They say they believe, but their lives are independent of Him. In my opinion, there is no worse sin than this "pious atheism." It is at the heart of many other sins, and it is the soul-cancer eating away inwardly at so many "good people" who are living well-adjusted lives in one of the "advanced" nations of the world.

"In the pride of his face" (v.4). It is nothing but arrogant to think that because we "prosper," our self-management must be working well for us. And Christ's letter to Laodicea (Revelation 3:14-22) shows just how deluded Christians themselves can be about this.

"I shall not be moved . . . I shall not meet adversity" (v.6). If we've shoved God out of the way and gotten away with it, we may think we're bullet-proof. But "I shall not be moved" is a poor prophecy.

"God has forgotten, he has hidden his face, he will never see it" (v.11). We figure we can squeeze in some years of disobedience and get back on track later. God isn't paying attention. He won't notice.

"You will not call to account" (v.13). In our foolish pride we suppose that we won't have to answer to God, or if we do, that event is so far in the future it doesn't make any practical difference.

To say the least, living this way is a *foolish* enterprise (Psalm 14:1; Luke 12:20). In the long run, it will not succeed. It is a precarious life, a house of cards that is going to collapse eventually.

But this pride is also *satanic.* The man in Psalm 10 does not worship Satan directly, but he is doing the very thing Satan wants us all to do: *manage our own lives.* And that pride is what has led us onto the downward slope of destruction. Since he can make it look so respectable and progressive, I imagine Satan is quite proud of it.

For a thing to be satanic does not mean that it is abominable and
immoral; the satanically-managed man is . . . absolutely
self-governed and has no need of God.

OSWALD CHAMBERS

July 14

Incline Your Heart to the Lord

Then Joshua said to the people, "You are witnesses against yourselves that you have chosen the LORD, to serve him." And they said, "We are witnesses." He said, "Then put away the foreign gods that are among you, and incline your heart to the LORD, the God of Israel."
Joshua 24:22,23

HAVING CHALLENGED ISRAEL TO CHOOSE WHETHER THEY WOULD SERVE GOD, JOSHUA THEN CALLED ON THEM TO PUT THEIR CHOICE INTO ACTION. If it is your decision to serve God, Joshua said, then "incline your heart to the LORD, the God of Israel."

That is a powerful way of putting it, is it not? *Incline your heart to the LORD.* The NIrV renders it "Give yourselves completely to the LORD," and the CEV, "You must decide once and for all that you really want to obey the LORD God of Israel." In a related text, we read of David's charge to Israel at the end of his life: "Now set your mind and heart to seek the LORD your God" (1 Chronicles 22:19). In all such passages, we hear God commanding His people to think of Him as more than a "maybe." Their hearts must be *inclined* to Him. They must *fix* their minds on Him. They must — and here is the main idea — be *devoted* to Him. This devotion must be the result of a conscious, deliberate choice they have made.

Of course, we have language in the Scriptures where God is the one who is asked to incline the hearts of His people. For example, "May [the LORD] . . . incline our hearts to him, to walk in all his ways and to keep his commandments, his statutes, and his rules" (1 Kings 8:57,58). And, "O LORD, . . . keep forever such purposes and thoughts in the hearts of your people, and direct their hearts toward you" (1 Chronicles 29:18). There is no contradiction here. God will help us and surround us with good influences, but it is we who must make the decision. In the end, only we have the power to decide what (or Whom) we will incline our hearts to.

If we are deciding whether to obey the gospel of Christ, this is what it all comes down to: *having alienated ourselves from God, will we or won't we give Him back our ultimate loyalty?* Had we never sinned, He would have always had our loyalty. But now, in Christ, He is making it possible for us to "incline our hearts" to Him once again. This is good news, much too good not to embrace enthusiastically.

It is but right that our hearts should be
on God, when the heart of God is so much on us.

RICHARD BAXTER

July 15

The Hearts of the Children of Mankind

. . . then hear from heaven your dwelling place and forgive
and render to each whose heart you know, according to all his ways,
for you, you only, know the hearts of the children of mankind.
2 Chronicles 6:30

SOLOMON'S PRAYER WAS THAT, IN THE YEARS TO COME, GOD WOULD HEAR THE PRAYERS OF ISRAEL WHEN THEY CRIED OUT TO HIM IN DISTRESS. "Render to each whose heart you know, according to all his ways," he said, "for you, you only, know the hearts of the children of mankind." Solomon knew that one important facet of prayer is that *God knows the thoughts and motives of our hearts.*

Although it is not always true that our troubles are the result of God's chastening for our sins, sometimes that is precisely the case (Hebrews 12:5-11). In regard to Israel as a nation, Solomon foresaw the same thing that Moses had warned about: if the people were unfaithful, God would bring calamity upon them (Deuteronomy 28:15-68). At such times, their prayers for *relief* would need to be prayers for *forgiveness.* So Solomon hoped that God would "hear from heaven your dwelling place and forgive."

When we pray today, three thousand years removed from the days of Solomon, what kinds of things does God know about our hearts when we pray to Him, especially for His forgiveness? It is to be hoped that He sees sincere hearts, truly penitent and willing to accept whatever requirements He has set for our forgiveness. Unfortunately, God often sees today what He saw in ancient Israel: careless, complacent hearts that are deep in denial of the truth.

It has cost God an enormous sacrifice to be able to forgive us. Knowing that, we should at all costs avoid *presuming* upon His grace, flippantly tossing off requests for His forgiveness as if such requests were a casual thing. We are told that, in Jesus Christ, we may come confidently before God's throne of grace (Hebrews 4:16), *but we had better not come with anything less than a no-strings-attached commitment to change our ways.* "No creature is hidden from his sight, but all are naked and exposed to the eyes of him to whom we must give account" (Hebrews 4:13). We may fool others about our hearts, but God is not deceived. He knows our motives — and His mercy is a severe mercy that screens out the triflers and pretenders.

He has sounded forth the trumpet that shall never call retreat,
He is sifting out the hearts of men before His judgment seat.

JULIA WARD HOWE

July 16

WHOLEHEARTED REPENTANCE VS. PRETENSE

Yet for all this her treacherous sister Judah did not return to me with her whole heart, but in pretense, declares the LORD.
Jeremiah 3:10

AS CHILDREN, WE SOMETIMES EXCUSED OUR FAILURE TO KEEP A PROMISE BY SAYING THAT WE "HAD OUR FINGERS CROSSED." The promise was not binding (we said) because we didn't really mean it, as indicated by the secret crossing of our fingers. A lawyer would say the contract was not a *bona fide* commitment made in "good faith" — we never intended to do what we said.

In the days of Jeremiah, the people in Jerusalem and Judah had become guilty of idolatry just like the ten northern tribes of Israel. Having been called to repentance by the preaching of the prophets, there had been occasional reforms, but the repentance had not been genuine or thorough. "Judah did not return to me with her whole heart, but in pretense, declares the LORD."

Were their "fingers crossed" when they said they would return to God? Did they not even intend to repent? We don't know. But in any case, the Lord said that they did not return to Him with a "whole heart." The person lacking a "whole heart" is one whose mind is not made up. He may not be deliberately dishonest in the statement of what he plans to do, but his plans are complicated by doubts. Like a man in a wedding ceremony who pledges to love his wife with "all his heart" but has not really closed the door of his heart to a previous relationship, the people of Judah only pretended that they had put away every "god" except God.

The opposite of wholeheartedness is double-mindedness. It is the problem of the person whose mind is torn between competing loyalties — and it is a problem we are told to get rid of. "Draw near to God, and he will draw near to you. Cleanse your hands, you sinners, *and purify your hearts, you double-minded*" (James 4:8).

There is no damage to our souls that Christ cannot repair. But He will not be manipulated by fake repentance on our part. If we expect His forgiveness and help, we'd better lay it all down before Him, with extreme honesty. No exceptions and no excuses will be allowed, and if we have in mind anything other than complete repentance, we'd better not insult Him by saying that we're "sorry."

Christ can do wonders with a broken heart
if He is given all the pieces.

OLD SAYING

July 17

Josiah, the Tenderhearted

". . . because your heart was tender and you humbled yourself before the LORD when you heard what I spoke against this place and against its inhabitants that they should become a desolation and a curse, and you have torn your clothes and wept before Me, I truly have heard you," declares the LORD.
2 Kings 22:19 NASB

WHEN KING JOSIAH HEARD WHAT GOD HAD PROMISED TO DO IF ISRAEL BECAME UNFAITHFUL, HE WAS STRICKEN WITH GRIEF. A godly man himself, Josiah might have hoped he would be spared the horrors of what was going to happen, but it didn't matter. If the nation was going to suffer, that was cause for great sorrow. God put it this way: "Your heart was tender and you humbled yourself . . . you have torn your clothes and wept before Me." Unfortunately, that is not the response that is typical when people are confronted with the reality of God's judgment upon sin.

One dictionary defines *tenderhearted* as "easily moved by another's distress; compassionate" (*AHD*). By that definition, Josiah was tenderhearted. If he had been one of the few godly members left in the congregation at Sardis (Revelation 3:4), he would still have been torn with agony to hear the Lord say to the group as a whole, "I know your works. You have the reputation of being alive, but you are dead" (v.1). Tenderhearted people are *grieved* when others (family? community? church? nation?) are in sin.

But as important as this point is, there is another that is even more so. When it becomes obvious that *we ourselves* are among the unfaithful, what is our response? Do we repent or do we retaliate? Hearing the statement of the gospel that we are under the penalty of death for our sins, are we tenderhearted enough to cry out with those on Pentecost, "What shall we do?" (Acts 2:37,38), or will we, like the crowd that murdered Stephen after he charged them with sin by his presentation of the gospel (Acts 7:54-60), attack the messenger because we are offended by the message?

The gospel "breaks" all of us. Some are broken by the honest recognition of their sin, and in their sorrow they embrace the gospel of God's forgiveness. Others are broken by an anger and a defensiveness that leads only to destruction. *O God, please break us in such a way that You may heal us and give us Your eternal life.*

We must be broken into life.

CHARLES R. RAVEN

July 18

God Heard Their Cry

. . . and the people of Israel groaned because of their slavery and cried out for help. Their cry for rescue from slavery came up to God.
Exodus 2:23

It had been four hundred years since the days when Joseph enjoyed the favor of Pharaoh, and in the interim the people of Israel had been enslaved by the Egyptians. In the grief of their bondage and hard labor, they cried out to God — and God heard their cry. We all know the story of Moses being sent by God to deliver Israel from Egypt and lead them to freedom.

Whether we are students of the Old Testament, the New Testament, or both, we've heard the word *salvation* many times. But the word has become a term with such religious overtones, we may forget the basic meaning of it. To "save" is to "rescue." I well remember when I was a boy that Mike Williams, my best friend at the time, saved me from drowning. I had dived off the high diving board, had the wind knocked out of me, and was floundering. Mike saw it, quickly swam over, and pulled me to safety. In other words, he "rescued" me (and still it makes me nervous to think what would have happened had he not acted so quickly).

When God heard Israel's desperate cry, He sent them a rescuer, a deliverer — in other words, a "savior." Moses did for them what they were helpless to do for themselves; he pulled them out of a very bad situation. And it was God who made the arrangements, He being moved by compassion for their groaning.

Physical slavery is horrible, but the truth is, we've all been in a much worse slavery. Jesus put it very plainly: "Everyone who practices sin is a slave to sin" (John 8:34). And unlike physical slavery, slavery to sin reaches into eternity and produces a plight too terrible to contemplate — *if we are not rescued from it.* But, of course, that is exactly what the gospel is about. God has sent us a Deliverer, and we, like Israel in Egypt, have to decide whether to trust that our Deliverer is telling us the truth about His mission.

Israel's rescue was by God's grace. So is ours. As with theirs (Exodus 12), ours depends on doing certain things God requires before He delivers us (Acts 2:37,38). The gospel must be obeyed to be effective, *but it starts with a heart honest enough to cry for help.*

Speak to him, thou, for he hears, and Spirit with Spirit can meet —
Closer is he than breathing, and nearer than hands and feet.

Alfred, Lord Tennyson

July 19

When We Don't Want To Be Delivered

Is not this what we said to you in Egypt: "Leave us alone that we may serve the Egyptians"? For it would have been better for us to serve the Egyptians than to die in the wilderness.
Exodus 14:12

HAVE YOU NOTICED THAT DELIVERANCE FROM TROUBLE IS OFTEN A GREAT BOTHER? Our present situation may not be ideal, but compared to the hardship of getting out of it, it sometimes looks like the lesser of two evils. Perhaps the best thing would be just to tolerate the status quo. After all, it may get better eventually.

When Moses agreed to return to Egypt and deliver the people of Israel from their slavery in that land, he had some difficulty getting them to accept him as their deliverer. But the real trouble began after they got out into the desert and realized how hard it was going to be, even with God's help, to make the trek to Canaan. "Is not this what we said to you in Egypt: 'Leave us alone that we may serve the Egyptians'? For it would have been better for us to serve the Egyptians than to die in the wilderness." From our perspective, we can see the foolishness of their thinking. *They were completely out of touch with how desperately they needed to be delivered from Egypt.* If they had seen the seriousness of their situation, they would have accepted any hardship in the process of being rescued.

In the modern culture of wealth, progress, and comfort, very few people see the need to be saved from anything that might be called "sin." The motto of modernism might be this: "We've still got a few wrinkles left to iron out, but we're doing pretty well."

Occasionally, however, people do see the truth about their separation from God. Yet they don't find the cure proposed by the gospel very appealing. When they realize that God intends to completely rebuild their character from the inside out (with radical surgery instead of bandages and pain relievers), their reply is much the same as Israel's. *Leave us alone; we don't want to be delivered.*

So a choice has to be made. We can stay where we are, which is easier, at least in the short run, or we can let the Great Deliverer begin to break our chains. Between now and eternity, there is a "wilderness" that will have to be traversed. But even the wilderness is part of an extraordinarily good plan to set us free.

Many of our troubles are God dragging us, and they would end if we would stand upon our feet and go whither he would have us.

HENRY WARD BEECHER

July 20

Sin Is Always Against God

How then can I do this great wickedness and sin against God?
Genesis 39:9

WHAT DO YOU THINK IS THE GREATEST MOTIVATION TO AVOID SIN? For most people, it would be the prospect of terrible things happening to them in this life as a consequence of their sin. ("If I steal drugs from the hospital and get caught, my nursing license will be revoked.") A thing may be wrong in principle and should be avoided simply because it is wrong, but most of the time we are more concerned about the consequences of getting caught.

But Joseph had the right idea in Genesis 39:9. Tempted to indulge in sin with his employer's wife, he not only said no, but he said no for the very highest reason: "How then can I do this great wickedness and sin against God?" He was a young man at the time of this story, but even at that age he understood that sin is always against God. Yes, it may damage other people horribly, and yes, we may damage ourselves with consequences that follow us for the rest of our lives — but with or without those consequences, sin is always a dishonor to the love of the God who made us.

We may see ourselves as being nice people. We may treat our friends and loved ones well, avoiding most of the obvious things that would have bad consequences in our relationships. Our good reputation and the love of so many who know us may testify to the fact that we are decent people for whom sin is not a major problem.

But sin is a problem we are all involved in (Romans 3:23). When we recognize that sin is a violation (even privately) of what we know to be God's will, it is clear that *we are not innocent — not a single one of us.* And if the gospel is about the forgiveness of our sins and the restoration of a right relationship with God, it is also clear that *we all need the gospel.* We can't be forgiven without it.

The temporal consequences of sin are certainly serious, and I, of all people, would not advise you to disregard those. But the eternal consequences are far greater. And the fact that, as Joseph knew, sin is always against God should weigh more heavily in our thinking than any social consideration. Separation from God is the worst of the worst things that can happen. And the best of the best news is that in the gospel God is willing to bring us back to Him.

Sin is essentially a departure from God.

MARTIN LUTHER

July 21

LIFE IN THE SON

The Father loves the Son and has given all things into his hand. Whoever believes in the Son has eternal life; whoever does not obey the Son shall not see life, but the wrath of God remains on him.
John 3:35,36

THERE MAY NOT BE A MORE PREGNANT PHRASE IN THE SCRIPTURES THAN "ETERNAL LIFE." It conveys a wealth of meaning beyond our present ability to understand (and certainly beyond my ability to describe). At the very least, let's avoid the mistake of thinking that it is different only in that it lasts longer than our present life. It is indeed "eternal" because it is unending, but more than that, it is of a different quality. It is not only *longer,* but it is *better.*

Notice that Jesus unequivocally affirmed that eternal life is "in the Son." When Jesus said that he who "believes in the Son has eternal life," He made a claim we must either accept or reject. But the witness of the writings in the New Testament is unmistakably consistent: *Jesus Christ is the path to eternal life.* At the end of his book, John said that he had written of Jesus' signs and wonders "so that you may believe that Jesus is the Christ, the Son of God, and that by believing you may have life in his name" (John 20:31).

But notice the contrast John makes in 3:36: "Whoever believes in the Son has eternal life; whoever does not obey the Son shall not see life, but the wrath of God remains on him." Having separated ourselves from God by our sin, we stand in the realm of God's condemnation, and if we refuse the pardon God graciously offers, then condemnation is where we shall stay. If a person rejects God's forgiveness, he can only expect God's justice — "the wrath of God remains on him." Between the grace of forgiveness and the justice of punishment, there is no third, neutral category.

Which motivates you more? Is it the joy of eternal life or the horror of eternal death? It is fashionable these days to downplay the fear of God's wrath as if that motive were merely old-fashioned and not appropriate as a factor in modern people's thinking. But in the Scriptures, the wrath of God is presented as the stark alternative to His love. The fact is, the world stands under the judgment of God, and the gospel entreats us to turn to Jesus Christ "who delivers us from the wrath to come" (1 Thessalonians 1:10).

Life eternal is the supreme good,
death eternal the supreme evil.

AUGUSTINE OF HIPPO

July 22

A Distinction That Will Be Unavoidable

They shall be mine, says the LORD of hosts, in the day
when I make up my treasured possession, and I will spare them
as a man spares his son who serves him. Then once more you shall
see the distinction between the righteous and the wicked, between
one who serves God and one who does not serve him.
Malachi 3:17,18

THE PEOPLE OF JUDAH IN MALACHI'S DAY HAD BECOME CYNICAL ABOUT THE DIFFERENCE BETWEEN GOOD AND EVIL. They were failing to make the moral judgments God expected them to make. But there was coming a new day — the day of the Messiah — when valid distinctions would be made. "Then once more you shall see the distinction between the righteous and the wicked, between one who serves God and one who does not serve him."

It is true that making accurate distinctions requires hard work. It also requires humility, cautiousness, openness, and a courageous willingness to have our previous perceptions corrected. But the fact that we may sometimes err and need to be straightened out does not mean we can "play it safe" by the avoidance of any distinctions at all. It means we make the best judgments we can — and then improve our judgments as we go along.

Am I in a right relationship with God? What about my loved ones, friends, and neighbors? These are extremely important questions; they can't simply be waved aside as being unanswerable. With regard to my own salvation, no less than that of the people around me, it is vital to see the truth of the matter. The last thing I would want to do is defer thinking about it until it is too late to do anything about reconciliation to God, for myself and those I love.

We must not shy away from saying that there is a difference between those who serve God and those who do not (Malachi 3:18). Since this distinction will be so clear on the Judgment Day that it will be unavoidable, we need to be pursuing a more accurate assessment of the difference *right now.* Rather than dismissing the question by saying, "Only God knows who His people are," *we need to be prayerfully growing in our ability to make this distinction rightly.* Yes, we must be humble. But we must also be honest.

Grant to us, O Lord, to know that which is worth knowing, to love
that which is worth loving . . . Grant us with true judgment to distinguish
things that differ, and above all to search out and to do what is well
pleasing unto thee, through Jesus Christ our Lord.

THOMAS À KEMPIS

July 23

THOSE WHO TAKE REFUGE IN HIM

The LORD is good, a stronghold in the day of trouble; he knows those who take refuge in him. But with an overflowing flood he will make a complete end of the adversaries, and will pursue his enemies into darkness.
Nahum 1:7,8

IT IS A DIFFICULT WORLD. The expression "survival of the fittest" would never have been coined in a world where there was no resistance to be met, a world where everything was just right for every creature. But obviously, our world is anything but just right for *any* creature. To survive, and then to thrive, requires struggle, and to lose the struggle is to suffer in many heartbreaking ways.

In such a world, the God of the Scriptures presents Himself to us as a God in whom people can find "refuge" — safety, sanctuary, and sustenance. In this life, the promise is not that the struggles will disappear but that there will be His provision of help. And with His promise of *help,* we can see that He is a God of *hope.*

There are those, of course, who portray faith in God as nothing more than wishful thinking. The argument is that in a difficult world, people naively and superstitiously believe in an all-powerful "Heavenly Father" because they can't bear to accept the alternative. Unfortunately, there are many for whom faith is nothing more than this. But the fact is, faith can be — and *should* be — the deliberate, rational choice to trust a God who has revealed Himself to mankind and proven over and over again that He can be trusted to be our refuge. If the God of the Scriptures does not exist, we will just have to do the best we can on our own. But if He does exist, we are fools not to seek His wisdom and strength.

Really, it is no different today than it has been since the beginning of recorded history: human beings have always faced an ultimate choice. Do we lay aside our self-sufficiency and trust in our Creator, or do we double down on our self-sufficiency and trust in human effort and ingenuity? This is the basic choice we face.

Either way, our choice has momentous consequences. And the worst thing we can do is try to have it both ways. So to my fellow believers, I say: *do not say you "trust" God if you do not.* God "knows those who take refuge in him." So what does He know about you? Does He see trust? Or does He see just another worldly optimist?

God sends no one away empty except
those who are full of themselves.

DWIGHT LYMAN MOODY

July 24

You Never Know Who Will Be Receptive

And the people of Nineveh believed God. They called for a fast and put on sackcloth, from the greatest of them to the least of them.
Jonah 3:5

JONAH WAS RELUCTANT TO ACCEPT THE ASSIGNMENT TO GO TO NINEVEH AND PREACH A MESSAGE OF REPENTANCE. But finally he did go, and the people of Nineveh recognized that what Jonah said was true. They repented, turning away from what was sinful in their habits. If Nineveh existed today, it probably wouldn't be high on our list of places to preach the gospel — yet Nineveh repented.

I once knew an evangelist who frequently said, "Let the gospel do the culling." In other words, rather than predetermine who we think will be receptive to the gospel of Christ, those of us who are Christians need to broadcast the message far and wide — and let the message itself determine who will respond and who will not. We may be surprised that some are more receptive than we thought they would be. We should learn to "never say never."

The fact is, receptiveness to the gospel is determined by hidden factors within a person's heart. We can't see these, but God can. He knows who is ready to hear, whether it is someone we might recognize as an honest hearer or not. Even in a place like Corinth, whose depravity was known far and wide, God encouraged Paul: "Do not be afraid, but go on speaking and do not be silent, for I am with you, and no one will attack you to harm you, for I have many in this city who are my people" (Acts 18:9,10).

We tend to see people only through the lens of their past. That is understandable because, unlike God, we can't see their future; the only information available to us is historical. And unfortunately, if a person's past is so sinful (as was the case with Nineveh) that we deem them unfit candidates for God's grace, then we probably won't "waste the time" it takes to present the gospel to them.

But what about our own need for the gospel? Looking only at our past (which may be much like Nineveh's), we may not be able to see what God could make possible if we would repent and embrace the gospel wholeheartedly. But the gospel can be just as powerful for us as for anybody else. It will take courage and humility — but repentance is a doorway far too wonderful not to enter.

Repentance is another way of saying that the bad past is to be considered as the starting point for better things.

DOROTHY L. SAYERS

July 25

How Do We "Rend" Our Hearts?

"Yet even now," declares the LORD, "return to me with all your heart, with fasting, with weeping, and with mourning; and rend your hearts and not your garments."
Joel 2:12,13

JOEL'S MESSAGE FROM GOD, LIKE THAT OF ALL THE PROPHETS, WAS THAT THE PEOPLE SHOULD TURN AWAY FROM THE SINS THAT HAD CUT THEM OFF FROM GOD. Even when God's long-delayed judgment had fallen upon them, it was possible, as long as life lasted, for them to repent and be restored to God's favor and blessing.

True repentance from sin is a matter of serious sincerity — much more than a quick "Sorry about that; I guess I could have done better." With Israel, God pleaded for deep sorrow: "Return to me with all your heart, with fasting, with weeping, and with mourning." Hearts touched by the knowledge of sin will grieve in a way that shows up in things like weeping and fasting. But it is the heart that is the primary concern. An outward show of sorrow would mean nothing to God if the heart was not penitent. So God said to the wayward, "Rend your hearts and not your garments."

This does not mean that outward manifestations of godly sorrow are unimportant. The saying in Joel is an example of the familiar "not-but" construction found in the Scriptures: "Not [this], but [that]." When, for example, Jesus said, "Do not work for the food that perishes, but for the food that endures to eternal life" (Jn. 6:27), He was not denying the importance of working for our physical food; rather, He was giving priority to our spiritual concerns. So it is with repentance. Outward expressions of grief are not to be suppressed, but it is in our hearts, first of all, that God looks for sorrow.

So how, exactly, do we rend our hearts? We do it by confronting the awfulness of our sin, without self-pity or any evasion of responsibility. We grieve how we've selfishly rebelled against God's love. And we yearn — *we weep* — to be with Him in eternity, whatever we may have lost by our sins in the here and now.

Fallen man is not simply an imperfect creature who needs improvement; he is a rebel who must lay down his arms . . . This process of surrender — this movement full speed astern — is what Christians call repentance. Now repentance is no fun at all. It is something much harder than merely eating humble pie. It means unlearning all the self-conceit and self-will that we have been training ourselves into for thousands of years. It means killing part of yourself, undergoing a kind of death.

C. S. LEWIS

July 26

Job's Faith

For I know that my Redeemer lives,
and at the last he will stand upon the earth.
And after my skin has been thus destroyed,
yet in my flesh I shall see God.
Job 19:25,26

JOB WAS A MAN WHO RESOLUTELY REFUSED TO GIVE UP HIS FAITH IN GOD. Having seen, when the sun was shining, that there were strong, compelling reasons to trust God, he did not let go of those reasons when the darkness closed in. He hung on to hope: "I shall see God" was the confidence that held him steady.

It is always disappointing to me to hear people mock faith as nothing more than "wishful thinking." Granted, there are some who believe only because it makes them more comfortable (just as there are some whose doubt is mainly emotional), but faith, rightly considered, is not wishful thinking. It is confidence in unseen, intangible realities *based on solid evidence.* If the evidence is strong enough, there need not be anything flimsy about faith. It can be as strong as the reasons that support it. Faith "is a well-grounded assurance of that for which we hope, and a conviction of the reality of things which we do not see" (Hebrews 11:1 Weymouth).

It is an obvious fact that this life can be hard. I remember years ago being at Arnold's Country Kitchen in Nashville, Tennessee, sitting across the table from a crusty old drifter. Somehow we got to talking about death, and he said, "I ain't afraid to die; it's gettin' to that point that's got me worried." It reminded me of Napoleon Bonaparte's saying that "it requires more courage to suffer than to die." Job would have agreed. And today, we are naive if we think our faith is always going to be easy to maintain. To embark on the Christian life is to enter upon an endurance test in which our resolve will have to be very strong.

For all Job knew, he was going to die from his afflictions, but if so, he was unconcerned: "For I know that my Redeemer lives, and at the last he will stand upon the earth." Job knew God would be waiting for him on the other side. "And after my skin has been thus destroyed, yet in my flesh I shall see God." Ultimately, that is what faith always is: trust in the God who is — *for now* — unseen.

Faith is to believe what we do not see;
and the reward of this faith is to see what we believe.

AUGUSTINE OF HIPPO

July 27

Delivered by a Strong Hand

They are your servants and your people, whom you
have redeemed by your great power and by your strong hand.
Nehemiah 1:10

The people of Jerusalem of whom Nehemiah spoke had been delivered from their captivity in Babylon. But this deliverance, as great as it was, foreshadowed a much greater deliverance: the redemption of the human race from slavery to sin.

To "redeem" is to rescue someone from a plight in which they are helpless to deliver themselves. In Nehemiah's day, the Jewish exiles who had returned to Jerusalem had been able to do so only because God made it possible. So Nehemiah could pray to God, "They are your servants and your people, whom you have redeemed."

When it comes to the matter of our sins against God, none of us can deliver ourselves from the consequences of those sins. No amount of moral effort would ever be enough to restore the innocence we had before we sinned. Our efforts are good as far as they go, but a whole lifetime of self-improvement would not be enough. Our sins have alienated us from our Creator, and that alienation is a gulf we are simply not able to bridge by our own diligence.

But just as it was by God's "great power" and "strong hand" that the Jews were delivered from Babylon, the same strength is sufficient to bring us out from the captivity of sin and death. Indeed, the power required to deal with sin is greater than what was needed to release the Jews from Babylon. In both cases, however, it is God's power. He is our Deliverer just as much as He is our Creator.

So heaven will not be for those who have earned it by their own success in being good people; *it will be for those who have been rescued by the Great Redeemer.* Will we accept this rescue or reject it? Answering that question is the most crucial challenge we will ever face in our passage through this world. But we need not make it harder than it is. Jesus waits eagerly to welcome us to His forgiveness. He is not looking for perfect people. He is looking for sinful people humble enough to see how much they need His forgiveness.

If I had the wisdom of Solomon, the patience of John,
the meekness of Moses, the strength of Samson, the obedience of
Abraham, the compassion of Joseph, the tears of Jeremiah, the poetic skill
of David, the prophetic voice of Elijah, the courage of Daniel, the greatness
of John the Baptist, the endurance and love of Paul, I would still need
redemption through Christ's blood, the forgiveness of sin.

R. L. Wheeler

July 28

There Arose Another Generation

. . . there arose another generation after them who
did not know the LORD or the work that he had done for Israel.
Judges 2:10

THE LAND OF CANAAN FINALLY HAVING BEEN GIVEN TO ISRAEL, THEY ENTERED UPON A TIME OF PEACE. "The people of Israel went each to his inheritance to take possession of the land. And the people served the LORD all the days of Joshua, and all the days of the elders who outlived Joshua, who had seen all the great work that the LORD had done for Israel" (Judges 2:6,7). But then it says, "All that generation . . . were gathered to their fathers. And there arose another generation after them who did not know the LORD or the work that he had done for Israel" (v.10). Once the struggles were over, it did not take many generations before God was forgotten.

Despite the numerous negative aspects of "warfare," spiritual as well as physical, it is a fact that strength, not to mention gratitude, is generally built up through struggle and testing. (If you think danger is never one of the "good and perfect gifts" that might come from God, meditate on Judges 3:1-4 for a while.)

As far as our dealings with God are concerned, there are many kinds of ease that tend to weaken us spiritually. If there was no more contending for the faith that needed to be done (Jude 3), no more hard work for others' benefit (2 Corinthians 12:15), no more cost to our discipleship (Luke 14:28), and no more cross to be borne (Mark 8:34), we would be foolish to think that a generation would not arise that "did not know the LORD." No age, including our own, has ever been exempt from the law of spiritual entropy.

I fear that the very fact of social acceptability has hurt the Lord's people in countries where "Christianity" is the predominant religion. Couple that with the affluence, ease, and comfort that many of us have gotten used to, and the mixture is a lethal cocktail. This essay is not a recommendation for seeing how hard we can make our lives. It is intended to be a warning: *we are never in greater peril than when the war is over and peace has broken out.*

Events and circumstances awaken our religion, as though
there were no need to pray to God except in illness and sorrow.
As soon as affairs take a turn for the better and the danger is past, our
devotion vanishes; the most we think of doing is to thank God for
the successful end of our troubles; after a short act of gratitude
we forget him and think of nothing but our pleasures.

JEAN NICOLAS GROU

July 29

Once Saved, Is It Possible for Us to Be Lost?

For if, after they have escaped the defilements of the world through the knowledge of our Lord and Savior Jesus Christ, they are again entangled in them and overcome, the last state has become worse for them than the first. For it would have been better for them never to have known the way of righteousness than after knowing it to turn back from the holy commandment delivered to them.
2 Peter 2:20,21

PETER'S WORDS INDICATE THAT IT IS INDEED POSSIBLE FOR A SAVED PERSON TO RETURN TO A LOST CONDITION. In fact, he says that "the last state has become worse for them than the first." Despite what the Calvinistic "once-saved-always-saved" doctrine teaches, it is necessary for those who have obeyed the gospel to remain faithful to Christ — or they will forfeit their eternal salvation.

It is sometimes argued that if a person appears to fall away from the faith, he or she was never really saved in the first place. But this won't work. There are too many texts in the Scriptures where people who were in a saved relationship with the Lord either apostatized or were warned against doing so.

We might think of Simon the Magician (Acts 8:9-24), the heresy in Galatia (1:6-9), the exhortations in Hebrews (3:6,12-14; 4:1,11; 6:11,12; 10:23,29,35-39; 12:1; etc.), Peter's concern for his brethren (2 Peter 1:5-15; 3:17,18), or Paul's warnings while in Ephesus (Acts 20:31) — and these are just a sample. It cannot be said that these warnings against apostasy were not really warnings or that the people they were addressed to were not in a saved relationship with Christ. The scriptural evidence is clear: *after being saved from our sins, we will return to being lost if we do not remain faithful to Christ.*

It is no wonder, then, that we see so many exhortations in the Scriptures to keep the faith. These warnings are greatly needed. We should not be doubtful about our salvation, but as long as Satan is still in business, we can't afford to be complacent (1 Peter 5:8-11).

As you can see, the bottom line is *freedom of the will.* We are free to choose whether we'll obey the gospel. But freedom doesn't stop there. Having obeyed the gospel, we are free to remain saved or change our minds and go back to being lost. When He saves us, God does not take away our freedom — or its consequences.

Freedom of the will means that all who have the capacity to exercise their will freely are responsible for the decisions they make and the consequences that arise from those decisions.

DAVID MCCLISTER

July 30

Love's Fire

. . . for love is strong as death, jealousy is fierce as the grave. Its flashes are flashes of fire, the very flame of the LORD. Many waters cannot quench love, neither can floods drown it. If a man offered for love all the wealth of his house, he would be utterly despised.
Song of Solomon 8:6,7

JESUS SAID TO HIS DISCIPLES, "IF YOU LOVE ME, YOU WILL KEEP MY COMMANDMENTS" (JOHN 14:15). This is not only a *requirement* that those who love Jesus must keep His commandments; it is a statement of *result,* i.e., what will happen if we do, in fact, love Him. The doing of Jesus' will flows naturally from a heart that loves Him.

In a perfectly healthy spiritual state, our actions toward God would be moved by a beautiful blend of various motives. None of these motives would be insignificant or inappropriate. Yet while there are other honorable motives for doing God's will, most people would agree that love is the highest. No motive is more noble.

But we can just as easily say that love is the most *powerful* motive in our relationship to God. It is no wonder that the poets have always compared love to fire. As Solomon described it, love's "flashes are flashes of fire, the very flame of the LORD. Many waters cannot quench love, neither can floods drown it." If you're not a poet but an accountant or an engineer, you might prefer that Solomon had just said, "Love is very powerful." But Solomon knew, personally as well as poetically, the *fire* of love's power. (Tragically, he also knew how destructive that fire can be when it's not rightly governed.) There is simply no force in the world more potent than love — and when love is a holy passion for God, it is a force that will move us to do what is right with fiery energy. "Love in its essence is spiritual fire" (Emanuel Swedenborg).

As we reflect on obeying the gospel, we would do well to ponder what it is that we most truly love. Perhaps we love God sincerely but have been ill-informed on what the Scriptures teach about how one becomes a Christian. If so, we need to act on our new knowledge and continue learning to love God with more depth. But maybe our lives are what they are right now because, in all honesty, the love of God has not been our primary passion. If that be the case, it is urgent that we learn to love God. If not, the lesser things we love more than Him will be the death of us.

We are shaped and fashioned by what we love.
JOHANN WOLFGANG VON GOETHE

July 31

ISRAEL'S DAY OF ATONEMENT

Now on the tenth day of this seventh month is the Day of Atonement.
Leviticus 23:27

ONCE A YEAR, THE PEOPLE OF ISRAEL WERE TO OBSERVE A "DAY OF ATONEMENT." The Lord required them to make special sacrifices for sin on this day, and on this day only, once a year, the High Priest entered the Most Holy Place in the tabernacle with the blood of the sacrifices. All of the observances on this most special day of the year were detailed in Leviticus 16:1-34 and 23:26-32.

On this day, a day when Israel was vividly reminded of the seriousness of sin, the Lord said, "you shall afflict yourselves" Leviticus 23:27 ESV). The Hebrew word translated "afflict" denotes various forms of self-denial. The NIV renders it "deny yourselves" and the NASB, "humble yourselves." (See its use also in texts like Psalm 35:13 and Isaiah 58:3.) The most usual form of this self-denial would be fasting, of course, but it might involve other forms of abstinence that would reflect *a deeply humble and penitent frame of mind.* However much Israel might rejoice in the Lord's salvation and be grateful for His blessings, on this day each year they were to ponder the seriousness of sin and afflict their souls.

The blood of the animals that were sacrificed on the Day of Atonement could not by themselves provide the forgiveness of sins. That would require nothing less than the perfect sacrifice of God's own Son, a sacrifice that would reach back to provide their forgiveness just as it reaches forward to provide ours today.

The writer of Hebrews says, "For Christ has entered, not into holy places made with hands, which are copies of the true things, but into heaven itself, now to appear in the presence of God on our behalf. Nor was it to offer himself repeatedly, as the high priest enters the holy places every year with blood not his own, for then he would have had to suffer repeatedly since the foundation of the world. But as it is, he has appeared once for all at the end of the ages to put away sin by the sacrifice of himself" (Hebrews 9:24-26).

Israel was fortunate to have such a stark reminder of the price of sin's atonement. And today, we lose much of the depth that should characterize our godliness if we never think of sin except to say, "Sin? It's no big deal. God's grace has got me covered."

One reason sin flourishes is that it is treated
like a cream puff instead of a rattlesnake.

BILLY SUNDAY

August 1

CHRIST'S AMBASSADORS

Therefore, we are ambassadors for Christ, God making his appeal through us. We implore you on behalf of Christ, be reconciled to God.
2 Corinthians 5:20

SPEAKING AS ONE OF THE APOSTLES, PAUL SAID, "WE ARE AMBASSADORS FOR CHRIST." This is a statement worth contemplating.

An ambassador is an authoritative spokesman for a government. When he speaks for the government that is behind him, his words carry the full weight of the government itself. In this way, the apostles were Christ's ambassadors, commissioned to speak with His full authority as the foundation of the church was being laid (Ephesians 2:20). If you had heard an apostle present the gospel, there would have been no need to worry whether he got it exactly right. When the apostles spoke, it was as if Christ Himself were speaking, and they had the credentials to prove their ambassadorship: the "signs of a true apostle" (2 Corinthians 12:12).

So where does that leave us today? The apostles are dead, and Christ never said anything about a chain of apostolic succession. In the most important sense, however, we still have the apostles — *we have their teaching in the New Testament.* And that teaching is what everything must be measured against (Galatians 1:8,9).

But, someone says, aren't all Christians ambassadors for Christ? Perhaps we could say so in a very general sense (just as we could say that every American is an "ambassador" of the United States when he travels, expected to represent his country well). But in an age when people tend to think there is nothing to the gospel except each person's individual opinion, we need to keep the emphasis on the *authoritative* statement of the gospel by those who were, in the truest sense, the ambassadors of Christ.

Today, we would not be able to know anything definitive about salvation from sin if Christ had not made arrangements for there to be an authoritative deposit of the gospel in the writings of the apostles. So if someone tries to teach you and he says he's an "ambassador" of Christ, be sure to test the conclusions his study has led him to against the teaching of Christ's emissaries, the apostles. *But if you are satisfied that what you have heard is, in fact, the gospel, then by all means obey it. Accept God's offer. Do not turn it down!*

The gospel is not so much a demand as it is an offer,
an offer of new life to man by the grace of God.

E. STANLEY JONES

August 2

The Church Manifests God's Wisdom

. . . so that through the church the manifold wisdom of God might now be made known to the rulers and authorities in the heavenly places.
Ephesians 3:10

If God's glory is seen in the heavens, His wisdom is seen in the church. And as Paul points out, it is not just to human beings that the church reveals God's wisdom; it is also "to the rulers and authorities in the heavenly places." To every being God ever created, even in the heavenly realms, the church stands as an exhibition of just how wise the Creator (and Redeemer) truly is.

The plan of salvation. When we see how God worked out His plan to save us, we stand amazed at the wisdom of it all. None of it happened by accident. Every bit of it was "according to the eternal purpose that he has realized in Christ Jesus our Lord" (v.11).

The local church. The design of the local church reflects God's wisdom. The very idea that there needed to be such a thing as the local church was so wise that only God could have thought of it.

Incidentally, one of the most striking things about the church in the New Testament is its simplicity. Universally, it consisted of all of God's saved people, with Christ as their head (Ephesians 1:22,23). And locally, it was simply the saints in a particular area, led by bishops and served by deacons (Philippians 1:1). There was no ecclesiastical hierarchy that stood between Christ and the local church: no pope, no collegium of cardinals, no denominational structure — in fact, nothing like the complex religious "machinery" of today.

The wisdom manifested in the church as God created it will not always seem wise to the world. As Joe Fitch observed one time, God created the buzzard as well as the bald eagle, and neither reflects the glory and wisdom of God any more than the other. It is only the wisdom of the world that would turn all buzzards into eagles. And so it is with the church. There are some things about God's plan for the church that to our "common sense" seem unworkable, but those things reflect the "manifold wisdom of God" just as much, if not more so, than the parts we like. Let us beware of trying to create the church along the lines of our own wisdom. It was meant to reflect God's wisdom, not ours.

The whole history of the world is discovered to be but a contest between the wisdom of God and the cunning of Satan and fallen men. The outcome of the contest is not in doubt.

A. W. Tozer

August 3

After Becoming a Christian, Then What?

Rather, speaking the truth in love, we are to grow up in every way into him who is the head, into Christ, from whom the whole body, joined and held together by every joint with which it is equipped, when each part is working properly, makes the body grow so that it builds itself up in love.
Ephesians 4:15,16

THE MOMENT A PERSON PASSES FROM SPIRITUAL DEATH TO LIFE IS A GREAT MOMENT. No small part of the new Christian's rejoicing is a sense of *relief.* He has escaped, by God's grace, the greatest of enemies, and it is right to celebrate, just as it was right for Israel to celebrate when God brought them through the Red Sea and destroyed the armies of Pharaoh (Exodus 15:1-21). But after the singing died down, Israel's question would have been, "What happens now?" It was great to be alive, but there was work to be done and a wilderness to be crossed before Canaan could be reached. And so it is with the new Christian. The joy of deliverance is appropriately followed by the question, "What do I do now?"

The new Christian needs to understand that he has embarked on *a process of spiritual growth.* Yes, baptism marks the end of a person's old life, but it is the beginning of the work God intends to do to remake that person's character and restore it to the perfect image of His Son. Many texts speak of this, but none more clearly than Ephesians 4:15,16 where Paul says that "we are to grow up in every way into him who is the head, into Christ."

But Paul also emphasizes the importance of the church in the Christian's life and growth. The body of Christ needs — *and is needed by* — every Christian. It is "joined and held together by every joint with which it is equipped, when each part is working properly, makes the body grow so that it builds itself up in love."

So to the new Christian, I say this: *your relationship to God is your primary concern, and your relationship to the church is secondary.* But don't underestimate *either* of these parts of God's plan. (1) Your contribution to the church won't be what it ought to be if your individual, private walk with God is not rich and vibrant. (2) Neither will your relationship to God be what it ought to be if you don't participate in the mutual strengthening that takes place in the church. Congregations are given for our good. They are part of God's means of producing mature, heaven-ready individuals.

Churches: Soulariums.

P. K. THOMAJAN

August 4

Grace to Help in Time of Need

Let us then with confidence draw near to the throne of grace,
that we may receive mercy and find grace to help in time of need.
Hebrews 4:16

FOR THOSE WHO HAVE OBEYED THE GOSPEL, THE THRONE OF GOD SHOULD ALWAYS BE THOUGHT OF AS "THE THRONE OF GRACE." Needing help in so many ways and wanting our obedience to Christ to be steadfast, we can't do without the confidence of which the Hebrew writer speaks. In order to keep from faltering in our faith, we'll need to stay close to the throne of God's grace.

It is a marvelous thing that we may have this confidence, but in Christ, that is the good news. As a gracious God, He wanted to save us from our sins, and to do so, He made a sacrifice of unimaginable love. Having done that, there is nothing else He wouldn't do to help us, in whatever way we need Him. "He who did not spare his own Son but gave him up for us all, how will he not also with him graciously give us all things?" (Romans 8:32).

The character of God, then, is the key to the assurance of our salvation. God being who He is, we do not doubt that He desires for us to overcome every discouragement thrown at us by the enemy (1 Peter 5:8). *God will give us the help we need — abundantly.*

The prayer at the end of Jude's letter to his embattled brethren is appropriate to our point: "Now to him who is able to keep you from stumbling and to present you blameless before the presence of his glory with great joy, to the only God, our Savior, through Jesus Christ our Lord, be glory, majesty, dominion, and authority, before all time and now and forever. Amen" (Jude 24,25).

"A Mighty Fortress Is Our God" is surely one of the greatest hymns ever written. In it Martin Luther powerfully captured the essence of the Christian's faith: "Did we in our own strength confide, our striving would be losing; were not the right Man on our side, the Man of God's own choosing: Dost ask who that may be? Christ Jesus, it is He; Lord Sabaoth His Name, from age to age the same, and He must win the battle." It is, after all, a battle. But we do not doubt that we will "receive mercy and find grace to help."

Beneath the shadow of Thy throne,
Thy people are by faith secure;
Sufficient is Thine arm alone
To make the soul's defenses sure.

ISAAC WATTS

August 5

The Household of God

. . . the household of God, which is the church
of the living God, a pillar and buttress of the truth.
1 Timothy 3:15

THIS MEANINGFUL PASSAGE POINTS TO THE IDENTITY OF THOSE WHO ARE CHRISTIANS. Let's look at it phrase by phrase.

Household of God. It is not the church building but the members of the family who make up God's "house," as made clear by the translation "household" (ESV). This marvelous household is referred to by Paul as "the household of faith" (Galatians 6:10).

Church of the living God. The church is God's. It belongs to Him and can rightly be called "the church of God, which he obtained with his own blood" (Acts 20:28). The "church of God" is not a denominational name; it is simply a description of ownership.

Pillar and buttress of the truth. In a building, both a pillar and a buttress ("ground" in the KJV, or "support" in the NASB) serve a foundational purpose. But how does this relate to the church? It does not mean that the church is the source of the truth, for the authority of God's truth is derived not from God's people but from God Himself (John 17:17; James 4:12). The idea in 1 Timothy 3:15 is that the people of God exhibit the truth in an objective way, demonstrating its power observably. The truth is not produced by the church, but the church is produced by the truth, in order "that through the church the manifold wisdom of God might now be made known" (Ephesians 3:10). As the product of God's truth, the church shows just how true — and powerful — God's wisdom is.

Doing this is the privilege of the church, the people who, like Israel, have been redeemed from slavery (not to Pharaoh but to sin). Paul urged his brethren to live consistently with the gospel in the midst of those who are still rejecting God, "among whom you shine as lights in the world" (Philippians 2:15). And not just by their example, it is by their words that members of the "household of God" are to be "a pillar and buttress of the truth." To the Thessalonians, Paul said that "the word of the Lord sounded forth from you" (1 Thessalonians 1:8). This, then, is how God's family "supports" the truth — by living it truly and speaking it clearly.

No other organization on the face of the earth is
charged with the high calling to which the church is
summoned: to confront men with Jesus Christ.

J. W. HYDE

August 6

I WILL BUILD MY CHURCH

And I tell you, you are Peter, and on this rock I will build my church, and the gates of hell shall not prevail against it.
Matthew 16:18

PETER HAD JUST CONFESSED THAT HE BELIEVED JESUS WAS THE MESSIAH. When Jesus had asked His disciples, "Who do you say that I am?" (v.15), Peter had spoken up and said, "You are the Christ, the Son of the living God" (v.16). Following Peter's confession, Jesus said He would build His church on this "rock" — not Peter himself, but the truth confessed by Peter. This truth, that Jesus is the Son of God, is the foundation on which the church is built.

In the New Testament, the word *church* is a translation of the Greek *ekklesia,* which meant an assembly or gathering. Literally, it meant a "called-out" group, a convening of people who left whatever they were doing to answer the call to come together. So in Matthew 16:18, the Lord said that He would have *a group of people who would be His church, His assembly* — they would be separated from the world in order to belong to Him. We read in the Book of Acts about the fulfillment of this, where after the gospel was first preached following Jesus' resurrection, many people were baptized and began living as members of the Lord's church (Acts 2:1-47).

So the Lord did just what He promised He would do: He built His church. The very word *build* signifies solidity and permanence. The church's foundation is the truth about Jesus — *the truth that He loved us and died to forgive us so that we could become His people.* And because this truth is indestructible, the church built upon it is indestructible. *The gates of hell shall not prevail against it.* Satan could not prevent God's Son from accomplishing His mission, and he cannot destroy the church which the Son built.

We err tragically when we minimize the church and fail to appreciate it. Shame on us if we think the church is nothing more than a topic that unbalanced preachers of a bygone era felt they needed to stress. If Christ built His church, it deserves our awe. Let us not "damn with faint praise" (to use Alexander Pope's expression) that which ought to be gloriously and joyously exalted.

I love thy church, O God!
Her walls before thee stand,
Dear as the apple of thine eye,
And graven on thy hand.

TIMOTHY DWIGHT

August 7

CHRIST TO HIS PEOPLE: CONGREGATE!

For a whole year they met with the church and taught a great many people. And in Antioch the disciples were first called Christians.
Acts 11:26

MANY THINGS ARE NOW SEEN AS UNNECESSARY (AND EVEN HARMFUL) THAT USED TO BE VIEWED AS ESSENTIAL. One of these is marriage. Chelsea Sullivan, a friend who used to manage a Starbucks in Vermont, said that when customers would hear that she was married, they would express shock and disbelief. "Yes, a committed relationship is okay, but at this date why in the world would a seemingly normal person like you want to be *married?"*

Another now-seen-as-unnecessary concept is "church." When "organized religion" is spoken of today, it is usually not with admiration. As with marriage, many argue that the benefits can be enjoyed without the traditional obligations. "Yes, be a believer if you wish, but why would a spiritual person want to go to church? Nowadays, being spiritual doesn't require you to be religious."

First of all, I agree that the "institutional" concept of salvation is wrong. The church does not stand between us and God or dispense salvation on His behalf. But on the other side of the road is an equally dangerous ditch: the notion that there is no collective or "together" aspect of Christianity at all. Our vertical relationship with God is primary, but that doesn't mean that a horizontal relationship with other Christians is merely optional. So let's break this issue into two questions, the answer to both of which is "Yes."

(1) Does it matter if I "go to church" at all? You can't read what happened in Antioch in Acts 11:19-26 and imagine those people downplaying their duties to the Lord's church in their locality. And this is not an isolated text. The entire New Testament assumes that Christians will be members of local groups of saints.

(2) If I go, does it matter where I go? In the first century, it wasn't long before people began departing from the apostles' teaching (1 John 2:18,19; 2 John 7-11). Today, the problem is even worse. So we need to be careful. *Not every church we might check out is one the Lord would recognize as being true to Him.* And studying the Scriptures is the only way to know what markers we ought to be looking for.

The New Testament does not envisage solitary religion; some kind of regular assembly for worship and instruction is everywhere taken for granted in the Epistles.

C. S. LEWIS

August 8

Wanting to Associate with Faithful Disciples

And when [Saul] had come to Jerusalem, he attempted to join the disciples.
Acts 9:26

In today's reading and tomorrow's, I want to raise two important questions, both of which have to do with the idea of "church." The first is this: when a person obeys the gospel, is it necessary to associate oneself with a congregation of Christians?

I'd be less than honest if I didn't tell you that the answer is "Yes." As far as the New Testament goes, there is no connection to Christ available to us that does not involve responsibilities to Christ's people (1 Corinthians 1:2; 1 John 4:20-5:2). For one thing, we will need to partake of the Lord's Supper every first day of the week, and in the New Testament, the Lord's Supper was a congregational activity (Acts 20:7; 1 Corinthians 11:17-34).

But I must be honest with you on another point. The brief days in the New Testament when all congregations were holding to the truth of the gospel are long gone. Most churches now professing Christianity are practicing a religion that is not even a forty-second cousin to the first-century faith. So today, you will need to look carefully for a group that takes the lordship of Christ seriously.

Please know that I'm willing to help you. Wherever you live, I can put you in touch with brothers and sisters who are committed to the simple, unadulterated gospel found in the New Testament. Feel free to contact me, and I will do everything I can to assist you.

If you're a new Christian looking for a faithful congregation, you may feel as if you're looking for a needle in a haystack. It is sad but true that most churches claiming to follow Christ are not doing that — they're following their own preferences about what "seems right" (Proverbs 14:12). But don't give up. It took you a while to find the true Messiah, and in a confused world, it may take you a while to find the Messiah's faithful people. Don't be misled by the attractions of modern entertainment masquerading as religion. You are searching for the Lord's people, so "examine everything carefully; hold fast to that which is good" (1 Thessalonians 5:21 NASB).

It is scarcely possible in most places to get anyone to attend a meeting where the only attraction is God. One can only conclude that God's professed children are bored with him, for they must be wooed to meeting with a stick of striped candy in the form of religious movies, games, and refreshments.

A. W. Tozer

August 9

WHAT ABOUT THE "CHURCHES OF CHRIST"?

Paul, an apostle of Christ Jesus by the will of God,
To the saints who are in Ephesus, and are faithful in Christ Jesus.
Ephesians 1:1

WE HAVE LOOKED AT THE IMPORTANCE OF THE "TOGETHER" PART OF CHRISTIANITY. Now let's tackle another, more specific, question: if a new convert to Christ is searching for a faithful congregation (as we talked about yesterday), one that works together and worships God in the manner revealed in the New Testament, what about the groups that call themselves "churches of Christ"? Is it, more or less, among the "churches of Christ" that a person is most likely to find the individuals who are the people of the Lord?

First of all, if there is such a thing as the "church of Christ" denomination (and unfortunately, there is), that is something I would steer you away from. The concept of denominational Christianity is foreign to the New Testament, and I share no more spiritual DNA with members of the "church of Christ" denomination than I do with people in any other denomination (and in some cases less).

But, as you may know, I worship with a group that calls itself a "church of Christ," so let me explain. When Paul said, "All the churches of Christ greet you" (Romans 16:16), he was merely saying that those churches belonged to Christ, which the CEV makes clear: "All of Christ's churches greet you." Any church that *follows the Lord obediently* is "of" Him, but how it identifies itself to the public is a question of expediency, as long as the identification is scriptural.

That said, I must be transparent. Of the congregations that I know of personally, many, if not most, of those that *are* faithfully following the Lord (at least in the United States) do wear the name "church of Christ," not as a denominational label but as a generic descriptor. They just want to be congregations that are "of Christ."

So yes, by all means investigate the "churches of Christ." But when you visit, you'll need to look deeper than the name and ask lots of questions. *Sad to say, most of the "churches of Christ" departed from the gospel long ago.* That designation expresses a noble idea, but a congregation is not "of Christ" just because it says it is. As at Sardis long ago, the Lord would say to some today, "You have the reputation of being alive, but you are dead" (Revelation 3:1).

The people of God wear the name of Christ because they are His people;
they are not His people because they wear His name.

ROBERT F. TURNER

August 10

Faith: What End Is It Meant to Have?

. . . obtaining the outcome of your faith, the salvation of your souls.
1 Peter 1:9

FAITH IS A PRINCIPLE OF SUCH IMPORTANCE, WE MIGHT HOPE THAT EVERYBODY WOULD UNDERSTAND IT. But many people do not. And one of the most misunderstood things about it is what Peter here calls the "outcome" of faith. Before we go any further, surely we can see that this point is important. *If we fail to grasp what the outcome of our faith is supposed to be, we are bound to have trouble.*

In 1 Peter 1:9, the word translated as "outcome" by the ESV is *telos,* a common Greek noun which usually meant something like goal or purpose. The corresponding verb meant to set out for a definite point or goal. Even in English, however, these words are very flexible and can have different connotations; within a single usage, they can carry more than one meaning at the same time.

When Peter wrote that the "salvation of your souls" is the *telos* of our faith, he may have meant that heaven is the *end point* of our journey. Our salvation will be the culmination of our earthly sojourn. Also, he may have meant that salvation is the *consequence* of our faith. For some other result to be produced, a person would have to do something besides follow Christ. And lastly, he may have meant that salvation is the *meaning* of our faith. When we say that history is "going somewhere," we're stating that it has a meaning and is not purposeless. Similarly, the faith of the Christian is not random or absurd; it will have a meaningful outcome.

But if you've read the New Testament, you know something else about heaven: *it is the reason why people become Christians.* At least, that is what life in Christ was about in the apostolic age. Its purpose or intended goal was not a better world in the here-and-now; it was, as Peter saw clearly, "the salvation of your souls."

Stephen Covey said we should "begin with the end in mind." And the New Testament leaves absolutely no doubt: *the "end" we're trying to get to is heaven.* That's the meaning of my life, and I hope it's yours. Any other outcome will not have been worth the journey.

My life, as his,
slips through death's
mesh,
time's bars,
joins hands with heaven,
speaks with stars.

LUCI SHAW

August 11

If God Commands It, We Can Be Courageous

Have I not commanded you? Be strong and courageous.
Do not be frightened, and do not be dismayed, for the
LORD your God is with you wherever you go.
Joshua 1:9

FACING THE FEARS THAT LAY AHEAD OF HIM, JOSHUA WAS TOLD TO BE "STRONG AND COURAGEOUS." I can hardly ever read this text without thinking of my son Brock, whose favorite song as a child was "Dare to Stand Like Joshua." And I suppose there are few admonitions in the Bible of more practical value than what God said to Joshua. "Be strong and courageous" is extremely good advice.

But today, what I want you to pay attention to is God's question to Joshua. Just before telling him to take courage, God said, "Have I not commanded you?" This might mean that God was commanding Joshua to be courageous, but it might have another meaning as well. The situations in which Joshua would need courage were those that he would be in *as a result of carrying out God's commands.* And I believe God was saying, "Joshua, as long as you are doing what I expect of you, you need not fear. I will always give you the help you need to do what I have commanded."

In one of his books, C. S. Lewis had an entire chapter called "Is Christianity Hard or Easy?" And in typical Lewis style, his answer was: it is both hard and easy, depending on how you look at it and how you go about it. But Lewis would have been the first to admit that even when it is approached in the right way, Christianity still requires some very hard things. There is no way around this fact, and ironically, we only make the Lord's commands harder when we try to take the hardship out of them.

But if doing the Lord's will is hard, so what? If He has commanded it, then we need to be brave. There is no such thing as a command of God that is doomed to fail due to a lack of resources. He is God, and He will help us do whatever He requires us to do.

So as you consider obeying the gospel, many of the *what ifs* will be frightful. I won't insult you by saying that your path will be easy. But what I will do is share my own experience: *if God commands it, it can be done.* Our prayer is not for ease but for boldness.

I do not ask to walk smooth paths
Nor bear an easy load,
I pray for strength and fortitude
To climb the rock-strewn road.

GAIL BROOK BURKET

August 12

The Value of the Gospel Is in the Resurrection

If in Christ we have hope in this life only,
we are of all people most to be pitied.
1 Corinthians 15:19

IT'S AN AGE-OLD QUESTION WHETHER THE MAIN PURPOSE OF THE GOSPEL HAS TO DO WITH THIS LIFE OR THE LIFE TO COME. In our age, the emphasis is so lopsided in favor of the here and now, one hardly ever hears from the pulpit about eternity, and there are many who say that if the gospel gives us a happier life right now, the question of the afterlife really doesn't matter that much. Paul tackled this issue in 1 Corinthians 15, and he maintained, with all the other apostles, that the resurrection of Christ, and consequently our own resurrection, is the heart of the gospel. Leave out the preaching of the resurrection, and whatever it is that you have left, it is not the gospel of Jesus Christ. And Paul didn't duck the implications of this. If it turns out that there is no resurrection, Christians are pathetic to have believed such a lie. "If in Christ we have hope in this life only, we are of all people most to be pitied."

Make no mistake: there are many earthly (or "temporal") blessings that may accompany life in Christ. Yet none of these is guaranteed to every Christian. Some of us, for example, enjoy three meals a day, but many Christians, equally faithful to the Lord, do not. The fact is, the only blessing promised by Christ to *all* of His faithful people is *reconciliation to God,* leading to eternal fellowship with Him when our earthly tribulations have been left behind.

In this life, the Lord may deliver us from some of our earthly problems. He certainly is capable of doing so. But sometimes it is His wisdom to allow us to suffer hardship, as He did with Paul's "thorn in the flesh" (2 Corinthians 12:7-10). When we are called upon to endure, we do so with the promise that He will help us.

So if we are Christians, our hopes should not be pinned on deliverance from earthly hardships. The value of the gospel does not lie in its power to remove the pains and difficulties of this life; its power is the promise of resurrection to eternal life when Christ returns (1 Peter 1:3-5,13). May God help us, against the spirit of our age, to put the emphasis where the apostles put it. May we not destroy Christianity in the process of making it "relevant."

Christianity is in its very essence a resurrection religion. The concept of resurrection lies at its heart. If you remove it, Christianity is destroyed.

JOHN R. W. STOTT

August 13

God's Wrath Is a Part of His Character

Since, therefore, we have now been justified by his blood,
much more shall we be saved by him from the wrath of God.
Romans 5:9

HAVING BEEN JUSTIFIED BY CHRIST'S BLOOD IN THE PRESENT, WE SHALL BE SAVED FROM THE WRATH OF GOD IN THE FUTURE. It's true that salvation in Christ is a present reality (Ephesians 2:8), but Paul is speaking in Romans 5:9 of a future event: our being spared from the judgment that is coming upon the world. In 2 Thessalonians 1:7-9, Paul wrote of the time when Christ will be "revealed from heaven with his mighty angels in flaming fire, inflicting vengeance on those who do not know God and on those who do not obey the gospel of our Lord Jesus. They will suffer the punishment of eternal destruction, away from the presence of the Lord and from the glory of his might." Until that time, we wait "for [God's] Son from heaven, whom he raised from the dead, Jesus who delivers us from the wrath to come" (1 Thessalonians 1:10).

Paul is clear in Romans 5:9 that it is "by him" that we shall be saved. In Christ, we are assured of being protected from the wrath that will be poured out on the rebellious and disobedient. But even in Christ, we must not fail to take God's wrath seriously. There are none among us who don't need to be warned.

It is a mistake to think of God's wrath as something that needs to be apologized for — and it is hazardous to hurry past the many Scriptures that speak of this. The devil would love for us to forget the foundational truth that Solomon learned the hard way: "Fear God and keep his commandments, for this is the whole duty of man. For God will bring every deed into judgment, with every secret thing, whether good or evil" (Ecclesiastes 12:13,14).

Let us remember, then, that wrath is a part of God's character. If He treated evil as a trifle to be overlooked, God would not be the perfectly good God the Scriptures reveal Him to be. *I would even suggest that God's wrath is a part of His love.* Very likely, it is nothing more than our immature concept of love that sees a conflict between the punishment of evil and the blessing of righteousness.

God is love, not, God is loving. God and love are synonymous.
Love is not an attribute of God, it *is* God; whatever God is, love is.
If your conception of love does not agree with justice and judgment
and purity and holiness, then your idea of love is wrong.

OSWALD CHAMBERS

August 14

Which Sins Do We Preach Against the Most?

For all that is in the world — the desires of the flesh and the desires of the eyes and pride of life — is not from the Father but is from the world.
1 John 2:16

SOME SINS OPENLY FLY THE FLAG OF CORRUPTION AND REBELLION, WHILE OTHERS DO THEIR DAMAGE MORE PRIVATELY. Sins like pride and greed, for example, are every bit as destructive as unchastity (if not more so), but those of us who preach don't preach against them nearly as often. We ought to ponder why this is so.

Sins come in all shapes and sizes. They are all equal in that they will separate us from God, and that fact should make us treat every sin, even the "least" of them, as a deadly serious matter. But in other ways, sins may be different. Some are oriented toward God while others are more in the direction of society. Some we confine to our hearts while others erupt into outward action. Some have greater temporal consequences attached to them than others.

Admit it or not, all of us "prioritize" sins. If you're a parent, there are some sins you would be more greatly concerned about, if you saw them beginning to take root in your children's lives. Such a prioritization of sins can hardly be avoided, I think. My concern is not that we view some sins as more serious — it's that we get our priorities from the popular culture. Our "righteous indignation" is determined not by the scale of values in the Scriptures but by the ever-changing dictums of social stigma, political correctness, and modern psychology. *So the problem is not that we have a list but that our ranking of the most dangerous sins didn't come from Jesus.*

Looking into our own hearts, what do we see? Whatever mistakes we might make in our concern for others, we certainly don't want to underestimate the danger of the sins that beset us personally. So what would alarm you most if you took an honest look inside and saw different kinds of sin in your heart?

In heaven there will be no marriage and in hell, no fornication. But in heaven there will be love and in hell, hatred. *Even now, hatred will take you closer to hell than fornication will.* Sexual sin is an abomination and it will damn your soul, but if things like pride, anger, and selfishness are in your heart, you are already farther down the road to hell than if lasciviousness was your only problem.

The sins of the bedroom are not the only ones. The sins of the boardroom should be just as much a matter of concern.

RICHARD HARRIES

August 15

What If We Deny the Incarnation?

For many deceivers have gone out into the world, those who do not confess the coming of Jesus Christ in the flesh. Such a one is the deceiver and the antichrist.

2 John 7

WE CANNOT ACCEPT THE GOSPEL WITHOUT EMBRACING WHAT JESUS TAUGHT ABOUT HIS BEING GOD. This may go against the modern mindset, where there is no proposition that is not negotiable, but when it comes to the salvation of our souls, the truth about Jesus Christ is necessary. There are some facts such that if we leave them out, what we have left is not the gospel of Christ.

When John wrote, probably toward the end of the first century, what would later be called Gnosticism was beginning to influence Christians. Central to this teaching was a denial of the Incarnation: God actually taking upon Himself human form in the person of Jesus (John 1:14; 5:18; 10:30; 14:7-9; 19:7). To deny this, John says, is to be a "deceiver." This is a strong term, obviously, and John does not use it lightly. There may have been some who were sincere in their denial that Jesus was God in the flesh, but sincere or not, the effect of such teaching is always the same. If Jesus was (and is) the Son of God, to deny that fact is to be deceived — and to teach such a denial to others is to deceive people concerning the way of salvation. The consequences of doing that are frightening indeed.

It is interesting how John describes this denial. He says it is a failure to "confess" the coming of Jesus Christ in the flesh. Here, then, is a truth that must be *acknowledged* — at whatever cost. It is not an optional truth; it is what it is, and our choice is simply whether to confess it or not. If we deny it, it still remains true.

It would be impossible to overestimate the importance of believing in the Incarnation. The entire gospel depends on it. God could not have died an atoning death for our sins if He had not become a human being who was capable of being killed. So to leave this out of our "gospel" is to drain the gospel of its main meaning.

Admittedly, the idea of the Incarnation is unpopular today. It is viewed as anachronistic and unsophisticated. As were people in the first century, we might easily be drawn to a more philosophical rendition of the gospel. But an idea is not false simply because its "appearance" seems ungainly. Appearances can be misleading.

The handsomest flower is not the sweetest.

OLD ADAGE

August 16

The Essential Truth about God's Son

Everyone who goes on ahead and does not abide in
the teaching of Christ, does not have God. Whoever abides
in the teaching has both the Father and the Son.
2 John 9

THE GNOSTICS IN THE FIRST CENTURY, WHO DENIED THAT JESUS WAS GOD IN THE FLESH, PRESENTED THEIR TEACHING AS BEING MORE ADVANCED. But John was emphatic: *if we leave the teaching of Christ, we do not go forward; we go backward.* In fact, we separate ourselves from God. We do "not have God," as John put it.

The "teaching of Christ" is a teaching we must "abide in" if we hope to be saved from our sins. And whatever else the teaching of Christ may include, it certainly includes the fact that He was God in the flesh. This was the principal point of dispute between the Gnostics and the apostles of Christ. The apostles were the authoritative bearers of Christ's teaching (John 14:25,26; 15:26,27; 16:12-15), and as one of those apostles, John did not back down. *Either we adhere to the teaching of Christ and His apostles concerning the miracle of His Incarnation or we have departed from God.*

If there is one constant in human history it is that human beings always make things more complex as time goes along. So with regard to the gospel, it should be no surprise that very soon after it began to be preached, it began to be corrupted by those who wanted to make it more advanced — supplementing it with layers of increased complexity and making it more appealing to those who would be turned off by its original message. In this world, nothing stays in its original condition for very long. The tendency to "go beyond" seems almost irresistible. But to return to our point, John, along with all of the apostles, warned that to go beyond the teaching of Christ is not to improve the gospel; it is to degrade it.

"Everyone who goes on ahead and does not abide in the teaching of Christ, does not have God." That is one of the starkest warnings in the Scriptures. Elsewhere, John wrote, "If we reject the Son, we reject the Father" (1 John 2:23 CEV). But on the other side of this warning is a hope that is the very heart of the gospel. *If we have Christ, and hold on to the truth about Him, then God is not only His Father but ours as well.* It is amazing what doors truth opens.

Who stumbles upon Christ (who is a granite stone)
Lies shattered; grasp him and be led securely home.

ANGELUS SILESIUS

August 17

Reverence vs. Pick and Choose

But if you judge the law, you are not a doer of the law but a judge.
James 4:11

CONFRONTED BY GOD'S LAW, THERE IS A CHOICE WE MUST MAKE BETWEEN TWO ATTITUDES. Will we submit to it (and be "under" the law) or will we pick and choose which commandments to obey (and be "above" the law)? Most people obey God's law occasionally, when it suits them, but very few are willing to make an unconditional commitment to obedience and submit to the Father with a simple "not my will, but yours, be done" (Luke 22:42).

Those of us who live in the United States are heirs to several historical traditions, and we are often bound by these even in our attitude toward God's law. First, we are heirs of the democratic tradition, which today has morphed into the egalitarian idea that hierarchies (and their requirement of submission) are never anything more than a necessary evil. Rulers only rule with the consent of the governed, and only the people have the right to say what the laws are going to be. Second, we are heirs of the Enlightenment, in which human reason became the test of all knowledge. And third, we have inherited the theory of capitalism, with its modern concept of consumerism, in which the customer is always right and the market exists to give him what he wants.

Having breathed this atmosphere all our lives, it is hard for any of us to come to the Scriptures with a completely submissive attitude. Trained by egalitarianism, we are suspicious of the very idea of authority, and as children of the Enlightenment, we view human reason as the final judge of what is true and good. As capitalistic consumers, we simply shop the religious "marketplace" for doctrines, duties, and worship styles that please us. If there are any that don't, we pass them by just as conveniently as we would pass by a product at Trader Joe's that didn't fit our lifestyle.

These days, "reverence" has come to be a meaningless word. The idea that God is the sovereign Ruler of the universe — *and that He has the right to govern everything about us* — is hard for us to swallow. But we must rise above our culture. If God is indeed our Creator, we are not free to sit in judgment on His laws. The truth must be embraced and acted upon. Not just some of it, but all of it.

If you believe what you like in the gospel, and reject what you don't like, it is not the gospel you believe, but yourself.

AUGUSTINE OF HIPPO

August 18

IS IT POSSIBLE TO "DRIFT" AWAY FROM CHRIST?

Therefore we must pay much closer attention to what we have heard, lest we drift away from it. For since the message declared by angels proved to be reliable, and every transgression or disobedience received a just retribution, how shall we escape if we neglect such a great salvation?
Hebrews 2:1-3

IN CHRIST, WE ARE SECURE IN HIS LOVE AND PROTECTION, BUT OUR VERY GRATITUDE FOR GOD'S GRACE CAUSES US TO BE ALL THE MORE CAREFUL TO MAINTAIN OUR SALVATION. After affirming that God's "divine power has granted to us all things that pertain to life and godliness," Peter wrote, "Therefore, brothers, be all the more diligent to confirm your calling and election, for if you practice these qualities you will never fall" (2 Peter 1:3-11). Both of these points of emphasis are needed. Each makes the other more meaningful.

But think carefully. After obeying the gospel, we may cease being faithful to Christ and end up being rejected by Him. But under what circumstances might that happen? Is it only open defiance and rebellion that would cause Christ to turn away from us?

Most of us would say we're "doing our best" and any problems we have are only those of "weakness." So if we believe that a deliberate, premeditated choice to leave Christ is the only way we can be lost, most of us will overestimate our security (Revelation 3:17).

But even a quick look at the Scriptures shows that there are other ways we might turn away from Christ, short of outright rebellion. One is the problem of "drift." As Hebrews 2:1-3 warns, we will lose our salvation if we "neglect" it. The writer hoped his readers would not be "sluggish, but imitators of those who through faith and patience inherit the promises" (Hebrews 6:12). Since the way is hard (Matthew 7:14), sluggishness can be deadly.

In Christ's letters to the churches of Asia, there were warnings against a lack of love (Revelation 2:4,5), doctrinal error (2:14-16), lukewarmness (3:16), etc. If they didn't repent, these Christians were going to be disowned by Christ. Today, we need the same message of caution. Rebellion is a temptation for all of us, no doubt, but it is not the only way we may depart from Christ. In a dangerous world, our confidence needs to be balanced with carefulness — *so don't let the devil tell you that "drift" won't ever be a problem for you.*

The condition upon which God hath given liberty to man is eternal vigilance.

JOHN PHILPOT CURRAN

August 19

None of Us Has Anybody We Can Look Down On

The Pharisee, standing by himself, prayed thus: "God,
I thank you that I am not like other men, extortioners, unjust,
adulterers, or even like this tax collector."
Luke 18:11

OUR "FORGETTER" IS A BLESSING, BUT IT CAN ALSO BE A CURSE. Some things it is best not to forget. In the above text, for example, the Pharisee felt good when he compared himself to the tax collector. But his good feelings were ill-founded. Having forgotten the seriousness of his own sins, he had a false self-image.

The sins we were forgiven of. Gratitude for God's grace means that we rejoice in our salvation. We do not allow our past to drown us in despair. But even so, we must not forget how indebted to God's grace we really are. Our gratitude (and hence our joy) will always be in proportion to our remembrance of the debt that was erased (Luke 7:40-47). If we forget the sins we were forgiven of, our joy will dry up and turn into the boredom of self-satisfaction.

The sins that remain in our lives. Most of us are out of touch with the amount of sin that still resides in our hearts. It may have been many years ago that we obeyed the gospel and began walking with the Lord, and we may have grown a good bit in the meantime. When we compare ourselves to others, it may seem that we are doing pretty well, but compared to the Lord, it's obvious that we still have a long way to go. We need to be humbled by the recognition of how sinful our motives often are, even when our outward behavior meets the standards of Christian conduct.

There is nothing about any of us that is not known to God. "The word of God is living and active, sharper than any two-edged sword, piercing to the division of soul and of spirit, of joints and of marrow, and discerning the thoughts and intentions of the heart. And no creature is hidden from his sight, but all are naked and exposed to the eyes of him to whom we must give account" (Hebrews 4:12,13). What if God made known to the public everything He knows about us, even the "thoughts and intentions" of our hearts? Who among us would not be disgraced and ashamed?

Thanks be to God for His offer of mercy in Jesus Christ! But if we have obeyed the gospel and received that mercy, let's be careful in our thinking. None of us has anybody we can look down on.

The best of us are but poor wretches just saved from shipwreck.

GEORGE ELIOT

August 20

Humbly Receiving the Word

. . . take into your souls without pride the word which,
being planted there, is able to give you salvation.
James 1:21 Bible in Basic English

God's word, communicated to us in the Scriptures, is extremely powerful. But in addition to His word, God has also given us freedom. Depending on the choices we make as we respond to the Scriptures, we will become either more receptive or more resistant. So in regard to our dealings with God's word, James uses the word *receive* — or as some other translations render it, "take into your souls" (BBE), "welcome" (NET), "accept" (NIV), etc. The NIrV aptly paraphrases the entire sentence, "Don't be too proud to accept the word that is planted in you. It can save you."

In our approach to God, all of us are hindered by pride. It comes in such subtle shapes and sizes, we may not see it for what it is, but none of us can truthfully say we don't have any problem with pride. And pride never presents any worse problem for us than when it hinders us from "receiving" God's word obediently. When we study the Scriptures, if we reject what the text clearly teaches, put up our defenses, or make excuses to convince ourselves that it's not applicable to us, then the devil need not expend any more effort trying to claim our souls. He has got us already.

As we've already seen, whether or not we're receptive hearers is a matter of choice. If pride is hindering our hearing, we can change that. Doing so will be hard, even with God's help, but the first step must be our decision to heed James' advice: "take into your souls without pride the word which, being planted there, is able to give you salvation." God's word does not automatically save anyone — it is "able" (that's the word James uses) to save only those *willing to receive it*. And ultimately, it is by our deeds that we show how receptive we've been. As James says, "Be doers of the word, and not hearers only, deceiving yourselves" (v.22).

In these days when Bibles are so plentiful, many of us know a good many things about the Scriptures. Indeed, some of us have studied the Scriptures all of our lives. But frankly, out of all we have "learned," only a fraction of that has truly been "received." Today, let's determine that we will not let pride keep God's word from pricking our conscience and moving us to greater obedience.

The Bible was not given for our information but for our transformation.

Dwight L. Moody

August 21

HUMBLING HIMSELF, HE BECAME OBEDIENT

And being found in human form, he humbled himself by becoming obedient to the point of death, even death on a cross.
Philippians 2:8

GOD COULD NOT HAVE DIED AN ATONING DEATH FOR OUR SINS WITHOUT BECOMING A HUMAN BEING. There was only one sacrifice that could save us, and He had to take upon Himself human form in order to make that sacrifice. From our limited viewpoint, we have no idea what it cost Him to humble Himself in this way.

The word *humility* is the only word that can describe it, of course, but what we know of humility in our human relationships hardly seems sufficient. When God "humbled himself" by diving into the cesspool of the human race and allowing Himself to be killed on our behalf, He engaged in an act of sacrificial service that should make any of us reluctant to say that we've ever really given up anything for anyone. In eternally unfathomable ways, He "emptied himself, by taking the form of a servant" (Philippians 2:7).

But it was not merely by being humble that Jesus procured our salvation — it was "by becoming obedient." We have learned nothing of Jesus Christ and His gospel if we have not learned the necessity of *obedience.* Our ears are deaf if we can't hear the courage of His submission to His Father's will on the eve of His execution: "Abba, Father, all things are possible for you. Remove this cup from me. Yet not what I will, but what you will" (Mark 14:36). *But oh, how thankful we are for His obedience. We would be lost without it, would we not?* "Although he was a son, he learned obedience through what he suffered. And being made perfect, he became the source of eternal salvation to all who obey him" (Hebrews 5:8,9).

In the Roman Empire, there was no more humiliating death than crucifixion. Jesus was not the only person executed by Rome in this way, but the uniqueness of His crucifixion was that the most humiliating form of death was meted out to *the most powerful Being in the universe: God Himself.* And if God would submit to such a thing, what are the implications for us? At the very least, it means we cannot "follow" Christ or "accept" Him without emulating His example of obedience — even when it is costly.

To be like Christ. That is our goal, plain and simple. It sounds like a peaceful, relaxing, easy objective. But stop and think. He learned obedience by the things he suffered. So must we.

CHARLES R. SWINDOLL

August 22

Every Knee Will Bow, Every Tongue Confess

Therefore God has highly exalted him and bestowed on him the name that is above every name, so that at the name of Jesus every knee should bow, in heaven and on earth and under the earth, and every tongue confess that Jesus Christ is Lord, to the glory of God the Father.
Philippians 2:9-11

CHRIST'S HUMILIATION WAS FOLLOWED A FEW WEEKS LATER BY HIS EXALTATION. The writer of Hebrews pointed his brethren to the example of Jesus, "who for the joy that was set before him endured the cross, despising the shame, *and is seated at the right hand of the throne of God*" (Hebrews 12:2). This is a reference to the prophecy of David in Psalm 110:1, a prophecy alluded to several times in the New Testament and always linked to the ascension of Jesus back to heaven following His resurrection: "So then the Lord Jesus, after he had spoken to them, was taken up into heaven and sat down at the right hand of God" (Mark 16:19).

In Philippians 2:9, Paul said that "God has highly exalted him and bestowed on him the name that is above every name." The majestic rule of Jesus as God's Son exceeds that of any other power or authority "in heaven and on earth and under the earth." As Jesus Himself said on the occasion when He commissioned His apostles to preach the gospel of God's forgiveness in His name, "All authority in heaven and on earth has been given to me. Go therefore and make disciples of all nations, baptizing them in the name of the Father and of the Son and of the Holy Spirit, teaching them to observe all that I have commanded you. And behold, I am with you always, to the end of the age" (Matthew 28:18-20).

Paul said that God has given this authority to His Son so that "every knee should bow . . . and every tongue confess that Jesus Christ is Lord." The gospel now invites us to accept our Lord's rule voluntarily and lovingly. If we refuse to do so, the time will come when He will return and bring the history of this world to a close. At that time, the reality of His rule will be unavoidable and there will be none who do not confess the truth. But if we have not done so before that day of judgment, it will be too late for our acknowledgement to save us. In reality, Christ *is* the Lord. But will we *accept* His lordship? That is what the gospel asks us to decide.

If Shakespeare should come into this room, we would all rise; but if Jesus Christ should come in, we would all kneel.

CHARLES LAMB

August 23

Christ's Weapons Are Not Fleshly

For the weapons of our warfare are not of the flesh but have divine power to destroy strongholds. We destroy arguments and every lofty opinion raised against the knowledge of God, and take every thought captive to obey Christ.
2 Corinthians 10:4,5

THE STRONGHOLDS DESTROYED BY JESUS CHRIST ARE NOT MILITARY OR GOVERNMENTAL. It is true that Jesus was victorious over the Roman Empire, but His victory was not gained on 28 October 312 (when Constantine won the Battle of the Milvian Bridge) or on 24 August 410 (when the Visigoths sacked Rome). No, in fulfillment of Daniel 2:44, Jesus broke in pieces the Roman Empire (and every other earthly empire) on the morning of His resurrection — and a few weeks later on the Day of Pentecost when the truth about salvation in His name began to transform the hearts of human beings.

As Paul put it so clearly, the purpose of the gospel is not to tear down earthly tyrannies or take over the halls of worldly power. It is to "destroy arguments and every lofty opinion raised against the knowledge of God." And if any captives are to be taken, the gospel will "take every thought captive to obey Christ."

We do not diminish the seriousness of the struggle when we say that the war between good and evil is an *ideological* warfare. Ideas are powerful, and you cannot think of a serious problem in the world that is not the result of some *untruth* that somebody has bought into. The devil's main weapon is the lie, and Christ's victory over His adversary consists of putting the truth back in its rightful place. Perhaps we may put it this way: Christ does not waste time hacking at the leaves of the tree; He goes to the very root of the trouble and cuts it off. And as the Great Physician, He is not primarily concerned with *symptoms;* He is going for the *cure.*

This being the victory Christ came to win, He did not resort to any of the means that are needed to win a political contest. The kingdom that resulted from His victory can't be measured by any of the criteria the world uses to judge how powerful something is. And because it is spiritual, Christ's kingdom is not vulnerable to any of the threats that earthly kingdoms have to worry about. This kingdom doesn't need weapons. *It's a different kind of kingdom.*

Girded for war, humility his mighty dress,
He moves into the battle wholly weaponless.

MADELEINE L'ENGLE

August 24

Willful Refusal to Obey

For rebellion is as the sin of divination, and presumption is as iniquity and idolatry. Because you have rejected the word of the LORD, he has also rejected you from being king.
1 Samuel 15:23

IN DESCRIBING SIN, ONE OF THE MAIN ILLUSTRATIONS USED IN THE BIBLE IS "REBELLION." This gives us the picture of a subject who commits treason against his rightful king. Rather than submit to the laws of the kingdom, he rebels. Willfully and treacherously, he declares independence from the kingdom with an attitude that says, "I don't care what the king says, I'll do as I please."

After all our rationalizations have been refuted by the facts, this is what sin always amounts to. It is rebellion. When we sin, we willfully refuse to obey God. Paul cuts through all the nonsense of our excuses in Romans 2:5 when he says "Because of your hard and impenitent heart you are storing up wrath for yourself on the day of wrath when God's righteous judgment will be revealed."

On the judgment day, there will only be two classes of people: "to those who by patience in well-doing seek for glory and honor and immortality, [God] will give eternal life; but for those who are self-seeking and do not obey the truth, but obey unrighteousness, there will be wrath and fury" (Romans 2:7,8). If we are lost, it will not be a miscarriage of justice. "Sin is not weakness, it is not disease; it is red-handed rebellion against God" (Oswald Chambers).

Even in what we *know* of God's will, there is often an element of rebellion in our ignorance. As Eric Hoffer said, "Far more crucial than what we know or do not know is what we do not want to know." So when the Scriptures speak of "ignorance," it is often a reference to the moral blindness that comes from refusing the light that was available to us (Romans 1:28-32; Ephesians 4:17-19).

It marks a huge step in our return to God when we acknowledge that our sins against Him have been deliberate. If all we can say is, "What I did was inadvisable, but I couldn't have done otherwise," we are a long way from seeing our need for forgiveness. It is only when we acknowledge that we have *chosen* to disobey God that we are ready to begin thinking about repentance.

That is the inner nature of sin always, willful refusal to obey God. But still men go on trying to get conviction upon sinners by telling them they sinned because they could not help it.

A. W. TOZER

August 25

Refreshment in the Lord

Yes, brother, I want some benefit from you in the Lord.
Refresh my heart in Christ.
Philemon 20

IN THE SHORT LETTER OF PAUL TO PHILEMON, PAUL MADE A BROTHER-TO-BROTHER REQUEST OF HIS FELLOW CHRISTIAN. Hoping the request would be favorably considered, Paul said, "Refresh my heart in Christ." Today let's meditate on this aspect of becoming a Christian. Not only do we assume new responsibilities to the Lord, but we acquire a new connection to others who, like us, have obeyed the gospel. As we see with Paul and Philemon, we have the opportunity to "refresh" our brothers and sisters in Christ.

The concept of "refreshing" another person is helpful. Perhaps it goes without saying that we all need to be refreshed from time to time, but most of us probably underestimate the extent to which we can have this effect on others. By our words and deeds, we can energize those around us, breathing new life into them.

But Paul hoped that Philemon would refresh his heart "in Christ," i.e., as a Christian. It is certainly possible for anyone, whether a Christian or not, to have a refreshing effect on other people, but in Jesus Christ this effect is deepened in significant ways. It is only in Christ that we have the ability to be refreshing in the ways that people need it the most. But here is the point that all of us who are Christians need to ponder: we need to see being a Christian not only in terms of what we can get (*being* refreshed) but also in terms of what we can give (refreshing *others*).

When all is said and done, we will act in rightful love toward others only when we have a right relationship with God and think about His nature as we should. As someone has said, our "sociology" flows out of our "theology." If we think there is no God at all, that will have an obvious impact on our relationships with other human beings. But even if we are believers, if our view of God is in conflict with God's revelation of Himself in the Scriptures as a whole — for example, if it is skewed in the direction of either His judgment or His forgiveness — our relationships will be hampered by that imbalance. So here is a very practical reason for learning about God as He truly is: it is the truth about God that will enable us to be genuinely "refreshing" as Christians.

There is no brotherhood of man without the fatherhood of God.

HENRY MARTYN FIELD

August 26

WHEN WE REACH GOD'S GOAL

And we all, with unveiled face, beholding the glory of the Lord, are being transformed into the same image from one degree of glory to another. For this comes from the Lord who is the Spirit.
2 Corinthians 3:18

IF WE ARE IN CHRIST, WE ARE BEING TRANSFORMED. Beginning with our initial obedience to the gospel and the forgiveness of our past sins, we are being renovated and rehabilitated. When we reach the place that Christ has gone to prepare for us (John 14:1-4), we will enjoy an absolutely perfect relationship with God forever. The damage of our sins will have been totally repaired, the flaws in our character removed, and even our innermost thoughts and motives completely conformed to our Father's holiness.

The apostle John envisioned the completion of this process of character growth when he said, "Beloved, we are God's children now, and what we will be has not yet appeared; but we know that when he appears we shall be like him, because we shall see him as he is. And everyone who thus hopes in him purifies himself as he is pure" (1 John 3:2,3). What a glorious vision of what we can be!

At present, however, we are still in "rehab." We ought to be powerfully pulled toward God by the vision of what we will be when the process is finished, but the fact is, we're not there yet. Paul put it in the present tense when he said that we "are being transformed into the same image from one degree of glory to another." As long as this life lasts, we'll always be works in progress.

But it is critically important to keep one thing in mind: *God will not be content until He has finished doing what He has begun to do with us.* Although His scheme of redemption obviously benefits us personally, the plan is primarily about God and His intention to redeem His creation from the ravages of sin. In Christ, He is transforming us into the sons and daughters that human beings were meant to be. He is, in effect, restoring our humanity to us.

Sin marred God's creation, taking creatures made in His image and defacing that image. As a result, we have never experienced what it is to be a human being — not fully and perfectly. At best, we have been stumbling along with lives that are only a faint echo of real life. But God does not plan to leave His masterpiece broken. In Christ, He proposes to bring us all the way back to life.

The glory of God is man fully alive.

IRENAEUS

August 27

What Trust Moves Us to Do

For my thoughts are not your thoughts,
neither are your ways my ways, declares the LORD.
For as the heavens are higher than the earth,
so are my ways higher than your ways
and my thoughts than your thoughts.
Isaiah 55:8,9

ONE OF LIFE'S GREATEST CHALLENGES IS TO TRUST GOD ENOUGH TO ACCEPT HIS MEANS AND HIS METHODS. Many are those who say they love God and trust Him, but in an age when human feelings are the ultimate source of authority, most people are willing to disregard anything in the Scriptures that does not seem reasonable to them. We say we believe God is non-negotiable, but when it comes to "means and methods," we often see those as flexible.

Few of us would have set up the gospel plan of salvation as God did. Even in the apostolic age, the gospel met with resistance from many who saw it as either ineffective or unsophisticated. Speaking as one who knew what it was like to reject the gospel as being unreasonable, Paul said, "For the word of the cross is folly to those who are perishing, but to us who are being saved it is the power of God. For it is written, 'I will destroy the wisdom of the wise, and the discernment of the discerning I will thwart.' Where is the one who is wise? Where is the scribe? Where is the debater of this age? Has not God made foolish the wisdom of the world? For since, in the wisdom of God, the world did not know God through wisdom, it pleased God through the folly of what we preach to save those who believe" (1 Corinthians 1:18-21).

But what about us today? Are we willing to accept God in general matters like love and faith, but when it comes to His instructions in the Scriptures about how these principles are to be carried out, do we balk? The unavoidable fact is, if we do not trust God's revealed instructions, we do not trust God Himself.

We see no better example of someone yielding to God's plan than Jesus yielding in the matter of His crucifixion (John 12:27,28). He went to the cross not because it was easy or because it was His preference, but simply because He trusted His Father's plan. He trusted the plan because He trusted His Father. And make no mistake: it was His obedience that showed that He trusted Him.

Faith reposes on the character of God, and if we believe that God is perfect, we must conclude that his ways are perfect also.

A. W. TOZER

August 28

Confessing Our Sins

If we confess our sins, he is faithful and just to forgive us
our sins and to cleanse us from all unrighteousness.
1 John 1:9

GOD'S GRACE IS A SOURCE OF JOY TO US. Where would we be if He were not "faithful and just to forgive us our sins and to cleanse us from all unrighteousness"? But God's forgiveness requires honesty on our part. Writing to Christians, John said, "If we confess our sins," God will accept our honesty and forgive us.

What does it mean to "confess" our sins? It means acknowledging what the sins are that we need to be forgiven of. This is far more than a generic statement that we "haven't done as well as we should." In confession, we specifically name the sins we are guilty of, acknowledging the full, unvarnished truth about our disobedience. Rather than pleading *extenuating* circumstances that might diminish our guilt, we confess the *aggravating* circumstances that make our guilt even worse than it might have been otherwise. In our own "trial," so to speak, we accuse ourselves more thoroughly than any of the witnesses — saying exactly what the sin was and why it was so wrong, sparing no detail and offering no excuse.

Anyone who has ever done this knows how painful it is. It comes from "a broken and contrite heart" (Psalm 51:17), and it hurts. But the joy of forgiveness is on the other side of this sorrow, and the process of confessing our sins and properly grieving them should not be rushed through. One reason many Christians have so little joy is that they have paid too little attention to the process of confession and grief for their sins. Eager to be happy, they have avoided the very thing that could have made them truly rejoice.

But in addition to God, is there anyone else to whom we should confess our sins? In some cases, yes. If anyone else has suffered loss or damage by our sin, we must acknowledge how we have hurt them and seek to make whatever restitution is possible. In addition, there may be others we will want to confess our sins to because they love us and will be a great help to us as we learn to repent and live differently. Hard though it is, confession is one of the best parts of God's plan for our redemption. It is a blessing because it is a courageous step in the direction of *truth.*

Confession, which means to agree with God regarding our sin, restores our fellowship. It is a form of discipline which God requires.

ERWIN W. LUTZER

August 29

Seeking the Kingdom of God First

But seek first the kingdom of God and his righteousness,
and all these things will be added to you.
Matthew 6:33

A FIRM DECISION MUST BE MADE TO "SEEK FIRST THE KINGDOM OF GOD." Very few people are willing to do this, even among those who profess allegiance to Christ. "Everyone wants the kingdom of God, but few want it first. Everyone wants high achievement, but few want to pay the price. Everyone wants God, but few want to put him first" (Charles L. Venable). Especially in the modern culture of so-called "Christian nations," very few do anything more than add a little "Christianity" to their busy lifestyles.

But Jesus was clear: we cannot serve two masters (Matthew 6:24). He said, "Whoever is not with me is against me, and whoever does not gather with me scatters" (Luke 11:23). When it comes to our discipleship to Jesus Christ, a radical choice has to be made. He will have all of our hearts or none of them at all.

But did you notice the last part of Jesus' statement in Matthew 6:33? If we put the kingdom first, "all these things will be added to you." Whatever other needs we have, these will be supplied — but we have to be willing to do without them, if need be, in order to maintain the priority of the kingdom. And, of course, the very worst thing we could do is to "put the kingdom first" because secretly we think this will be the best way to get "all these things."

Whether to put God's kingdom first in our hearts is a hard decision, hard because of the sacrifice required and the carefulness demanded by the decision. Consequently, we often dither about it and procrastinate. (I love the *American Heritage Dictionary's* definition of *dither:* "to be nervously irresolute in acting or doing.")

We need to hear Joshua's challenge: "If it is evil in your eyes to serve the LORD, choose this day whom you will serve" (Joshua 24:15). Or Elijah's exhortation: "How long will you go limping between two different opinions? If the LORD is God, follow him; but if Baal, then follow him" (1 Kings 18:21). Or Moses' plea: "I have set before you life and death, blessing and curse. Therefore choose life, that you and your offspring may live" (Deuteronomy 30:19). In this life, it pays to be careful what we grasp and what we give up.

If you have not chosen the kingdom of God first, it will in the end
make no difference what you have chosen instead.

WILLIAM LAW

August 30

WHAT THE LORDSHIP OF CHRIST MEANS

Not everyone who says to me, "Lord, Lord," will enter the kingdom of heaven, but the one who does the will of my Father who is in heaven.
Matthew 7:21

IF WE THINK THAT OBEDIENCE HAS NOTHING TO DO WITH OUR CITIZENSHIP IN GOD'S KINGDOM, WE ARE MISTAKEN. For Jesus Christ to be our Savior, He must be our Lord. And the lordship of Christ involves more than just *saying* He is our Lord. "Not everyone who says to me, 'Lord, Lord,' will enter the kingdom of heaven, but the one who does the will of my Father who is in heaven."

The first hearers of the gospel two thousand years ago would have been more familiar with the word *lord* than we are. It simply meant "one who is in authority." But used in reference to Jesus Christ it had a special meaning. In Matthew 28:18-20, He claimed that *all authority in heaven and on earth* had been given to Him. He was the "King of kings and Lord of lords" (Revelation 19:16).

Remember that we have defined the problem of sin as the problem of rebellion against God. If that is the problem, it makes obvious sense that for our sins to be forgiven we are going to have to lay down our rebellion, come back to the rightful King, and once against submit ourselves to His rule. Wonder of all wonders, He is willing to forgive us of our treason, but His grace requires that we begin doing what we have not been doing: *obey His will.* He must be our Master, our Ruler . . . *our Lord.*

But how do we know if Jesus is our Lord? We know by taking a look at whether we're actually obeying Him or not. Whatever we may say, if we are not obeying Him, He is not our Lord.

Perhaps we could not do better than to end these thoughts with Jesus' vivid conclusion to the Sermon on the Mount: "Everyone then who hears these words of mine and does them will be like a wise man who built his house on the rock. And the rain fell, and the floods came, and the winds blew and beat on that house, but it did not fall, because it had been founded on the rock. And everyone who *hears these words of mine and does not do them* will be like a foolish man who built his house on the sand. And the rain fell, and the floods came, and the winds blew and beat against that house, and it fell, and great was the fall of it" (Matthew 7:24-27).

What gets me into the kingdom, from Christ's own statement,
is not saying, "Lord, Lord," but acting "Lord, Lord."

JIM ELLIOT

August 31

CHOICES THAT EXCLUDE EACH OTHER

No one can serve two masters, for either he will hate the one and love the other, or he will be devoted to the one and despise the other. You cannot serve God and money.
Matthew 6:24

WHEN WE ARE MAKING UP OUR MINDS ABOUT A TOUGH CHOICE, THERE MIGHT BE MANY REASONS WHY WE DELAY THE DECISION. Perhaps we're still unsure which fork in the road to take. Or maybe we're mustering the courage the decision is going to require.

At other times, however, we have a different problem. We have managed to make the decision, but we try to hold on to the circumstances we would have had if we had chosen the other option. As the saying goes, we try to have our cake and eat it too.

In the gospel, Jesus asks us to make life's ultimate choice. Whether or not to follow Him is the most radical decision that will ever confront us — it requires making Him the Lord of everything about us, even our innermost thoughts and motives. To say the least, such a decision requires the sacrifice of every previous allegiance we've ever had. Whatever has been our ultimate priority up to now, that priority must be subordinated to the will of our new Master. We will follow the path that leads us to Him in eternity, forsaking every other path and every other preference.

However, the time comes when we look back longingly at our past priorities — and we return to them. Without openly rejecting the Lord, we simply start following our own will in the "secular" parts of our life, thinking that maybe our way and Jesus' way are not so incompatible after all. He will still be our primary Lord, we tell ourselves; we will make sure we keep the other things from getting out of hand. But we are deceiving ourselves, as anybody can see who really knows us (including our children). We have let something else sneak back onto the throne of our hearts.

On this point, Jesus cut to the heart of the matter: "No one can serve two masters, for either he will hate the one and love the other, or he will be devoted to the one and despise the other." It is impossible to keep two ultimate priorities. Ultimate priorities, by definition, are mutually exclusive. They cannot coexist peacefully.

So "no one can serve two masters" is a challenging saying, all the more so for those of us today who believe we can "have it all."

The first duty of every soul is to find not its freedom but its Master.

P. T. FORSYTH

September 1

ENTER BY THE NARROW GATE

Enter by the narrow gate. For the gate is wide and the way is easy that leads to destruction, and those who enter by it are many. For the gate is narrow and the way is hard that leads to life, and those who find it are few.
Matthew 7:13,14

HERE IS ONE OF JESUS' MORE UNPOPULAR SAYINGS. Compared to the wide gate and the easy way, the gate is narrow and the way is hard that leads to life. Reconciliation to God, according to Jesus, requires a choice not many will be willing to make.

The "natural" path is always easier than any other — and it never goes anywhere but downhill. By definition, "natural" means what will happen if no effort is exerted to alter the outcome — we call it "taking the course of least resistance." Even in our daily lives, we are not usually happy with the degradation that takes place when we simply do nothing. But taking the natural path is even more disastrous in the spiritual realm. Some hard choices have to be made, and we are the ones who must make them.

God will help us, of course. Surrounding us with resources and circumstances that urge us in the right direction, God will open doors of opportunity for us. Without His help we could do nothing. In His love, He will even "discipline" (or "chasten") us, as Hebrews 12:5-11 indicates. But having been disciplined by God, we will have to discipline ourselves. To be godly people, we will have to exert ourselves to go uphill rather than downhill — and the choice will usually involve more than doing what comes naturally.

Comparing our situation as Christians to that of the athlete, for whom self-discipline is obviously necessary, Paul said, "Every athlete exercises self-control in all things. They do it to receive a perishable wreath, but we an imperishable. So I do not run aimlessly; I do not box as one beating the air. But I discipline my body and keep it under control, lest after preaching to others I myself should be disqualified" (1 Corinthians 9:25-27).

It does no good to deny this challenging aspect of godliness. If we take God seriously, we won't seek to soften the force of texts like Matthew 7:13,14 with a quick "yes but." The fact is, relatively few will be interested in the life that leads to heaven. But whatever others may do, each of us must make our own choice. *What will we do?*

Sanctification means . . . a life of discipline such as nine out of ten of us will have nothing to do with.

OSWALD CHAMBERS

September 2

NOMINAL CHRISTIANS

But I have this against you, that you have abandoned the love you had at first. Remember therefore from where you have fallen; repent, and do the works you did at first. If not, I will come to you and remove your lampstand from its place, unless you repent.
Revelation 2:4,5

THE CHRISTIANS IN EPHESUS, TO WHOM THE ABOVE WORDS WERE WRITTEN, WERE IN A DANGEROUS POSITION. Having been faithful to Christ in the past, they no longer loved Him as they used to. And Christ was clear: if they did not repent and come back to Him in their hearts, He would sever His connection to them.

If Christ did end up removing their "lampstand," the members of the church in Ephesus probably continued to call themselves Christians, at least for a while. They would have listed "Christian" as their religious affiliation, and might have thought of their salvation as being secured by their allegiance to "Christianity" rather than some other religion. But in reality, the word "Christian" would have been only a label and nothing more.

Today, when we speak of "nominal" Christians, that is what we mean: people who are Christians in "name only." They self-identify as Christians, and may even attend a few church services now and then. When it comes to defending the "true faith," they may be militant, but inwardly there is no substance to their faith. They are the modern embodiment of the mentality God spoke of in Isaiah's day: "[They] draw near with their mouth and honor me with their lips, while their hearts are far from me" (Isaiah 29:13).

Wherever Christianity becomes safe and socially acceptable, the number of name-only Christians will grow. They're not truly religious, but Christianity will be their "religious preference." And nothing could be more offensive to the Lord. To the Laodiceans, the Lord said, "So, because you are lukewarm, and neither hot nor cold, I will spit you out of my mouth" (Revelation 3:16).

So in cultures where there are many nominal Christians, evangelism often amounts to converting the "Christians" to Christ. This is the hardest kind of evangelism by far. But think of the power that would be unleashed if even a few of those who have been wearing Christ's name actually became His people.

If we were willing to learn the meaning of real discipleship and actually to become disciples, the church in the West would be transformed and the resultant impact on society would be staggering.

DAVID WEST

September 3

Sensitivity to Sin

They have no sense of shame. They live for lustful pleasure and eagerly practice every kind of impurity.
Ephesians 4:19 NLT

IT IS NOT A GOOD THING IF OUR SINS DON'T BOTHER US. Just as you wouldn't want to be unable to feel physical pain, you wouldn't want to be insensitive to the pangs of conscience. The "warning system" provided by our conscience is one of the most valuable assets in our spiritual toolkit. We should give thanks for it.

As important as it is, however, a sense of shame seems to be an endangered species of emotion in the culture that surrounds us. If we care about the world our children are going to have to live in, we can't help but be concerned about current trends. But there is something else I want you to pay attention to: *each of us needs to be more concerned about our lack of sensitivity to the sins that we know are in our own hearts.* Whatever may be going on in the world, are we as sensitive to our own sins as we should be?

Oswald Chambers spoke perceptively when he said, "Measure your growth in grace by your sensitiveness to sin." The more we learn to love our Father, the more our hearts are going to hurt when we realize we've failed Him. The person who rarely sees any sin in his life — or seeing it, is not bothered by it — is not a spiritual senior but only a sophomore. As we gain wisdom, our conscience becomes more keen, rather than more comfortable.

And, of course, our increasing sensitivity to sin causes us to yearn all the more fervently for the perfection of our character in eternity. Thomas D. Bernard's comment that our "sense of sin is in proportion to our nearness to God" sounds contradictory, but it's not. The nearer we are to God, the more we see the gap between us and Him — and the more we long for that gap to be taken away.

So where are you, my friend, in regard to this subject? If the painful awareness of sin seems to be growing rather than diminishing, does that mean you are becoming a more wicked person? Not knowing you, I can't say for sure. But your pain may just mean that your conscience is becoming more healthy. And if that be the case, you are moving in God's direction. Frankly, I'd be more worried about you if you thought you were doing just fine.

It is not when we are conscious of our faults that we are the most wicked; on the contrary, we are less so.

FRANÇOIS FÉNELON

September 4

CONFORMITY TO CHRIST: BOTH A FACT AND A PROCESS

... seeing that you have put off the old self with its practices
and have put on the new self, which is being renewed
in knowledge after the image of its creator.
Colossians 3:9,10

FOR TODAY'S MEDITATION, CONTEMPLATE THE CONCEPT OF "CHRISTLIKENESS." Surely it is obvious that the Christian is to demonstrate a likeness to the character (or "mind") of Christ. Having obeyed the gospel and entered the realm of God's grace, we are to be people in whom the beauty of Christ can be seen.

But is Christlikeness an accomplished fact or is it a goal we're to grow toward? It is both, and Paul makes this point in two passages that are strikingly similar. In Colossians 3:9,10, he puts conformity to Christ in the past tense. He says that we *have* "put off the old self . . . [and] put on the new." But in Ephesians 4:22-24, he puts it in the form of a *command:* "put off your old self . . . [and] put on the new self." These texts are not contradictory; each contains an important truth. What we *are* in Christ imparts a sense of rest — and what we *must become* gives us a sense of responsibility. So the gospel has two sides to it: the *indicative* and the *imperative.*

I suggest that both the indicative and the imperative parts of the gospel require a decision on our part; neither is automatic. It will not be true to say that we have put on Christ if we have not made a commitment to doing that. And we certainly will not grow in our conformity to His character if we don't devote ourselves to that process. In both cases, we must exhibit the kind of decisiveness reflected in the song: "I have decided to follow Jesus. No turning back. No turning back." To put it another way, we must choose to become the people that, in fact, we are in Christ.

Anyone who has been a Christian for very long will tell you that this is hard. There will never be a time in this life when the past does not try to pull us back — and sometimes the pull can be very strong. After all, we wouldn't have been what we used to be if there weren't some very pleasant aspects of being that kind of person. But we can't have it both ways. A choice has to be made.

Growth is one of the best things in life, but it is also one of the most challenging. To put it plainly: *growth requires sacrifice.* But the choice we make is worth every bit of what it costs us in this world.

To be another than I am, I must abandon that I am.
JOHN CHRYSOSTOM

September 5

GOD'S WAY IS CONDUCIVE TO HUMILITY

By faith Abel offered to God a more acceptable sacrifice than Cain, through which he was commended as righteous, God commending him by accepting his gifts. And through his faith, though he died, he still speaks.
Hebrews 11:4

WE DO NOT KNOW SPECIFICALLY WHY ABEL'S OFFERING WAS MORE ACCEPTABLE TO GOD, BUT WE ARE TOLD THAT HE DID WHAT HE DID "BY FAITH." Unlike his brother, he trusted God enough to do things God's way — whatever that might have involved — rather than substitute his own preferences in the matter.

When we look over the entire history of God's dealings with mankind recorded in the Scriptures we see an interesting pattern. Whenever people have decided to follow their own inclinations, we see two differences between their way and God's way:

(1) God's way is more simple. Human beings have a tendency to complicate things. Our projects are usually complicated at the start, and they grow even more complex as time goes along. In contrast, God's way of doing things is more plain and unadorned — His plan is so simple that we often see it as "simplistic."

(2) God's way is conducive to humility. Precisely because God's way is more simple, it takes trust for us to believe it will work. To follow God's instructions, we have to bow before His wisdom and rely on methods that seem insufficient, if not completely silly.

If somehow we were able to build the kingdom of God according to our own blueprint, the result would be pride — and rightly so, because the achievement would have resulted from our own wisdom. Until our house of cards came crashing down (Psalm 127:1), we possibly could have said, "Look at what we have accomplished." But when we follow God's plans there can never be any pride in it. His way goes against our ideas and opinions, and the honest person will always have to admit, "Well, I didn't think such a plan would work, but I was wrong. Although I would have set things up differently, God's way turned out to be the best."

The wisdom of God is revealed to us today in the Scriptures (2 Timothy 3:16,17). We should study the Scriptures with a reverent, childlike trust in our Father. Such a trust is not naive; it is based on His proven reliability. He is the God of ultimate truth and reality, and reality is a thing that requires humility on our part.

Humility is nothing but truth, while pride is nothing but lying.

VINCENT DE PAUL

September 6

Human Progress Is Perilous

And as people migrated from the east, they found a plain in the land of Shinar and settled there. And they said to one another, "Come, let us make bricks, and burn them thoroughly." And they had brick for stone, and bitumen for mortar. Then they said, "Come, let us build ourselves a city and a tower with its top in the heavens, and let us make a name for ourselves, lest we be dispersed over the face of the whole earth."
Genesis 11:2-4

THE "TOWER OF BABEL" IS A FAMILIAR STORY, BUT ITS POINT IS OFTEN MISUNDERSTOOD. The problem was not the height of the tower but the presumption of the builders. Refusing to acknowledge their need for God, they declared their independence and said, in effect, "We will do as we please; there is no problem we can't overcome and no goal we can't achieve on our own."

Today, the effects of the Enlightenment, the Industrial Revolution, and Progressivism have combined to produce a presumption bolder by far than that of Babel. Our culture is built on the premise of human progress and perfectability. There is no inward unrest that can't be calmed by mindfulness and meditation, and there are no outward problems that can't be solved by science and technology. Even in the realm of spirituality, God is no longer essential. Our faults and foibles can be eliminated by looking deep within ourselves. Our authentic lives are waiting to be discovered by the wisdom and love that are already in our hearts.

Postmodernism (to its credit) rejected the unbridled optimism of modernism, but we are currently seeing a resurgence of interest in the Enlightenment. Bestselling books are once again praising the Enlightenment, arguing that human reason and science have given us a world that is very good — and getting awesomely better.

Yet despite the diminishing danger of war, hunger, and disease, the global incidence of suicide is increasing dramatically. Clearly, our "progress" has left many people deeply disturbed. Can it be that our profoundest problems have no human solution?

The truth is, we can't help ourselves where we need help the most. Yes, we can "science" our way out of some of life's lesser problems, but the potential of human self-help is limited. *We do not have it within us to solve the problem of sin.* We cannot get back to God on our own — and that is what the gospel of Christ is about.

The cross has revealed to good men that
their goodness has not been good enough.

JOHANN H. SCHROEDER

September 7

The Power of Pentecost

And behold, I am sending the promise of my Father upon you. But stay in the city until you are clothed with power from on high.
Luke 24:49

In the final days of His life, Jesus prepared His apostles for the work they would do after He ascended back to heaven. They would be eyewitnesses of His resurrection, and they would be the authoritative proclaimers of His gospel. But He told them not to leave Jerusalem "until you are clothed with power from on high." This clothing with power began to take place on the Day of Pentecost just a few weeks after Jesus' ascension. We have a record of it in Acts 2, and that record is crucial to our grasp of the gospel.

In Acts 2, we are told that the apostles began to speak of "the mighty works of God" (v.11). Miraculously, they spoke in languages they had never learned, but the greater miracle, no less miraculously empowered, was the content of that which was preached: *the saving message of Jesus Christ.* The "speaking in tongues" facilitated the message that day, and it certainly underscored the authority of the apostles, but the emphasis in Acts 2 is on the content of the preaching. We would seriously fail in our appreciation of this text if we were so amazed by the signs and wonders that we didn't pay attention to the message the signs were pointing to.

In his sermon, Peter alluded to God's promise in Joel 2:28-32: "I will pour out my Spirit on all flesh . . . [and] everyone who calls on the name of the Lord shall be saved." The subject of the sermon was salvation, so we're not surprised that the hearers cried out, "Brothers, what shall we do?" (Acts 2:37). Peter's reply was clear: "Repent and be baptized every one of you in the name of Jesus Christ for the forgiveness of your sins, and you will receive the gift of the Holy Spirit" (Acts 2:38). In other words, as you call on the name of the Lord you will receive that which the Holy Spirit has made possible through the miraculously empowered preaching of the apostles: *salvation from your sins.* So the power that went forth from Jerusalem that day was not the miracles (those lasted only for a while), but the saving gospel of Jesus Christ (Isaiah 2:2,3).

God hides nothing. His very work from the beginning
is revelation — a casting aside of veil after veil, a showing unto men
of truth after truth. On and on from fact divine he advances,
until at length in his Son Jesus he unveils his very face.

George MacDonald

September 8

We Don't Get to Design the Path to God

You have plowed iniquity; you have reaped injustice; you have eaten the fruit of lies. Because you have trusted in your own way and in the multitude of your warriors . . .
Hosea 10:13

TRUSTING IN OUR OWN WAY IS A PROBLEM THAT SHOWS UP IN MANY DIFFERENT CIRCUMSTANCES. The basic problem is always pride, of course, but pride can wear many different disguises. Some of those disguises are so subtle that we don't see the danger of them.

In regard to our relationship to God, for example, we tend to view things as we wish them to be. The existence of God? We may believe there is a God because it makes us feel better. The nature of God? We may envision God in ways that harmonize with our personal preferences. The will of God? We may feel the need to reinterpret any text that seems unreasonable to us. In all of these things, rather than bow humbly before the objective truth about God, whatever the evidence indicates, we tend to accept only the "truth" that pleases us subjectively. We trust in our "own way."

Yet our track record (both individually and as a species) shows that our own opinions and judgments have not been sufficient to meet the challenges of life in this world. If we're honest, we have to agree with Jeremiah when he said, "I know, O LORD, that the way of man is not in himself, that it is not in man who walks to direct his steps" (Jeremiah 10:23). The essence of faith has always been trust in God's wisdom — *especially when it runs counter to our own.* "For my thoughts are not your thoughts, neither are your ways my ways, declares the LORD. For as the heavens are higher than the earth, so are my ways higher than your ways and my thoughts than your thoughts" (Isaiah 55:8,9). We are wise if we heed Solomon's advice: "Trust in the LORD with all your heart, and do not lean on your own understanding" (Proverbs 3:5).

The gospel is not a travel brochure showing various paths to choose from; it simply offers the "way of God" (Acts 18:26). The path that leads to God in eternity — the one He has laid out — will often seem narrow and illogical to us (Matthew 7:13,14). But that doesn't matter. It only matters whether it is, in fact, "the Way" (Acts 24:14).

The question is not whether a doctrine is beautiful but whether it is true. When we wish to go to a place, we do not ask whether the road leads through a pretty country, but whether it is the right road.

AUGUSTUS HARE

September 9

"In the Right Church" and Still Lost?

. . . you still live as the people of this world live. When there is jealousy among you and you quarrel with one another, doesn't this prove that you belong to this world, living by its standards?
1 Corinthians 3:3 Good News Bible

THE QUESTION "HOW DO YOU KNOW YOU ARE SAVED?" IS AN IMPORTANT QUESTION. Paul urged the Corinthians, "Examine yourselves, to see whether you are in the faith. Test yourselves" (2 Corinthians 13:5). But we need to be careful what standard we use to make this test. Some suppose that salvation is on the group plan and that as long as their names are on the roster of a congregation that is faithful to the Lord, their salvation is assured. Such individuals would say to themselves, "I have obeyed the gospel, the Lord has added me to His church, and I am saved — end of discussion." But the truth of the matter requires a deeper look.

Some of the Christians in Corinth had not grown much since they became Christians. Their conduct showed that their hearts were the same as before they obeyed the gospel. As Paul said, "You are still of the flesh . . . and behaving only in a human way" (1 Corinthians 3:3 ESV). And if they didn't repent, their salvation would be in jeopardy. The conclusion is sobering: it is possible to be "in the right church" (at least outwardly) and still be lost.

Having obeyed the gospel, we certainly need to find a fellowship of faithful Christians to be a part of. Christ does have some requirements concerning the collective (or "together") part of our discipleship. But while the faithfulness of others will encourage us, merely being attached to a faithful congregation won't save us. We won't go to heaven just because we were "in the right group."

Each of us needs to have a sense of personal responsibility. If after studying the Scriptures we realize that the religion we've been practicing is wrong, we need to leave that religion. If we find that we've been a part of a network of churches whose beliefs and practices are unscriptural, we need to disassociate ourselves. And if the particular congregation we've been a part of is not faithful to Christ, we need to worship elsewhere. But even if we're surrounded by others who are faithful to Christ, the more important question is still about our *own* responsibilities before the Lord.

Keep us, Lord, so awake in the duties of our callings
that we may sleep in thy peace and wake in thy glory.

JOHN DONNE

September 10

If We're Not Disturbed, We're Not Listening

There was again a division among the Jews because of these words.
Many of them said, "He has a demon, and is insane; why listen to him?"
John 10:19,20

WHEN JESUS SPOKE, PEOPLE WERE STIRRED. As Eric Hoffer put it, "Jesus was not a conservative." Even after He was gone, the teaching of His apostles continued to have a disruptive effect. When Paul and his coworkers went to Thessalonica, for example, the city was soon in an uproar. Some shouted, "These men who have turned the world upside down have come here also" (Acts 17:6).

J. B. Phillips once said, "Of all the epithets that could be applied to Christ, 'mild' seems one of the least appropriate." If Jesus is now seen as being tame and temperate, it is because His religion has been legalized. He has become familiar to us. We may believe the gospel is still revolutionary, but we think it is other people (the "wicked") who should be disturbed by it. "Oh, how society would be transformed if people would just listen to Jesus," we think.

But are *we* listening? If we're not disturbed by the "hard sayings" of Jesus (John 6:60), it may be that we're not paying attention. Like the self-righteous scholars who came to hear John the Baptist preach (Matthew 3:5-8), perhaps we don't see that what is being said applies to us as much as it does to anyone else.

One reason we're not disturbed by Jesus is that our *outward* lives are, for the most part, in conformity with His teachings. We don't feel personally challenged because we think we've already made the adjustments that Jesus' teaching calls for. We're kind, we help the needy, we attend worship services, and we say thanks before eating our meals — so we feel pretty good about ourselves.

But the external aspect of the gospel is easy compared to the harder part, which has to do with the *heart*. However "nice" my outward life may be, when I measure my heart (my thoughts, attitudes, and intentions) against Jesus' teaching, I am ashamed. His teaching disturbs me greatly, if I have the least bit of self-honesty. So may we all — every one of us — listen to Jesus with a new attentiveness. We must be disturbed before we can be redeemed.

The teaching of Jesus Christ does not appear at first to be what it is.
At first it appears to be beautiful and pious and lukewarm; but before
long it becomes a ripping and tearing torpedo which splits to atoms
every preconceived notion a man ever had.

OSWALD CHAMBERS

September 11

TRUST, THE ONLY PATH TO TRUTH, IS DANGEROUS

Commit your way to the LORD.
Psalm 37:5

IN OUR SECULAR WORK AS WELL AS OUR SPIRITUAL JOURNEY, WE FIND THAT "REWARDS REQUIRE COMMITMENT." If we are so averse to risk that we won't trust anything enough to commit ourselves to it, we will, wanting mainly to avoid being wrong, never know the joy that could have been ours if the commitment was right. Nothing good comes from the commitment-free life. Commitments are scary, to be sure, but as the saying goes, he who hesitates is lost.

We might say, "Well, yes, commitments are necessary, but before we make them, we need to make absolutely sure there is no possibility of our being wrong." In the real world, however, there are no such scenarios. We *never* have enough information to be *absolutely* certain about our decisions, and even if we did, that kind of decision-making would not require any faith. For faith to be faith, there must be some risk, some element of uncertainty.

Obviously, we need to be *careful* in our commitments. Even if complete information is not available, we need to gather all the evidence we can, so that our faith is not blind faith but serious trust based upon consideration of the best information we could get.

But to return to our main point, all the good things in life require *committing* ourselves to them. Hesitancy, doubt, and tentativeness will cut the very heart out of our discipleship to Christ. Distrusting God, we will never get the answers to our questions.

In her book on the practice of mindfulness, Kim Davies says, "The foundation of any practice is a certain level of commitment: you have to not only make a clear decision to try mindfulness but also to maintain your practice and awareness." I agree. And when it comes to godliness, a practice much higher than mindfulness, the principle of "rewards require commitment" is even more true.

David said in Psalm 37:5, "Commit your way to the LORD." This means counting the cost, accepting the risk, and putting our trust in God. *It also means binding ourselves resolutely to the practice of godliness.* Not only is this the right thing to do, but it is, in the end, the only way to know if the Lord's way is good. The path to truth requires trust — the kind of trust that knows what *commitment* is.

There is no discovery of the truth of Christ's teaching, no unanswerable inward endorsement of it, without committing oneself to his way of life.

J. B. PHILLIPS

September 12

SALVATION BY BAPTISM ONLY?

And the hand of the Lord was with them,
and a great number who believed turned to the Lord.
Acts 11:21

THE "FAITH ONLY" DOCTRINE IS NOT TAUGHT IN THE SCRIPTURES. Merely believing that Jesus is the Christ is not enough to save us from our sins. In the words of James, "As the body apart from the spirit is dead, so also faith apart from works is dead" (2:26).

But neither will we be saved by "baptism only." The person who thinks his only problem is that he was attending services at the wrong church, and that he is now saved because he "got baptized" and the Lord added him to the "church of Christ," is out of touch with reality. His problem was far deeper than attendance at an unscriptural church. It was the problem of sin — *sin in his heart as well as in his actions.* And if that problem is going to be corrected, a radical turning (or "conversion") will have to occur.

Baptism without faith. For baptism to result in the forgiveness of sins, it must be an act of faith, or trust, in God (Ephesians 2:8).

Baptism without confession. Baptism is meaningless if it does not result in a life which confesses Christ in deed as well as word.

Baptism without repentance. Like John the Baptist (Matthew 3:7-9), Jesus would rebuke us if we wanted to be baptized but were not willing to repent of the sins that had separated us from God.

Baptism without conversion. In Acts 2:38, Peter told his hearers, "Repent and be baptized." In the very next chapter, he told another audience in Acts 3:19, "Repent and be converted" (NKJV) or "turn back" (ESV). Baptism is the crucial turning point at which we pass from being lost into the state of being "in Christ" (Romans 6:3; Galatians 3:27; Colossians 2:12). But if faith without works is insufficient (James 2:14-26), *so is baptism without conversion.* If we do not walk in "newness of life" (Romans 6:4), it is to be wondered whether we really did die with Christ when we were baptized.

In 1 Thessalonians 1:9, Paul wrote that the believers in Thessalonica had "turned to God from idols to serve the living and true God." And today, even if we've never worshiped a physical idol, this is what must happen. We must *turn to God.* We must cease from our old lives and live as those who are truly "in Christ."

Conversion may occur in an instant, but the process of coming from sinfulness into a new life can be a long and arduous journey.

CHARLES COLSON

September 13

Forgiveness and Transformation

We are to grow up in every way into him who is the head, into Christ.
Ephesians 4:15

When we obey the gospel of Christ, God's forgiveness opens the door to our transformation. Not only does God want to forgive us of our sins; He wants to repair sin's damage and rebuild our character, transforming us into creatures who can enjoy a perfect relationship with Him in eternity. The great importance of forgiveness is that it leads to this transformation. Our being molded, shaped, and conformed to God's character is the main goal of all that He has done (and is doing) in Jesus Christ.

A gradual process. When we are baptized into Christ, we rejoice in the forgiveness of God — *but we dare not underestimate the work that remains to be done.* The sins of our past, which God has now forgiven, were produced by *character traits* that must be gotten rid of. These must be replaced by the virtues of God's character (2 Peter 1:3-11) or else we will continue to live as we used to. Such a drastic rebuilding of our character does not happen overnight. It takes time. But while there is a need for patience, we also need to be diligent. Our transformation will not take place automatically, by divine decree. We have to embrace the process actively and wholeheartedly, submitting to God's training for however long it takes.

A painful process. Most kinds of growth in this world require discipline, and we should not expect our spiritual growth to be any different. When we need chastening, that is exactly what God will do. "He disciplines us for our good, that we may share his holiness. For the moment all discipline seems painful rather than pleasant, but later it yields the peaceful fruit of righteousness to those who have been trained by it" (Hebrews 12:10,11).

A glorious process. The gradual, and often painful, process of being transformed into godly creatures is one that we submit to because of its goal: we are on our way to becoming the sons and daughters of God, in the very highest sense. He created us in the first place, and through the gospel He is now *re-creating* us in the glorious image of His Son, Jesus Christ. Only God could do this, and if we persevere, one day we will see His face (Revelation 22:4). Sin will have been destroyed, and we will have forever to rejoice.

Thus we enter through our heart into the heart of God, who embraces all of history with his eternally creative and recreative love.

Henri J. M. Nouwen

September 14

WHAT IF "REASON" WERE JUST A "NATURAL" PROCESS?

Did any people ever hear the voice of a god speaking out of the midst of the fire, as you have heard, and still live? . . . To you it was shown, that you might know that the LORD is God; there is no other besides him.
Deuteronomy 4:33-35

WHEN GOD SPOKE TO ISRAEL ON MOUNT SINAI, SOMETHING HAPPENED THAT HAD NO NATURAL CAUSE. Assuming that what is recorded actually took place, the event was not triggered by any natural event that preceded it — it was the introduction of something "new" or "extra" into nature's progression of cause and effect, something from outside that closed, deterministic system.

I suggest that the operations of our own reason are similar, not that they are divine communications, but that they cannot be explained as the result of natural causes producing natural effects. Many neuroscientists today, of course, dispute this; they argue that what we call human "reason" is nothing more than the brain at work as a physical organ. When science has learned more about the brain, they say, we will recognize that a person never has any thought that cannot be accounted for neurologically and biochemically. Every firing of every neuron is the result of something *within nature.* Nothing freely decided upon ever comes into the sequence — whatever happens, it was determined materialistically.

But think about this from Douglas Groothuis: "if materialism were true, we could never grant *reasons* for holding beliefs since all our brain states would be rigorously determined in a materialistically *caused* fashion. Thought would be reduced to a mere reflex action on the order of a muscle twinge. But can glorified muscle twinges weigh evidence and reach warranted conclusions?"

We ought not to minimize what is required if our reasoning is to be objectively valid. It must be the working of something *personal* — an independent force not chained to the sequence of *physical* cause and effect. And in the biblical account, that is exactly the case: *we are dual creatures who straddle the physical and spiritual worlds.* We have a brain, but we also have a mind — a reasoning faculty that reaches far beyond what the brain (which is its servant) can do.

The validity of our reasoning depends upon the transcendence of reason itself. Reason must stand outside of nature in order for it to give us truth about nature. Our thinking, if we are to regard it as true or false, must be a shot from Something beyond nature, a beam from the Light beyond the sun, a participation in the eternal *Logos.*

JOE RIGNEY

September 15

Appraising Jesus

From now on, therefore, we regard no one according to the flesh. Even though we once regarded Christ according to the flesh, we regard him thus no longer.
2 Corinthians 5:16

SOMETIMES WE SAY, "THERE'S MORE TO THAT PERSON THAN MEETS THE EYE." In reality, that is true of everybody we've ever met. We never see anything more than the tip of the iceberg in anyone's life, and it is hazardous to form conclusions about their character if all we have is a first impression or a superficial acquaintance.

With people (and even with situations and circumstances), discovering the whole truth requires more digging than many of us are willing to do. First impressions may get us started down the road to understanding, but finding out what is really going on usually takes patience and fact-finding. It can be hard work.

In 1 Corinthians 5:16, Paul admits that his previous rejection of Jesus as the Messiah was the result of having judged Him "according to the flesh." Eventually, however, Paul came to see that the truth about Jesus was something that could not be seen if all one did was look at outward, worldly appearances. So as we form our own opinions about Jesus, let's think of two important principles:

(1) Sometimes we need to find out more of the *facts* before we draw a conclusion. Given the far-reaching implications of the question, it is amazing how many people reject Jesus while knowing very little of His life and teachings from the original sources. Whatever our ultimate decision turns out to be, surely that decision needs to be based on more than a few tidbits of information.

(2) But also, we need to be careful about the *criteria* we use to make our evaluation. Even when we have a lot of information about a person, our assessment of their character is determined by the value system we apply to them, and this is especially critical when it comes to Jesus. If Jesus truly was the Son of God, we would not expect that truth to be obvious to us if our "eyes" can only see things that *this* world considers to be important.

So may we avoid judging Jesus "according to the flesh." There is more to Him than meets the eye. May we appraise Him *carefully* — and appraise His inner character the most carefully of all.

Jesus Christ always speaks from the source of things; consequently those who deal only with the surface find him an offense.

OSWALD CHAMBERS

September 16

In Christ, What Are We Saved From?

For the grace of God has appeared, bringing salvation for all people.
Titus 2:11

When we're honest, we see that our sins against God have put us in a desperate situation. In our most private moments, we all have known the agony of Paul's cry, "Who will rescue me from this body of death?" (Romans 7:24 NRSV). Surely, we need not only to be saved, but we need a Savior.

But if you and I made a list of all the things we'd like to be saved from, it would be a long list, would it not? There is much about our lives in this world that we find disappointing, disagreeable, and difficult. What is it, then, that we desire to be saved (i.e., delivered or rescued) from? When we come to Jesus Christ, what is the help we're seeking more than any other kind of help?

Eternal condemnation. Even if there could be no relief in this world from all the things that have gone wrong, we would surely long to be with our God in eternity rather than banished from Him. So heaven is the highest and most important promise of the gospel. This, above all, is what we should be seeking from Christ.

Our disobedient actions. The gospel involves not only forgiveness but reformation, and it should be this deliverance from our sinful habits and weaknesses that we long for. It is not enough to be protected from the *punishment* for sin; we need to be saved from the *practice* of sin. This desire for obedience should move us deeply.

Our wayward hearts. Since our actions flow from our hearts, it is our hearts that are the main problem. Whatever outward sources of difficulty may disturb us, we should be more concerned about the darkness that is still in our thoughts and motives. We ought to long fervently for the hearts that can be ours in heaven.

The thread running through every mention of the gospel in the New Testament is the idea of a unity being restored that was broken by sin. Sin has broken apart everything that was meant to be together, but through Christ all is being brought back into harmony. Our disintegration — our broken-to-pieces-hood — is being healed. In Christ, our hope is for eternal health and wholeness.

The terms for *salvation* in many languages are derived from roots like *salvus, saos, whole, heil,* which all designate health, the opposite of disintegration and disruption. Salvation is healing in the ultimate sense; it is final, cosmic, and individual healing.

Paul Tillich

September 17

RESCUING ALL THREE PARTS OF THE HUMAN MIND

I will give them a heart to know that I am the LORD,
and they shall be my people and I will be their God,
for they shall return to me with their whole heart.
Jeremiah 24:7

ONE WAY OF LOOKING AT WHAT GOD WANTS TO DO WITH US IN JESUS CHRIST IS TO THINK ABOUT ALL THREE PARTS OF OUR "HEART" BEING REHABILITATED. Sin starts on the inside and works its way outward; so if the problem of sinful behavior is going to be corrected, the thing that most needs to change is *inside* of us.

Our minds are complicated and not easily described, but for our meditation today, let's say that our thinking falls into three categories: intellect, emotion, and will. To be redeemed from sin, all three of these must be rescued, not just one or two of them:

Intellect. With our intellect, we process information: we learn, analyze, and store "facts." But obviously, much of the "information" in our minds is incorrect, and that information, if we act on it, will produce behavior that is dysfunctional and destructive. Biblically speaking, untruth on the inside produces sinful behavior on the outside. So the first thing the gospel must do is establish truth in the intellectual part of our minds (John 8:32; Acts 26:18).

Emotion. As important as our intellect is, our emotions (or feelings) also play a critical role. Since our feelings grow out of our thinking (if I believe a burglar is in my basement, feelings appropriate to that thought will be generated automatically), it is critical that our thinking be based on truth. However, since our actions will mostly be determined by our feelings, we need to make sure our feelings are appropriate to the realities we're dealing with.

Will. Our will is our decision-making ability, and *freedom* of the will means we can choose our actions individually. Here, then, is where the gospel of Christ makes the greatest difference. *The disastrous conflict between our will and God's will needs to be removed.*

Putting all of this together, we see an amazing plan. In Christ, we can make better *decisions* because our *feelings* are more appropriate, and we can do that because our *thoughts* are more truthful. In bringing us back to God, the gospel leaves no stone unturned.

Three things are necessary for the salvation of man:
to know what he ought to believe; to know what he ought
to desire; and to know what he ought to do.

THOMAS AQUINAS

September 18

Freedom from Slavery to Sin

Jesus answered them, "Truly, truly, I say to you, everyone who practices sin is a slave to sin. The slave does not remain in the house forever; the son remains forever. So if the Son sets you free, you will be free indeed."
John 8:34-36

WE STRUGGLE TO BE FREE FROM SIN — NOT JUST IN ONE WAY BUT IN TWO. In addition to the *penalty* of sin (eternal death), we also need deliverance from the *practice* of sin in our lives. The old hymn "Rock of Ages" prayerfully expresses these two things we need from Christ: "Be of sin the double cure, save from wrath and make me pure." The second is no less important than the first.

We should not be under any delusion about the seriousness of the sins we have committed. Sin is much more than a slight inconvenience or an unhealthy habit — *it ties us in bondage to a death-dealing slavemaster from whom we are helpless to deliver ourselves.* As Paul reminds us, "Christ died for us at a time when we were helpless and sinful" (Rom 5:6 *Bible in Basic English*). Jesus was not exaggerating when He said, "Everyone who practices sin is a slave to sin." When we are thinking soberly, we see that no one is capable of enslaving us more terribly than we have enslaved ourselves.

Concerning those who advocated the "freedom" of a licentious lifestyle for Christians, Peter said, "They promise them freedom, but they themselves are slaves of corruption. For whatever overcomes a person, to that he is enslaved" (2 Peter 2:19). Beginning in the Garden of Eden, that has always been Satan's lie. Promising freedom, he delivers slavery. Such is the nature of sin.

And there is no middle ground. If we're not in a right relationship with God, we are the slaves of sin. "Do you not know that if you present yourselves to anyone as obedient slaves, you are slaves of the one whom you obey, either of sin, which leads to death, or of obedience, which leads to righteousness?" (Romans 6:16). Deciding which path we'll take is life's most consequential decision.

All sin comes down to pride and self-will, of course, and so deliverance from sin is deliverance from the bondage of selfishness. Having demanded to do as we please, we've sold ourselves into slavery. And as painful as it is, there is no better day than when we have the honesty to say, with Paul, "Wretched man that I am! Who will deliver me from this body of death?" (Romans 7:24).

He is a slave of the greatest slave who serves nothing but himself.

ANONYMOUS

September 19

What "Christlikeness" Means

For those whom he foreknew he also predestined to be conformed to the image of his Son, in order that he might be the firstborn among many brothers.
Romans 8:29

SOMETIMES WE SET OUR SIGHTS TOO LOW. Even in our relationship to God (which we say is the highest of all pursuits in life) we settle for far less than what is really offered to us in Jesus Christ.

For example, think about our concept of "Christlikeness." When we think of "Christianity," too often we think only of how it can make us nicer people. What we need, however, is not merely forgiveness but transformation — at the deepest level, from the inside out. The gospel recognizes this, and to become "Christlike" is not merely to become more well-behaved. It is to have imparted to us a new order of existence in which we become nothing less than "sons of God." Before you underestimate what Christ intends to do to you if you obey the gospel, ponder texts like these:

(1) "And we all, with unveiled face, beholding the glory of the Lord, are being transformed into the same image from one degree of glory to another" (2 Corinthians 3:18).

(2) "By which he has granted to us his precious and very great promises, so that through them you may become partakers of the divine nature, having escaped from the corruption that is in the world because of sinful desire" (2 Peter 1:4).

(3) "Just as we have borne the image of the man of dust, we shall also bear the image of the man of heaven" (1 Corinthians 15:49).

If we're honest, we have to admit that we need what these texts are talking about. It is not just our behavior that needs improving. *We ourselves — our deepest thoughts and motives — need fixing.* So Christ came into the world to bring an entirely new kind of life. If we are in Christ, a life that is "eternal" is being created within us, and one day it will reach its perfection. "You therefore must be perfect, as your heavenly Father is perfect" (Matthew 5:48).

Of all the errors we might make with regard to the gospel, the worst would be misunderstanding what its purpose is. The miracle of the Incarnation is that in Jesus a new kind of life has broken into this world. *Are we ready for what this kind of life means?*

Salvation means the incoming into human nature of the great characteristics that belong to God.

OSWALD CHAMBERS

September 20

KEEP YOURSELVES IN THE LOVE OF GOD

But you, beloved, building yourselves up in your most holy faith and praying in the Holy Spirit, keep yourselves in the love of God, waiting for the mercy of our Lord Jesus Christ that leads to eternal life.
Jude 20,21

LIVING IN A HARD WORLD, THERE ARE SOME DECISIONS THAT HAVE TO BE MADE. If we have obeyed the gospel of Christ, we must decide to grow strong enough to meet life's challenges. It is good that we have started the journey, but we need to be doing what Jude recommended: "building yourselves up in your most holy faith." Peter wrote that it is by the addition of certain strong virtues to our faith that "there will be richly provided for you an entrance into the eternal kingdom of our Lord and Savior Jesus Christ" (2 Peter 1:5-11), and he said that we must "grow in the grace and knowledge of our Lord and Savior Jesus Christ" (2 Peter 3:18).

Keep yourselves in the love of God. There is a sense in which God's power must keep us (1 Peter 1:5), but there is also a sense in which we must keep ourselves (2 Peter 1:10). Paul's advice to young Timothy was this: "Keep a close watch on yourself and on the teaching. Persist in this, for by so doing you will save both yourself and your hearers" (1 Timothy 4:16). *It is, above all, in the love of God that we must keep ourselves* — determining not to leave its shelter or the commands that flow from it (1 John 2:4-6).

Waiting for the mercy of our Lord Jesus Christ that leads to eternal life. As we keep ourselves in the love of God, one thing is always uppermost in our minds: *Christ is coming back.* Even though the Christian stays busy helping others in the here and now and sharing with them the gospel of salvation, it is not wrong to say that the Christian's life is one of *waiting.* And John says, "Everyone who thus hopes in him purifies himself as he is pure" (1 John 3:3).

Life will always have its ups and downs. Although we know God's purposes will surely be accomplished in the end, what will happen to us between now and the end has not been revealed. But regardless of what happens, there is one thing we can always do: we can determine that we will be faithful. *We can keep ourselves in the love of God.* That is the decision we can — and must — make. And it is not just a one-time decision. It must be made every day.

God has not called me to be successful;
he has called me to be faithful.

TERESA OF CALCUTTA

September 21

No Other Name by Which We Must Be Saved

And there is salvation in no one else, for there is no other name under heaven given among men by which we must be saved.
Acts 4:12

JESUS WAS BORN WHILE AUGUSTUS CAESAR WAS RULER OF THE ROMAN EMPIRE. Augustus was seventy-six when he died in AD 14 on the afternoon of August 19. Far away in the provincial hinterlands that afternoon, Jesus of Nazareth would have been about eighteen or nineteen. Augustus was succeeded by his stepson Tiberias, who was on the throne later when Jesus, then about thirty-three years old, was sentenced by the Roman governor Pontius Pilate to die by crucifixion just outside the city of Jerusalem.

The era of Augustus-Tiberias (and for quite some time afterward) was an age of boiling religious ferment, a time when many people throughout the empire were wondering about the "salvation of the soul." Wherever you went, there were orators, teachers, scholars, professors, philosophers, prophets, priests, rabbis, miracle workers, magicians — and even many "messiahs" — who claimed to teach how death could be defeated and eternal life obtained. Every one of them was right, and all the others wrong — or so they claimed — and many of them had devoted disciples.

Into this mix came Jesus, a nobody whose only credential was a rural pedigree from despised Galilee. He claimed, like many others, to teach the only way to salvation, but even His message of being sent by God to die for mankind and then be resurrected, thereby procuring salvation, was a narrative familiar in Greco-Roman mythology. Hearing Jesus, a cynic would have said, "Oh no! Not another dying-and-rising-savior cult. The last thing we need is one more guru claiming to teach the 'only way' to eternal life."

In those days, there were many savior gods in whose "name" salvation was offered, based on their alleged resurrection. Yet Jesus' resurrection was the only one backed up by *multiple eyewitnesses* — people who would never have submitted to brutal martyrdom if they knew their story was not true. The apostles, when threatened, never backed down: *the gospel is true and "there is no other name under heaven given among men by which we must be saved."* Others may help us with lesser problems, but only Christ can get us to heaven.

A person may go to heaven without health, without riches, without honors, without learning, without friends; but he can never go there without Christ.

JOHN DYER

September 22

Obeying the Gospel Means Trusting in Christ

. . . that we who first trusted in Christ should be to the praise of His glory. In Him you also trusted, after you heard the word of truth, the gospel of your salvation; in whom also, having believed, you were sealed with the Holy Spirit of promise.
Ephesians 1:12,13 NKJV

In the New Testament, the act of becoming a Christian is described in several ways, each of them instructive. One of these is "trusting (or hoping) in Christ." In the NKJV, Paul spoke of the Jews as those "who first trusted in Christ," and then he said that Gentiles in places like Ephesus had "also trusted." For today's meditation, let's think about what it means to trust in Christ.

If you compare several translations of v.12, you will notice that many render the verb not as "trusted" but as "hoped." But while the literal meaning of the Greek verb is to "hope before" or to "be the first to hope," the ideas of hope and trust are so intertwined that "trusted in Christ" is not a bad translation.

Faith, trust, and hope all have to do with intangible ("unseen") realities, usually because these are in the future. Based on evidence, we believe that certain things are true and that certain things are going to happen. Belief engenders trust, and trust is the thing that makes hope possible. Faith is, as the Hebrew writer described it, "the assurance of things hoped for" (Hebrews 11:1).

There is no better example of faith than Abraham. "Under utterly hopeless circumstances he hopefully believed . . . being absolutely certain that whatever promise [God] is bound by He is able also to make good" (Romans 4:18-21 *Weymouth*). So today, when we *obey* the gospel we *trust* in Christ. Believing God's promise of salvation, we stake our lives on the reality of the promise.

If you're like me, you may have found that trusting Christ is an ongoing work. Yes, we know that Christ has proven His trustworthiness. And yes, when we were baptized we made a commitment to trust Him. But life wears us down, and our trust runs low. So we have to go back, remember the foundations of our faith, and remake our commitment to trust Him. As life unfolds, our decision to trust has to be repeated frequently and fervently. That's not a lack of faith — it's how serious commitments always work.

Relying on God has to begin all over again every day as if nothing had yet been done.

C. S. Lewis

September 23

INDIVIDUALLY . . . AND TOGETHER

And day by day, attending the temple together and breaking bread in their homes, they received their food with glad and generous hearts, praising God and having favor with all the people. And the Lord added to their number day by day those who were being saved.
Acts 2:46,47

THE LAST SECTION OF ACTS 2 INDICATES HOW IMPORTANT THE COLLECTIVE ASPECT OF THE GOSPEL WAS TO THE EARLIEST CHRISTIANS IN JERUSALEM. Their "together" activities were not the sum total of their lives in Christ; nevertheless, they entered into this part of the gospel with great engagement and enthusiasm.

Today, *religiosity* has been cut off from *spirituality*. Disillusioned by "organized religion," many wish to be spiritual but not religious. In practical terms, this means they do not "go to church," preferring to have a relationship with God that is strictly private. Yet in the New Testament, in texts like Acts 2:41-47, we see Christians giving heed to *both* parts of the faith. *To be blunt, we can't be Christians without doing what they did, which they did under the direction of the apostles.*

There is something else that must be said, and I fear to say it, but I believe I must. If we resist the idea of "church" because it is so frustrating and messy, that is probably an indication of how much we stand in need of it. Yes, it certainly would be easier not to have to adjust ourselves to other people, submit to them, and work out the inevitable conflicts that arise. But that is precisely the point. If there is one thing the gospel wants to do, it is to teach us humility — and the local congregation is a big part of what the Lord has designed for that purpose. There are many things about C. S. Lewis that I disagree with, but I have always appreciated the honesty with which he saw that he needed to "go to church." So if you find the "people" part of Christianity a turnoff, I invite you to contemplate the quotation below. Then look in the mirror and ask yourself *why* the spiritual-but-not-religious approach is so appealing to you. While you're doing that, I'll go look in my mirror too.

When I first became a Christian . . . I thought that I could do it on my own, by retiring to my rooms and reading theology, and I wouldn't go to the churches and gospel halls . . . But as I went on I saw the great merit of it. I came up against different people of quite different outlooks and different education, and then gradually my conceit just began peeling off. I realized that the hymns (which were just sixth-rate music) were, nevertheless, being sung with devotion and benefit by an old saint in elastic-side boots in the opposite pew, and then you realize that you aren't fit to clean those boots.

C. S. LEWIS

September 24

ETERNAL GLORY

Therefore I endure everything for the sake of the elect, that they also may obtain the salvation that is in Christ Jesus with eternal glory.
2 Timothy 2:10

BY THE TIME PAUL WROTE HIS SECOND LETTER TO TIMOTHY, HE HAD SUFFERED A GREAT DEAL OVER A PERIOD OF MANY YEARS. And why had he done so? In the text above, he said that his labor had been motivated by a desire to see others "obtain the salvation that is in Christ Jesus with eternal glory." The glory that awaits, of course, is glorious just because it is *God's glory.* In a similar passage in Romans 5:1,2, Paul had said, "Since we have been justified by faith, we have peace with God through our Lord Jesus Christ. Through him we have also obtained access by faith into this grace in which we stand, and we rejoice *in hope of the glory of God."*

Contrary to what we often hear today, this "eternal glory" is what the gospel of Christ is primarily about. Yes, those who have this hope in Christ will do all they can to alleviate suffering in the world, but if we downplay — or leave out altogether — the main point of the gospel, we have not shown true love to our neighbor. On this battlefield we call "life," people do have many needs, and it's sometimes hard to know what kind of help to render first. But God's glory is far and away the most *important* need that anyone has. More attention needs to be paid to the greatness of that need.

The "eternal glory" of which Paul spoke is of more worth than everything else we will ever have the privilege of enjoying. That is not to say the joys of this world are trivial, for they are very good. But since we lack in this world the main thing we were created for — *full, complete, perfect fellowship with our Creator* — any of the joys available to us right now must be classified as lesser joys. Even if we could have them all, they wouldn't come close to the One Thing waiting for the faithful when Christ returns: *eternal glory.* Paul was not wrong to spend his lifetime working so others might have that. And we are not fools if we can say, as he did, "Brothers, I do not consider that I have made it my own. But one thing I do: forgetting what lies behind and straining forward to what lies ahead, I press on toward the goal for the prize of the upward call of God in Christ Jesus" (Philippians 3:13,14).

I would not give one moment of heaven for all the joys and riches of the world, even if it lasted for thousands and thousands of years.

MARTIN LUTHER

September 25

Longing to Put On Our Heavenly Dwelling

For we know that if the tent that is our earthly home is destroyed, we have a building from God, a house not made with hands, eternal in the heavens. For in this tent we groan, longing to put on our heavenly dwelling.
2 Corinthians 5:1,2

HEAVEN IS A TOPIC THE CHRISTIAN FINDS IT IMPOSSIBLE TO BE INDIFFERENT ABOUT. If he accepts the account of the gospel given in the New Testament, it is a subject he is intensely interested in, because he realizes that eternity with God is what the gospel is primarily about. It's the reason he became a Christian in the first place, and without that hope, the gospel is a cruel fraud.

Paul spoke of our physical bodies as a "tent" or "tabernacle," which is a temporary dwelling. And knowing (as we all do in our more honest moments) that this life is hard and heartbreaking, he said, *"In this tent we groan, longing to put on our heavenly dwelling."* He looked forward to eternity with a longing that he described as "groaning." Paul had more than a mild interest in heaven.

Just a few verses later, he said that "while we are at home in the body we are away from the Lord" (v.6). While Paul was obviously willing to stay in this world and work as an evangelist as long as the Lord wanted him to, he did not hesitate to say what his preference was: "Yes, we are of good courage, and we would rather be away from the body and at home with the Lord" (v.8). As he put it in his letter to the Philippians, "My desire is to depart and be with Christ, for that is far better" (Philippians 1:23).

For one thing, our lives in this world wear us out. We grow weary. If we're as busy as we ought to be, we become "exhausted" in the sense of being "drained" or "depleted." So one reason the Christian looks forward to heaven so longingly is that it is the *rest* God has prepared for His people. In the visions which John recorded in Revelation, he said, "And I heard a voice from heaven saying, 'Write this: Blessed are the dead who die in the Lord from now on.' 'Blessed indeed,' says the Spirit, 'that they may *rest from their labors,* for their deeds follow them!'" (Revelation 14:13).

Until we "put on our heavenly dwelling," however, we press toward the goal (Philippians 3:14). God helped Israel through the wilderness, and He will help us also. If the journey is hard, that will just make our home all the sweeter when we get there.

The Promised Land always lies on the other side of a wilderness.

HAVELOCK ELLIS

September 26

THE KINGDOM OF OUR LORD AND OF HIS CHRIST

Then the seventh angel blew his trumpet, and there were loud voices in heaven, saying, "The kingdom of the world has become the kingdom of our Lord and of his Christ, and he shall reign forever and ever."
Revelation 11:15

THIS TEXT CONTAINS ONE OF THE MOST MAJESTIC STATEMENTS IN THE SCRIPTURES. It appears halfway through Revelation, the last book in the Bible, at a point where God's enemies have been defeated: *"the kingdom of the world has become the kingdom of our Lord and of his Christ."* The last half of Revelation recapitulates the story of triumph portrayed in the first "movement" (to put it in musical terms) and climaxes with a fervent expression of eternal hope.

Following the statement of Revelation 11:15, this song of praise is given before God's throne: "We give thanks to you, Lord God Almighty, who is and who was, for you have taken your great power and begun to reign. *The nations raged, but your wrath came, and the time for the dead to be judged, and for rewarding your servants,* the prophets and saints, and those who fear your name, both small and great, and for destroying the destroyers of the earth" (vv.17,18). These phrases lead me to believe that the great announcement of God's victory in Revelation 11:15-19 refers not to His rule over the nations of men right now (though He certainly does rule over them), but to *His ultimate victory — a victory that has not yet been finalized.*

The outcome of the war, of course, is not in doubt. But since Satan's power has not yet been completely taken away, Paul could speak of the "end" when Christ "delivers the kingdom to God the Father after destroying every rule and every authority and power. *For he must reign until he has put all his enemies under his feet.* The last enemy to be destroyed is death" (1 Corinthians 15:24-26).

That triumph is going to take place. But until then, what is our response to the lordship of Christ? He is "longsuffering toward us, not willing that any should perish but that all should come to repentance" (2 Peter 3:9 NKJV). However, He has promised that He will return. When He does, there will be an accounting — a rendering of His judgment upon our decision concerning His kingship. If we need to change our decision, let's do that. While we can.

In the day when all men will stand before God,
the significant question for each of us will no longer be
what we think of Christ, but what he thinks of us.

ELVA J. HOOVER

September 27

THEY SHALL SEE HIS FACE

Then the angel showed me the river of the water of life,
bright as crystal, flowing from the throne of God and of the
Lamb through the middle of the street of the city; also, on either
side of the river, the tree of life with its twelve kinds of fruit, yielding
its fruit each month. The leaves of the tree were for the healing of the
nations. No longer will there be anything accursed, but the throne of
God and of the Lamb will be in it, and his servants will worship him.
They will see his face, and his name will be on their foreheads.
Revelation 22:1-4

WE DON'T KNOW WHAT KIND OF INTERACTION ADAM AND EVE HAD WITH GOD IN THE GARDEN PRIOR TO THEIR SIN. It seems they may have had a direct, face-to-face fellowship with Him. But whatever it was, they lost a great deal of their contact with God when, after they decided to reject His rule over them, they were cast out of the Garden. They became alienated from their Creator.

One morning not long ago, I was reading in Exodus 33 where Moses pleaded with God, "Please show me your glory" (v.18). But God said, "You cannot see my face, for man shall not see me and live" (v.20). However, God agreed to hide Moses in a cleft in the rock while He passed by. "Then I will take away my hand, and you shall see my back, but my face shall not be seen" (v.23).

Given the tragic consequences of mankind's sin, there is no more precious promise in the Scriptures than the promise of what heaven will be like for those who have been redeemed and reconciled to God: "They will see his face" (Revelation 22:4).

Whoever you are and whether you even believe that there is a God who created you, I want to suggest that you long to see the face of God. We *all* long for God, whether we realize that He is the object of our longings or not. Created in His image, we are "hard-wired" to need Him — and to need Him *deeply*. If, as I hope, Adam and Eve are in heaven (if they are, it will be the result of the sacrifice Christ made to enable their sins to be forgiven), don't you know they will be thrilled to see the face of the God they foolishly turned their backs on so long ago? And don't you know that the best part of heaven for them, as for every one of the saved, will be the fact that God's face is the face of a Friend?

Deep calleth unto deep, and though polluted and landlocked
by the mighty disaster theologians call the Fall, the soul
senses its origin and longs to return to its source.

A. W. TOZER

September 28

FATHER, SON, AND HOLY SPIRIT

Go therefore and make disciples of all nations, baptizing them in the name of the Father and of the Son and of the Holy Spirit.
Matthew 28:19

GOD IS ONE, BUT HIS UNITY IS A TRI-UNITY. That is to say, the Father, the Son, and the Holy Spirit are all parts of the oneness of God. While this challenges even our best efforts to understand, it is clearly what the Scriptures reveal about God. We are not free to dispense with the unity of God, but neither are we free to deny that the Father, Son, and Holy Spirit are all parts of the one God.

The unity of God. The first text that comes to mind is probably Moses' declaration: "Hear, O Israel: The LORD our God, the LORD is one" (Deuteronomy 6:4). But many other texts also affirm this, in both the Old and the New Testaments (Malachi 2:10; 1 Corinthians 8:4-6; etc.). So let us not waver: God — and God *alone* — is God.

The complexity of God. Even in the Old Testament, God's personhood was not simple. At Sodom, "the LORD" on the scene that morning rained down fire from "the LORD" still in heaven (Genesis 19:24). This is consistent with the New Testament, where the Father, Son, and Spirit are seen doing different things simultaneously but in different locations, as at Jesus' baptism (Matthew 3:16,17).

People often attempt analogies to show *how* God could be three Persons and still be one God, but with deep theological truths, analogy-making is dangerous. It is best for us to simply affirm what the Scriptures teach. It is our privilege to be the recipients of *every bit of information about Himself that God has revealed.*

We must courageously accept God's self-disclosure, even the parts that seem to us not to "fit." It would be wrong to delete any of it for the sake of logic or harmony. Yet in addition to being courageous, we must also be humble. It is a part of the majesty of God that He is complex beyond our ability to analyze or describe. As tempting as it is to reject complexities our minds can't handle, we need to humble ourselves — in both wonder and gratitude — before the truth about God. Even in eternity His deep and various nature will be beyond our creaturely understanding. Yet our part will be not to tame Him but to enjoy Him . . . in all His diversity.

In fact, it is spiritually healthy for us to acknowledge openly that God's very being is far greater than we can ever comprehend. This humbles us before God and draws us to worship him without reservation.

WAYNE GRUDEM

September 29

BAPTISM IS FOR BELIEVERS

Crispus, the ruler of the synagogue, believed in the Lord,
together with his entire household. And many of the Corinthians
hearing Paul believed and were baptized.
Acts 18:8

THERE IS IN THE NEW TESTAMENT A STRONG LINK BETWEEN BELIEF AND BAPTISM. I would go so far as to say that the link is inseparable. The only people who were baptized were those who believed in Jesus Christ (Mark 16:15,16) and had repented of the sins they were seeking to be forgiven of (Acts 2:37,38). Their baptism was preceded by the "good confession" (1 Timothy 6:12,13), an oral affirmation that, yes, they were in fact believers in Christ (Romans 10:9,10). As to who was to be baptized, the New Testament is clear.

Without faith, baptism only gets a person wet. It is not a ritualistic act, effective regardless of what is going on in the recipient's heart. Rather, its efficacy depends on "faith in the powerful working of God" (Colossians 2:12) — the active ingredient is trust in God: dependence on (a) what He *has* done, and (b) what He *will* do.

"Infant baptism" is the act of "baptizing" (not really baptizing but only sprinkling) infants shortly after they are born. This having been done, it is said that the children are now "Christian" children, rather than "unbaptized" or "pagan." This is more common in Europe, where most countries have a state church. Birth in one of those countries means that you are a citizen of that country politically, and religiously, you are enrolled in the national church. In such cases, your "baptism" is often a mere formality. A very secular Englishman once told me, "We only go to church twice in life: when we're hatched and when we're dispatched." He made that remark humorously, but even so, he seemed to be glad not to be one of the "unbaptized" in the world. As we have seen, however, in the New Testament, *baptism was meaningless without faith.*

I hesitate to take up a page to talk about infant baptism. But unfortunately, there are many misconceptions about baptism in people's minds — and this is one of the most prevalent. Yet it only takes reading the New Testament to see what baptism was originally: the appeal of a believer for a good conscience (1 Peter 3:21).

Those who were baptized [in the New Testament] were men and women
who were able to make a decision to commit their lives to Jesus. This and
other requirements for baptism indicate that baptism is for those
old enough to know what they are doing.

OWEN OLBRICHT

September 30

THE PROSPECT OF PERSECUTION

Then Haman said to King Ahasuerus, "There is a certain people scattered abroad and dispersed among the peoples in all the provinces of your kingdom. Their laws are different from those of every other people, and they do not keep the king's laws, so that it is not to the king's profit to tolerate them. If it please the king, let it be decreed that they be destroyed."
Esther 3:8,9

ONE OF THE UGLIEST REALITIES OF HUMAN HISTORY IS THE PERSECUTION OF GROUPS OF PEOPLE. Perhaps we shouldn't be surprised at this, since the first and most obvious result of sin is strife (Gen. 3:12; 4:8; 6:11; etc.). Still, it is a sad fact in this world that discord between groups of people often results in persecution. As we see in the example from Esther, the pretext for persecution is usually the charge that a group has become a threat to "us." Wanting to get rid of the Jews, Haman knew exactly which argument to make to the king: *"It is not to the king's profit to tolerate them."* In other words, they are a menace, so do away with them.

The group seen as disadvantageous to society may be a religious or ethnic group, or the difference may be racial, ideological, or economic. The particular difference doesn't matter. All it takes is for one group that has enough power to look upon another group as being "others" and exercise its power to marginalize them, if not exterminate them altogether. This is simply a fact of the world we live in. Christians are certainly not the only ones who have ever been persecuted (and sadly, they have sometimes been the persecutors), but anyplace where Christians are seen as being socially disadvantageous, persecution is likely to happen.

So if you obey the gospel of Christ, you should take seriously the prospect of persecution (Acts 14:21,22). In the United States (at least for the time being), it is not likely that you would be in physical danger, but as Christians become a shrinking segment of the population — and our views become despised by the mainstream culture — it is likely that you will be mocked and demeaned. And it may be that this is, for many of us, the threat we fear most of all. Many people would die for the Lord who would not stand up to the threat of social shame. So let us pray for the courage not only to be put to death for the Lord but also to be made fun of.

A man who has faith must be prepared not only to be a martyr, but to be a fool.

G. K. CHESTERTON

October 1

A Living Hope

Blessed be the God and Father of our Lord Jesus Christ! According to his great mercy, he has caused us to be born again to a living hope through the resurrection of Jesus Christ from the dead.
1 Peter 1:3

WITH HOPE, ALMOST NO OBSTACLE IS INSURMOUNTABLE, BUT WITHOUT HOPE, IT DOESN'T TAKE MUCH TO DESTROY US. That being true, it should stir us deeply to hear Peter tell us in this text about what has been made possible in Jesus Christ: *a living hope.*

It is only by God's "great mercy" that the hope Peter speaks of has become a possibility for sinful people like us. Having rebelled even once against God's will by doing that which we knew to be wrong, we have forfeited the privilege of fellowship with God. Alienated from Him, not all the righteousness we could exhibit would be enough to reestablish a state of perfect holiness on our part. So when God opened up the door of reconciliation, He did something we did not deserve to have done for us. And mark it well: it was "through the resurrection of Jesus Christ from the dead" that this happened. Everything about the gospel of Christ depends on the fact that His resurrection took place historically.

In v.4, Peter continued by saying that the object of our hope is *"an inheritance that is imperishable, undefiled, and unfading, kept in heaven for you."* If this is true — and as an eyewitness of Jesus after His resurrection, Peter was in a position to know the facts of the case — it means the Christian's hope is in an absolutely unique category. There is nothing in this world that won't have to be given up when we die, and even before we die, there is nothing we can do or have that isn't perishable, tentative, and subject to disappointment. But unlike all these treasures, our hope in Christ is "pure and undefiled, beyond the reach of change and decay" (NLT).

Finally, Peter says in v.5 that we *"by God's power are being guarded through faith for a salvation ready to be revealed in the last time."* Christ's resurrection is proof that God can be counted on to help us. His power, through our faith, will guard and keep us until our hope is finally realized. So when discouragement hits us (as it surely will), one thing is to be recalled: *the resurrection of Christ.*

If Jesus rose from the dead, then you have to accept all that he said; if he didn't rise from the dead, then why worry about any of what he said? The issue on which everything hangs is not whether or not you like his teaching but whether or not he rose from the dead.

TIMOTHY KELLER

October 2

THE CHURCH IN CORINTH

To the church of God that is in Corinth, to those sanctified in Christ Jesus, called to be saints together with all those who in every place call upon the name of our Lord Jesus Christ, both their Lord and ours.
1 Corinthians 1:2

TODAY AND TOMORROW, WE WILL BE LOOKING AT TWO CHURCHES IN THE NEW TESTAMENT. First, we turn our attention to the fascinating group which Paul addressed as "the church of God that is in Corinth." Together, the two letters that we have from Paul to Corinth take up more pages in the New Testament than we have from him to any other congregation. Notice how he refers to them:

The church of God that is in Corinth. The "church of God" refers to those whom He has saved. As a church (an assembly or collection of saved ones), the Christians in Corinth *belonged* to God.

Those sanctified in Christ Jesus, called to be saints. To be "sanctified" means to be reserved for a special purpose. In Corinth, then, the Lord had some "saints" — people who had answered the call of the gospel to be dedicated solely to His purposes in Christ.

With all those who in every place call upon the name of our Lord Jesus Christ. The Christians in Corinth were not the only saints in the world. As followers of Jesus, the brothers and sisters there would have felt a kinship to those "in every place" who called upon the name of the Lord, even if they had never met many of those people face to face. And when they engaged in the Lord's work (1 Corinthians 15:58), they would have known that many others were also doing the same work in other localities.

Perhaps the thing that strikes us most dramatically about the Corinthians is that Paul addresses them as "saints" despite the seriousness of their problems. This illustrates how the term *saint* has changed since the first century. In the New Testament, a saint was a person who was "in Christ"; he or she was simply a Christian, one of the Lord's people. And the defining characteristic of the Lord's people is not that they have reached a stage of sinless perfection in the here and now, but that, having obeyed the initial terms of the gospel, they are now living under the mercy of God. Forgiven of their past and now having access to God's grace, *they are in the process of being remade into creatures that will be with God in eternity.*

A saint is a creature of vast possibilities,
knit into shape by the ruling personality of God.

OSWALD CHAMBERS

October 3

The Church in Philippi

Paul and Timothy, servants of Christ Jesus,
To all the saints in Christ Jesus who are at Philippi,
with the overseers and deacons.
Philippians 1:1

IT IS OBVIOUS THAT PAUL HAD A SPECIAL LOVE FOR THE CHRISTIANS IN THE CITY OF PHILIPPI. The church there had begun in unusual circumstances (Acts 16:11-40), and the brethren had kept in touch with Paul, helping and encouraging him generously. In the text above, we have the salutation of a letter that Paul and Timothy sent to the Philippians. It is a good snapshot of what a local congregation of Christians was in the days of the New Testament.

The saints in Christ Jesus who are at Philippi. As we noticed yesterday, "saints" is one of the ways the Lord's people are referred to in the New Testament. The saints were not a special group of Christians; all Christians were saints. But the word *saint* points to something special about the identity and character of Christians: *as Christ's people, they are "sanctified" to Him.* That is, they are set apart exclusively for His purposes. Certainly, to be sanctified involves moral purity, but the idea is not limited to that. In every possible way, the saint is to belong uniquely to the Lord and to be held in reserve for use in the accomplishment of His purposes. In Philippi, there were such people. They had obeyed the gospel and received the forgiveness of their past sins. Beginning at that point, they were living as disciples of Christ and doing His work in the city of Philippi. They were the Lord's church in that place.

With the overseers and deacons. This text encapsulates what the New Testament teaches about the makeup of the local church. In the Lord's wisdom, it was simple but very effective. The Christians or "saints" as a whole were led by "overseers" and served by "deacons." The overseers, known elsewhere as "elders" or "shepherds" (1 Peter 5:1-4), were responsible for the leadership of the congregation, and the "deacons" (or "servants") were appointed to assist the church in specific ways. A simple plan? Yes. But this was the church in Philippi — and three things resulted: the Lord was glorified, the church was strengthened, and the city heard the gospel.

A Christian church is a body or collection of persons,
voluntarily associated together, professing to believe what
Christ teaches, to do what Christ enjoins, to imitate his example,
cherish his spirit, and make known his gospel to others.

R. F. SAMPLE

October 4

The Washing of Water with the Word

. . . that he might sanctify her, having cleansed her
by the washing of water with the word.
Ephesians 5:26

To accomplish the purposes of Christ, the church must be "sanctified." This word sounds like nothing more than religious lingo to some, but its concept is important and not hard to understand. To be "sanctified" is to be set apart for special use.

For example, I have an iron skillet in which I have never made anything but cornbread. When I bought it long ago, I "set it apart" for that purpose, and it has had to be content to be "different" from my other skillets. To maintain the magnificence of the cornbread that is cooked in it, it simply cannot come into contact with certain other things. (Knowing skillet nature as I do, I am sure the others accuse the cornbread skillet of being self-righteous.)

Now, on a more serious note, Christ gave Himself up for the church *in order that "he might sanctify her."* The whole plan by which Christ was able to have a "set apart" people depended on His dying for those people. Not in fifty lifetimes could any of us have kept enough *mitzvoth* ("commandments") for even one of our sins to be forgiven. The Messiah had to die for our atonement (Isaiah 53:4-6).

Also in v.26, we see that Christ "cleansed her by the washing of water with the word." This is a reference to the baptism (an immersion in water) in which all who are now in Christ came to be so (Romans 6:3; Galatians 3:27), as a result of hearing the word of the Lord concerning the forgiveness of their sins. Paul makes the point in triplicate in 1 Corinthians 6:11 where, after referring to those whose lives were given to sin, he said, "And such were some of you. But you were *washed*, you were *sanctified*, you were *justified* in the name of the Lord Jesus Christ and by the Spirit of our God." How, then, does Christ sanctify the church? He does it *individually.* One day the process will be finished, but only for those who have entered that process individually in the here and now.

We note that some seem to think there is a future time when, by some process undefined, Christ will cleanse the present filthy, sinful church. Current imperfections are thus excused. We beg to differ with this traditional interpretation. We do not question the future reception of the church as the bride of Christ (2 Corinthians 11:2,3; Revelation 21:2), but we believe the "setting apart" and "cleansing" is *now* taking place, and has been in process ever since the gospel of Christ was first preached.

Robert F. Turner

October 5

A Ransomed People

And they sang a new song, saying, "Worthy are you to take the scroll and to open its seals, for you were slain, and by your blood you ransomed people for God from every tribe and language and people and nation."
Revelation 5:9

THE LAMB THAT WAS SLAIN! Reminiscent of the Passover lamb in Israel, Jesus was a greater sacrifice, enabling God to justify mankind from its sins. John the Baptist said on one occasion as he saw Jesus coming toward him, "Behold, the Lamb of God, who takes away the sin of the world!" (John 1:29). In Revelation, no one but this Lamb is worthy to open the scroll containing God's purposes for mankind (Revelation 5:4,5). And He is qualified to do so — "for you were slain, and by your blood you ransomed people for God from every tribe and language and people and nation" (v.9).

To "ransom" is to redeem. When people are in trouble and can't deliver themselves, a redeemer is one who offers to pay the price to solve the problem for them. So it was that by offering His life, Jesus Christ ransomed us. He allowed us to be forgiven and released from the penalty of death. As a result of the ransom price being paid, our chains are now broken. God has a people who once were slaves but now are free to belong to Him in the most special sense. It is "for God" that we've been ransomed.

Revelation 5:9 emphasizes that this ransomed people will be made up of those "from every tribe and language and people and nation." Jesus had said to the Jews, "I have other sheep that are not of this fold. I must bring them also, and they will listen to my voice. So there will be one flock, one shepherd" (John 10:16).

There are many scriptural ways Christians may view themselves, but none is any more beneficial than to think of ourselves as having been ransomed. It is dangerous to forget that *we are only able to be God's people because He rescued us.* If gratitude for grace is the most motivating force in the world, then Christians should be the most motivated people in the world, for they are reminded, at least once a week when they partake of the Lord's Supper, that when God delivered them from their slavery to sin, it was an act of sheer grace. It would be a hardhearted person indeed who could know this and not respond with both awestruck reverence and the gratitude which leads to faithful obedience.

Grace is love that cares and stoops and rescues.

JOHN R. W. STOTT

October 6

And They Will Be His People

And I heard a loud voice from the throne saying, "Behold, the dwelling place of God is with man. He will dwell with them, and they will be his people, and God himself will be with them as their God."
Revelation 21:3

When God took upon Himself human flesh, He dwelled ("tabernacled") among us for a while. The Gospel of John makes this point in 1:14, where it says that in Jesus Christ, God "lived here with us" (CEV). This is a staggering thought, that God would dwell among human beings, even those forgiven of their sins and living faithfully unto Him. And yet this is the language used to describe God's relationship with His people. The words are used of Israel in the Old Testament (Leviticus 26:11,12), they are used of the church today (2 Corinthians 6:16), and they are used, in their most far-reaching sense, of the perfect relationship God will have with the redeemed in heaven (Revelation 21:3).

It can't be emphasized enough that God's people are a *people.* In today's culture, where it's so easy to get trapped in our own personal silos, we need to keep in mind that those who are in a right relationship with God are involved in *something much bigger than their own private fellowship with Him.* For one thing, there is the local congregation of Christians to think about, the welfare of which each of us needs to be actively concerned about. But beyond that, there is the body of Christ in its universal sense (Ephesians 1:22,23; Colossians 1:18). And we need not be totally agnostic as to who those people are. They are those who have obeyed the gospel of Christ and are adhering to the New Testament. That standard is not so hard to understand that we can't look around us and recognize people in various localities as being God's people — or not.

Above all, we need to keep the focus on God and His eternal purposes. If He has a people, which He certainly does in Jesus Christ, it was not without *purpose* that He made them His people. On our side of the relationship, the promise that "they will be his people" was not made to give us a merely honorary position. God dwells with us in order that we may *know* Him — and knowing Him, that we might experience *the joy of living within His wisdom.*

The greatest blessing of heaven will be unhindered fellowship with God himself. The goal of God's covenant, "Immanuel (God with us)" in Isaiah 7:14, foreshadowed in the Old Testament tabernacle and temple, will be achieved.

Dennis E. Johnson

October 7

A People for His Own Possession

But you are a chosen race, a royal priesthood, a holy nation,
a people for his own possession, that you may proclaim the excellencies
of him who called you out of darkness into his marvelous light. Once you
were not a people, but now you are God's people; once you had
not received mercy, but now you have received mercy.
1 Peter 2:9,10

In this text in the King James Version, Christians are described as "a peculiar people." One of the meanings of peculiar is "belonging distinctively to one person," so the idea is not that Christians are odd or strange (although some of us certainly are!); it is that they are *the unique possession of God*. Here are several more recent translations: God's "special people" (CEV), "people who belong to God" (ERV), and "a people of his own" (NET).

Peter's words, of course, are a reference to what God had said to Israel after He had brought them out of their long bondage in Egypt. Gathered at Mount Sinai, Israel heard God say to them through Moses, "Now therefore, if you will indeed obey my voice and keep my covenant, you shall be my treasured possession among all peoples, for all the earth is mine; and you shall be to me a kingdom of priests and a holy nation" (Exodus 19:5,6).

Even in the case of Israel, God prefaced His statement with an "if." Physical parentage might be automatic, but only "if you will indeed obey my voice" would they remain a part of God's "treasured possession." And if that was true then, it is even more true now. God has a people, to be sure, but faithfulness is required.

The people who are God's own possession have accepted His plan to restore them to His glorious image (2 Corinthians 3:18), and make them people through whom He can accomplish the initial purpose He had when creating mankind. For this process to occur, the alienation of sin must be removed — and it is God's choice that this reconciliation can only be done through the atonement of His Son, Jesus Christ. But in Christ, let us not undervalue what it is possible for us to be: *a people set aside for God to possess*. There is no higher privilege than to be a part of this people.

All who believe that the Creator revealed Himself to His creatures confidently look to that revelation for His purpose. Whatever His purpose may be, we believe man's greatest good can be realized in achieving that end. In God's Word . . . those who through God's grace seek to satisfy His divine purpose are called the "people of God" in a very special sense.

Robert F. Turner

October 8

I Will Be Their God

For this is the covenant that I will make with the house of Israel after those days, declares the Lord: I will put my laws into their minds, and write them on their hearts, and I will be their God, and they shall be my people.
Hebrews 8:10

THIS VERSE IS PART OF THE HEBREW WRITER'S QUOTATION OF JEREMIAH 31:31-34, WHICH IS THE LONGEST OLD TESTAMENT QUOTATION IN THE NEW TESTAMENT. For today's study, let's focus on God's statement, "I will be their God, and they shall be my people."

In the Old Testament, God was the God of the Jews. There were certainly people outside of Israel who worshiped Him as the true God, but at Mount Sinai God entered into a covenant with Israel that set up a special relationship between Him and Israel (Exodus 19:1-6). This was in fulfillment of God's promise to Abraham (Genesis 12:1-3), and it was to prepare Israel to be the physical family through whom the Messiah would be born into the world — the One anticipated all the way back in Genesis 3:15 who would crush Satan and reverse the damage done by sin.

Even the "old" covenant itself had spoken of a "new" one that God would put into place: "Behold, the days are coming, declares the LORD, when I will make a new covenant" (Jeremiah 31:31). This new covenant would be "not like" (v.32) the old one; it would be different. Some things seem similar, however. In the new covenant, according to v.33, God would say, "I will be their God, and they shall be my people," but He had said the same thing to Israel (Leviticus 26:12). We need to consider carefully how this language might be different in the new covenant as opposed to the old.

For one thing, "I will be their God" had reference in the old covenant to Israel, but in the new it would encompass people from every nation. And amazingly, even this had been anticipated in the Jewish prophecies of the Messiah's reign, like Daniel 7:13,14.

But "I will be their God" would also have a more personal meaning in the new covenant. God would not just be the deity acknowledged by a group of people as the true God — He would be the God whom they actually loved and worshiped and trusted. In Latin terms, He would be their God *de facto* as well as *de jure.*

The Greek [in Hebrews 8:10] expresses it cryptically —
"I will be to them as God, and they will be to me as people."
The relationship was to be intimate and mutual.

DONALD GUTHRIE

October 9

A People for God's Name

Simeon has related how God first visited the Gentiles,
to take from them a people for his name.
Acts 15:14

A PERSON'S "NAME" COMMUNICATES HIS CHARACTER OR TRUE NATURE. Hence, "a good name is better than precious ointment" (Ecclesiastes 7:1). In the case of God's name, of course, much more is involved than with any human name. God's name stands for not only His character but also His power — especially His power to deliver and to save. When the apostles were pressured by the Jewish authorities, they said concerning Jesus Christ, "There is salvation in no one else, for there is no other name under heaven given among men by which we must be saved" (Acts 4:12).

In Acts 15:14, when James said that God had dealt with the Gentiles so as to take from them "a people for his name," what did he mean? In the Old Testament, the expression "a people for his name" always referred to the Israelites; here we are told that it is also from among the Gentiles that some will be His people. But what does it mean to be a people "for his name"? I am still pondering this, but at least two things are clear to me so far:

(1) God's people "wear" His name. If we are called by God's name that means we belong to Him. More important, it means we partake of His character (2 Peter 1:4). In heaven, God's people will have been perfected completely in the godliness of their character — "and his name will be on their foreheads" (Revelation 22:4).

(2) God's people "bear" His name. In a sense, God has put His reputation in the hands of those who are "a people for his name." Knowing that the world is watching, we live so as to reflect favorably on God's character and His power (Matthew 5:13-16).

The glory of the gospel is that God has such a people as this: *a people for his name.* Whether Jewish or Gentile, we may be a part of that people by obeying the gospel. In Christ, not only is our alienation from God removed, but so is the alienation between Jew and Gentile (Galatians 3:27,28). No matter who we are, we have *an equal need* for God's forgiveness, and in Christ, we receive that forgiveness *on exactly the same basis.* No one receives favoritism, and no one is excluded. May the good news be both your joy and mine.

God's concern is for His name, His glory, His people,
His unfolding eternal purpose and for His Kingdom.

ALISTAIR BEGG

October 10

THE WAY

But Saul, still breathing threats and murder against the disciples of the Lord, went to the high priest and asked him for letters to the synagogues at Damascus, so that if he found any belonging to the Way, men or women, he might bring them bound to Jerusalem.
Acts 9:1,2

AS THESE VERSES INDICATE, "THE WAY" IS HOW THE CHRISTIAN FAITH WAS KNOWN IN ITS EARLY DAYS. The fact that the faith was known by that description says several things. First, a "way" indicates *a manner of living* and not merely a set of doctrines. Second, "the Way" is the language of choice and boundaries (since we can't follow a particular path and still go everywhere else too). And third, the narrowness of *one* way — *the* Way — is objectionable to modern culture. Its exclusiveness is thought to be ungracious.

But R. C. Sproul made a perceptive comment when he said, "The question is not, 'Why is there only one way to God?' but 'Why is there even one way?'" It is a token of just how gracious God is that He opened up any way for us to come back at all, when justice could have been served by simply letting us reap the harvest we had sown. Seen from this perspective, it seems outrageous of us, guilty of treason and standing before the King, to complain that He is narrow and judgmental if He does not allow us to reconcile ourselves to Him in any way we think is appropriate.

There is also another thing to ponder. We often frame the question of "the Way" in terms of *our* journey, when in reality, the better analogy is just the reverse. If we are reconciled to God, that will not be the result of our making a "journey" that got us to heaven; it will be the result of God coming to our rescue. He is the One who takes the initiative, reaching down to us in our lost condition and offering us His saving hand. *If He does that at all, it will certainly be on His terms.* Being who He is, and having the nature that He does, He cannot be other than what He is. He could not reconcile Himself to us in simply any way that "felt good" to Him; it would have to be in a way that is consistent with His divine attributes, which are fixed and very definite. So let's quit talking about "man's journey to God." It is God who condescends to save us; humility on our part will gladly accept "the Way" provided by Him, which is through obedience to the gospel of His Son.

God cannot come to me in any way but his own way.

OSWALD CHAMBERS

October 11

Everywhere in Every Church

That is why I sent you Timothy, my beloved and faithful
child in the Lord, to remind you of my ways in Christ,
as I teach them everywhere in every church.
1 Corinthians 4:17

THE THINGS PAUL TAUGHT AS AN APOSTLE, HE TAUGHT EVERYWHERE IN EVERY CHURCH. And the statement Paul makes here is like others in the same letter indicating that the order he imposed on the Lord's work and worship in Corinth did not vary from what he imposed on any other congregation (1 Corinthians 7:17; 14:36). As he indicated in 16:1, he had the authority, as an apostle, to "direct" the churches to do certain things. His were not just suggestions; they were commands. As an apostle, he could make this kind of statement, which no one but an apostle would have dared to make: "I do not permit . . ." (1 Timothy 2:12).

Not only was Paul's teaching the same wherever he went; his teaching was the same as that of the other apostles. When he found himself under attack for taking the gospel to the Gentiles, he argued that the other apostles were in agreement with his practice (Galatians 2:6-10). He made it clear that he, like the other apostles, had received the teaching from God by direct revelation (Galatians 1:11,12). Coming from the same source, the teaching of all the apostles would naturally be in agreement (2 Peter 3:15,16).

Have you ever wondered how congregations in the New Testament period resembled one another so strongly in their faith and practice? It was not by following a historical tradition, for in those early days there was no tradition. It was not by taking orders from the home office of a denomination or association of churches, for there was no such thing. And it wasn't by copying one another. It was simply by following *the teaching of the apostles.* And today, if we go back to the teaching of the apostles and use that as our template, *the congregations you and I worship with will resemble those congregations in the very same ways they resembled one another.*

The point here is not that likeness is a value in and of itself; it is that when we yield to the authority of Jesus Christ, mediated to us by the teaching of His apostles in the Scriptures, we will be what He wants us to be, both individually and congregationally.

Market-driven churches? Whatever
happened to gospel-driven churches?

WALTER B. SHURDEN

October 12

The Apostles

. . . built on the foundation of the apostles and prophets, Christ Jesus himself being the cornerstone, in whom the whole structure, being joined together, grows into a holy temple in the Lord.
Ephesians 2:20,21

THE CHURCH OF WHICH CHRIST IS THE CORNERSTONE HAS A SOLID FOUNDATION: THE APOSTLES AND PROPHETS. Prophecy was important, obviously, but since it was a gift of the Spirit (1 Corinthians 12:8-10), it was imparted by the apostles (Acts 8:14-19). So the work of the apostles was primary (1 Corinthians 12:28). It was to them that Christ gave the "keys of the kingdom of heaven" (Matthew 16:19). There would come a time when prophecies (and the other miraculous gifts) would no longer be present in the church (1 Corinthians 13:8,9), but the teaching of the apostles, uniquely revealed to them by God's Spirit (John 14:25,26; 16:4-15), would serve as the permanent constitution of the Lord's church. Beginning on Pentecost and continuing afterward until Christ returns, Christians would need to ground their faith and practice in the apostles' teaching. As John, who was one of the apostles, wrote toward the end of the apostolic age, "Let what you heard from the beginning abide in you. If what you heard from the beginning abides in you, then you too will abide in the Son and in the Father" (1 John 2:24).

The apostles were, first of all, eyewitnesses of Jesus after His resurrection (Acts 1:21-26). But second, Jesus had said to the apostles alone that they would be guided into "all the truth" by the Holy Spirit (John 16:13). And to guarantee their authority as Christ's emissaries, they were given distinctive abilities which served as "the signs of a true apostle" (2 Corinthians 12:12).

In the New Testament, the second half of Luke-Acts is often called "Acts of the Apostles," and that is an excellent name for it. Endowed with nothing less than Christ's own authority, the apostles were *those through whom Christ continued His work* after He ascended to heaven. If we think we're exalting Christ when we downplay the work of the apostles, we're mistaken. Christ's work is inseparable from the teaching of those men; it is the very foundation of the church — and the wise will take it utterly seriously.

This doctrine of Christ and of the apostles, from which the true faith of the primitive church was received, the apostles at first delivered orally, without writing, but later, not by any human counsel but by the will of God, they handed it on in the Scriptures.

MARTIN CHEMNITZ

October 13

THE APOSTOLIC TRADITIONS

So then, brothers, stand firm and hold to the traditions that you were taught by us, either by our spoken word or by our letter.
2 Thessalonians 2:15

IS TRADITION A GOOD THING OR A BAD THING? The word is neutral; it simply means "that which has been received." So tradition can be good or bad, depending on several things: the *source* from which it was received, the nature of *what* has been received, and what is *done* with it after it is received. But the traditions of which Paul spoke — the teachings of Christ revealed to His apostles — are good in the highest sense. And Paul urged the church in Thessalonica to stand firm and hold to these traditions. To depart from them would be to abandon the gospel and depart from Christ.

The teaching of the apostles carried the full weight of Christ's authority, as we see in the terminology used by Peter: *"the commandment of the Lord and Savior through your apostles"* (2 Peter 3:2). Thus, the apostles' teaching was in a special category as far as its authority was concerned (2 Corinthians 10:8; 13:10). It was the definitive guide for churches wherever they might be, revealed directly to the apostles (Galatians 1:11,12) and completing what Christ had begun to teach them during His earthly ministry (John 16:12,13). *Not even the apostles themselves could depart from this standard without their souls being in jeopardy (Galatians 1:8,9).* And when other people did begin to depart (as predicted in 2 Timothy 4:3,4 and other passages), the apostles exhorted their brethren to remember "what you heard from the beginning" (1 John 2:24). There was an unalterable standard to which they needed to adhere.

The authority of the apostles was not handed down to successors who would hold their office after they died. Once laid, the foundation of the church did not need to be laid again (Ephesians 2:20,21) — *the truths that form the foundation laid by the apostles will be available in the Scriptures until Christ returns.* So I believe Paul would say to us exactly what he said to the Thessalonians: "stand firm and hold to the traditions that you were taught by us." *Return* must be the church's watchword, now as it was back then. Return to Christ Jesus. Return to the apostolic traditions. Return to the Scriptures.

What does this reestablishment of the authority of the Scriptures and the abolition of all the foreign norms really signify for the church? Is it not, purely and simply, a return to the apostolic type of church?

ALFRED KUEN

October 14

Restoration as a Principle

Let what you heard from the beginning abide in you.
If what you heard from the beginning abides in you, then
you too will abide in the Son and in the Father.
1 John 2:24

THE CONCEPT OF "RESTORATION" IS OF FUNDAMENTAL IMPORTANCE IN BOTH THE OLD AND THE NEW TESTAMENTS. We can't read the Scriptures seriously and not see that if we intend to be God's faithful people, "restoration" must be a work we engage in. God has never — in any age of the world — left people without any standard which must be adhered to, in both belief and practice. "Restoration" means (a) being reminded of the standard, and (b) making constant efforts to bring things back in line with it.

If you have any acquaintance with basic science (or if you have ever looked at your teenager's bedroom), you are familiar with the law of "entropy": *left to themselves, things descend into greater and greater disorder.* This law is as true in the spiritual realm as it is in the physical. Over time, things degrade. Without constant monitoring, maintenance, and "restoration," we drift away from the standard God has set. And the descent into disorder is so gradual we often don't admit to ourselves what is happening.

In our individual lives, we see the need for realignment with the Scriptures more easily, but perhaps we don't recognize it as much *at the congregational level.* Local assemblies of Christians must commit themselves to a restoration of the apostolic order. If not, they will descend into greater "entropy" with each passing year — *and there is no congregation where this tendency is not present.*

If you're a new Christian, look for a congregation that is committed to the principle of restoration. And if you've been a Christian for some time, remind the brothers and sisters where you worship that it is dangerous to be content with their past restoration efforts, as if New Testament Christianity has been fully restored and they can put things on autopilot from now on. Look for elders who are not afraid to lead their brethren in congregational acts of repentance and restoration. And look for brethren who know they need to be warned. "We must pay much closer attention to what we have heard, lest we drift away from it" (Hebrews 2:1).

The life of the Church depends on one thing:
her return to biblical principles.

OTTO RIECKER

October 15

RESTORATION AS AN ONGOING WORK

Remember therefore from where you have fallen; repent, and do the works you did at first. If not, I will come to you and remove your lampstand from its place, unless you repent.
Revelation 2:5

IN YESTERDAY'S READING, WE TALKED ABOUT THE IMPORTANCE OF RESTORING THE FAITH AND PRACTICE THAT WE FIND IN THE NEW TESTAMENT. Today, let's reemphasize the fact that restoration must be *an ongoing work.* There will never come a time when we can say, "What is taught in the New Testament has been restored, so we won't have to work on that any more; we can relax and enjoy it."

The church in Ephesus is a good example of what can happen. The brethren there had been zealous in defending the apostolic faith against corrupters and compromisers (Revelation 2:2,3). But toward the end of the first century, they themselves were in need of returning to the standard. They didn't love the Lord as they used to (v.4), and the problem was deeper than just not "feeling it" anymore (as this text is sometimes taught). They weren't *doing* what they once did, and the Lord said, "Remember therefore from where you have fallen; *repent, and do the works you did at first.* If not, I will come to you and remove your lampstand from its place, unless you repent" (v.5). This church needed to come back to Christ!

Both individually and congregationally, restoration requires constant vigilance. We must reassess and return. Reassess and return. Reassess and return. If our forebears did this, we are blessed to have their example. *But like them, we need to reassess and return.*

It is uncomfortable to have it brought to our attention (either individually or congregationally) that we stand in need of restoration — just as what your cardiologist tells you may not be fun to hear. But God forbid that we should react as Isaiah's people who, when they heard calls for restoration, said, "Do not prophesy to us what is right; speak to us smooth things, prophesy illusions" (Isaiah 30:10). Granted, the preacher who frequently emphasizes returning to the standard may be more of an irritant than a comforter, but any preacher worth his salt will have the attitude that Peter had: "It seems right to me, as long as I am in this tent of flesh, to keep your minds awake by working on your memory" (2 Peter 1:13 BBE).

Better the discomfort that leads to repentance and restoration than temporal comfort and eternal damnation.

FRANCINE RIVERS

October 16

Apostasy Was Foretold

Now the Spirit expressly says that in later times some will depart from the faith by devoting themselves to deceitful spirits and teachings of demons.
1 Timothy 4:1

PREDICTIONS OF APOSTASY, LIKE THE ONE ABOVE, ARE FOUND THROUGHOUT THE NEW TESTAMENT. It was a matter of great concern to all of the apostles. The fact that there would occur a departure from the foundational teachings of the gospel was not something they could think about except with a broken heart.

Here are some other texts that reveal the concern of the New Testament writers about the crisis that was coming (and I hope you'll take the time to look these up and think about them): Acts 20:29-31; 2 Thessalonians 2:3-5; 1 Timothy 6:20,21; 2 Timothy 3:1-7; 4:3,4; 2 Peter 2:1-3; 3:1-4; 1 John 2:18,19; 4:1; Jude 3,4.

Today, it is not hard to see that the apostles were right to be concerned. A great apostasy did, in fact, take place. And it is sobering to realize that most of what goes on in the modern world under the name of "Christianity" is a result of that apostasy.

Martin Luther, of course, is known for having sparked the Protestant Reformation. But although he saw that Catholicism was a departure from the Scriptures, Luther's work did not result in a complete return to the apostolic faith, and the Protestantism of today is just as much a part of the apostasy foretold by the apostles as the Catholicism against which the Protestants protested.

Clearly, we need to be warned just as strongly as the brethren to whom the apostles wrote in the first century. *We need constant reminders and admonitions.* Given the human propensity for drifting (Galatians 1:6), there is no hope for us if restoration is not an ongoing priority — and not just congregationally but individually.

Apostasy can be dealt with only by the testing of everything by God's standard (1 Thessalonians 5:21) and monitoring ourselves with great honesty (1 Corinthians 10:12; 2 Corinthians 13:5; Hebrews 2:1). The key is constant recourse to the teachings of Christ and His apostles, coupled with a love that simply refuses to let go of our Savior. If we wish to be God's people, in this or any other age, we must radically respect His plan for our salvation — and the Scriptures are our only means of knowing what that plan is.

There is no broader way to apostasy than to reject God's sovereignty in all things concerning the revelation of himself and our obedience.

JOHN OWEN

October 17

Accept Forgiveness, Grow in Godliness

Like newborn infants, long for the pure spiritual milk, that by it you may grow up into salvation.
1 Peter 2:2

If we are outside of Jesus Christ, in a lost condition because we've never obeyed the gospel, God would say two things to us. He would say, first, that we need to accept His forgiveness by obeying the gospel. But He would say also that, having been forgiven, we need to start growing in godliness each day.

The first is the most immediate need, obviously. If a person is lost in sin, the most pressing question he or she must ask is, "What must I do to be saved?" (Acts 16:30). If that is our situation, the passages in the New Testament we need to be focusing on are those that tell us what is required in order to pass from death to life, spiritually speaking. *What are the initial things a person must do? What is required by God in order to come into a saved, forgiven, and reconciled relationship with Him?* If we're honest in our search, we will let passages like Acts 2:37,38 and Romans 10:9,10 speak to our need. Without letting our own opinions intervene, we will let the Scriptures tell us what God's conditions for salvation are.

But growing in godliness is no less important than our initial obedience to the gospel. Peter was speaking to Christians when he said, "Like newborn infants, long for the pure spiritual milk, that by it you may grow up into salvation" (1 Peter 2:2). The point of becoming a Christian is not just to receive the forgiveness of our past sins; it is to enter the process of having the damage of sin repaired. It is to start becoming less like the old person who died when we were baptized (Romans 6:1-4) and more like the new person Christ will enable us to be (Ephesians 4:22-24).

It is regrettable that so many seem to view salvation as nothing more than being saved from their past sins. In reality, however, it is also being saved from the person we used to be. Outgrowing that old person is a *process* — and it takes time.

So, spiritual growth needs to be established as a priority in our lives, and the earlier we establish it, the better. Neglecting this is not just undesirable; it is dangerous. As Christians, there is no safe plateau where we may complacently sing "Just As I Am." Either we grow toward God's likeness, or we go back to being dead.

All growth that is not toward God is growing to decay.

George MacDonald

October 18

JESUS IS FAIRER, JESUS IS PURER

He is the image of the invisible God, the firstborn of all creation.
Colossians 1:15

DARKNESS CAN HAVE A DARKENING EFFECT ON US MENTALLY. If you were to live underground long enough, you would almost forget that there is such a thing as sunshine, and when you finally saw it again, you would be exhilarated. In a similar way, those who heard Jesus Christ might have had a hard time putting it into words, but they would have felt somewhat as a person feels who comes into the light after a long stay in the darkness. In fact, Peter, writing to his fellow Christians, spoke of God as "him who called you out of darkness into his marvelous light" (1 Peter 2:9). *Marvelous light* is exactly what it is. Those who have long endured the darkness and then experienced the beauty of what Jesus makes possible know very well what Peter was talking about.

I recently bought a little oil lamp that I light each night after I've turned off all the other lights in my apartment. It has come to mean a great deal to me because of what it reminds me of when I look at it in the dark hours. Its little flame is a comforting reminder that the darkness in this world will not last always, and even while it does, there is a Savior who is now reigning in a realm of light. He is my Beautiful Friend, the One who will one day come for me and take me to that wonderful place (John 14:2,3).

In Colossians 1:15, Paul affirms that Jesus Christ is "the image of the invisible God, the firstborn of all creation." The point is not that He was the first thing created but that He is the unrivaled Ruler over all that was made through Him (vv.16,17). And if He is, as Weymouth translates it, "the visible representation of the invisible God," it is a most beautiful God that He represents to us. As the Lord of all creation, He rules over a cosmos that reveals the *glory* of its Creator (Psalm 19:1). What touches our hearts so deeply is that *He is even more fair and pure than the creation which He has made.* And the grandest truth of all is that the One who created the beauty around us is able to fix our broken hearts and create a beauty *within* us — one that is nothing less than His own beauty.

Fair are the meadows, fairer still the woodlands,
Robed in all the blooming garb of spring;
Jesus is fairer, Jesus is purer,
Who makes the woeful heart to sing.

GERMAN FOLK HYMN

October 19

His Wonderful Passion and Purity

When he went ashore he saw a great crowd, and he had compassion on them, because they were like sheep without a shepherd. And he began to teach them many things.
Mark 6:34

ONE OF OUR GREAT ENDOWMENTS AS HUMAN BEINGS IS THE CAPACITY TO FEEL THINGS EMOTIONALLY. Whatever "emotions" any of the lower creatures may seem to have, these are indescribably far below the emotional abilities of human beings. We are able to feel things the way we do because we are made in the image of a personal Creator. Emotions are the unique province of personal beings, and we are personal because God is personal.

The word *passion* simply means strong feeling. It may be good or bad, depending on what the feeling is about and what is done with that feeling. But the world would be a poorer place if there were no passionate people. All of us can feel, but some people seem to feel things more deeply and vividly. In the case of Jesus, who was God our Creator in the form of a human being, He felt things perfectly — which meant that at times He felt them very strongly. In the passage in Mark 6:34, for example, we see Him being moved with compassion for the multitudes who followed Him. He did not find their needs merely "interesting"; He was passionately moved by them. He cared, and He cared very deeply.

Yet Jesus' passion was never anything less than pure. It was always governed by eternally valid *principles*. Even when we see Him demonstrating anger, as in John 2:13-17, His anger was never out of control. I do not doubt that the purity of His passion (along with the passion of His purity) would have caused many to think, "Here is a person unlike any who has ever appeared in the world."

When we study Jesus, is it not His combination of passion and purity that is so powerful? As with all His other characteristics, the blend of these two in such a harmonious way is what allowed Him to have the influence that He did. And does this not remind us that we were created to be *whole* persons, not people with our various traits at war with each other? This wholeness was the beauty of Jesus, and my prayer must be: *let this beauty be seen in me.*

Let the beauty of Jesus be seen in me,
All His wonderful passion and purity.
May His Spirit divine all my being refine;
Let the beauty of Jesus be seen in me.

ALBERT W. T. ORSBORN

October 20

IMMANUEL

Therefore the Lord himself will give you a sign. Behold, the virgin shall conceive and bear a son, and shall call his name Immanuel.
Isaiah 7:14

ONE OF THE FUNDAMENTAL TRUTHS OF THE GOSPEL IS THE INCARNATION. From the Latin for "flesh," the Incarnation means that God took fleshly form. In order to deal with human sin at its deepest level, God allowed Himself to be born into the world as a human being. In the person of Jesus Christ, the Son of God was both true God and true man. "And the Word became flesh and dwelt among us, and we have seen his glory, glory as of the only Son from the Father, full of grace and truth" (John 1:14).

In Isaiah 7:14, the birth of One who could rightly be called *Immanuel* ("God with us") was foretold. This is one of the many "messianic" prophecies in the Old Testament, predictions that anticipated the coming of a great king (Messiah means "Anointed One") who would inaugurate the kingdom of God and rule with divine sovereignty. In addition to Isaiah 7:14, we think of other texts like Psalm 2:1-12; 110:1-7; Isaiah 52:13-53:12; and dozens more.

One of the solid evidences of Jesus' identity as the Messiah is *the fulfillment in His life and death of every one of these messianic prophecies.* They are fulfilled in such minute detail, and so many centuries after the prophecies were made, no one person could have arranged his life in such a way as to fulfill them all. How could Jesus have decided to be born in Bethlehem (Micah 5:2), be of the tribe of Judah (Genesis 49:10), be a descendant of David (Isaiah 9:6,7; 11:1), be put to death in such a gruesome manner (Psalm 22:1-18), and then be brought back from the grave (Psalm 16:10)? No one merely pretending to be the Messiah could have done all these things.

But in regard to "God with us" in Isaiah 7:14, it is an important part of the gospel that God did, in fact, enter our world and live among us as He did. He loved us and saved us, not from a distance but by becoming one of us. Jesus, as God in the flesh, is our Lord, but He is also our Brother and Friend. We worship and adore Him knowing that He knows what it is like to be "us." How could such a thing as this be possible? We do not know; we simply give thanks that our salvation has been wrought by "God with us."

Jesus, name above all names: Beautiful Savior, glorious Lord,
Emmanuel, God is with us, Blessed Redeemer, Living Word.

NAIDA HEARN

October 21

Christ in Us, the Hope of Glory

To them God chose to make known how great among the Gentiles are the riches of the glory of this mystery, which is Christ in you, the hope of glory.
Colossians 1:27

ALTHOUGH THE GOSPEL WAS FORESHADOWED IN THE OLD TESTAMENT, IT WAS A "MYSTERY" UNTIL GOD FULLY REVEALED IT IN THE LIFE OF JESUS CHRIST AND THE TEACHING OF THE APOSTLES. It was not mysterious in the sense of being weird or arcane, but it was a "mystery" in that it could not have been known until God disclosed it. In Colossians 1:27, the mystery was not just God's plan in general but a specific part of the plan: that it would be for the whole world and not just Israel (cf. Ephesians 3:4-6). In our text above, Paul said that God chose "to make known how great among the Gentiles are the riches of the glory of this mystery."

Which is Christ in you. In the New Testament, Christians are spoken of as being in Christ (2 Corinthians 5:17; 1 Peter 5:14) — and likewise, He is said to be in them (John 14:20; Romans 8:10). The surprise, to some at least, was that the expression "Christ in you" would ever be applied to Christians who were not Jewish.

The hope of glory. If the remission of sins is found only in Christ, then our hope of sharing God's glory in eternity is tied to Him. But that is precisely what the gospel offers: *the hope of a glory beyond the boundaries of this world.* "When Christ who is your life appears, then you also will appear with him in glory" (Colossians 3:4).

As the unveiled mystery now shows, the "hope of glory" in Christ is for all of mankind, the Gentile no less than the Jew. The inclusion of the Gentiles in God's redemptive plan had been hinted at in prophecies about the Messiah (Isaiah 56:6-8; Amos 9:11,12), but no one could have known how it would happen until God revealed it in the gospel of Christ. Now that we know, however, we stand amazed at "how vast a wealth of glory for the Gentile world" (Weymouth) is stored up in the hope of the gospel.

In Christ, then, is the very summation of all that we need and aspire to. There is nothing about our broken relationship with God that He is not able to repair, no void in our hearts He cannot fill. He is God, who came from heaven to save us. And the rest of our lives would not be time enough to praise Him sufficiently.

Jesus, LORD God Almighty, Wonderful Couns'lor, Light of the world,
The Prince of Peace, Hope of glory, Man of Sorrows, Lamb of God.

DANE K. SHEPARD

October 22

IF FAITH DOES NOT ACT, IT DOES NOT SAVE

For as the body apart from the spirit is dead,
so also faith apart from works is dead.
James 2:26

FAITH IS ABOUT AS BASIC A CONCEPT AS THERE IS IN THE GOSPEL. Its importance in our response to God is immense (Philippians 3:8,9). But faith, or trust, is not easy. It requires a good deal of courage. For example, it takes faith to accept whatever the Lord's commandments are in cases where what He requires goes against our preferences and preconceived notions. *But if we do not trust the Lord enough to comply with His instructions, it is vain for us to think that He will save us anyway.* Think about it: if the attitude that led us into sin initially was "I don't think I really *have* to do what God commanded," what possible hope of salvation do we have if we exhibit the same attitude about what the gospel requires of us? Like it or not, distrust of God is at the root of sin — *and deciding to trust Him again is at the heart of how we must respond to the gospel.*

Genuine faith will always show up in action, often at great risk. We see this in each of the amazing examples in Hebrews 11 of people in the Old Testament who did what they did because they trusted God. We do not earn our salvation by our works, but the fact remains, if faith does not obey God, it is not real faith. James put it unmistakably: "Faith apart from works is dead" (2:26).

"The road to hell is paved with good intentions" may be a crude saying, but it is true. Many a good-intentioned person knows what he should do, but not many make the choice to carry out their intentions. And this failure to act on our best impulses is a serious matter; it compounds our sin. "Whoever knows the right thing to do and fails to do it, for him it is sin" (James 4:17). So I would suggest that the gospel calls us to do not one but two things: we must *think* rightly and then *do* what our thinking tells us is right.

If you're not a Christian, it may be you don't yet agree that the gospel is true. If so, I hope you'll keep studying. But if you *are* convinced Jesus is the Messiah and you know what the gospel requires for your salvation in Him, my prayer is that your newfound faith will move you to humble, obedient action.

Faith and works are bound up in the same bundle. He that obeys God trusts God; and he that trusts God obeys God. He that is without faith is without works; and he that is without works is without faith.

CHARLES SPURGEON

October 23

WE MUST ALL APPEAR

For we must all appear before the judgment seat of Christ so that each one may receive what is due for what he has done in the body, whether good or evil.
2 Corinthians 5:10

IT IS A VERY SERIOUS THING THAT PAUL SAYS HERE. There is not a single one of us who will not have to account for himself or herself before Christ at the judgment. That accounting will be an absolutely accurate assessment of our life-choices, whether good or evil. There will be no favoritism and no miscarriage of justice. Each one will "receive what is due for what he has done." An equally honest picture of the judgment is found in Romans 2:5-11.

In v.9, the verse preceding our text in 2 Corinthians 5:10, Paul had spoken of his desire to please Christ: "we make it our aim to please him." The wonder of the gospel is that this is possible. Outside of Christ, our sins would doom us and judgment would hold nothing but fear, but thanks to Christ's sacrifice and our having died with Him in obedience to the gospel, "There is therefore now no condemnation for those who are in Christ Jesus" (Romans 8:1). The apostle John wrote to his brethren, "By this is love perfected with us, so that we may have confidence for the day of judgment, because as he is so also are we in this world" (1 John 4:17).

But don't be deceived: if our sins haven't been forgiven by the blood of Christ and we're not living in a faithful relationship with Him, the judgment that is coming will be an occasion of terror for us. The fact that God's grace has provided salvation will do us no good if we have not accepted that grace on His terms, by complying with the conditions upon which we could have "passed from death to life" (John 5:24). As Christians, knowing that we will be judged, while not paralyzing us with fear, is a healthy incentive to take God seriously. But without a right relationship with God through Christ, we have good reason to fear (1 Peter 4:17,18).

In summary, then, judgment before God is inevitable for all of us. It is coming — and the only question is whether we'll be ready. So Solomon was exactly right: "The end of the matter; all has been heard. Fear God and keep his commandments, for this is the whole duty of man. *For God will bring every deed into judgment,* with every secret thing, whether good or evil" (Ecclesiastes 12:13,14).

All roads lead to the judgment seat of Christ.

KEITH GREEN

October 24

WHAT WAS WRITTEN IN THE HEBREW SCRIPTURES

Thus it is written, that the Christ should suffer and on the third day rise from the dead, and that repentance for the forgiveness of sins should be proclaimed in his name to all nations, beginning from Jerusalem. You are witnesses of these things.
Luke 24:46-48

THIS STATEMENT WAS MADE BY JESUS TO A GROUP OF HIS DISCIPLES ON THE EVENING OF THE SAME DAY ON WHICH HE HAD BEEN RAISED FROM THE DEAD. As He appeared to them in the room in Jerusalem where they were gathered, the disciples were frightened, but Jesus assured them they were not seeing a ghost and asked if they had anything to eat. Then He began to talk to them about the momentous events of His death and resurrection.

He said, "These are my words that I spoke to you while I was still with you, that everything written about me in the Law of Moses and the Prophets and the Psalms must be fulfilled" (Luke 24:44). Not one detail of what had happened in the previous week should have been surprising to the disciples. All of it was a part of what had been written about the Messiah in the three divisions of the Tanakh (the Torah, the Prophets, and the Writings). And then "he opened their minds to understand the Scriptures" (v.45).

Now we come to our text in vv.46-48. Specifically, what Jesus showed His disciples from the Hebrew Scriptures is that (a) the Messiah would suffer, (b) He would rise from the dead, and (c) repentance for the forgiveness of sins would be preached in His name to all the nations, beginning from Jerusalem. And when the apostles themselves began their work, they preached from the Hebrew Scriptures, showing that what the prophets had foretold about the Messiah was perfectly fulfilled in Jesus of Nazareth (Acts 3:22-26; 9:22; 10:43; 17:2,3; 18:5; 24:14; 26:22,23; 28;23,24; etc.).

There is no greater study for us than to immerse ourselves in the Hebrew Scriptures, reverently looking there for every detail which God revealed about the coming of His Messiah. The Messiah was to be a King, obviously, but as it turned out, He was a very different King than anyone expected. In particular, His horrible death and victorious resurrection caught everyone by surprise. But that is the way it often is with events that shake the world.

What happened on that day [of Jesus' resurrection] became, was, and remained the center around which everything else moves.

KARL BARTH

October 25

WHY SAUL, THE RABBI, OBEYED THE GOSPEL OF CHRIST

. . . in order that I may gain Christ and be found in him, not having a righteousness of my own that comes from the law, but that which comes through faith in Christ, the righteousness from God that depends on faith — that I may know him and the power of his resurrection, and may share his sufferings, becoming like him in his death, that by any means possible I may attain the resurrection from the dead.

Philippians 3:8-11

FOR THE TASK OF TAKING THE GOSPEL TO THE GENTILES, GOD SELECTED A MOST UNLIKELY CANDIDATE. Saul of Tarsus was a firebrand. He was a strict and conscientious Pharisee, a protégé of Gamaliel, one of the leading rabbis in Jerusalem with an influential seat on the Sanhedrin. Before his conversion to Christ, Saul was an ardent persecutor of the fledgling church, traveling even to distant cities to imprison those of "the Way" (Acts 9:1,2).

Saul, later known as Paul, was on track to become one of the leading scholars and defenders of the Jewish faith of his generation. He had a great deal to give up. When he became convinced that he had to become a Christian, it was not as if he had nothing to lose. And the life he had as a Christian, at least in this world, was a life so hard most of us can hardly imagine it (just read 2 Corinthians 11:23-28 if you think Paul made his life more comfortable when he obeyed the gospel). When he was baptized for the remission of his sins (Acts 22:16), Paul was not switching his "religious affiliation" — he was moving from condemnation to salvation, from death to life, from Satan to the Savior of the world.

After turning to Christ, Paul was as fiery a preacher as he had been a persecutor, which goes to show that the Lord is not looking for timid people without any intensity but for those who, when they finally see the truth, will take a bold and passionate stand for it. And why will people take such a stand, even going so far as to die for Christ? *Because of how good the good news really is.* So today, our motivation needs to be just as passionate. My own prayer is that I obeyed the gospel in order "that I may gain Christ and be found in him, . . . becoming like him in his death, that by any means possible I may attain the resurrection from the dead."

The best news of the Christian gospel is that the supremely glorious Creator of the universe has acted in Jesus Christ's death and resurrection to remove every obstacle between us and himself so that we may find everlasting joy in seeing and savoring his infinite beauty.

JOHN PIPER

October 26

The Good Confession

Fight the good fight of the faith. Take hold of the eternal life to which you were called and about which you made the good confession in the presence of many witnesses.
1 Timothy 6:12

OPENNESS, TRANSPARENCY, DISCLOSURE. These are words with a very high social value these days. We tend to see them positively (at least as far as other people's conduct is concerned).

But what about openness with regard to our religious convictions, especially those that might get us into trouble if they were publicly known? When we might be persecuted for our beliefs, we often find it convenient to be quiet about them. And perhaps even more than persecution, we fear social disapproval and ostracism. As the world becomes increasingly secular, religious beliefs of any kind will come to be viewed as contemptible. Whatever other religious people may do, how is a Christian to deal with this pressure?

Well, the gospel is clear on this point. Jesus said, "Everyone who acknowledges me before men, I also will acknowledge before my Father who is in heaven, but whoever denies me before men, I also will deny before my Father who is in heaven" (Matthew 10:32,33). Openly acknowledging that we are the Lord's people is a part of our faith in Him. We cannot hide our identity and still expect that He will acknowledge us on the Judgment Day.

In 1 Timothy 6:12, Paul reminded Timothy that he had made "the good confession." Surely the verbal confession that Jesus is Lord is a good confession — the best of all possible acknowledgements that a person could make. *And it is a required part of becoming a Christian.* "With the heart one believes and is justified, and with the mouth one confesses and is saved" (Romans 10:10).

But to confess Christ goes beyond merely saying the words "I believe that Jesus is the Son of God." We must truly believe those words — and they must be confessed in our deeds as well as our words. We can't have Jesus as our "Savior" without obeying Him as our "Lord." And in the end, doing that may require the greatest courage of all: confessing by our actions that we have accepted His lordship — both when it is convenient and when it is not.

One of the greatest errors in the church today is the artificial distinction we have created between accepting Christ as Savior and confessing Him as Lord. We have made two experiences of it, but the New Testament makes them one.

VANCE HAVNER

October 27

EACH MUST CHOOSE

Now therefore fear the LORD and serve him in sincerity and in faithfulness. Put away the gods that your fathers served beyond the River and in Egypt, and serve the LORD. And if it is evil in your eyes to serve the LORD, choose this day whom you will serve, whether the gods your fathers served in the region beyond the River, or the gods of the Amorites in whose land you dwell. But as for me and my house, we will serve the LORD.
Joshua 24:14,15

THE LONGER I LIVE, THE MORE I SEE THE IMPORTANCE OF DECISIVENESS. If we don't train ourselves to make decisive choices, we will self-destruct. So Joshua could not have challenged Israel more profitably than by saying, "Choose this day whom you will serve." He knew they would serve one god or another; he just hoped it would be the true God they chose — *deliberately and decisively.*

What are we to make of Joshua's saying, "But as for me and my house, we will serve the LORD"? Did Joshua have the power to choose for his family that they would serve God? No, at least not in the strictest sense. I believe he was saying, "As the leader of my clan, I am making the choice to serve the LORD, and to the best of my ability I will influence each member of the family to do likewise." In his day, Joshua would have had the authority to enforce certain rules in his clan (at least externally). But in truth, Joshua could not make this, the greatest decision of life, for anyone but himself. Then, as now, we cannot compel; we can only influence.

As important as choice is, then, it must be exercised *individually*. This powerful gift of freedom that God has given us is perhaps the most private of all our gifts. We can influence other human beings and they can influence us, but no human being can enter the secret chambers of another's heart and make even the slightest decision for him. Even if I say to you, "I can't make up my mind; you decide," you are not really making my decision. I have simply made the decision to follow your lead. And as we all know, "not making a decision" is a misnomer. Not to decide is really just one kind of decision: the decision to do nothing and hope for the best.

In regard to God, we must say a decisive *Yes!* — or we'll not like where we end up. As I heard someone say, "God lives upstream from us, and we're not going to get to where He is by just drifting." The most disastrous thing we can do is "not decide."

There is a time when we must firmly choose the course we will follow, or the relentless drift of events will make the decision.

HERBERT V. PROCHNOW

October 28

The Faith Is Worth Contending For

Beloved, although I was very eager to write to you about our common salvation, I found it necessary to write appealing to you to contend for the faith that was once for all delivered to the saints.
Jude 3

JUDE MAKES TWO POINTS ABOUT THE GOSPEL, EACH OF WHICH OUGHT TO IMPRESS US. First, he calls it "the faith." And second, he says that it was "once for all delivered to the saints." The faith is not an ever-evolving system of belief, supplemented in each generation by continuing revelation from God. Instead, it is a body of teaching completely and definitively revealed to the apostles in their generation, just as Christ said it would be (John 14:26; 16:12,13). Having been delivered, it stands complete — once for all.

Although he wanted to write about the salvation he and his brethren were blessed to enjoy, Jude says he found it necessary to urge them to "contend for the faith." They were being assailed by teachers promoting a false gospel, and the content of this teaching needed to be contradicted in no uncertain terms.

"Contending" can be an ungodly activity, but it is not necessarily so. Paul urged Timothy to avoid the ugly side of controversy: "And the Lord's servant must not be quarrelsome but kind to everyone, able to teach, patiently enduring evil, correcting his opponents with gentleness" (2 Timothy 2:24,25). Nevertheless, the faith must be contended for. Paul himself "had no small dissension and debate" (Acts 15:1,2) with the false teachers who came to Antioch.

Here is a bold affirmation, but one I believe needs to be made: the gospel is not only true, but it can be rationally and objectively *known* to be true. It is not something that should be swallowed naively; in fact, it requires careful evaluation. But if the message of Christ is true, it is by far the most important truth in the world — *and it is worthy of being defended.* Just as surely as the gospel is preached, there will be those who corrupt it. When they speak up, those who know the Scriptures must speak up also.

Seek the truth
Listen to the truth
Teach the truth
Love the truth
Abide by the truth
And defend the truth
To the death.

JOHN HUSS

October 29

THERE ARE THOSE WHO PERVERT GOD'S GRACE

For certain people have crept in unnoticed who long ago were designated for this condemnation, ungodly people, who pervert the grace of our God into sensuality and deny our only Master and Lord, Jesus Christ.
Jude 4

THERE WAS AN URGENT PROBLEM AMONG THE CHRISTIANS TO WHOM JUDE WROTE. Having urged them to "contend for the faith" (v.3), in v.4 Jude gave the reason why such a defense of the faith was necessary: it was because "certain people have crept in unnoticed . . . who pervert the grace of our God." These were teachers who, based on their view of God's grace, minimized the seriousness of immoral behavior among Christians.

Sadly, the problem faced by Jude and his fellow Christians has not disappeared from the earth. Today, as then, there are those who present God's grace in such a way that it becomes a license to sin. Advocating what they say is a more advanced spirituality, these teachers promise freedom from the simple dos and don'ts of "legalism." But Peter, like Jude, saw this teaching for what it was: a perversion of the gospel, based on a lie. "For, speaking loud boasts of folly, they entice by sensual passions of the flesh those who are barely escaping from those who live in error. They promise them freedom, but they themselves are slaves of corruption. For whatever overcomes a person, to that he is enslaved" (2 Peter 2:18,19).

It is indeed sad that false versions of the gospel have to be dealt with, but they do. When the truth is twisted and people are being influenced, the only responsible thing is to "contend for the faith." The little letter of Jude is a strong dose of medicine, but Jude was not alone. Peter (2 Peter 2:1-3), Paul (2 Timothy 3:13,14), and John (1 John 2:18,19) were no less concerned.

When we obey the gospel of Christ, we commit ourselves to walking "in newness of life" (Romans 6:3,4), and this eliminates the very idea of continuing to live in sin (Romans 6:1,2). Granted, as Christians we will continue to fall short and our only hope of salvation is in God's forgiveness. But forgiveness requires godly sorrow and repentance. In the absence of "a broken and contrite heart" (Psalm 51:17), grace offers no freedom to continue in sin.

Grace abounds only when there is genuine repentance and we cannot simultaneously will sin and repentance since this involves a contradiction in terms.

DOROTHY L. SAYERS

October 30

In a World of Futility, How Should We Live?

The end of the matter; all has been heard. Fear God and keep his commandments, for this is the whole duty of man.
Ecclesiastes 12:13

IN ECCLESIASTES, WE ARE CONFRONTED WITH OUR POWERLESSNESS. Neither the human race collectively nor any of us individually can ever be sure that performing actions "A" and "B" will lead to "C" in this life. It might, but it might not. But if what we do can't be counted on to give us the life we want, what difference does it make how we live? Let's summarize the advice given in Ecclesiastes, and then pay special attention to the conclusion:

Do the best that we know to do. Wisdom is no guarantee of success, but that doesn't mean it's worthless — wisdom will give our plans their best chance of succeeding (11:1-6), and only a fool would disregard wisdom. Even at our wisest, however, we humbly recognize that we're not in control. God may overrule even the best of our projects, based on His greater wisdom.

Enjoy each day's happiness. Rather than basing our happiness on our (very weak) ability to make the future turn out the way we want, Ecclesiastes recommends that we simply enjoy today's pleasures for their own sake (3:12,13,22). As far as earthly joys are concerned, God means for us to enjoy them and then let them go.

Fear God and keep His commandments. After advising us to act wisely and relish the joys of daily living, Ecclesiastes ends with a profound conclusion: no matter what happens, we should fear God and stay within the boundaries of His laws. Doing this is "the whole duty of man" (12:13). The meaning of this statement is aptly rendered in the CEV paraphrase, "This is what life is all about."

The key to human conduct, therefore, lies not in figuring out what will produce this or that result tomorrow — it lies in the fear of God and obedience to what He has commanded. By frustrating our ability to create the future we want in this world, even by the means of religious activity (7:15), God is calling us back to the main thing that was lost in Eden: simple, unconditional *reverence.*

We must adjust our minds to the doing of what is right because it is right, and not because it will turn earthly events in our direction. The sooner we give up our "comprehend and control" approach to life, the sooner we'll be ready to hear the gospel.

Duty is ours and events are God's.

ANGELINA GRIMKÉ

October 31

Every Deed Will Be Tested

For God will bring every deed into judgment,
with every secret thing, whether good or evil.
Ecclesiastes 12:14

THE LAST VERSE IN ECCLESIASTES GIVES US THE REASON WHY WE SHOULD FEAR GOD AND KEEP HIS COMMANDMENTS. Reverence and obedience must define the way we live because "God will bring every deed into judgment." All that we do is going to be tested, not by the trial of any human evaluation, but by the judgment of God Himself. Not wanting to deal with it, we may pretend this testing won't come, but we will be tried by it nevertheless.

It is not just some of our deeds, but "every deed" that will be brought into judgment by God. Even "every secret thing" will be judged by Him. "No creature is hidden from his sight, but all are naked and exposed to the eyes of him to whom we must give account" (Hebrews 4:13). This truth should jolt us. We may present to other human beings only what we want them to know, but God knows even the most secret contents of our hearts.

Our deeds will be judged "whether good or evil." Just as we may temporarily deny God's judgment itself, we may also deny the existence of objective right and wrong, but our denial doesn't make it go away (any more than closing the blinds makes the sun go away). There is an eternal, unalterable difference between good and evil, and it has its origin in God's own character.

Because He is our Creator, God has a right to bring us into judgment. Having given us life and a free will, He will hold us accountable for the use of our freedom of choice between good and evil. Think of it in terms of "stewardship." Having been entrusted with great gifts, we will answer for our faithfulness in using them. Surely it is the right of the Giver to conduct such a reckoning.

At the final judgment, and even before, we won't be able to hide from that which Thomas Merton called "the implacable light of judgment." Apart from the forgiveness of God, which is what the gospel of Christ is about, none of us has any hope at the judgment. But if we won't face reality, not even the gospel can help us.

What we need is not a false peace which enables us to evade
the implacable light of judgment, but the grace courageously to accept
the bitter truth that is revealed to us; to abandon our inertia, our egotism
and submit entirely to the demands of the Spirit.

THOMAS MERTON

November 1

After Baptism, What's Different?

. . . but declared first to those in Damascus, then in Jerusalem and throughout all the region of Judea, and also to the Gentiles, that they should repent and turn to God, performing deeds in keeping with their repentance.
Acts 26:20

In this text, Paul gives us a summary of the message God sent him to preach. To one and all, he preached that "they should repent and turn to God, performing deeds in keeping with their repentance." This preaching called for a change much deeper than simply changing one's "religious affiliation." If the only thing that is different after we've been baptized is that we "now go to the right church," it may be that we've still got some changing to do.

Attending a different church. Some have the idea that heaven is simply the reward given by God to those who have identified the right religious group to be a part of. For them, baptism means little more than the doorway between the wrong church and the right church. On this point, let us be clear: unscriptural religious affiliations will jeopardize our souls. But there is more to the gospel — and to salvation — than getting into the right church.

Becoming a different person. In the text above, Paul said that he called on hearers to "turn to God." This is the heart of the gospel: *turning to God.* If we have been religious people and have been affiliated with a group whose doctrines and practices are out of sync with the Scriptures, that will need to be corrected. But those things are *symptoms* of the problem. The problem the gospel addresses is that our *hearts* have been taking a disobedient, self-willed stance with regard to God, not just in our religious affiliation but in everything else. The gospel, therefore, calls on us to turn to God, seeking the gracious forgiveness He offers and committing ourselves to a completely new life in Him. This new life will come from an admission that the problem with our previous life was not merely the church we were attending; the problem was *us.* So yes, the matter of "church" will need to be addressed, but the deeper (and much harder) issue is whether we're ready to die to what we used to be and learn to be a person with a very different kind of heart. Without this kind of turning to God, baptism is an empty act.

Conversion is a deep work — a heart work. It goes throughout the man, throughout the mind, throughout the members, throughout the entire life.

Joseph Alleine

November 2

SELF MUST BE CRUCIFIED

Then Jesus told his disciples, "If anyone would come after me, let him deny himself and take up his cross and follow me. For whoever would save his life will lose it, but whoever loses his life for my sake will find it."
Matthew 16:24,25

FOR JESUS, THE JOY WAS ON THE OTHER SIDE OF THE CROSS. The "joy that was set before him" could only be His after He "endured the cross" (Hebrews 12:2). If we wish to follow Jesus, what will we do? We want the joy He now has with the Father, but will we follow Him to the cross? "If anyone would come after me, let him deny himself and take up his cross and follow me."

There have been some of the Lord's disciples who have died by crucifixion as Jesus did. Peter seems to have suffered such a death (John 21:18,19). But that is not what the Lord was talking about when He said we must "take up our cross." Regardless of what happens to our physical bodies, there is something else about us that must die. There is something that must be "denied."

"If anyone would come after me, let him deny himself." For all of us (at least those old enough to have committed sin), it is "self" that must be crucified. Paul said of his own conversion, "I have been crucified with Christ. It is no longer I who live, but Christ who lives in me. And the life I now live in the flesh I live by faith in the Son of God, who loved me and gave himself for me" (Galatians 2:20).

God created us for the joy of living inside the limits of His love. He never wanted anything for us but "life." Yet we rebelled. We threw off His restraints. And what we found was not greater life, but "death" in all of its many forms. So this "self" — this stubborn, greedy demand to grasp what is "ours" — is what got us into trouble. If we're to be saved, it will have to be gotten rid of.

If we're not willing to put our self-will to death, we make a tragic and foolish mistake. Jesus said, "Whoever would save his life will lose it, but whoever loses his life for my sake will find it." It is life's ultimate irony that *we only get what we've given up.*

It sounds like a good thing to be "resurrected," doesn't it? But there is some dying that has to be done before a resurrection can take place. If there is anything other than God that we can't or won't give up, then the devil has our heart. "Give it up," Jesus says. "Hold on to it, and you will die. But die, and you will live."

Without sacrifice there is no resurrection.

ANDRÉ GIDE

November 3

HENCEFORTH

I have fought the good fight, I have finished the race, I have kept the faith. Henceforth there is laid up for me the crown of righteousness, which the Lord, the righteous judge, will award to me on that day, and not only to me but also to all who have loved his appearing.
2 Timothy 4:7,8

A CURIOUS THING HAPPENS AS THE YEARS GO BY AND WE GROW OLDER IN CHRIST. Toward life's end, we grow weary; the body deteriorates and the toll taken by the struggles of life can no longer be ignored. But at the same time, we become more excited and enthusiastic. The thought that we're getting close to the goal for which we've always lived fills us with a zest that simply can't be experienced any earlier in life. With each passing day, Paul's words become ever more real to us: "Though our outer self is wasting away, our inner self is being renewed day by day" (2 Corinthians 4:16).

Paul was getting close to the end of his life when he wrote the words we find in 2 Timothy 4:7,8. Meditate with me on the phrases in this text. They tell us much about what life in Christ is about.

Fought the good fight. Our adversary, Satan, will make our path to heaven as hard as he can make it. He cannot separate us from God against our will (John 10:28,29; 16:33), but Jesus Himself said that the way would be hard (Matthew 7:14). In this world, there happens to be a war going on, and we need to be able to say, as we come to the end of life, that we have fought the good fight.

Finished the race. If life is a war, it's also a race. Unless we die when we're young, it will be a *long* race, one in which we'll often be tempted to give up and quit running. Lately, I have found myself saying almost every day, "Feet, don't fail me now."

Kept the faith. Of all the things Paul could have said, this is the grandest. To be able to utter these words as we come down to the end is, in a sense, the principal goal in life. To say that we have "kept the faith" does not mean that we never betrayed the Lord. It means that when we saw that we had betrayed Him, we sought His forgiveness, got back on our feet, and kept striving forward.

"Henceforth," Paul wrote, "there is laid up for me the crown of righteousness." It is only the rugged who will receive this crown, those who have fought and run and been tested in the fire.

The devil tempts that he may ruin;
God tests that he may crown.

AMBROSE

November 4

Choose Life!

I call heaven and earth to witness against you today, that I have set before you life and death, blessing and curse. Therefore choose life, that you and your offspring may live, loving the LORD your God, obeying his voice and holding fast to him.
Deuteronomy 30:19,20

WE ARE ABLE TO CHOOSE OUR DESTINY. If the alternatives are obedience to God (which leads ultimately to life) and disobedience (which leads to death), it is possible to "choose life," as Moses urged Israel to do. And God, who gave us the power to choose, is always hoping that life is the choice we will make. As He instructed Ezekiel, "Say to them, As I live, declares the Lord GOD, I have no pleasure in the death of the wicked, but that the wicked turn from his way and live; turn back, turn back from your evil ways, for why will you die, O house of Israel?" (Ezekiel 33:11).

When we come to the New Testament, we hear Jesus exhorting people to make the same choice: to reject death and choose life. But since the road to life requires sacrifice, many people — indeed, *most* people — turn away from it, preferring instead a course of less resistance. "Enter by the narrow gate," He said, "for the gate is wide and the way is easy that leads to destruction, and those who enter by it are many. For the gate is narrow and the way is hard that leads to life, *and those who find it are few*" (Matthew 7:13,14).

Even in the little decisions of daily life, the power of choice is amazing. But those who know its power know that *choosing is more than simply having a preference — it requires action.* And certainly with regard to God, we haven't "chosen life" if we're not doing the kinds of things Moses commanded Israel to do in Deuteronomy 30: "loving the Lord your God, obeying His voice and holding fast to him" (v.20). Choosing life is not a passive experience.

I have lived for threescore and ten years in this world, and among the things I am most sure of is this: when you come down to the end, the thing that will break your heart will not be the choices you made; it will be the choices you *didn't* make. And if we spend eternity away from God, never having chosen to accept His forgiveness in Christ, the worst part of it will be knowing that we didn't have to end up this way. *We could have chosen life.*

When you have to make a choice and don't make it, that is in itself a choice.

WILLIAM JAMES

November 5

TESTING EVERYTHING BY THE SCRIPTURES

Now these Jews were more noble than those in Thessalonica; they received the word with all eagerness, examining the Scriptures daily to see if these things were so.
Acts 17:11

THE PROPHETS IN ISRAEL HAD PREDICTED THE COMING OF A MESSIAH. This Messiah or Christ (literally, the "Anointed One") would reign over a kingdom superior to any of the kingdoms of mankind (Daniel 2:44). But Jesus of Nazareth was not the only individual in the first century (or even later) to claim to be the Messiah. Messianic pretenders were a dime a dozen, as we might say. So how could a person know? How could one be sure?

When Paul came as a former Jewish rabbi and spoke in the synagogue at Berea, he proclaimed that Jesus of Nazareth was the Messiah, the very One who had been predicted in the Jewish Scriptures. Paul was an eyewitness that Jesus had been resurrected (Acts 9:1-9), and Paul could perform miracles to verify his claims (2 Corinthians 12:12). But to their credit, the Berean Jews knew that the ultimate test of Jesus' messiahship was *scriptural* in nature: if this Jesus truly was the person the Hebrew prophets had spoken of, then everything about Jesus would interlock with what had been said about the Messiah in the prophecies themselves.

So listening respectfully to Paul's claims, they were "examining the Scriptures daily to see if these things were so." In the final analysis, that is the test every religious teaching has to pass. *Does this teaching match up with what God is known to have revealed in the past?* God does not contradict Himself, and any new revelation has to be consistent with what we know God has already said. (The shocking story in 1 Kings 13 makes this point very dramatically.)

Fortunately, there is an abundance of Jewish Scripture against which Jesus can be measured (Psalm 16 & 22; Isaiah 53; Micah 5:2; etc.) — and there is no detail of Jesus' life, death, and resurrection that does not match up. For His part, Jesus was willing to be tested against the Scriptures, and He even upbraided those who had not done this. "O foolish ones, and slow of heart to believe all that the prophets have spoken! Was it not necessary that the Christ should suffer these things and enter into his glory?" (Luke 24:25,26).

In the Old Testament the new lies hidden,
in the New Testament the old is laid open.

AUGUSTINE OF HIPPO

November 6

TURNING FROM THE POWER OF SATAN TO GOD

. . . to open their eyes, so that they may turn from darkness to light and from the power of Satan to God, that they may receive forgiveness of sins and a place among those who are sanctified by faith in me.
Acts 26:18

PAUL WAS AN APOSTLE AND WE ARE NOT, BUT THE MISSION ASSIGNED TO HIM IS ONE WE CAN LEARN FROM. He was given the task of taking the gospel to the Gentiles, and in the text above, God was telling Paul what the purpose of his preaching would be. We, no less than Paul, need to understand the purpose of the gospel. Indeed, there is nothing more important for us to understand.

To open their eyes. The gospel provides the solution to our worst problem, the remedy to our worst illness. But in order to help us, the first thing the gospel has to do is open our eyes to the truth about our situation. We must see our *need* for the gospel.

So that they may turn from darkness to light and from the power of Satan to God. If our problem is sin, and if God is offering forgiveness, what we need to do is *turn around.* In denial of the truth about God, we've been going in the wrong direction. We've submitted ourselves to the power of Satan. That can change — and God will forgive us — but not without a real *conversion* (or "turning").

That they may receive forgiveness of sins and a place among those who are sanctified by faith in me. Here are the two things that result from the gospel. First, the forgiveness of sins. This is why Jesus died, and it is what the gospel is about. Second, those forgiven have "a place among those who are sanctified by faith in me." This is what is unique about those who are faithful to Jesus Christ. They still struggle, as all do, but they have a hope based on "the righteousness from God that depends on faith" (Philippians 3:9).

All of this is a wonderful plan, of course, but it requires life's most serious choice and its greatest love. For those living under the deadly power of Satan, no moderate remedy will do. Jesus Christ can save us, but we must turn to Him decisively. In sin, we took our hearts away from our God. We must give them back. For after all, there are only two alternatives, only two possible "fathers" waiting for us in eternity. We must choose between them.

There is no heaven with a little of hell in it — no plan to retain this or that of the devil in our hearts or our pockets. Out Satan must go, every hair and feather!

GEORGE MACDONALD

November 7

HASTENING THE COMING

. . . waiting for and hastening the coming of the day of God,
because of which the heavens will be set on fire and dissolved,
and the heavenly bodies will melt as they burn!
2 Peter 3:12

THE APOSTLE PETER SPEAKS IN THIS PASSAGE OF SOMETHING THAT PEOPLE TODAY RARELY THINK ABOUT, IF THEY THINK ABOUT IT AT ALL. The "day of God" is coming, he says, and it will be a day when the present universe will come to an end. Having been created by God, it will be brought to its conclusion by Him.

We don't know (and it's wrong to try to predict) when this cataclysm will occur. Peter said it will arrive unexpectedly: "the day of the Lord will come like a thief" (v.10). But it would be foolish to be lulled into complacency. The past is not always the key to the future — one-of-a-kind events do take place, as the people in Noah's day found out. Those today who say, "Where is the promise of his coming? For ever since the fathers fell asleep, all things are continuing as they were from the beginning of creation" (v.4) are dangerously forgetting that God always keeps His promises, the long passage of time notwithstanding. "The Lord is not slow to fulfill his promise as some count slowness" (v.9).

But for the faithful in Christ, the coming of this day is not to be dreaded. In his first letter, Peter had spoken of the "living hope" that has been made possible (1 Peter 1:3). Because of Christ's resurrection, those who have responded obediently to His gospel have "an inheritance that is imperishable, undefiled, and unfading, kept in heaven for you, who by God's power are being guarded through faith for a salvation ready to be revealed in the last time" (vv.4,5). In this great hope, he said, "you rejoice, though now for a little while, if necessary, you have been grieved by various trials" (v.6).

So, as Peter teaches us, we should be "waiting for and hastening the coming of the day of God." Paul said that "the Lord himself will descend from heaven with a cry of command, with the voice of an archangel, and with the sound of the trumpet of God" (1 Thessalonians 4:16). Oh, to hear the glorious, triumphant sound of that trumpet! May we hear it much sooner rather than later!

There's a great day coming,
A great day coming,
There's a great day coming by and by.

WILL L. THOMPSON

November 8

TAKE MY YOKE UPON YOU

Come to me, all who labor and are heavy laden, and I will give you rest. Take my yoke upon you, and learn from me, for I am gentle and lowly in heart, and you will find rest for your souls. For my yoke is easy, and my burden is light.
Matthew 11:28-30

THE INVITATION OF JESUS IS AN INVITATION TO THE WEARY. The satisfied may find Him "interesting," if even that, but those who recognize the toll that sin has taken upon them are desperate for relief. Poor in spirit, mourning for their sins, and hungering and thirsting for righteousness (Matthew 5:3-6), they long to hear more of what He meant when He said, *"I will give you rest."*

It may seem odd that what Jesus offers the weary is a yoke. *"Take my yoke upon you, and learn from me."* But He knows the nature of our problem. We have worn ourselves out running away from reality and refusing to accept the rule of our Creator. Rebellion is, after all, an extremely exhausting enterprise, and we have found it to be so (despite the lie we were told by the tempter, who said that disobedience would be the way to real "life"). So what we need is not the "freedom" of more lawlessness; we need to return to the will of God and find our rest therein. In comparison to the yoke of the enemy, the yoke that Jesus offers is easy. It requires nothing but what contributes to our true and lasting good.

Jesus' invitation is to *learn* from Him. The rest and refreshment He wants to give us can only be ours if we learn to think differently. Untruth must be replaced by truth. Dysfunctional concepts must be replaced by healthy ones. In short, we must learn a new "mind" (Philippians 2:5). "Do not be conformed to this world," Paul wrote, "but be transformed by the renewal of your mind, that by testing you may discern what is the will of God, what is good and acceptable and perfect" (Romans 12:2).

The truth will liberate us from what has enslaved us (John 8:32), but only if we *submit* to it — not just intellectually but in our deeds. Submission is hard, at least at first, since old habits die hard. But if rejecting the King's rule is what killed us in the first place, *we should not expect peace of mind if we won't relearn the laws of obedience.*

It is not in understanding a set of doctrines, not in outward comprehension of the scheme of salvation, that rest and peace are to be found, but in taking up, in all lowliness and meekness, the yoke of the Lord Jesus Christ.

FREDERICK WILLIAM ROBERTSON

November 9

A Decision Only We Can Make

"Return to me . . . and I will return to you," says the LORD of hosts.
Zechariah 1:3

THE MESSAGE PREACHED BY THE PROPHETS WAS THE MESSAGE OF REPENTANCE. Despite their blessings, Israel had frequently strayed from God, and they needed to turn back. This was not a popular message. Nobody ever likes to be told that they have departed from God, but in Israel's case, this would have been especially true. Given the privileges of their special role in God's plan to save the world, there would have been many who presumed that Israel's unique relationship with God guaranteed that His favor was automatically theirs. So when the prophets called upon the Jews to return to God, many in the audience might have said, "What in the world are you talking about? We've never *left* God."

Yet Israel *did* need to return to God. The preaching of the prophets was desperately needed (even if it was not wanted). And today, we need to hear God's appeal no less: "Return to me . . . and I will return to you." It does no good to suppose that (a) we have such a privileged status before God, or (b) we are such good people, there could never be a breach between us and God. Both John the Baptist and Jesus preached, "Repent, for the kingdom of heaven is at hand" (Matthew 3:1,2; 4:17), Peter preached repentance on Pentecost (Acts 2:38), and Jesus even called upon several of the congregations in Asia to repent (Revelation 2:5, etc.). And not only is there a universal *need* for repentance; there is a universal *possibility* of repentance. The fact that it is commanded presumes that it is possible for us to do it. While there is still breath in our lungs, none of us is a hopeless case. We are never so distant from God that, by His grace, the trip back home can't be made.

As long as we sojourn in this world, God will never give up on us. He will always, always, always be calling us to come back home, just as He called Israel through Zechariah. Since God gave us a free will, the decision to return is one that only we can make, but we shouldn't underestimate the desire with which He longs for us to make that choice. He loves us more than we can imagine, and He will pursue us down all the hard pathways of life, persistently pleading, "Return to me . . . and I will return to you."

I strayed, and yet I remembered you. I heard your voice behind me, telling me to return.

AUGUSTINE OF HIPPO

November 10

THE SAMARITAN SYNDROME

So these nations feared the LORD and also served their carved images. Their children did likewise, and their children's children — as their fathers did, so they do to this day.
2 Kings 17:41

THE PEOPLE DESCRIBED IN THIS TEXT ARE THOSE WHOSE DESCENDANTS WERE KNOWN IN THE NEW TESTAMENT PERIOD AS THE SAMARITANS. Descendants of intermarriage between Israelites and the foreigners imported by the Assyrians in 722 BC into Samaria, the central section of Israel, the Samaritans practiced a religion that was a mixture of elements from Judaism and the religions of the lands from which the foreigners had come.

Today, we might say the approach of the Samaritans to the worship of God was *eclectic* ("combining elements from a variety of sources"). A religious historian might call it *syncretism* ("reconciliation or fusion of differing systems of belief").

By whatever name it might be called, however, it was a dishonor to God and a clear violation of the covenant He had made with Israel at Sinai: "The LORD made a covenant with them and commanded them, 'You shall not fear other gods or bow yourselves to them or serve them or sacrifice to them . . . you shall not forget the covenant that I have made with you. You shall not fear other gods'" (2 Kings 17:35-38). It might have been expected that the polytheists imported into Israel would incorporate the God of Israel into their pantheon of deities, but for the Israelites to reciprocate by adding the practices of these nations into their worship of God was the very kind of idolatry they had been warned against for centuries. Before they even crossed the Jordan, Moses had said, "If your heart turns away, and you will not hear, but are drawn away to worship other gods and serve them, I declare to you today, that you shall surely perish" (Deuteronomy 30:17,18).

But what bearing does this have on our study of obeying the gospel of Christ? Just this: Jesus calls on us to make a radical choice. The choice Israel needed to make was a prefiguring of the greater choice that confronts us today. *The very worst decision we can make is to try to have every possibility at once.* It is no more possible to serve two masters now (Matthew 6:24) than it was in Samaria ages ago.

Progress always consists in taking one or another of two alternatives, abandoning the attempt to combine them.

ALBERT SCHWEITZER

November 11

DON'T LIMP! DECIDE!

And Elijah came near to all the people and said, "How long will you go limping between two different opinions? If the LORD is God, follow him; but if Baal, then follow him." And the people did not answer him a word.
1 Kings 18:21

ELIJAH DID NOT PULL ANY PUNCHES. Challenging the people to choose between the worship of God and the worship of Baal, he mocked their wishy-washiness: "How long will you go limping between two different opinions?" Or as the ERV so colorfully paraphrases it: "You must decide what you are going to do. How long will you keep jumping from one side to the other?"

In this book, we've been discussing the importance of obeying the gospel of Christ — both the "how" and the "why" of that obedience. I hope I've made it clear that the commitment to follow Christ is not one to be entered into lightly. The question of whether the gospel is true is extremely — indeed, *eternally* — important and should be considered carefully. But sooner or later, a decision has to be made. If you've seen that the gospel is true, and you know what the New Testament teaches about how to obey it, the question is unavoidable: *What do you choose to do?* You can't limp between obeying the gospel and rejecting it any more than Israel could limp between God and Baal. You must decide.

When we're faced with momentous decisions, we sometimes think we have decided when, in reality, we have not. Often, we think we've decided when all we've done is congratulate ourselves on knowing what we *should* do, thinking, "I'll do it as soon as a good opportunity presents itself." In an age that worships feelings, substituting feelings for thinking (and even for action), we suppose that we've made a choice simply because we feel a certain way. But ponder this statement by Eric Greitens, with which I agree: "Remember that deciding is not doing, and wanting is not choosing. Transformation will take place not because of what you decide you want, but because of what you choose to do."

Dietrich Bonhoeffer famously said, "It is the characteristic excellence of the strong man that he can bring momentous issues to the fore and make a decision about them." The weak waver, vacillate, and procrastinate. But the people of strong character decide. And they know that backing away is always the *wrong* decision.

Not to decide is to decide.

HARVEY COX

November 12

No Christianity without Correctability

They hate him who reproves in the gate,
and they abhor him who speaks the truth.
Amos 5:10

THE PROPHETS SENT BY GOD TO CALL FOR REPENTANCE IN ISRAEL DID NOT ALWAYS FIND A RECEPTIVE AUDIENCE. Israel, desperately in need of a radical return to God, often rejected the pleas of the prophets for a change of heart. Apparently this was characteristic of the attitude of many of them about correction in general. Even when it came to listening to the daily wisdom of their elders in the community, they were incorrigible. "They hate him who reproves in the gate, and they abhor him who speaks the truth."

In the New Testament, we hear Jesus lamenting the fact that Jerusalem had for so long rejected those sent by God to call them back from their sin, "O Jerusalem, Jerusalem, the city that *kills the prophets and stones those who are sent to it!* How often would I have gathered your children together as a hen gathers her brood under her wings, and you were not willing!" (Matthew 23:37).

But what about you and me? Are we innocent of this error? Honestly, can any of us say that we've listened any more openly when confronted with the need for change at the deepest level? Israel's tendency to "abhor him who speaks the truth" is, unfortunately, a *human* tendency. Every one of us resists being reproved.

And if the Hebrew prophets were hard to hear, the gospel of Jesus Christ is hard also — for the very same reason. It requires enough honesty to admit that our fellowship with God is broken: unless we change direction and seek God's forgiveness on His terms, we will remain alienated from Him forever. Frankly, not many people are "correctable" enough to listen as humbly as the Bereans did in Acts 17:11: "they received the word with all eagerness, examining the Scriptures daily to see if these things were so."

Wisdom is a curious thing in that it hurts us before it helps us. Although its benefits are enjoyable, wisdom usually requires some painful adjustments at first — starting with the admission that our present situation is not all right. And so it is with the gospel of Christ. It promises eternal salvation, but only to those bold enough to leave behind their current state. It's a journey that many will not make because it is far too uncomfortable and costly.

Wisdom is a good purchase though we pay dearly for it.

OLD PROVERB

November 13

The Gospel Is True, but We Must Pay Attention

. . . how shall we escape if we neglect such a great salvation? It was declared at first by the Lord, and it was attested to us by those who heard, while God also bore witness by signs and wonders and various miracles and by gifts of the Holy Spirit distributed according to his will.
Hebrews 2:3,4

THE RESULTS OF THE SURVEY STRUCK ME. In a recent poll, people in Western Europe who have abandoned religion after being raised in a religious home were asked why they became unreligious. The most frequent reason, cited by 68% of those surveyed, was that they just "gradually drifted away from religion."

In the New Testament, the Letter to the Hebrews was written to a group of Christians whose commitment was wavering. In 2:3,4, there is a reminder of the strong foundation on which the gospel of Christ rests. Whether we are Christians or we're just considering Christianity, we would do well to ponder these points:

Declared at first by the Lord. Jesus preached, "The time is fulfilled, and the kingdom of God is at hand; repent and believe in the gospel" (Mark 1:14,15). But Jesus said not only that the "good news" had come to pass, but that, in fact, He *was* the good news. "Come to me," He said, "and I will give you rest" (Matthew 11:28).

Attested to us by those who heard. The apostles were eyewitnesses. They had been with Jesus for three years, hearing everything He said, and they had seen Him after His resurrection. Even under threat of persecution, they could not remain silent: "We cannot but speak of what we have seen and heard" (Acts 4:20).

God also bore witness. Paul said that he had performed the "signs of a true apostle" (2 Corinthians 12:12). So the witness of the apostles to the gospel's truth was further backed up by the miracles they could perform. These miracles provided a final, conclusive proof, as if God Himself was saying, "This message is true."

Shall we neglect such a great salvation and simply drift away from it? The evidence that the gospel is true has never changed since the days of Jesus and the founding of His church. Our circumstances may have altered. Our emotions may have fluctuated. But here is one thing that has not changed: *the powerful three-fold witness to the truth that Jesus is the Christ, the Son of God.*

If you examined a hundred people who had lost their faith in Christianity, I wonder how many of them would turn out to have been reasoned out of it by honest argument? Do not most people simply drift away?

C. S. Lewis

November 14

The Power (and Beauty) of Commitment

But Ruth said, "Do not urge me to leave you or to return from following you. For where you go I will go, and where you lodge I will lodge. Your people shall be my people, and your God my God. Where you die I will die, and there will I be buried. May the LORD do so to me and more also if anything but death parts me from you."
Ruth 1:16,17

THERE IS NOT IN THE SCRIPTURES A MORE BEAUTIFUL EXPRESSION OF FAITHFUL "FOLLOWERSHIP" THAN THE WORDS OF RUTH TO HER MOTHER-IN-LAW, NAOMI. Not knowing what the future might hold, she pledged to stay with Naomi and help her — no matter what might happen. And while this is a touching statement of the faithfulness of one human being to another, it reminds us of the even greater power and beauty of our commitment to our God.

For one thing, Ruth's commitment did not depend on whether it would be easy to keep. And just as Ruth's commitment to Naomi was unconditional, our commitment to God needs to be so. We will surely fail in our discipleship to Christ if we're not willing to bind ourselves with a do-or-die pledge of faithfulness.

All of the serious commitments in life are costly. They rarely end up being kept if we're not willing to make significant sacrifices. Jesus had sacrifice in mind when He said, "If anyone would come after me, let him deny himself and take up his cross and follow me" (Matthew 16:24). What that cross will require of us, we don't know. What we do know is that heaven will be worth more than anything it may cost us in this world (Mark 10:28-31).

It is obvious that Ruth loved Naomi very dearly — and her pledge to follow Naomi was motivated by a love that showed up in faithful action rather than mere feelings. In the end, it is only love for God that will hold us steady as we make life's hard choices.

Most of us (or at least many of us) will do what is right in the big tests of life, especially if the test is public and other people are watching to see what we will do. But it may be that the truly "big" tests of life are the "little" ones, the many daily decisions that call for us to remember our promises to the Lord and faithfully do the best we can do. Over the long haul, that is how godly character comes into being. And that is how, if we are followers of Jesus Christ, most of the good is done that we hope to do in our lives.

Faithfulness in little things is a big thing.

JOHN CHRYSOSTOM

November 15

The Church in Splendor

. . . so that [Christ] might present the church to himself
in splendor, without spot or wrinkle or any such thing,
that she might be holy and without blemish.
Ephesians 5:27

IT IS INTRIGUING TO THINK OF CHRIST "PRESENTING THE CHURCH TO HIMSELF." The basic image is that of a bride being presented to her bridegroom (as in 2 Corinthians 11:2; Revelation 21:2), but here Christ is pictured as presenting His own bride to Himself. Christ gave Himself up for His bride, in the words of Richmond Lattimore's translation, "so as to *set the church next to himself* in glory, with no spot or wrinkle or anything of the sort upon her, but to be holy and without flaw." Or as Ronald Knox renders it, "[Christ] would *summon it into his own presence,* the Church in all its beauty, no stain, no wrinkle, no such disfigurement." The idea is that if the church is at any time to be a bride worthy of the Lord's own purity, He Himself will have made her so.

In the ESV, "splendor" is the word used to describe the Lord's bride, the church. Other possible translations would be "glory" or "radiance." These are words that all refer, in their literal sense, to things that shine brightly, but we often use words like "glory" to mean "majestic beauty" (*American Heritage Dictionary*). And that phrase — *majestic beauty* — wouldn't be a bad way to characterize the church which Christ died to cleanse and set apart for Himself.

The object of Christ's sacrifice was a bride "without spot or wrinkle or any such thing, that she might be holy and without blemish." This object will be fully realized in heaven, but even now those who have been washed from their sins in baptism (Acts 22:16; Ephesians 5:26) are in a process leading to that goal: *"beholding the glory of the Lord,* [we] are being transformed into the same image from one degree of glory to another" (2 Corinthians 3:18). For after all, Jesus Christ is the key to the church's splendor, both now and in eternity. The bride's beauty is that of her Bridegroom.

The enemies of Christ are triumphant, Christianity is
a failure, they say, and the church of God herself looks on in pain
at the shortcomings in her midst. But lo, at length from the very heart
of the shadows appears the majestic figure of Jesus, his countenance is as
the sun shining in his strength, around those wounds in brow and
side and hands and feet — those wounds which shelter countless
thousands of broken hearts — are healing rays.

OSWALD CHAMBERS

November 16

OPPORTUNITY TO SEEK GOD

For this reason every one of your faithful followers
should pray to you while there is a window of opportunity.
Psalm 32:6 NET

GOD GRANTS US THE TIME TO SEEK HIM, BUT HE DOES NOT OWE ANY OF US UNLIMITED TIME. Eventually, our time in this world comes to an end; after that, there will be nothing left but the rendering of God's judgment on the way we responded to His salvation. "Just as it is appointed for man to die once, and after that comes judgment, so Christ, having been offered once to bear the sins of many, will appear a second time, not to deal with sin but to save those who are eagerly waiting for him" (Hebrews 9:27,28).

In Hebrews 3:13, the writer encouraged his fellow Christians with these words: "But exhort one another every day, as long as it is called 'today,' that none of you may be hardened by the deceitfulness of sin." There are many reasons to do what is right in a timely way and not postpone it, but one of the most practical reasons is that waiting to obey God always puts us in danger of being hardened by our sin. The longer we delay, the more our conscience becomes callous. For all practical purposes, the window of opportunity closes for us on the day when we start telling those who try to get through to us to mind their own business.

Just days before His death, Jesus stood outside Jerusalem, surveying the city: "O Jerusalem, Jerusalem, the city that kills the prophets and stones those who are sent to it! How often would I have gathered your children together as a hen gathers her brood under her wings, and you were not willing! *See, your house is left to you desolate*" (Matthew 23:37,38). To be lost, then, is a double tragedy. It is to have separated ourselves from God by our sins and then to have refused the salvation which He tried to offer us.

If we are cut off from God, standing under the penalty of eternal death which He has justly decreed, we need to obey the gospel of Christ. But, to use an old idiom, we need to "strike while the iron is hot." If we fail to use the opportunity which His grace has provided, the word *regret* will crush us with horrible force. There is no love more painful than the love that dies untold. So tell Jesus Christ that you love Him. Tell Him today — by your obedience.

You cannot repent too soon because
you do not know how soon it may be too late.

SIR THOMAS FULLER

November 17

Even in Christ, We Are Not Yet Fully Alive

And this is the promise that he made to us — eternal life.
1 John 2:25

When God entered this world and took upon Himself human form, a never-before thing began to happen. The miracle of the Incarnation was not just that God became man but that in the person of His Son, Jesus Christ, God brought into this world a new kind of life. This new life is nothing less than the kind of life that God Himself has always had, and based on what Jesus did, God has been offering this life to all who will agree to be delivered from the death of sin and made alive in this new way. "This is the promise that he made to us — eternal life."

When we obey the gospel of Christ, we receive the forgiveness of our past sins and there is a sense in which we pass, at that point, from death to life. We who "were dead . . . God made alive together with him, having forgiven us all our trespasses" (Colossians 2:13). But there is a greater sense in which obedience to the gospel puts us into *a process of growth that will lead to life,* the kind of life that, in its fullness and perfection, will only be ours when Christ returns. "For you have died, and your life is hidden with Christ in God. When Christ who is your life appears, then you also will appear with him in glory" (Colossians 3:3,4).

Right now, God is working on our character with a hammer and chisel, as it were. The ravages of sin are being chipped away, sometimes painfully. The hearts we were meant to have are being created anew by our Father. What a thrill it is to get a glimpse of the joy that will be ours when the process has finally been completed and we think and act as creatures perfectly alive in every way. No more damage, no more death — just perfect, unending *life.*

In Christ, therefore, we live in great anticipation. And since we live in anticipation, we also live with *focused concentration* and *resolute patience.* Excited, enticed, and intrigued by the foretaste of what real life will be, we can hardly wait. But wait we must. So Peter says, "Preparing your minds for action, and being sober-minded, set your hope fully on the grace that will be brought to you at the revelation of Jesus Christ" (1 Peter 1:13).

This world is a great sculptor's shop. We are the statues and there is a rumor going around the shop that some of us are someday going to come to life.

C. S. Lewis

November 18

Confident in Christ . . . and Careful

Watch yourselves, so that you may not lose what we have worked for, but may win a full reward.
2 John 8

TOWARD THE END OF JOHN'S LIFE, THE CHRISTIANS IN ASIA WERE IN DIRE STRAITS. Threatened with persecution, heartbroken at the doctrinal apostasy that was taking place, disturbed about the prevalence of moral corruption among Christians, and concerned about the complacency of so many churches, the faithful brothers and sisters were hard pressed. And John was concerned about these faithful disciples: "Watch yourselves, so that you may not lose what we have worked for, but may win a full reward."

To be watchful does not mean to be afraid. It does not require paranoia, anxiety, or uncertainty as to our salvation in Christ. But it does require vigilance. Given the problems that confront us (no less today than in the first century), it would be dangerous not to guard our faith carefully — there are none more vulnerable to the devil's malice than those who are not paying attention.

Like it or not, we have an enemy whose intent is to destroy us. Peter compares him to a lion looking for his next meal. "Be sober-minded; be watchful. Your adversary the devil prowls around like a roaring lion, seeking someone to devour" (1 Peter 5:8). This enemy is no match for the power of the King, of course. But until the last battle has been fought, we need to be cautious. As long as it is possible for us to become lackadaisical and drift away from the Lord (Hebrews 2:1), we need to be very careful (Ephesians 5:15).

In Christ's letters to the seven churches of Asia, we hear Him warning even the most faithful of these churches to be steadfast. To Philadelphia, He said, "Hold fast what you have, so that no one may seize your crown" (Revelation 3:11). The "armor" that Christ has given us (Ephesians 6:10-20) is quite capable of guarding us against the devil, but only if we strap it on . . . *and use it.*

Unguarded strength is double weakness, as the saying goes. Even with our strengths, blessings, and advantages, we must take care. Being naive is not a virtue. So Jesus said to His apostles, "Behold, I am sending you out as sheep in the midst of wolves, so be wise as serpents and innocent as doves" (Matthew 10:16).

The thing we have to watch most of all is our strength, our strong point. We all tend to fail ultimately at our strong point.

D. MARTYN LLOYD-JONES

November 19

When the Feeling of Salvation Fails Us

Paul, a servant of God and an apostle of Jesus Christ, for the sake of the faith of God's elect and their knowledge of the truth, which accords with godliness, in hope of eternal life, which God, who never lies, promised before the ages began and at the proper time manifested in his word through the preaching with which I have been entrusted by the command of God our Savior.
Titus 1:1-3

FEELINGS ARE IMPORTANT, BUT THEY ARE NOT INFALLIBLE. If our feelings are based on erroneous thoughts, those feelings will be inappropriate. So the constant challenge in life is to make sure our thoughts (and our actions) are *based on truth and not on fiction.*

As indicated in the text above, the hope of eternal life rests on the promise of God. (What Paul says about it is similar to what Peter said in 1 Peter 1:3-5.) And dependence on God's promise is the main component of faith — the decision to trust His promise.

Since life can be a hard business, there are times when we won't "feel" forgiven. What should we do at such times? *We should go back to the Scriptures.* It is only in the Scriptures that we will find a dependable, objective assessment of our relationship to the Lord.

Looking into the Scriptures, we may find that having accepted God's salvation on His terms, our hope in Him is well-founded. Despite our feelings, we must count on the dependability of what God has said.

But looking into the Scriptures, we may find that we are not, in fact, in a right relationship with the Lord. In that case, we need to repent and seek His forgiveness. When Paul said, "Examine yourselves, to see whether you are in the faith" (2 Corinthians 13:5), he raised the possibility that some of his brethren in Corinth might not have as secure a relationship with Christ as they thought they had.

Either way, the Scriptures need to be our guide. Our feelings may err on the high side or the low side, but the only reliable basis for our confidence is God's promise. And never forget: *the only thing we know about God's promise is what we find in the Scriptures.*

Someone asked Luther, "Do you feel that you have been forgiven?"
He answered: "No, but I'm as sure as there's a God in heaven.
For feelings come and feelings go, and feelings are deceiving;
My warrant is the Word of God, naught else is worth believing.
Though all my heart should feel condemned for want of some sweet token,
There is One greater than my heart whose Word cannot be broken.
I'll trust in God's unchanging Word till soul and body sever;
For though all things shall pass away, his Word shall stand forever!"

MARTIN LUTHER

November 20

Jesus Christ, Our Example

For I have given you an example, that you also
should do just as I have done to you.
John 13:15

CERTAIN PARTS OF JESUS' WAY OF LIFE ARE POPULAR AND FREQUENTLY PRAISED. When we want support for our viewpoint, there always seems to be some aspect of Jesus' teaching and lifestyle that we can appeal to. And whatever our theology or sociology, we can find a favorite angle from which to admire Jesus.

The problem is, we tend to "cherry pick" the examples of Jesus, taking the ones we like and leaving the others aside. If there is something Jesus did that seems extreme, unrealistic, or unreasonable, we respond to that text with a quick "yes but." To an objective outsider, it would almost seem that we limit our imitation of Jesus' example to what is "trending" at the present moment.

Today, of course, we face many dilemmas that have no specific precedent in Jesus' life two thousand years ago. "What would Jesus do?" is always the right question to ask, but getting a helpful answer to that can be difficult. It requires wisdom and discernment — and these things come from much study, thought, and prayer, not to mention a good deal of hard and painful experience.

Rightly answering "What would Jesus do?" requires, above all, learning the *character* of Jesus. When we study the stories of His teaching and His behavior, we are wanting to learn His principles, His values, His likes and dislikes. We won't follow Jesus' example faithfully if we haven't learned to *think* as He does. And learning to think as He does is what growth in Christ is all about.

Jesus, however, must be more than just our Example. He came into the world, first and foremost, to be our Savior. And if we have not accepted His salvation from our sins, His example will do us little good. But if He is first our Savior and then our Example, look at what happens. By coming penitently to Jesus — seeking first the forgiveness of our sins and then committing ourselves to live by His example — we become an example that helps other people come to Christ. *The process repeats itself from person to person.*

In his life, Christ is an example, showing us how to live.
In his death, he is a sacrifice, satisfying for our sins.
In his resurrection, he is a conqueror.
In his ascension, he is a king.
In his intercession, he is a high priest.

MARTIN LUTHER

November 21

HAVE WE "PUT ON" CHRIST?

For as many of you as were baptized into Christ have put on Christ.
Galatians 3:27

IN THE NEW TESTAMENT, ONE WAY CHRISTIANS ARE DESCRIBED IS TO SAY THAT THEY ARE PEOPLE WHO HAVE "PUT ON" CHRIST. The image, of course, is that of taking off one set of clothes and putting on another. In his new relationship with Jesus Christ, the Christian has "put on" His Lord — he has adopted Christ's virtues and character in such a way as to have "clothed" himself in Christ.

(1) Baptized into Christ. Paul wrote that "as many of you as were baptized into Christ have put on Christ." Attempts to explain away this clear statement are futile. It is in baptism, and not before, that we enter into this new relationship with Christ, not because it earns us salvation as a meritorious work, but simply because Christ commanded it as a condition of His grace (Acts 2:38).

(2) Putting on Christ. Baptism is followed by the living of a new life (Romans 6:4), so there is a vital link between baptism and putting on Christ. But the second does not automatically follow from the first — it is a choice on the part of the one who has been baptized. For that reason, the Christian is not just *said* to have put on Christ (Galatians 3:27), but he is *commanded* to do so (Ephesians 4:24). In Colossians 2:6, Paul put it simply: "Therefore, as you received Christ Jesus the Lord, so walk in him."

Suppose a person studies Jesus' teachings and emulates His character, but does not obey the command to be baptized for the remission of his sins. He will have a better life in this world (and others will benefit from that), but he will die with no scriptural basis upon which to expect anything but separation from God in eternity.

But turn the situation around. Suppose a person is baptized but never chooses to "put on" Christ. His lifestyle would suggest that, despite his baptism, his heart still belongs to the devil. His old rebellious self was not "buried" as it should have been (Romans 6:1-4).

So for those who have been baptized, the critical question is this: *have we put on Christ?* Have we been truly *converted* to Him, discarding our old life and clothing ourselves with the fresh, clean garments of our Lord's heart, mind, and character? If not, perhaps our commitment to Christ is lacking. He deserves better from us.

Christianity can be condensed into four words:
admit, submit, commit, and transmit.

SAMUEL WILBERFORCE

November 22

O TO BE LIKE THEE!

Beloved, we are God's children now, and what we will be has not yet appeared; but we know that when he appears we shall be like him, because we shall see him as he is. And everyone who thus hopes in him purifies himself as he is pure.
1 John 3:2,3

IN HIS DEALINGS WITH US, GOD HAS A GREAT GOAL. It is not merely to rescue us but to reform us. For all who will accept His plan, God intends to repair the damage sin has done to our character and make us into nothing less than perfect reproductions of His gloriously perfect Son: "Those whom he foreknew he also predestined to be conformed to the image of his Son, in order that he might be the firstborn among many brothers" (Romans 8:29). Making this possible is why Christ died for us. And whatever secondary or intermediate blessings may be involved, we ought never to lose sight of what God is really after: *our likeness to Jesus Christ, His Son.*

We see this in the life-choices of Paul. He wanted to be like Christ in everything, even in suffering: "That I may know him and the power of his resurrection, and may share his sufferings, becoming like him in his death, that by any means possible I may attain the resurrection from the dead" (Philippians 3:10,11).

Today, we would do well to ponder the advice of the 18th-century Anglican, William Law, who said, "From morning to night keep Jesus in your heart, long for nothing, desire nothing, hope for nothing, but to have all that is within you changed into the spirit and temper of the Holy Jesus." If this is not a driving force within us, we are settling for something less than the gospel of Christ.

To the Christians in Corinth, Paul wrote, "We all, with unveiled face, beholding the glory of the Lord, are being transformed into the same image from one degree of glory to another" (2 Corinthians 3:18). Far more than comfortable circumstances or emotional inspiration, to be conformed to the virtues of Christ's character is what we want — at any cost. And not only is this our highest hope; it must be the goal we pursue more actively and energetically than any other. What did John say in our beginning text? *"Everyone who thus hopes in him purifies himself as he is pure."*

O to be like Thee! blessed Redeemer;
This is my constant longing and pray'r;
Gladly I'll forfeit all of earth's treasures,
Jesus, Thy perfect likeness to wear.

THOMAS O. CHISHOLM

November 23

OBEDIENCE IS A CHOICE

Although he was a son, he learned obedience through what he suffered. And being made perfect, he became the source of eternal salvation to all who obey him.
Hebrews 5:8,9

ONE OF THE MOST IMPORTANT LESSONS WE CAN LEARN FROM JESUS IS THE LESSON OF VOLUNTARY OBEDIENCE TO GOD. Even with His unique relationship to the Heavenly Father, Jesus still had to *choose to obey.* "Although he was a son, he learned obedience through what he suffered." In making this difficult choice, "he became the source of eternal salvation to all who obey him."

In the New Testament, we are urged to have the same attitude toward obedience that Jesus had, even if it means setting aside personal preferences (Philippians 2:5-8). We can't claim to be Jesus' followers if we don't emulate His reverence in doing what is *right.* For Jesus, the question "What is God's will?" was the only question worth asking. It was the end of every discussion.

But also like Jesus, we must understand the *decisiveness* of obedience. If He always did what was right, it wasn't because He was carried along by some irresistible force. Instead, he "learned obedience," freely and voluntarily making the choice to submit to God's will. And nowhere do we see His agony in this choice any more painfully than in Gethsemane: "And he withdrew from them about a stone's throw, and knelt down and prayed, saying, 'Father, if you are willing, remove this cup from me. Nevertheless, not my will, but yours, be done'" (Luke 22:41,42).

No matter how complicated the scenario, doing what is right is always an option. When we face hard decisions, it will be helpful if we've established habits of obedience previously. But even so, obedience is a choice that must be made moment by moment. In the life of obedience, there is no such thing as "autopilot."

There is no way around it: *obedience requires discipline.* And discipline comes from deciding what is most important to us. So if you're a Christian, I recommend that you meditate on Paul's exhortation: "Set your minds on things that are above, not on things that are on earth" (Colossians 3:2). Valuing our hope more highly than anything else, we will pursue that hope with passionate discipline. *Turning back is a choice we will choose not to make — period.*

The Christian life is never automatic.

ERWIN W. LUTZER

November 24

A Sobering (and Encouraging) Thought

Do not be deceived: God is not mocked, for whatever one sows, that will he also reap. For the one who sows to his own flesh will from the flesh reap corruption, but the one who sows to the Spirit will from the Spirit reap eternal life. And let us not grow weary of doing good, for in due season we will reap, if we do not give up.
Galatians 6:7-9

Ideas have emotional consequences, and the impact they have on us can be complex. Sometimes a single idea may produce effects that are on opposite ends of the emotional spectrum. For example, there are a number of ideas that are both *sobering* and *encouraging* at the same time. This is not a problem; it is a blessing.

Writing to the Galatians, Paul wanted to encourage them to remain faithful and keep doing the Lord's work even when they were persecuted. But he also wanted to warn them of the consequences of unfaithfulness. So he pointed to the process of sowing and reaping: "whatever one sows, that will he also reap." What emotional effect would it have on these Christians to realize that we will reap what we have sown? If they thought about it, they would be both *sobered* (a person can't sow to the flesh and not reap corruption) and *encouraged* (if we keep sowing to the Spirit, we will reap eternal life; so whatever happens, we must not give up).

Why do texts like this have such a balanced effect on us? It is because both of their points of emphasis are inherent in the character of God. A simplistic view of God would see Him as either a God of love or a God of judgment. The truth, however, is that He is both, and if either component of His character is left out of our thinking, we will be worshiping not the real God but an imaginary God that we have constructed in our own minds.

Even after obeying the gospel, we still need to be reminded of the sobering side of God's truth (1 Corinthians 10:12). But what if you have not yet obeyed the gospel? What do you need to hear? You need to hear *all of the truth that God has revealed about Himself.* So study all of the Scriptures. You will be encouraged, but you will also be sobered. To repeat, this is not a problem; it is a blessing.

The judgment of God is the reaping that comes from sowing and is evidence of the love of God, not proof of his wrath. The penalty of an evil harvest is not God's punishment; it is the consequence of defying the moral order which in love he maintains as the only environment in which maturity of fellowship and communion can be achieved.

Kirby Page

November 25

If We Have Died to Sin

What shall we say then? Are we to continue in sin that grace may abound? By no means! How can we who died to sin still live in it?
Romans 6:1,2

ONE OF OUR GREATEST CHALLENGES IS TO RESPOND RIGHTLY TO GOD'S GRACE. Surely there is no greater gift than the forgiveness of our sins in God's Son, Jesus Christ. But we must determine not to "receive the grace of God in vain" (2 Corinthians 6:1).

In Romans 6:1,2, Paul was dealing with the false notion that if God forgives our sins by grace then it doesn't matter how we live: we may sin with impunity, knowing that grace will save us anyway. But if a Christian thought this way, he or she would obviously have a confused concept of what it means to obey the gospel. "How," Paul asks, "can we who died to sin still live in it?"

When we are baptized into Christ, we are baptized into His death. We die to the sins that separated us from God, and we dedicate ourselves to walking in "newness of life" (Romans 6:4). But what does this mean at the practical level? What qualities of character will regulate the life of one who is obeying the gospel?

Commitment. At the very least, we must commit ourselves to obedience to Christ. Words like "promise" and "vow" are not too strong to describe the decisiveness of our new life in Christ.

Confession. When we fail to think or act as we know Christ would want, we are to confess our sin to Him honestly. Most of us would do well to make the specific confession of our actual sins more of a daily practice. Dying to sin means confessing our sins.

Repentance. Just as confession should be our habit, so should repentance. Like David, we should seek God's help in seeing our sins so that we can correct them immediately (Psalm 19:12-14). In this life, dying to sin does not mean perfection — it means repentance.

If commitment, confession, and repentance are not a part of our daily walk with God, we need to go back and remember the "death" we died when we were baptized. If at that time we did not honestly decide to turn our backs on sin — *no ifs, ands, or maybes* — then we need to do so. There is no hope of defeating the enemy if we still dine at his table from time to time. If we have died to sin, the only word sufficient to keep it out of our hearts is "No!"

It is the great moment of our lives when we decide that sin must die right out, not be curbed or suppressed or counteracted, but crucified.

OSWALD CHAMBERS

November 26

HONEST ABOUT OUR TRANSGRESSIONS

For when I kept silent, my bones wasted away
through my groaning all day long.
Psalm 32:3

WE NEED TO ACCEPT THE LORD'S VERDICT CONCERNING OUR SINS. Our sins can be forgiven if we accept His plan for their forgiveness, but a part of the plan is repentance — and repentance includes taking honest responsibility for what we've done. To the best of our present understanding, we must see the seriousness of our sins and enter a plea of "guilty as charged." When we fail to do this, by hiding our sin or trying to minimize it, our situation just keeps getting worse. "When I kept silent," David said, "my bones wasted away through my groaning all day long."

It is interesting to contrast the honesty of David (2 Samuel 12:13) with the excuse-making of Saul (1 Samuel 15:15,24). Unlike Saul, who wanted to rationalize his deeds and soften the blow as much as possible, David wanted to hear the worst-case indictment of his character by the God of truth — *so that he could repent.* The truth can be painful, as we all know, but David wanted only the truth. "Who can understand his errors? Cleanse me from secret faults" (Psalm 19:12 NKJV). "Search me, O God, and know my heart! Try me and know my thoughts! And see if there be any grievous way in me, and lead me in the way everlasting!" (Psalm 139:23,24).

All of us want other people to see us favorably, but I'll tell you something else: *we want to see ourselves favorably.* When we have sinned, we will spare no effort to make the situation seem as innocent as possible *in our own thinking.* What we did may not have been the best, we think, but the "mistakes" we made were "understandable." But the more time we waste trying to spin the story to our advantage, the longer it will be before we can be forgiven.

Thanks to the gospel of Christ, there is no sin we can't be forgiven of. But forgiveness is only for the honest. Like the penitent tax collector in Luke 18:9-14, we must be willing to say, "God, be merciful to me, a sinner!" It may seem more comfortable to stay in the darkness and try to preserve our flattering self-image with denials of the truth, but there is nothing but death in that cave. To be forgiven, we're going to have to come out of hiding. In Jesus Christ there is life — but it is only in the light of *truth* that we can live.

If my hangups and negatives are called sin by our Lord, then sin it is.

BOB TURNBULL

November 27

FAITH HAS CONSEQUENCES

For this very reason, make every effort to supplement your faith with virtue, and virtue with knowledge, and knowledge with self-control, and self-control with steadfastness, and steadfastness with godliness, and godliness with brotherly affection, and brotherly affection with love. For if these qualities are yours and are increasing, they keep you from being ineffective or unfruitful in the knowledge of our Lord Jesus Christ.

2 Peter 1:5-8

THERE IS A "JUDICIAL" ASPECT TO THE GOSPEL, BUT SALVATION IN CHRIST INVOLVES FAR MORE THAN GOD'S PRONOUNCEMENT THAT WE ARE "JUSTIFIED." Having obeyed the gospel we do indeed stand in a right relationship with God, having been pardoned from our past sins (Romans 5:1,2). At that point, however, we begin learning to be *very different people* than we used to be. As forgiven ones, living under God's mercy, we participate in the process of "bringing holiness to completion in the fear of God" (2 Corinthians 7:1).

In particular, we begin living on the basis of *faith.* Paul was quoting from Habakkuk when he said, "The righteous shall live by faith" (Romans 1:17). In contrast to our previous self-will, our decisions are now governed by God's will. Our operative principle is confidence in the One "whom I have believed" (2 Timothy 1:12).

As we learn to live by faith, things begin to happen that would not happen if it were not for faith. For one thing, faith commits us to a life of spiritual growth. It is the foundation upon which all of the Christ-like qualities of character are built — and the addition of these virtues to our faith is not optional. "Therefore, brothers, be all the more diligent to confirm your calling and election, for if you practice these qualities you will never fall. For in this way there will be richly provided for you an entrance into the eternal kingdom of our Lord and Savior Jesus Christ" (2 Peter 1:10,11).

Believing, then, is not a simple one-time decision after which we drift through life automatically, taking it for granted that we have been saved. True faith is a "walk," a way of living (Colossians 2:6,7). At the heart of it all is a *trust* in God that causes us to obey Him readily and reverently. It is a soul-deep dependence on the Father who has loved us and saved us. To believe is not only to believe, but to take the risks that only trust will take.

The temptation to make our relationship to God judicial instead of personal is very strong. Believing for salvation has been reduced to a once-done act that requires no further attention.

A. W. TOZER

November 28

Called, Beloved, Kept

Jude, a servant of Jesus Christ and brother of James,
To those who are called, beloved in God the Father and kept for
Jesus Christ: May mercy, peace, and love be multiplied to you.
Jude 1,2

Being a Christian is a reality that can be looked at from more than one angle. In other words, a person who is a Christian can describe his identity in various ways. Let's look at the three expressions Jude used to address his fellow Christians.

Those who are called. Through the gospel, God calls everyone to accept the salvation that He is offering in Jesus Christ. To obey the gospel is, in effect, to answer God's call, and to live faithfully as a Christian is to be among the called. It was God alone who had the right to decide what the terms of His salvation would be; on our own, we could never have worked our way back to Him. So when we submit to the terms of His forgiveness in the gospel, we can rejoice in the privilege of being among those whom He has called out of the darkness to be His own possession (1 Peter 2:9).

Beloved in God the Father. While God obviously loves every person He has ever created, He has a very specific love for those who have said yes to His plan of salvation, i.e., the individuals who have responded to His love with gratitude, obedience, and faithfulness. In the salutation to his letters, Paul often spoke of God's love for those whom He has saved: "To all those in Rome who are loved by God and called to be saints: Grace to you and peace from God our Father and the Lord Jesus Christ" (Romans 1:7).

Kept for Jesus Christ. In a world of obstacles and temptations, we could not survive, even after obeying the gospel, if it weren't for the help God gives us in Christ. Peter wrote of those "who by God's power are being guarded through faith for a salvation ready to be revealed in the last time" (1 Peter 1:5). And Jude ended his letter with this: "[God] is able to keep you from stumbling and to present you blameless before the presence of his glory with great joy" (Jude 24). Well might he say, "May mercy, peace, and love be multiplied to you." There is simply no higher joy available to us.

True joy is not a thing of moods, not a capricious emotion,
tied to fluctuating experiences. It is a state and condition of the soul.
It survives through pain and sorrow and, like a subterranean spring,
waters the whole life. It is intimately allied and bound up with love
and goodness, and so is deeply rooted in the life of God.

Rufus Matthew Jones

November 29

Judged by Our Response to Jesus' Word

I have come into the world as light, so that whoever believes in me may not remain in darkness. If anyone hears my words and does not keep them, I do not judge him; for I did not come to judge the world but to save the world. The one who rejects me and does not receive my words has a judge; the word that I have spoken will judge him on the last day.
John 12:46-48

WHEN WE HEAR THE WORDS OF JESUS CHRIST WE HAVE A DECISION TO MAKE. The question we must answer is actually two questions: *Is it true? And if it is true, what are we going to do about it?* No decision we ever make in this life has greater consequences.

In these daily meditations, we have emphasized that our response to God's initiative is a matter of choice on our part. The gospel comes to us in the form of an invitation. From the depths of His great heart, our Lord is saying to each of us, "Come to me" (Matthew 11:28). But while the freedom our Father has given us is a magnificent blessing, it entails a serious responsibility.

Looking back at John 12, observe how Jesus describes the two paths that we must choose between. In v.46, He had spoken of "whoever believes in me." That is the first path. Then, in vv.47,48, He speaks of the other path, the path of disbelief. Hearing Jesus' words, this person "does not keep them." Refusing to believe, he "rejects me" and "does not receive my words." So to disbelieve is not merely to be uninterested or unconvinced: the decision not to "receive" or to "keep" Jesus' words is a decision to "reject" Him. If what He taught is false, that is precisely what we should do. But what if it is true? In that case, we will have rejected the message that could have saved us and sentenced ourselves to eternal death. "The word that I have spoken," Jesus said, "will judge him on the last day." If we are lost, it will not be because we couldn't be rescued, but because we rejected our Rescuer.

The picture in John 12 is not simply that of a person distrusting a set of doctrines. When the words of the gospel are rejected, it is Jesus Himself who is being refused. So let us look at our situation with clear eyes: *our eternal destiny hinges on our response to the person of Jesus Christ.* If His words are true, *He alone is our Savior.* How we respond to Him is the most important thing about us.

Jesus Christ never asks anyone to define his position or to understand a creed, but "Who am I to you?" . . . Jesus Christ makes the whole of human destiny depend on a man's relationship to himself.

OSWALD CHAMBERS

November 30

ENTRANCE INTO THE ETERNAL KINGDOM

Therefore, brothers, be all the more diligent to confirm your calling and election, for if you practice these qualities you will never fall. For in this way there will be richly provided for you an entrance into the eternal kingdom of our Lord and Savior Jesus Christ.
2 Peter 1:10,11

AS CHRISTIANS, IT IS EXTREMELY IMPORTANT FOR US TO GROW IN THE CHARACTER TRAITS OF GODLINESS. Just prior to the text above, Peter had encouraged his readers to work hard at growing in virtue, knowledge, self-control, steadfastness, godliness, brotherly affection, and love (vv.5-7). God will help us, obviously, but the process of renovating our character cannot take place without our active engagement and obedience. We must not only be *willing* to have our imperfections removed; we must *exert ourselves* in that direction. As Paul encouraged his young friend Timothy, "Meditate on these things; give yourself entirely to them, that your progress may be evident to all" (1 Timothy 4:15 NKJV).

In the text in 2 Peter 1:10,11, Peter says, "Be all the more diligent to confirm your calling and election." God's "chosen" and His "elect" are those who accept the terms upon which He has made salvation conditional. The invitation of God is open to all, but we must choose to be among the chosen. In Romans 1:5, Paul uses the expression "the obedience of faith" to summarize what is necessary on our part. Peter urges us to be "diligent" in this matter. Not taking our salvation for granted, we must be people who *grow.*

If we give ourselves wholeheartedly and lovingly to the strengthening of our character, we need not doubt our salvation. Peter said, "If you do these things you will never stumble" (NKJV). Having obeyed the gospel of Christ, we are in the kingdom which He established, but heaven is not yet our home. We await the *eternal* kingdom — and we wait for it with eager anticipation (Philippians 3:12-14; 2 Peter 3:11-13; 1 John 3:2,3; etc.).

It is helpful to think of our lives in Christ right now as a remedial process. We have been saved from our past sins, but we still have habits that need to be broken, ways of thinking that need to be changed, and attitudes that need to be adjusted. So God is disciplining us, teaching us, and helping us to grow in His direction. If we don't drop out, one day we'll graduate from this school.

Heaven is a place prepared for those who are prepared for it.

OLD SAYING

December 1

Jesus Christ and Him Crucified

For I decided to know nothing among you
except Jesus Christ and him crucified.
1 Corinthians 2:2

PAUL WAS GRATEFUL FOR HIS BRETHREN IN CORINTH, BUT HE WAS WORRIED ABOUT THEM. They had divided into factions, each group following its favorite teacher of the gospel (1 Corinthians 1:10-13). This kind of sectarianism was very common in cities like Corinth, of course, where the public forum was filled with philosophers, orators, and teachers — each wooing followers by showing himself to be more on the intellectual cutting edge than the others.

Yet this was the very kind of attractiveness Paul had tried to avoid. "I decided," he said, "to know nothing among you except Jesus Christ and him crucified." And his reason was both clear and practical: "My speech and my message were not in plausible words of wisdom . . . so that your faith might not rest in the wisdom of men but in the power of God" (1 Corinthians 2:4,5).

Jesus Christ. It is hard for human reason to accept the fact that the Creator of the universe took human form in the person of Jesus of Nazareth, but that is exactly what the gospel affirms. Only once in history did such a thing happen — and having happened, the Person in whom it happened, Jesus, is now the One through whom God is offering to reconcile human beings to Himself.

And him crucified. When God became a man, He did so in order to die for our sins. It was not to be a great prophet or a perfect moral example but to die *an atoning death* that God entered our world as a human being. Speaking of Himself, Jesus said, "The Son of Man came not to be served but to serve, and to give his life as a ransom for many" (Mark 10:45). So the gospel is not just the message of Christ; it is the message of Christ *crucified.* If God, in the person of Jesus Christ, did not die for our sins, then we are still lost.

When we come to Christ, accepting His invitation, we come empty-handed, recognizing our own insufficiency and lack of power to procure our own salvation. But more than that, we come yielding to His decision as to our greatest need. Whatever other gifts our "wisdom" might say are more needful, we are content to receive that for which He was crucified: *the forgiveness of our sins.*

Nothing in my hand I bring,
Simply to thy cross I cling.

AUGUSTUS MONTAGUE TOPLADY

December 2

PUTTING OUR HAND TO THE PLOW

Yet another said, "I will follow you, Lord, but let me first say farewell to those at my home." Jesus said to him, "No one who puts his hand to the plow and looks back is fit for the kingdom of God."
Luke 9:61,62

ONE COMMON THREAD RUNNING THROUGHOUT THE NEW TESTAMENT IS COMMITMENT. Will we follow Jesus? Our answer must be more than "maybe" or "if I don't change my mind."

Decisiveness. Too many so-called "Christians" have never decisively "put their hand to the plow." But a true disciple is one who has considered the alternatives and made an actual commitment.

Sacrifice. Commitments are nearly always hard to keep. Circumstances arise that test our resolve. So we must be prepared to sacrifice and suffer rather than go back on our promise.

Trust. When tested, the only thing that will keep us steady and true is a deep trust that God is not going to let us down. We must believe that heaven will be worth any amount of loss.

The trust required to make our commitment to Christ, along with its attendant sacrifices, is based on God's *worthiness* of trust. Everything He has ever revealed about Himself shows that He *can* be counted on. His promises *can* be trusted. So we must not look back wistfully at the things we have given up; our Father has much better things waiting for us at the end of the road.

It was a strong, forward-looking faith that moved Abraham to leave his home in Ur of the Chaldeans. He may have had fears, but he "obeyed when he was called to go out to a place that he was to receive as an inheritance" (Hebrews 11:8). And he was not alone in trusting God's promises. Through the centuries, many others have "died in faith, not having received the things promised, but having seen them and greeted them from afar, and having acknowledged that they were strangers and exiles on the earth. For people who speak thus make it clear that they are seeking a homeland. If they had been thinking of that land from which they had gone out, they would have had opportunity to return" (11:13-15).

So, my dear friends, may we "put our hand to the plow" in faith, love, and confident hope. May we *commit* ourselves to following Jesus Christ wherever He leads. *And may we never look back.*

Has this world been so kind to you that you would leave it with regret? There are better things ahead than any we leave behind.

C. S. LEWIS

December 3

GOD WILL JUDGE THE WORLD IN RIGHTEOUSNESS

The times of ignorance God overlooked, but now he commands all people everywhere to repent, because he has fixed a day on which he will judge the world in righteousness by a man whom he has appointed; and of this he has given assurance to all by raising him from the dead.
Acts 17:30,31

THE IDEA OF A "JUDGMENT DAY" IS UNPOPULAR THESE DAYS. Even among Christians, a declining percentage believes that such a thing will actually happen. And yet, if we take Jesus seriously, along with the teaching of the apostles whom He selected to communicate His message, we must accept the fact that eventually God is going to call each of us to account for how we have lived.

In the text above, Paul was speaking to a group of Greek philosophers in Athens. Notice the emphasis he places on repentance: *"the times of ignorance God overlooked, but now he commands all people everywhere to repent."* Sin is the problem, the gospel is the solution, and repentance is a part of the plan. It can't be left out.

But even though God has commanded repentance, why should we do what He says? *"Because he has fixed a day on which he will judge the world."* As our Creator, God has the sovereign right to require an accounting for how we've used the freedom He gave us. The wise have always known this to be true (Ecclesiastes 12:13,14).

God will judge the world *"in righteousness by a man whom he has appointed."* Paul is speaking here of Jesus Christ, the Son of God. We should be encouraged (and also sobered) by the fact that God's judgment by His Son will be "in righteousness." No mistakes will be made. God's judgment will be infallibly right.

And what is the evidence these things will happen? *"Of this he has given assurance to all by raising him from the dead."* You may not have thought of the resurrection in connection with God's judgment, but Paul connects the two here. The resurrection of Christ guaranteed all of the promises of God, and the Day of Judgment is one of the most important. It is perilous to ignore this promise.

If judgment seems to us inconsistent with God's character, we need to reconsider our concept of God. And it's worth asking: would God be good if He did not punish unrepentant rebellion?

Nobody can judge men but God, and we can hardly obtain a higher or more reverent view of God than that which represents him to us as judging men with perfect knowledge, unperplexed certainty, and undisturbed compassion.

FREDERICK WILLIAM FABER

December 4

We Are Not Saved by Those We Are Connected To

Bear fruit in keeping with repentance. And do not presume
to say to yourselves, "We have Abraham as our father," for I tell you,
God is able from these stones to raise up children for Abraham.
Matthew 3:8,9

IF THE JEWISH LEADERS THOUGHT OF SALVATION IN "INSTITUTIONAL" TERMS, THEY WERE NOT ALONE. Very few of us can say we haven't made the same mistake. We are strongly tempted to think that our ticket into the eternal fellowship of God is automatically secured by our membership in the *group* we think God is going to save. As long as we're in that group, it doesn't matter what's in our heart or what we do individually. The "institution" is what dispenses salvation, and if we're in fellowship with that group, we are saved.

The truth, however, is that we will be judged on an individual basis. "For we must all appear before the judgment seat of Christ, so that each one may receive what is due for what he has done in the body, whether good or evil" (2 Corinthians 5:10). Our human connections will not save us. It is *our own deeds* that will matter.

This does not mean that our human connections are not important. The New Testament clearly teaches that having obeyed the gospel and come into a right relationship with God, we will need to seek out others who have also been reconciled to God through Christ, so that we can pursue the communal life God has designed for His people in this world (Acts 2:41-47). We cannot be connected to Christ without having some serious brotherly and sisterly duties. *But our group relationship grows out of our personal connection to Christ, and not vice versa.* The distinction is important.

In regard to God, we all need a stronger sense of personal responsibility. In the end, if we stand before God unforgiven and in a lost condition, it will not be for the sins of others but for our own. We should be thankful that we won't be lost for the wickedness of others, but we should be sobered by the other side of that truth: *we will not be saved by the righteousness of others.* Are we helped in this life by the good lives of those we come in contact with? Yes. And should we give thanks for the helpful influence of godly people? Certainly. But those folks can't save us. We do not go to heaven on the group plan. The "obedience of faith" (Romans 1:5) required by the gospel is a matter of personal choice.

Souls are not saved in bundles.

RALPH WALDO EMERSON

December 5

Made in God's Image, We Long for His Fellowship

So God created man in his own image, in the image of God
he created him; male and female he created them.
Genesis 1:27

HUMAN BEINGS HAVE ALWAYS MARVELED AT THEIR UNIQUENESS. Compared to differences that separate the lower creatures, we are so different from even the highest of other living beings, the difference can hardly be described. But how and why are we so different? Until the 18th century in Western Europe, almost every person in the world took seriously the explanation that we correspond in a special way to the God who created us. This is what Genesis 1:27 affirms: "God created man in his own image, in the image of God he created him." Let us think about what this means — and why it is so important in "obeying the gospel."

Perhaps we can summarize our uniqueness by saying that we are *personal* beings. We have "consciousness" and "mind," and the more we contemplate this, the more marvelous it is. We have a *will* that is free to choose our behavior. We can make decisions that are independent of our genetic makeup, our instincts, or our external influences. And if, in fact, we have this freedom because our Creator gave it to us, look at what this means: it means we have both *responsibility* and *accountability* to Him. He has the right to direct our conduct — and bring us into judgment.

Every one of us knows we have not used our freedom rightly. We know that at times we have *rebelled* against our Creator. Knowing full well what our Father's will was, we deliberately went the other direction. We know this because we have something else that is unique to personal beings: *conscience.*

With freedom, responsibility, and conscience, therefore, come the problem of *sin.* By rebelling, we have cut ourselves off from our Creator spiritually. We stand under His penalty for our actions, and we desperately need Him to do what only He can do to redeem us and reconcile us to Himself. We need His *salvation.*

As we ponder whether we will say yes to God's redemption, we recognize another fact about us. *We need our God deeply.* Created in His image, we yearn for Him. Whatever else we may accomplish, this truth can't be denied: *cut off from the God in whose image we were made, we are the most unsatisfied of all creatures.*

Naught but God can satisfy the soul.

PHILIP JAMES BAILEY

December 6

A Gentle Knock at the Door

Behold, I stand at the door and knock. If anyone hears my voice and opens the door, I will come in to him and eat with him, and he with me.
Revelation 3:20

IT MAY STRIKE US AS UNUSUAL THAT WHEN GOD CAME INTO THE WORLD, HE CAME IN SUCH A GENTLE WAY. Perhaps He could have landed with an invading army and compelled our submission with brute force. But he appeared as a gentle Teacher, asking us to open the doors of our hearts to Him. In saying this, we do not question His power or authority; we are simply noticing that the call of the gospel comes to us in the form of an *invitation.*

In my life, there have been times when I wondered why the truth about God and His Son, Jesus Christ, is not more compelling. If these things are true, why are they not so obvious that everybody would see them? Why do we have to be reasoned with and persuaded? As I have grown older, it has become clearer to me that God wants to have a relationship with us that is based on love — and if love is forced upon us, it ceases to be love.

Think about the combination of *truth* and *love* that is involved in our response to the gospel. The truth will always be the truth, of course, and the truth about God is majestically powerful. It tingles our spine when we contemplate even the edges of it. But the problem of sin is the problem of our rebellion against God's love. In self-will we have refused to abide within the limits that our Creator's love placed around us for our protection. Yet the wonder of the gospel is that He loved us enough not to leave us in our alienated condition. He made it possible for us to be reconciled to Him. But it would defeat the whole purpose of His love to compel us to come back. So He "knocks at the door," so to speak, inviting us to let Him come in. If we respond to the *truth* of the gospel, it must be an act of voluntary *love.* We must choose to say yes.

This means that our eternal destiny is in our hands. If the gospel is an invitation, everything hinges on our response to it. Will we accept our Father's love? Or will we reject it? If we are lost, we will probably spend eternity blaming God for not being more forceful to break down our resistance. But if it's not love that brings us back home, what good would it do for us to return to God anyway? What He desires is our love . . . or nothing at all.

Jesus Christ will never strong-arm his way into your life.

GRADY B. WILSON

December 7

The Deadliest Temptation

And as he reasoned about righteousness and self-control and the coming judgment, Felix was alarmed and said, "Go away for the present. When I get an opportunity I will summon you."
Acts 24:25

Temptation comes to us in various ways. Sometimes we are tempted to engage in acts of deliberate disobedience. Knowing full well what God's will is, we are persuaded to do what God has said we must not do, as Eve did when she ate of the forbidden fruit (Genesis 3:1-6). At other times, however, we simply procrastinate doing what is right. We don't see ourselves as being defiant or rebellious; we just can't bring ourselves to obey today — *we will take care of it tomorrow.* But while weakness may seem preferable to outright defiance, I suggest that the temptation to put off obedience until tomorrow is a worse problem than some people realize.

When we don't want to do what is right. It may be that we delay doing God's will because, deep down, we don't want to do it. Like Augustine who prayed "Lord, make me chaste, but not yet," our delay may be a sign that we actually prefer our present situation.

Hoping what is right will be easier tomorrow. If there is likely to be some pain or difficulty in doing what's right, it's tempting to think that the decision might get easier at some future date. In the real world, hard decisions only get harder the longer we wait, but somehow we think our present situation is an exception to the rule. "Tomorrow," we think, "it will be easier. I will do it then."

The temptation to procrastinate is, as I said, worse than the temptation to rebel because it deludes us into a false sense of security. Feeling sure that "our hearts are right," we are lulled into a pattern of default and neglect. As time goes by, our postponement becomes a permanent habit, and we find that what began as innocent procrastination has hardened into outright rebellion. All the while, we were telling ourselves that we truly "wanted" to obey God; we just couldn't muster the strength to do it right then.

As a wise observer of life once said, "There is nothing any more permanent than a temporary solution." If that's true anywhere, it's certainly true in our spiritual lives. So while we are trying to avoid deliberate revolt against God, we must also be on guard against that most deadly of disobedient words: *later.*

When God says today, the devil says tomorrow.

German Proverb

December 8

Flee! Don't Look Back!

Then the LORD rained on Sodom and Gomorrah sulfur and fire from the LORD out of heaven. And he overthrew those cities, and all the valley, and all the inhabitants of the cities, and what grew on the ground. But Lot's wife, behind him, looked back, and she became a pillar of salt.
Genesis 19:24-26

THE ADMONITION TO FLEE IS SOMETIMES MORE IMPORTANT THAN WE REALIZE. If we were in a difficult situation, the advice to "get out of there" might not sound very savvy or sophisticated. But we should not underestimate the wisdom of simply . . . *fleeing.*

As we have seen in previous readings, repentance is a crucial part of the gospel. It is not reasonable, even at the level of common sense, to expect God's forgiveness if we're not willing to give up the sins we want God to forgive us of. But repentance is hard, especially when sinful habits are deeply ingrained in our way of life. From a practical standpoint, there is not much chance of getting away from the clutches of sin if we don't flee from it — decisively rejecting it and pointing ourselves in a new direction. Even more important, our discipleship and consecration to the Lord require us to flee. The Lord's invitation to "forsake all and follow Me" is diametrically opposed to "stay where you are." It's time we realized that discipleship is an adventure, not a "staycation."

Flee. When we leave "Sodom," we ought not to leave there in a leisurely way; disaster is on our heels, and we must make haste. And we should keep this in mind: we aren't just fleeing punishment or judgment; we are fleeing sin itself. In our daily lives, that means we should avoid temptation as much as possible, cutting ourselves off from any influence that might drag us back into sin.

Don't look back. For repentance to be genuine, sin must be rejected decisively — a firm "no" must be said to the very thought of going back. If we "look back" by letting ourselves long for the nightlife in Sodom, it won't be long before we go back to live there. This does not mean we won't ever think about the past, but when we do, we will gently bring our minds back to where they need to be in the present. Tempted to reminisce, we will remember the decision we made to flee, and no matter what it costs, we will keep going toward God. Returning to Sodom is simply not an option.

When you from Sodom flee, the judgment to escape,
Salvation will depend on never looking back.

ANGELUS SILESIUS

December 9

JESUS, THE CRISIS-PRODUCER

Do not think that I have come to bring peace to the earth.
I have not come to bring peace, but a sword.
Matthew 10:34

IN RESPONSE TO JESUS, PEOPLE DID MANY DIFFERENT THINGS, BUT ONE THING NOBODY DID WAS REMAIN NEUTRAL. Jesus' teaching authoritatively called for a decision, and those who did not make a decision for or against Jesus were making the worst decision of all. As Jesus said, "Whoever is not with me is against me, and whoever does not gather with me scatters" (Matthew 12:30).

Jesus is often referred to as the Prince of Peace, and that is certainly what He was. (The description comes from the messianic prophecy in Isaiah 9:6.) But the peace that Jesus brought into the world was rejected by many. Not everybody agreed with what He said, and those who did agree often found themselves estranged from friends and family members who had rejected Him. It is not hard to imagine the bitter disputes that arose wherever Jesus went. "And there was considerable complaining about him among the crowds. While some were saying, 'He is a good man,' others were saying, 'No, he is deceiving the crowd'" (John 7:12 NRSV).

If today it seems that not many are interested in Jesus' teaching one way or the other, it is probably because Jesus' followers have tamed His teaching and turned it into something far less disruptive than it used to be. The "gospel" has become so bland that not even the devil pays much attention to it anymore.

But if we go back to the Scriptures and grapple seriously with the teachings of Jesus and His apostles, we will be challenged just as people were back then. Our conscience will be pricked, and we will feel the same urge to declare ourselves — either as devoted disciples of the Son of God (Matthew 16:15,16) or the murderous friends of Beelzebub (Luke 11:15). When we hear Jesus honestly, a crisis is produced deep within our hearts. *Is this teaching true? And if it is true, what are we going to do about it?* The most tragic thing we can do is run away from this crisis. Painful though it may be, a decision must be made, either to follow Jesus or fight against Him.

Wherever [Jesus] went he produced a crisis. He compelled individuals to decide, to make a choice. In fact, he struck me as the most crisis-producing individual I had ever encountered . . . Nearly everyone clashed with Jesus, whether they loved him or hated him.

REBECCA MANLEY PIPPERT

December 10

The Most Disturbing Message in the World

Now when they heard this they were cut to the heart, and said to Peter and the rest of the apostles, "Brothers, what shall we do?"
Acts 2:37

WOULD YOU SAY BEING "CUT TO THE HEART" IS A GOOD THING? These days, most people wouldn't. We want, at all costs, to experience happy feelings, and we would be turned off by any sermon that called on us to pass through the wilderness of godly sorrow. We only want to hear how much God loves us (forget the sorrowful things God's love might require of us), and if our wonderful "self" needs any change, it just needs to be "actualized."

But the gospel — preached first by John the Baptist, then Jesus, and later the apostles — was *disturbing.* The first thing it produced, at least in the hearts of honest hearers, was not joy but grief. When people heard about "Jesus Christ and him crucified" (1 Corinthians 2:2), they contemplated His death with tears of repentance, asking fervently, "What shall we do?" (Acts 2:37).

There is a sense in which *conservatism* ("preservation of the status quo") is our deadliest spiritual enemy. The truth is, we are lost in sin and alienated from God, but we think we're doing fine. If the gospel can't break through that complacency, it can't save us. Not even the gospel can save those who see no need to be saved.

Our "house of cards" is unstable. The gospel wants to disrupt our assumption that the lives we've built are secure (Luke 12:16-21). Eventually, our "house of cards" is going to come crashing down, and if we're not shaken up by the prospect of that, we should be.

Our sins are serious. In Luke 18:9-14, the Pharisee would have admitted that he had a few imperfections, but he was out of touch with how serious those shortcomings were. He needed nothing quite so much as to be troubled by the truth about himself.

Our character is far from God's character. Those who have been Christians for many years often overestimate how much they have grown spiritually. If we keep listening to the gospel, it will often disturb us with the reminder of how far we still have to go.

The bottom line is this: if the seed of the kingdom is going to grow within us, the fields of our hearts have to be plowed up. And the harder the ground, the more painful the plowing is going to be.

If Christianity has never disturbed us,
we have not yet learned what it is.

WILLIAM TEMPLE

December 11

Obedience Is Not a Negative Concept

By this we know that we love the children of God, when we love God and obey his commandments. For this is the love of God, that we keep his commandments. And his commandments are not burdensome.
1 John 5:2,3

NOWADAYS, MOST PEOPLE THINK OF EQUALITY IN SUCH A WAY THAT THEY BELIEVE HIERARCHIES ARE EVIL AND ARE TO BE AVOIDED WHEREVER POSSIBLE. The very word *obedience* evokes an image of pre-modern times, before equality came to be viewed as it is today. As a result, when we delve into the Scriptures and encounter words like *lord, master, ruler, king,* and *lawgiver,* we have a knee-jerk reaction against the very idea conveyed by such words.

To "obey," of course, means to yield to the command of someone else. The idea may be unwelcome in our culture, but Jesus was not averse to it. During His sojourn in this world, for example, He submitted to baptism as an act of obedience, despite having no sins that He needed to repent of (Matthew 3:13-17). And on one occasion, He said simply, "I have come down from heaven, not to do my own will but the will of him who sent me" (John 6:38).

When the gospel of Christ was preached on the Day of Pentecost in Acts 2, Peter concluded his sermon by saying, "Let all the house of Israel therefore know for certain that God has made him both Lord and Christ, this Jesus whom you crucified" (v.36). *Both Lord and Christ.* To be Christians, we will have to accept not only the messiahship but also the lordship of Christ — and that will require us to get comfortable with the idea of obedience.

So we need to view obedience in a more kindly light. And even in our relationships with other human beings, we should not think of hierarchies and submission as inherently evil. Without so much as a word of resistance or resentment, Jesus submitted to the authority of a Roman governor and allowed Himself to be put to death. And even in the years of His youth, He had been submissive to Joseph and Mary, although as their Creator He would have had the right to command their behavior (Luke 2:51,52). Wherever we look in the New Testament, we see Jesus recommending obedience as something to be honored and appreciated. He showed us that it was not obedience that got us into trouble, but obedience to *sin.*

Thirty years of our Lord's life are hidden in these words of the gospel: "He was subject to them."

JACQUES-BÉNIGNE BOSSUET

December 12

Looking Beyond Our Salvation to the Savior

The next day he saw Jesus coming toward him, and said,
"Behold, the Lamb of God, who takes away the sin of the world!"
John 1:29

As the "Lamb of God," Jesus Christ is the one who "takes away the sin of the world." The words "looking to Jesus" (Hebrews 12:2) are powerful. If our sins are to be taken away, it is to Him that we must look. We have no other hope (Acts 4:12).

However, there is a subtle danger in focusing on our need for salvation. I hate to mention it, because the last thing some people need is to pay less attention to their need for forgiveness. But if we're not careful, we may put the emphasis in the wrong place. It is true that we are a needy people and only God can save us. Without God's grace, we are lost. But something is wrong if we think of God as existing for the purpose of serving our needs.

So I want to recommend an adjustment to the way in which many of us think about God. As the gospel first begins to do its work, we are most conscious of our sinfulness and need for salvation. Then, if we obey the gospel, we start living on the basis of gratitude for our salvation. That surely marks a huge step forward. But the third stage is even more important: the stage in which we forget ourselves and are focused on God. As wonderful as it is to see that we've been saved, it is better to think of the God who saved us. And frankly, I'm not there yet. Are you?

When we get to heaven, we will be completely happy. But I believe our thoughts will not be centered on how happy we are. We will be so completely caught up in the glory and majesty of God that *our happiness will simply be a byproduct of thinking rightly about God.* The truth about God will have set us free — free from, among other things, any preoccupation with our own salvation.

For now, our thoughts are often about ourselves: our needs and the Lord's ability to supply them. But we need to be growing toward a greater maturity. When our salvation has reached its final perfection at the foot of God's throne, we won't be thinking about ourselves or even the fact that we were saved. *We'll only be thinking of the Savior Himself.* And even now, it is beneficial to think less about what we desire from God and more about who He is.

Looking at the wound of sin will never save anyone.
What you must do is to look at the remedy.

Dwight Lyman Moody

December 13

God, the Support of the Saved

Now to him who is able to keep you from stumbling and to present you blameless before the presence of his glory with great joy, to the only God, our Savior, through Jesus Christ our Lord, be glory, majesty, dominion, and authority, before all time and now and forever. Amen.

Jude 24,25

JUDE'S CHRISTIAN FRIENDS NEEDED TO BE ASSURED OF GOD'S HELP. They faced difficulties that would test their allegiance to Christ, ordeals that might overwhelm them if they didn't have the faithful support of their Heavenly Father. So Jude ended his letter of warning to his brethren with this ascription of praise to God: "[He] is able to keep you from stumbling and to present you blameless before the presence of his glory with great joy."

On the night of Jesus' betrayal and arrest, He predicted that Peter would deny Him and forsake Him. But Jesus also assured Peter that he would come back from his failure, stronger for having fallen and gotten back on his feet. "Simon, Simon, behold, Satan demanded to have you, that he might sift you like wheat, but I have prayed for you that your faith may not fail. And when you have turned again, strengthen your brothers" (Luke 22:31,32).

A part of the help God gives us in Christ is that we have our fellow Christians' help in times of temptation and failure. Paul wrote, "Brothers, if anyone is caught in any transgression, you who are spiritual should restore him in a spirit of gentleness. Keep watch on yourself, lest you too be tempted. Bear one another's burdens, and so fulfill the law of Christ" (Galatians 6:1,2). And "we urge you, brothers, admonish the idle, encourage the fainthearted, help the weak, be patient with them all" (1 Thessalonians 5:14). In Christ, we are never alone in our struggles.

We can be grateful that God restricts Satan's power. "God is faithful, and he will not let you be tempted beyond your ability, but with the temptation he will also provide the way of escape, that you may be able to endure it" (1 Corinthians 10:13).

Having obeyed the gospel, our glorious hope is an eternal rest, one where all our stumblings will be behind us. Until then, we have the promise of God's steadfast love and constant support.

O Lord, support us all the day long, until the shadows lengthen and the evening comes and the busy world is hushed, and the fever of life is over, and our work is done. Then in thy mercy grant us a safe lodging and a holy rest, and peace at last.

JOHN HENRY NEWMAN

December 14

IN CHRIST, WE CAN BE EVERYTHING GOD INTENDED

For the creation waits with eager longing
for the revealing of the sons of God.
Romans 8:19

BOUND TO THE PRESENT MOMENT AS WE ARE, WE CAN'T SEE VERY FAR BACKWARD OR FORWARD. So we can only imagine what human beings were before they fell into sin, and it is beyond our dreams to envision what we will be, in Jesus Christ, when God has completed His future plans for us. Paul said "the revealing of the sons of God" is a thing being awaited with "eager longing."

If this perspective on our past, present, and future is true to reality, however, it is at odds with the account given by modernism. According to that account, human beings have arisen by the random process of genetic mutation (and more recently by their own efforts) from amoral organisms to those that can think and struggle morally. But just as the past is to be accounted for without recourse to any god, so the future, whatever it turns out to be, will be only what we are able to make of it and no more. Indeed, modernism looks upon religion, and especially theistic religion, as a part of the primitive past that must be discarded if humanity is going to overcome its problems and achieve its best future.

If the account of modernism is true, it should be accepted. But if it is not true, it is nothing less than the most devastating blow in history to the hopes of the human heart. If we can rise no higher than the heights made possible by our own ingenuity, the results so far do not give us cause for anything but great worry.

We do not, of course, choose between modernism and the gospel of Christ merely on the basis of which ideology gives us the greater comfort. The gospel makes its case historically, hanging everything on the credibility of the resurrection of Christ.

If the resurrection happened, the gospel is true and there is great glory both behind us and ahead of us. Created in God's image, human beings were glorious, but they fell into sin. In Christ, our humanity can be restored — and what Christians are now waiting for is what Paul described as "the glorious liberty of the children of God" (Romans 8:21 NKJV). So God, if He exists, is not a hindrance to human progress. *He is our only hope of becoming fully human.*

By his first work God gave me to myself; and by the next he gave himself to me. And when he gave himself, he gave me back myself that I had lost.

BERNARD OF CLAIRVAUX

December 15

Will All Be Saved?

Or do you presume on the riches of his kindness and forbearance and patience, not knowing that God's kindness is meant to lead you to repentance? But because of your hard and impenitent heart you are storing up wrath for yourself on the day of wrath when God's righteous judgment will be revealed.
Romans 2:4,5

MOST PEOPLE BELIEVE THAT EVERYBODY IS GOING TO HEAVEN. At almost every funeral service, the speaker comforts the family by saying that the deceased (no matter how irreligious or immoral) is now at peace with God. Somehow we find a way to believe that, in the end, all of us will find our way to heaven.

If God is an objective reality, that reality is independent of our personal preferences. Whatever is the truth about God, we must be prepared to accept it. And we ought to decide what the truth is by consulting God's revelation of Himself in the Scriptures.

When we consult the evidence, what we find is that God is a God of grace. This is good news, to say the least. God wants to save us from our sins, repair the damage sin has done to our character, and then have us enjoy eternity with Him (John 3:16).

But the evidence also indicates that God will not take away our free will. He will not force us to accept His salvation. Instead, God makes salvation available to all (John 3:17), and grants the gift to those who accept it on His terms (John 5:39,40). If we reject the gospel, we won't share the same destiny as those who obey it.

God "will render to each one according to his works: to those who by patience in well-doing seek for glory and honor and immortality, he will give eternal life; but for those who are self-seeking and do not obey the truth, but obey unrighteousness, there will be wrath and fury. There will be tribulation and distress for every human being who does evil, the Jew first and also the Greek, but glory and honor and peace for everyone who does good, the Jew first and also the Greek. For God shows no partiality" (Romans 2:6-11). Having given us Christ, God has put the choice in our hands. Will we surrender and submit to our Savior?

I would pay any price to be able to say truthfully, "All will be saved." But my reason retorts, "Without their will, or with it?" If I say, "Without their will," I at once perceive a contradiction; how can the supreme voluntary act of self-surrender be involuntary? If I say, "With their will," my reason replies, "How if they will not give in?"

C. S. Lewis

December 16

What Happens When We Say No?

As I live, declares the Lord God, I have no pleasure in the death of the wicked, but that the wicked turn from his way and live; turn back, turn back from your evil ways, for why will you die, O house of Israel?
Ezekiel 33:11

It would be a mistake to think that God is unaffected when we reject Him. It was He who gave us the freedom to choose, and He will not force His will upon us, but that does not mean He is impartial or indifferent as to which choice we will make.

Our Father loves us more than we have the ability to imagine. He gave His Son to save us (John 3:16; Romans 5:6-8). Surely, His preference is that we say yes to His offer of salvation and allow Him to reconcile us to Himself. Like the father of the Prodigal Son, God will not follow us into the far country, nor make us get up out of the pig pen and come back home — but when we come home, He will run to meet us and embrace us (Luke 15:11-32).

Can we not hear the sorrow in Jesus' voice when He said, "O Jerusalem, Jerusalem, the city that kills the prophets and stones those who are sent to it! How often would I have gathered your children together as a hen gathers her brood under her wings, and you were not willing!" (Matthew 23:37)? And do we not feel the urgency of God's concern when He said, "I have no pleasure in the death of the wicked, but that the wicked turn from his way and live; turn back, turn back from your evil ways, for why will you die, O house of Israel" (Ezekiel 33:11)? Our God is a God of tears.

At judgment there will be some to whom the Lord will have no choice but to say, "Depart from me" (Matthew 7:23), but it will break His heart to do so. In that moment, God will lose far more than we will. Having created us, He has far more invested in us than we have in Him. So the loss of even one person whom He has created in His image must of necessity be a tragic loss to Him.

Freedom is a fearful responsibility. It may be hard for us to wrap our minds around the fact that God has given us the power to break His heart — but the desire to love Him and *not* break His heart ought to be one of the prime reasons why we obey the gospel. Could there by anything worse than saying no to our Father?

There are only two kinds of people in the end: those who say to God, "Thy will be done," and those to whom God says, in the end, "Thy will be done." All that are in Hell, choose it. Without that self-choice there could be no Hell.

C. S. Lewis

December 17

We Can't Get Back to God on Our Own

For since, in the wisdom of God, the world did not know God through wisdom, it pleased God through the folly of what we preach to save those who believe.
1 Corinthians 1:21

It is obvious that the consequences of sin in the world are distressing to us. There are few rational people anywhere who do not understand the difficulties of the human condition: we struggle with loneliness, depression, anxiety, fear, anger, alienation, and irrelevance (to name just a few of our challenges).

But for all those who recognize the reality of these struggles, few see clearly that they are, indeed, the consequences of sin. It is not that every instance of suffering is the result of some sin in the life of the sufferer, but that suffering in general would not be in the world if all human beings were still in a right relationship with God.

We live in the age of optimistic "self-help." We may struggle, but we believe the answers lie within us, or at least that science and psychology will eventually find a way to alleviate our pain. So we keep searching, looking for the right technique or ideology.

But if the root of the problem is our alienation from God — and this is exactly what the gospel of Christ affirms — we will not be able to fix this problem on our own. Only God can open the door that would readmit us to His throne room. And the wondrous news is that He has done so. By giving His Son to die for us, He made an atoning sacrifice that did for us what we could never have done for ourselves. "For while we were still helpless, at the right time Christ died for the ungodly" (Romans 5:6 NASB).

But not only must we accept God's solution; we must accept it on His terms. If we could never have worked our own way back to Him, neither can we refuse, or attempt to modify, the conditions that God has attached to the granting of His salvation to us.

So the gospel requires the humbling of ourselves before God, the God against whom we have rebelled. And this makes sense, doesn't it? If the problem of sin is the problem of self-will, we must lay aside our self-will in order to be saved. If we insist on self-help, we may become nicer people, but our sins will still be unforgiven.

The love of God, with arms extended on a cross, bars the way to hell. But if that love is ignored, rejected, and finally refused, there comes a time when love can only weep while man pushes past into the self-chosen alienation which Christ went to the cross to avert.

Michael Green

December 18

Seeing the Truth, Deciding to Respond

But when he came to himself, he said, "How many of my father's hired servants have more than enough bread, but I perish here with hunger! I will arise and go to my father, and I will say to him, 'Father, I have sinned against heaven and before you.'"
Luke 15:17,18

THE LOST SON IN THIS STORY MADE A DECISION. Alienated from his father, and having abused every blessing he had ever been given, this young man "came to himself." Finally recognizing the foolishness of his previous choices, he decided to get up out of the pig pen, go back home, and seek his father's pardon.

There are those who would argue that such a thing is impossible. Deterministic views of life see everything about us as the product of forces beyond our control (divine predestination, genetic determinants, environmental pressures, psychological compulsions, and social restrictions, to name just a few).

But we are not helpless. As we see in the story in Luke 15, the positive choice is always available. *No matter how desperate the situation, there is always some step we can take in the right direction.* Are we influenced by the temptations around us? Yes. Are we weakened by our previous sins? Certainly. But we are not helpless. We have the freedom to choose repentance rather than further rebellion.

We can hear the sadness in Jesus' voice when He lamented His own people's rejection of Him. "O Jerusalem, Jerusalem, the city that kills the prophets and stones those who are sent to it! How often would I have gathered your children together as a hen gathers her brood under her wings, and you were not willing!" (Matthew 23:37). *You were not willing!* In another place, He said, "You refuse to come to me that you may have life" (John 5:40).

We have defined "obeying the gospel" as rightly responding to the gospel. To be morally "responsible" means "able to choose our response." So with the power to decide, let us decide. We've wasted enough time. Now is the time to quit being foolish.

Man is no helpless invalid left in a valley of total depravity until God pulls him out. Man is rather an upstanding human being whose vision has been impaired by the cataracts of sin and whose soul has been weakened by the virus of pride, but there is sufficient vision left for him to lift his eyes unto the hills, and there remains enough of God's image for him to turn his weak and sin-battered life toward the Great Physician, the curer of the ravages of sin.

MARTIN LUTHER

December 19

THE TWO GREAT ALTERNATIVES

He will render to each one according to his works: to those who by patience in well-doing seek for glory and honor and immortality, he will give eternal life; but for those who are self-seeking and do not obey the truth, but obey unrighteousness, there will be wrath and fury.
Romans 2:6-8

JESUS SAID THAT EVERY TREE IS KNOWN BY THE FRUIT IT BEARS. Our outward deeds are important because, in the end, they will have shown the kind of persons we were on the inside, in our hearts. God's judgment of us will be based on truth, and if the truth is that self-will was the principle we allowed to govern us, we need not fool ourselves that He will treat us the same as if we had lived otherwise. "He will render to each one according to his works."

Those who by patience in well-doing seek for glory and honor and immortality. Unlike the self-seekers in the next verse, these individuals "seek for glory and honor and immortality." And these things are more than just vague ideals; it is by actual deeds — "by patience in well-doing" — that these goals are pursued. The path of obedience was their choice, and to them God "will give eternal life."

Those who are self-seeking and do not obey the truth, but obey unrighteousness. Since salvation is by grace, many question the concept of "obeying the gospel," as if that attaches too much important to obedience. But clearly the choice between obedience and disobedience is critical. For those who "do not obey the truth, but obey unrighteousness, there will be wrath and fury."

Like every basic truth, this truth that God "will render to each one according to his works" is both comforting and sobering. It is comforting to know that God deals with individuals, based on their own choices — we don't have to fear being lost because of someone else's choices. But freedom of choice and personal responsibility are also sobering. People are not saved on the "group plan." Each of us must choose individually and personally.

And finally, there is something else that must be said: God's judgment will be on the basis of our actual works and not merely good "attitudes" or good "intentions." The lordship of Christ requires more than mere sentiment. "Why do you call me 'Lord, Lord,' and not do what I tell you?" (Luke 6:46).

You can be certain of this: when the Day of Judgment comes,
we shall not be asked what we have read, but what we have done;
not how well we have spoken, but how well we have lived.

THOMAS À KEMPIS

December 20

WHAT PROFIT?

For what will it profit a man if he gains the whole world and forfeits his soul? Or what shall a man give in return for his soul?
Matthew 16:26

IN THE LAST TWO THOUSAND YEARS, MANY DIFFERENT MESSAGES HAVE BEEN PREACHED BY THOSE CLAIMING TO UPHOLD THE GOSPEL OF CHRIST. Today, most of what goes by the name of "Christianity" is a far cry from what Jesus taught and what He instructed His apostles to teach. To be specific, the original emphasis on the removal of our sins so that we could have a right relationship with God, and the hope of eternal life, has been replaced by a modern emphasis on psychological uplift and social justice.

It should go without saying: *we need to rightly understand what the gospel of Christ is about.* If we misjudge the main point of the gospel (and even worse, misrepresent the main point to those we teach), the results of our misplaced emphasis will be tragic.

Surely there are many different problems in the world. To say that this world is "broken" is to say the painfully obvious. But when Jesus appeared, what was it about this world that He proposed to fix? If we let Jesus, the Great Physician, tell us what our very worst problem is, will we humbly accept His diagnosis?

In one of Jesus' most often-quoted statements He said, "For the Son of Man came to seek and to save the lost" (Luke 19:10). Whatever other problems He might have helped us with, He was clear that none of these benefits would matter if we failed to let Him restore us to the fellowship of our Heavenly Father. *"For what will it profit a man if he gains the whole world and forfeits his soul?"*

Jesus' priority was the forgiveness of our sins so that having been reconciled to God we could be conformed to His character and look forward to a perfect relationship with Him in eternity. If that was Jesus' priority, it ought to be ours. It ought to matter more than economic security, emotional well-being, or anything else.

Do we understand the horror of refusing God's redemption and dying in our rebellion against Him? If that happens, nothing we ever gained in this world will matter. If our souls are lost in eternity, the only thing — the *only* thing — we will regret missing in this life was a right relationship with the God who made us.

The essence of hell is complete separation from God, and that is the ultimate disaster.

W. R. MATTHEWS

December 21

Real Restoration to God

Create in me a clean heart, O God,
and renew a right spirit within me.
Psalm 51:10

IF WE WANT SALVATION AT ALL, MOST OF US ONLY WANT SALVATION FROM OUR CIRCUMSTANCES, NOT SALVATION FROM OUR SINS. We'd like help with the difficult, painful aspects of our lives, especially the unjust things other people have done to us. It is the unpleasantness and hardship of this broken world that we want God to fix.

Now and then, though, we do see that our own sins have contributed to the hardship of our lives, and we seek relief from the hurts we've inflicted on ourselves. Perhaps we even see with godly sorrow just how horribly our actions have broken the heart of our Father in heaven. Repentance becomes a priority with us.

But here is the point: even when we see that sin is what is hurting us, we often don't go deep enough to see the real problem. What needs fixing is not just our actions; *we need new hearts.* At the very deepest level inside of us, we need to be renovated, rebuilt, and renewed. Since our thinking is what has produced our deeds, our thinking needs to change. And the change will have to be *radical* (going to the "root" of the problem). We will have to see what David saw after his sin: more than forgiveness for the specific sin, he needed help with his heart. *Create in me a clean heart, O God.*

This is what the gospel of Christ aims to accomplish. And frankly, even those of us who have accepted Christ need to see more clearly *the newness of heart* that God is looking for. As Paul put it when he wrote to the Christians in Rome, "Do not be conformed to this world, but be transformed by the renewal of your mind" (Romans 12:2). And as he wrote to the Ephesians, those who have been forgiven need "to be renewed in the spirit of [our] minds, and to put on the new self, created after the likeness of God in true righteousness and holiness" (Ephesians 4:23,24).

Is this what we desire? When we come to Christ, is this what we're looking for? It should be. And the more we mature in Christ, the more this will be our passion. *Create in me a clean heart, O God.*

A heart in every thought renewed,
And full of love divine,
Perfect and right and pure and good,
A copy, Lord, of thine.

CHARLES WESLEY

December 22

A Victory Given by God

But thanks be to God, who gives us
the victory through our Lord Jesus Christ.
1 Corinthians 15:57

GRATITUDE IS ONE OF THE MAJOR MOTIFS THAT WE HEAR IN THE GREAT SYMPHONY OF THE GOSPEL OF CHRIST. The apostle Paul, for example, uses the expression "thanks be to God" six times in his letters. And he uses it in 1 Corinthians 15:57 as he reaches the climax of his magnificent discussion of the resurrection of Christ.

Victory is a powerful word, but it is exactly the right word to describe what the gospel is about. Succumbing to sin, we were defeated by Satan, and eternal death was the result. But God entered the world in the person of Jesus of Nazareth, died a vicarious death, and was then raised on the third day, defeating death, the worst weapon of the enemy. "Since therefore the children share in flesh and blood, he himself likewise partook of the same things, that through death he might destroy the one who has the power of death, that is, the devil, and deliver all those who through fear of death were subject to lifelong slavery" (Hebrews 2:14,15).

In 1 Corinthians 15:57, Paul is very clear: it is "through our Lord Jesus Christ" that the victory has been given. This echoes the statement of Peter in Acts 4:12, where, speaking of Christ, he said, "And there is salvation in no one else, for there is no other name under heaven given among men by which we must be saved."

But going back to Paul's emphasis on gratitude, he said that it is God "who gives us the victory." Salvation from sin is not a gift granted universally and unconditionally to all of mankind, without regard to how people respond or don't respond to the gospel. It was God's decision to limit the gift to those who would respond according to certain conditions that He set (Acts 2:37,38). *Nevertheless, the gift is still a gift, and it is one given by God.* When we were hopelessly defeated, God stepped in and won the victory for us.

We should never become so familiar with the gospel that we underestimate what God has done in Christ. Our salvation from sin is a gift much greater than mere survival, and to enjoy eternity with God is to do more than just get by. It will be the enjoyment of nothing less than the glorious triumph of God Himself.

God wants us to be victors, not victims; to grow, not grovel;
to soar, not sink; to overcome, not to be overwhelmed.

WILLIAM ARTHUR WARD

December 23

Come to Jesus, Do Not Tarry

You search the Scriptures because you think that in them
you have eternal life; and it is they that bear witness about me,
yet you refuse to come to me that you may have life.
John 5:39,40

When Jesus invites us to come to Him, it is possible to refuse. Tragic as such a refusal is, many do refuse. But many others simply delay, thinking an easier time will come later.

It is always important for us to see the seriousness of our plight as those who have departed from God. Sin is no trivial matter. Its punishment cannot be small. As our Creator, God is our rightful Sovereign, and to rebel against His will, as we have all done, is to put ourselves under the penalty of death. There can be no question about the justice of God's decree. Eternal death is the right consequence for rebellion against our Creator (Romans 6:23).

Remember what we said way back in January about our attitude in coming to Jesus? We come willing to *commit ourselves to His lordship.* Disobedience having gotten us into trouble, we are now ready to change from disobedience to obedience. But before our discipleship can begin, we must *seek the forgiveness of our sins.* This we are willing to do on whatever terms God has set, grateful for His grace. And we seek His forgiveness for no other reason than *godly sorrow* — grief that we have sinned against the One who loves us.

The word for *lost* is the saddest word in any language. And when the word applies to our *eternal* condition, that is a sadness beyond description, all the more sad in view of what God has sacrificed to save us. If we persist in our refusal of His grace and die in our rebellious state, the worst part of hell will be knowing that we chose it. It could have been otherwise, but we refused to be rescued. It just wasn't important enough for us to *act.*

Most of us know what it is to damage our lives by delaying our duty. Knowing what is right, we have procrastinated and done much harm. By God's grace, let's stop the damage right now. He gave His Son to make our forgiveness possible. More life than we can imagine is waiting for us, but we must accept His pardon on His terms and we must come back to Him . . . before it is too late.

Come to Jesus! do not tarry,
Enter in at mercy's gate;
O delay not till the morrow,
Lest thy coming be too late.

E. R. Latta

December 24

When You Return, Expect a Celebration

But the father said to his servants, "Bring quickly the best robe,
and put it on him, and put a ring on his hand, and shoes on his feet.
And bring the fattened calf and kill it, and let us eat and celebrate.
For this my son was dead, and is alive again; he was lost,
and is found." And they began to celebrate.
Luke 15:22-24

IT SHOULD GIVE US COURAGE TO READ THE WORDS "AND THEY BEGAN TO CELEBRATE." Among those old enough to discern right from wrong, there is not a one of us who has not "left home." We have broken our Father's heart, insisting on the freedom to go into a "far country" where His will would not restrict us and we could indulge our own desires. Coming to our senses, we've seen the tragedy of our decision, but perhaps we are reluctant to accept the invitation of the gospel to come back home to God. Perhaps we wonder what kind of reception we would receive if we did so.

A problem we all have. When we commit sin, we do something that everybody around us has also done. None of us is innocent. Deep in our hearts, we know Paul was right when he said that "all have sinned and fall short of the glory of God" (Romans 3:23).

The necessity of repentance. The gospel of God's forgiveness is a message that requires repentance. "From that time Jesus began to preach, saying, 'Repent, for the kingdom of heaven is at hand'" (Matthew 4:17). So there are two terrible mistakes we need to avoid: (1) presuming that God's grace will bless us whether we repent or not, and (2) presuming that if we don't repent today, there will be other days in the future when we can take care of that.

The joy of forgiveness. Moved by love to end our rebellion against God, we must summon our courage and do what the Prodigal Son did: go back home and offer our repentance to our Father. What a day that will be! If there is a joy any deeper than forgiveness, it is the joy of living in a right relationship with the Father who has given us back what we so foolishly threw away.

When we have wandered away from home, our Father fervently desires for us to come back to Him (Luke 15:20). It is not just that He will allow us to return — He *wants* us to return. And when we do, we can expect that, by His grace, there will be a banquet at which He will show us how much He has always loved us.

When prodigals return, great things are done.

A. A. Dowty

December 25

ARE YOU A CHRISTIAN?

Then Agrippa said to Paul, "You almost
persuade me to become a Christian."
Acts 26:28 NKJV

THE QUESTION "ARE YOU A CHRISTIAN?" IS PERHAPS MORE CONFUSING TO PEOPLE TODAY THAN IT WOULD HAVE BEEN IN THE FIRST CENTURY. But when Agrippa said, "You almost persuade me to become a Christian," he knew what a Christian was. He understood the word *Christian* in its original sense: *a disciple of Jesus Christ.*

Sadly, there is no evidence that Agrippa ever became a Christian, but he was certainly on the right track when he said that to be a Christian he would have to *become* one. No one has ever been a Christian (at least in the original sense) without having chosen to obey the gospel of Christ. Discipleship to Jesus is not a condition one stumbles into inadvertently (and it is certainly not a status one acquires by being born into a certain nation or family). To the contrary, it is a relationship to God one chooses to accept — and then it is a way of life one decides to pursue.

As we have seen, the gospel of Christ is the message of salvation from our sins (Luke 24:46,47). It is for the penitent (Matthew 4:17), those who have come to see the seriousness of their betrayal of their Father and who "mourn" (Matthew 5:4) and "hunger and thirst for righteousness" (Matthew 5:6). In their sorrow, they embrace the good news of the forgiveness that is offered in Christ. Believing that He is indeed the Savior, they are willing to openly confess what they believe about Him (Romans 10:9,10), and they are eager to be baptized into Christ so that their sins might be forgiven (Acts 2:38). And for the rest of their lives, they live "in newness of life" (Romans 6:4), looking forward to Christ's return and their life in eternity with God (2 Peter 3:10-13; 1 John 3:2,3).

And so, my friend, I ask you, "Where are you in regard to this process?" If you haven't already said an unalterable "No" to it, I hope you will give the gospel of Christ a chance to convince you of its truth. I hope the day will soon come when someone will ask and you'll be able to say enthusiastically, "Yes, I am a Christian!"

To the dead he sayeth: Arise!
To the living: Follow me!
And that voice still soundeth on
From the centuries that are gone,
To the centuries that shall be!

HENRY WADSWORTH LONGFELLOW

December 26

HAVE YOU ACCEPTED CHRIST?

Therefore, as you received Christ Jesus the Lord, so walk in him, rooted and built up in him and established in the faith, just as you were taught, abounding in thanksgiving.
Colossians 2:6,7

PAUL'S COUNSEL TO THE COLOSSIANS IS ONE THAT APPLIES TO ALL OF US WHO HAVE OBEYED THE GOSPEL. He said, "As you received Christ Jesus the Lord, so walk in him." Having accepted Christ, we need to live like persons who have actually done that.

We often hear people talk about having "accepted Jesus as their Lord" when a quick look at their lives makes us wonder if they even know the definition of *lord.* Jesus said, "Why do you call me 'Lord, Lord,' and not do what I tell you?" (Luke 6:46). Jesus Christ is not truly our Lord if it is not His will that governs us.

In Colossians 2:7, Paul used the analogy of a plant. Those who have received Christ must be "rooted and built up in him and established in the faith." This echoes Jesus' teaching about the kinds of soil into which the seed of God's word is sown. The seed must not only germinate; it must send down roots deep enough that the plant grows to maturity and produces fruit (Matthew 13:1-9,18-23). So we must not only accept Christ initially; we must accept Him for the rest of our lives — in our hearts and our deeds.

But let's make it personal. What would your next step be if you wished to accept Christ? If you still stand outside of God's forgiveness, not having obeyed even the initial terms of the gospel, you need to turn your heart toward God in godly sorrow and come before Him with the humble question, "What must I do?" And the answer of the gospel will be that you need to confess that you believe Jesus is the Christ (Romans 10:9,10), repent of your sins (Luke 13:3), and be baptized into Christ's death (Romans 6:3,4), trusting in God's promise to wash away your sins (Acts 22:16).

But if you have done these things in the past, what now? If you honestly have to admit that you haven't kept the commitment you made to Christ, then you need to repent of that and come back to Him with a deeper love (Revelation 2:4,5). Your "acceptance" of Christ needs to be more "accepting." And frankly, who among us (even those who have been Christians the longest) can say we don't need to open the doors of our heart more widely to Jesus Christ?

We get no deeper into Christ than we allow him to get into us.

JOHN HENRY JOWETT

December 27

Forgiven, Saved, Born Again

For if we have been united with him in a death like his, we shall certainly be united with him in a resurrection like his. We know that our old self was crucified with him in order that the body of sin might be brought to nothing, so that we would no longer be enslaved to sin. For one who has died has been set free from sin. Now if we have died with Christ, we believe that we will also live with him.
Romans 6:5-8

IT IS A POPULAR MISCONCEPTION THAT "BORN AGAIN" CHRISTIANS ARE DIFFERENT FROM ORDINARY CHRISTIANS. Let's look today at three biblical descriptions of what happens when a person obeys the gospel of Christ, all of which point to the same experience. These descriptions emphasize the deep, inward nature of the change that takes place when a person turns to Jesus Christ.

Forgiven. At the very least, accepting salvation in Christ means being forgiven of our past sins. But it also means having the comfort and hope that come from continual access to God's grace. "If we confess our sins, he is faithful and just to forgive us our sins and to cleanse us from all unrighteousness" (1 John 1:9).

Saved. This aspect of our conversion to Christ is probably not emphasized enough these days, but we dare not forget that if we are in Christ, we are among those who have been *rescued.* "Since, therefore, we have now been justified by his blood, much more shall we be saved by him from the wrath of God" (Romans 5:9).

Born again. In Christ, our "before" and "after" are so radically different it can be said that a new person has come to life. We died to our old self, and a new self has been born. And this is not just for some Christians; it is for all of us. Jesus said, "Unless one is born again he cannot see the kingdom of God" (John 3:3).

As you can see, to be forgiven/saved/born again is no small experience. When Peter said, "Repent therefore and be converted, that your sins may be blotted out, so that times of refreshing may come from the presence of the Lord" (Acts 3:19,20 NKJV), he was imploring his hearers to do nothing less than turn from death to life. *No greater — or more decisive — change is possible for us in this world.*

Have you made the following decision about sin — that it must be completely killed in you? It takes a long time to come to the point of making this complete and effective decision about sin. It is, however, the greatest moment in your life once you decide that sin must die in you — not simply be restrained, suppressed, or counteracted, but crucified — just as Jesus Christ died for the sin of the world.

OSWALD CHAMBERS

December 28

EXAMINING OURSELVES

Examine yourselves as to whether you are in the faith. Test yourselves.
Do you not know yourselves, that Jesus Christ is in you?
— unless indeed you are disqualified.
2 Corinthians 13:5 NKJV

GIVEN THE IMPORTANCE OF OUR RELATIONSHIP TO GOD, THERE IS NO HIGHER PRIORITY FOR US THAN SELF-EXAMINATION. Are we, or are we not, in a right relationship with Him? Do we, or do we not, have the hope of eternal life? And no less critical is this question: *by what standard are we going to judge these matters?* If we never question ourselves, we may spend our lives climbing the ladder and find that our ladder was leaning against the wrong wall.

Paul's instruction to "examine yourselves as to whether you are in the faith" was written to a group of Christians. One of the worst things a Christian can do is take his salvation for granted. Without self-examination, we may find ourselves in the same situation as the Corinthians, with a confidence about being "in the faith" that goes beyond what is warranted by the facts.

But what is the application of this principle to non-Christians? If you are presently committed to some other path, is self-examination something you are willing to do? If the gospel of Christ is true, your salvation depends on letting go of your present position.

No matter where any of us may be in relation to Jesus Christ, there are two qualities of character required of us: *honesty* and *courage.* Without the honesty to see where we've been out of sync with God's will, we won't change. And without the courage to change, honesty will only make our conscience more painful. So "examine yourselves" is a serious challenge to us all. It tests our integrity at the deepest level. Are we willing to question whether our relationship to God is really what we've been thinking it was?

None of us gets to any significant destination without making many mid-course corrections. Even in the humdrum activities of daily life, we have to be willing to make adjustments. How much more, then, must we be "correctable" when it comes to life's most important issue: *the status of our relationship to God.* While life lasts, there is no correction we cannot make — but making the changes that will lead us to God's presence in eternity requires *the honesty to admit we have been wrong and the courage to change for the better.*

Absolute candor is an indispensable requisite to salvation.

A. W. TOZER

December 29

Have You Died with Christ?

Do you not know that all of us who have been baptized into Christ Jesus were baptized into his death? We were buried therefore with him by baptism into death, in order that, just as Christ was raised from the dead by the glory of the Father, we too might walk in newness of life.
Romans 6:3,4

IN THE GOSPEL, THERE IS AN INSEPARABLE LINK BETWEEN CHRIST'S DEATH AND OUR BAPTISM. The death of Christ is obviously important; it is by His death that the forgiveness of our sins was made possible (Matthew 26:28). But to whom is this forgiveness granted? And at what point is the gift received? Paul gives us a clear answer when he says that when we are baptized into Christ, we are baptized into His death. *"We were buried therefore with him by baptism into death."* It is in baptism that we die with Christ, and it is when we submit to this command that God fulfills His promise to forgive us, based on Christ's sacrifice on our behalf.

Baptism is the crucial turning point in our obedience to the gospel. Separating "before" from "after," it is the point at which, dying with Christ, we are resurrected to our new life. Just "as Christ was raised from the dead by the glory of the Father," it is now our duty and privilege to "walk in newness of life."

How could there be a more radical turning point in a person's life? As Paul described it in another letter: "I have been crucified with Christ. It is no longer I who live, but Christ who lives in me. And the life I now live in the flesh I live by faith in the Son of God, who loved me and gave himself for me" (Galatians 2:20).

Baptism, then, is an act in which we become connected to Christ's death, burial, and resurrection. There is nothing meritorious about it as far as we are concerned; it is purely an act of faith, commanded by the Lord. "Having been buried with him in baptism," we are "raised with him through faith in the powerful working of God, who raised him from the dead" (Colossians 2:12).

In 2 Timothy 2:11, Paul spoke of the hope made possible by the gospel when he said, "If we have died with him, we will also live with him." It is no exaggeration to say that whether we have died with Christ is the most important question we will ever ask.

Buried with Christ and raised with Him too,
What is there left for me to do?
Simply to cease from struggling and strife,
Simply to walk in newness of life.

T. RYDER

December 30

HAVE YOU OBEYED THE GOSPEL?

For it is time for judgment to begin at the household of God;
and if it begins with us, what will be the outcome
for those who do not obey the gospel of God?
1 Peter 4:17

WHEN PETER SPEAKS OF "JUDGMENT," HE PRESENTS US WITH A SOBERING THOUGHT. The marvelous gift of the freedom of our will is accompanied by responsibility and accountability to our Creator. The time will come when we will be judged. In our conscience, we all know we are guilty of having rejected what we knew of God's will on many occasions. If there can be no forgiveness, the consequences of our sin will fall upon us inexorably.

In the gospel (or "good news") of Jesus Christ, forgiveness is the very thing that is offered. But the offer must be responded to. The gospel must be obeyed. And Peter's words offer no hope to those who, having heard the gospel message, refuse to obey it. *"What will be the outcome for those who do not obey the gospel of God?"*

The initial terms of obedience to the gospel have been looked at on many pages in this book, but let's review them. Believing that Jesus is the Christ, we must make an open confession of our faith to others (Romans 10:9,10). Then we must do what Peter instructed the audience to do on Pentecost: "Repent and be baptized every one of you in the name of Jesus Christ for the forgiveness of your sins" (Acts 2:38). In the act of baptism, we die with Christ, receiving God's forgiveness and also the strength and guidance He provides so that "we too might walk in newness of life" (Romans 6:4).

Have you obeyed the gospel? Whatever others may have done, have you responded rightly to the glad tidings of salvation in Jesus Christ? The gospel is the best news in the world, but the results of refusing it would be more tragic than we can imagine.

I know of no better way to view obedience than to see it in terms of God's *kingship.* The problem of sin is the problem of rebellion against the rule of God. Surely there can be no reconciliation without an honest return to obedience, starting with the initial terms of God's pardon and continuing for the rest of our lives. Are you willing to come back to the King and obey His gospel? If not, the only consequences you can expect are those of an outlaw.

I cannot say "Thine is the kingdom" if I do not give the King
the disciplined obedience of a loyal subject.

ANONYMOUS

December 31

What Hinders You?

And now why do you wait? Rise and be baptized
and wash away your sins, calling on his name.
Acts 22:16

When Ananias found Saul of Tarsus, the notorious persecutor of the church, Saul had been fasting and praying sorrowfully for three days. "And now why do you wait?" Ananias asked. "Rise and be baptized and wash away your sins, calling on his name." Saul did as he was instructed, received the forgiveness of his sins, and served Jesus Christ fervently for the rest of his life. We know him today as the apostle Paul.

"Why do you wait?" is a question that touches the conscience of us all. And it's a question that is exceedingly hard to answer. Even searching our hearts deeply, we don't always have the honesty to admit why we delay doing what we know we ought to do.

One thing, however, is certain: there is no *good* reason to wait. Once we see what we must do to be reconciled to God, waiting only worsens our problem. As Corrie ten Boom said, "An unrepented sin is a continued sin." Whatever the reason, it is never worth the loss of our souls. Nothing is worth that. "For what will it profit a man if he gains the whole world and forfeits his soul? Or what shall a man give in return for his soul?" (Matthew 16:26).

In the New Testament, as soon as people saw the seriousness of their sins and the joy of forgiveness that could be theirs in Christ, they wanted to be baptized immediately. In Acts 16:25-34, there is even the story of a group of people being baptized in the middle of the night. *Waiting was not something they wanted to do.*

Hindrances to the gospel come in many shapes and sizes. The world is full of obstacles, and some of them are fearful. God knows about all of these. He knows how hard it can be for us. But there is no hindrance He won't help us overcome, if we're willing.

So as we come to the end of our meditations on obeying the gospel, there is nothing left but the question of choice. What will we do — each of us — with the gospel? God has given His Son to save us from our sins, but He will not compel us. If we reject what our Father has done, we will have made the decision to be lost. So let us not wait. Let us do exactly what Saul of Tarsus did: obey.

He who created us without our help
will not save us without our consent.

Augustine of Hippo

A Prayer for Daily Meditation

I, a pilgrim of eternity,
stand before Thee, O Eternal One.

Let me not seek to deaden or destroy
the desire for Thee that disturbs my heart.
Let me rather yield myself to its constraint
and go where it leads me.

Make me wise to see all things today
under the form of eternity,
and make me brave to face all the changes
in my life which such a vision may entail.

Through the grace of Christ my Savior.
Amen.

— *John Baille*

Index of Daily Scripture Texts

Malachi

Matthew

Mark

Luke

John

Acts

Romans

1 Corinthians

2 Corinthians

Galatians

ACKNOWLEDGMENTS

THIS BOOK WAS WRITTEN IN DIFFICULT CIRCUMSTANCES, even more difficult than those of the previous four books. That being true, I am all the more indebted to those who have helped me.

Thanks to Becky Voyles and Jessica Keet, my editors for twenty years. Becky still endures my stubbornness with patience and grace. To survive, she has had to maintain a sense of humor about the whole thing. And Jessica continues to edit marvelously and encourage me personally. On this book especially, Jessica's willingness to read these pages with such sensitivity and empathy has been deeply appreciated. Thank you, Jess, for being so extraordinary.

This particular book contains more of the basic truths of the gospel of Christ than any other book I've written. So it is appropriate for me to thank those who helped me, even when I was a child, to begin understanding the gospel. My parents, Leroy and Charlene Henry, are at the top of the list, obviously. But I can hardly think of my parents' faith without thinking of Reg and Martha Ginn. Reg was the preacher in Meridian, Mississippi until I was about ten years old, so it was his preaching, along with Martha's winsomeness, that helped form my first understandings of God's truth and grace.

Those who support me financially are no doubt the most remarkable people in the world. I am a difficult person (please keep the chorus of amens down a bit), my personal life is an infuriating mixture of good and evil, and my work habits have been a lifelong demonstration of unpredictability. Supporting me has always been risky, but I pray that, in the end, your decision will have been blessed by God.

Above all, I want to thank those who pray for me. Now that I teach only by the written word ("You have gone," one reader said, "from preaching standing up to preaching sitting down"), I need your prayers even more. Some of you pray for me regularly, even daily, and words alone are not enough to express my gratitude. Without your faithful prayers, this work would have collapsed long ago.

With *Obeying the Gospel* now done, only two more books remain in the seven-volume *WordPoints Daybook Series*. Two more may not seem like much, but these are lengthy works and my strength and endurance are not what they used to be. I sometimes wonder if the years left to me are going to be enough. But I promise you this: *as long as the Lord gives me strength, I will continue to write one page at a time.* Who knows? If each of us redeems the time — just doing the "next thing" right in front of us — the Lord may surprise us all.

WordPoints Daybook Series

THE KIND OF BOOKS KNOWN AS "DAYBOOKS" HAVE A RICH LITERARY TRADITION. They are books containing a brief reading for each day of the year, and their value is that they sharply concentrate our thoughts on significant subjects once a day, every day.

The *WordPoints Daybook Series* has redefined the daybook for modern readers. Written by Gary Henry with his well-known blend of candor and courtesy, these volumes have become a familiar part of the daily routine of thousands of readers around the world.

The series as a whole takes the reader on a journey. We begin by thinking about elementary character issues and the importance of God, move toward the question of obedience to the gospel of Jesus Christ, and end with a consideration of heaven: the home of the soul.

Book 1 — ***Enthusiastic Ideas: A Good Word for Each Day of the Year.*** What are the time-tested ideas that should inform our character? (ISBN13 978-0-9713710-2-6)

Book 2 — ***More Enthusiastic Ideas: Another Good Word for Each Day of the Year.*** What are the helpful words that should motivate our conduct? (ISBN13 978-0-9713710-3-3)

Book 3 — ***Diligently Seeking God: Daily Motivation to Take God More Seriously.*** What difference does it make whether we seek God? (ISBN13 978-0-9713710-0-2)

Book 4 — ***Reaching Forward: Daily Motivation to Move Ahead More Steadily.*** Is there anything about tomorrow worth reaching for? (ISBN13 978-0-9713710-1-9)

Book 5 — ***Obeying the Gospel: Daily Motivation to Act on Our Faith.*** How do we make a genuine, scripture-based commitment to Christ? (ISBN13 978-1-936357-51-2)

Book 6 — ***Walking in Christ: Daily Motivation to Grow in Our Commitment.*** How do we lead lives of authentic discipleship to Christ? (In preparation)

Book 7 — ***Going Home: Daily Motivation to Make the Final Journey.*** What happens to our hearts as we get closer to the goal of heaven? (In preparation)

"The reader is in for a strong intellectual and spiritual challenge . . . The thought-provoking richness of the 366 essays is reminiscent of the wisdom-dense writings of C. S. Lewis." — Ellen Kennedy

"At once comfortable and elegant . . . a feast for the eye and hand, the soul and mind and heart." — Peggy Rosenthal

WordPoints.com

WordPoints.com is your main source for Bible studies by Gary Henry.

- Email subscriptions to daily devotions
- Monday-Friday family Bible study guides
- Articles, sermons, lectures, e-book downloads

Challenging every person to take God more seriously. These Bible studies are devotional helps of a different sort — they will challenge you to a higher concept of spiritual growth. Join us for a diligent, God-centered seeking of what is right and good in every area of life.

AreYouaChristian.com

A special sub-section of *WordPoints.com*, this website looks at the how and why of becoming a Christian.

(1) Is the message of Jesus Christ true?
(2) If it is, what should we do about it?

Rich, challenging Bible study resources for every person.

- Each day's page from *Obeying the Gospel* — with audio
- E-Study Courses, 9 Core Concepts, 20 Questions
- Small-group discussion guides

A unique characteristic of *AreYouaChristian.com* is that it asks Christians to re-examine whether they are, in fact, Christians. Have we truly responded to the gospel as people did in the New Testament?

SCAN ME

(1) Forgiveness
(2) Faithfulness
(3) Ultimate hope

Our need for these three things deserves our most careful attention. *AreYouaChristian.com* will help you study these from the perspective of the Scriptures. Visit the website today and become a regular reader.

CPSIA information can be obtained
at www.ICGtesting.com
Printed in the USA
LVHW040851171120
671900LV00002B/69

9 781936 357512